Imperialism, Crisis, and Class Struggle

Studies in Critical Social Sciences Book Series

Haymarket Books is proud to be working with Brill Academic Publishers (http://www.brill.nl) to republish the Studies in Critical Social Sciences book series, edited by David Fasenfest, in paperback editions. Other titles in this series include:

The Apprentice's Sorcerer: Liberal Tradition and Fascism
Ishay Landa

Dialectic of Solidarity: Labor, Antisemitism, and the Frankfurt School
Mark P. Worrell

The Destiny of Modern Societies: The Calvinist Predestination of a New Society
Milan Zafirovski

Engaging Social Justice: Critical Studies of 21st Century Social Transformation
edited by David Fasenfest

The Future of Religion: Toward a Reconciled Society
edited by Michael R. Ott

Globalization and the Environment
edited by Andrew Jorgenson and Edward Kick

Hybrid Identities: Theoretical and Empirical Examinations
edited by Keri E. Iyall Smith and Patricia Leavy

Imperialism, Neoliberalism and Social Struggles in Latin America
edited by Richard A. Dello Buono and José Bell Lara

Liberal Modernity and Its Adversaries: Freedom, Liberalism and Anti-Liberalism in the Twenty-first Century
Milan Zafirovski

Marx, Critical Theory, and Religion: A Critique of Rational Choice
edited by Warren S. Goldstein

Marx's Scientific Dialectics: A Methodological Treatise for a New Century
Paul Paolucci

Profitable Ideas: The Ideology of the Individual in Capitalist Development
Michael O'Flynn

Race and Ethnicity: Across Time, Space, and Discipline
Rodney D. Coates

Transforming Globalization: Challenges and Opportunities in the Post 9/11 Era
edited by Bruce Podobnik and Thomas Reifer

Western Europe, Eastern Europe and World Development 13th-18th Centuries
edited by Jean Batou and Henryk Szlajfer

IMPERIALISM, CRISIS, AND CLASS STRUGGLE

THE ENDURING VERITIES AND CONTEMPORARY FACE OF CAPITALISM: ESSAYS IN HONOR OF JAMES PETRAS

EDITED BY HENRY VELTMEYER

Haymarket Books
Chicago, Illinois

First published in 2010 by Brill Academic Publishers, The Netherlands
© 2006 Koninklijke Brill NV, Leiden, The Netherlands

Published in paperback in 2012 by
Haymarket Books
P.O. Box 180165
Chicago, IL 60618
773-583-7884
www.haymarketbooks.org

ISBN: 978-1-60846-146-2

Trade distribution:
In the US, through Consortium Book Sales, www.cbsd.com
In the UK, Turnaround Publisher Services, www.turnaround-psl.com
In Australia, Palgrave Macmillan, www.palgravemacmillan.com.au
In all other countries, Publishers Group Worldwide, www.pgw.com

Cover design by Ragina Johnson.

This book was published with the generous support of Lannan Foundation and
the Wallace Global Fund.

Printed in the United States.

10 9 8 7 6 5 4 3 2 1

Library of Congress Cataloging-in-Publication Data is available.

SUSTAINABLE FORESTRY INITIATIVE Certified Sourcing
www.sfiprogram.org
SFI-00993

CONTENTS

THE MAKING OF A REVOLUTIONARY AND
ANTI-IMPERIALIST

Chapter One   James Petras, Scholar and Revolutionary:
An Appreciation   3
Henry Veltmeyer

Chapter Two   James Petras and that 'Long Petal of Wine,
Sea and Snow'   19
Fernando I. Leiva

CAPITALISM AND MARXIST THEORY

Chapter Three   Trotsky and Latin American Development
Theory   41
Ronald H. Chilcote

Chapter Four   Capitalism, Primitive Accumulation and
Unfree Labour   67
Tom Brass

Chapter Five   Farewell to Imperialism? A Critical Sociological
Study of Empire   133
Ashok Kumbamu

CAPITALISM IN THE ERA OF NEOLIBERALISM:
A SYSTEM IN CRISIS

Chapter Six   The Class Nature of Neoliberal Globalization in
the Age of Imperialism   153
Berch Berberoglu

Chapter Seven   The Migration-Development Nexus:
A Marxist Class Perspective   171
Raúl Delgado Wise

Chapter Eight   The Financialization of the Capitalist Class:
Monopoly-Finance Capital and the New Contradictory
Relations of Ruling Class Power   191
John Bellamy Foster and Hannah Holleman

Chapter Nine   Food, Water and Fuel: The Crisis of Life
under Capitalism   203
Michel Chossudovsky

POLITICAL DYNAMICS OF US IMPERIALISM

Chapter Ten   'Not about to Lose Chile': Democratic
Socialism Confronts the Imperial State   221
Morris Morley

Chapter Eleven   The Rational Destruction of Yugoslavia   255
Michael Parenti

Chapter Twelve   James Petras on the Israeli Lobby,
Occupied Palestine and US-Israeli Militarism   273
Stephen Lendman

List of Contributors   285

James Petras—Selected Publications   289

References   293

Index   311

THE MAKING OF A REVOLUTIONARY AND
ANTI-IMPERIALIST

CHAPTER ONE

JAMES PETRAS, SCHOLAR AND REVOLUTIONARY: AN APPRECIATION

Henry Veltmeyer

Despite a decade and more of broadly distributed gains and relative prosperity, the 1960s were a period of revolutionary ferment, protest—against the Vietnam war, the alienation of life and work under capitalism, racism, sexism and labour exploitation—and civil as well as class-based movements for social change. By 1968 the labour movement in diverse contexts but particularly in Europe and Latin America had experienced a gradual but appreciable improvement in its capacity to negotiate with capital for improved wages and better working conditions, a power evident in the upheavals of 1968 as people across the world took to the streets in the demand for radical change. In Latin America and the Caribbean, and Asia and parts of Africa, advances in the class struggle and the labour movement were combined with anti-colonial or anti-imperialist movements of national liberation and the class struggle of the landless rural poor for land and a change in the prevailing capitalist system—a system labelled and conceptualized by insurgent sociologists at the time as 'US imperialism'.

It was in these times and the specific context of Chile, the subject of his doctoral thesis, that James Petras, a recent graduate from Political Science at the University of California at Berkeley, at the time a major centre of revolutionary ferment and radical ideas, materialized as a scholar, part of a university and broader community of a Marxist-oriented intellectual and political activists (on this see Fernando Leiva and Ron Chilcote's contributions to this volume) and took up, as it were, radical sociological and political thought. As Fernando Leiva reviews it, Petras' analysis of political developments in Chile was a fundamental crucible for the making of a 'revolutionary and anti-imperialist', and the first step in a life-time of enduring contributions to a critical Marxist tradition in the study of the dynamics of capitalist development.

Class Analysis in the Transition from Developmentalism to
Neoliberal Globalization

Political sociology in the late 1960s, more than other academic disciplines such as economics or political science in the liberal tradition, reflected the revolutionary temper of the times and a disposition for radical analysis and political change. This concern for radical change was reflected in the issues and pages of the *Insurgent Sociologist*, as well as the type of issues taken up in this and other publication outlets of Marxist social science such as *Monthly Review*. The revolutionary temper of the times, and a radical orientation of sociological and political analysis, was also reflected in the popularity of the book, *Latin America: Reform or Revolution?* that James Petras, together with Maurice Zeitlin, edited on political developments in Latin America. Together with Petras' *Latin America: Dependence or Revolution* (1973), this book became a touchstone of Marxist analysis of political developments in Latin America. On this see Fernando Leiva's succinct but revealing review of Petras' biography as a social scientist and revolutionary. Both books for decades remained academic 'bestsellers', selling well over a hundred thousand copies and used for decades as essential reference points for graduate studies in sociology and political science both in Latin and North America.

Of critical concern and a central focus of these studies was the regional and global dynamics of the production crisis, a crisis of overproduction that brought to an end the so-called 'golden age of capitalism'—two decades of system-wide economic growth (Schor and Marglin, 1990). As emphasised by Petras and Veltmeyer (2005) in their contributions to this book, the strategic-political responses to this crisis, and its 'structural' outcomes, can be put into six categories: (i) a technological conversion of the global production apparatus—the 'revolutionary path' of capitalist development according to Marx (although Petras disputes the notion of a 'third technological revolution'); (ii) a geographical displacement of global production, resulting in a 'new international division of labour' (Fröbel, Heinrichs and Kreye, 1980)' as well as the emergence of a group of 'newly industrialising countries' in Asia and Latin America; (iii) a transformation in the form of capitalist production at the level of labour regulation (Lipietz, 1987); (iv) the direct assault by capital on labour, launching what is now widely seen but that few scholars at the time (Petras being a notable exception) saw as a 'global class war', which took the form, and had the result, of reducing share of the labour in the social product and diminishing its organizational capacity and political power (Davis, 1984); (v) launching the idea and project of 'development' with 'international cooperation' as a means of dampening revolutionary ferment in the countryside, the demand for revolutionary change, to prevent the emergence of another Cuba in Latin America and elsewhere (Petras and Veltmeyer, 2005); and (vi) the construction of a 'new world order' in which the 'forces of freedom' would be freed from the regulatory constraints of the welfare-and-development state (Veltmeyer and Petras, 2000).

One of Petras' most substantial and enduring contributions at the level of Marxist social science has been to analyse in depth and from a social class perspective the fundamental economic, social and political dynamics of this economic restructuring process of capitalist development. As he theoretically reconstructs it this process is essentially a matter of imperialism in its diverse forms and faces. For example, as emphasized in *Unmasking Globalization* (2001), a path-breaking study of the contemporary dynamics of imperialism, the project of international cooperation for 'development' presented and presents the soft side of what might be termed the 'new imperialism', the velvet glove within which is found, and brought out and used when and where needed, the iron fist of military power or armed force.[1] As for 'globalization' as Petras sees it in *Unmasking Globalization* and elsewhere, it manifests the ideological power of capital—its capacity to sell an idea used to justify neoliberal policies of structural adjustment.

The 'new world order' of neoliberal globalization in Petras' theoretical discourse and empirical analysis, although presented by the World Bank in its 1995 *World Development Report*, a veritable capitalist manifesto, as the best and indeed only path towards prosperity was structured and designed as a pathway out of the crisis of the overproduction in the early 1970s—a means of reactivating the accumulation

---

[1] Within the Marxist tradition 'neoimperialism' generally refers to postcolonial forms of extraction of surplus value from the labour of the direct producers and workers on the periphery of the capitalist system, by means of foreign direct investment, trade and aid. But in the context of the neoconservative regime led by George W. Bush, particularly in the wake of 9/11 and the neoconservative project to re-establish US hegemony over the world economy by means of the direct unilateral projection of military power by the US state, the 'new imperialism' was associated with the unilateral projection of overt force and military force by the US state (Petras and Veltmeyer, 2005).

process. In Bello's analysis, a key aspect and dimension of this restructuring process—financialization—had within it the seeds of the current global financial crisis, which is understood by Petras as a crisis in the system of capitalist production, a crisis that reaches well beyond the economy of financial capital into the real economy, putting at risk the livelihoods, jobs and development prospects of the working class and people in the popular sector, and exposing the fragile foundations of the entire production system.

The current dynamics of this systemic crisis, anticipated by Petras in his 2005 treatise on the theme, are explored by Foster and Holleman. Like Petras and unlike many economists today in both the Marxist and liberal tradition, they examine the consequences of the 'financialization' of production and the crisis—phenomena that lead many analysts today to examine the dynamics of the global crisis today as a problem that can be addressed not as a systemic issue but merely by making a policy correction, a matter of reregulating the global movements of capital and good global governance. Foster and Holleman's penetrating analysis of the actual class dynamics of the global crisis (the 'financialization of the capitalist class') is in the best tradition of Marxist scholarship and class analysis shaped in considerable measure by James Petras.

From Marxism and Structuralism to the Postmodern Pivot in Social Analysis

In the 1980s much was made of an apparent 'theoretical impasse' that in fact was nothing more than the latest attack, from an idealist standpoint, on the methodology of positivism (liberalism) and historical materialism (Marxism) as forms of social science (Booth, 1985; Gulbankian Commission, 1996).[2]

On the basis of this idealist critique, and in the context of a global class war and the turn of events and developments related to an emerging 'new world order' and an ideological offensive of capital against labour—not a few academics abandoned class analysis and turned away from the global class struggle between capital and labour unfold-

---

[2] On the evolution and involutions of this materialism-idealism debate see Veltmeyer (2002).

ing in diverse theatres across the world. Some turned away not only from Marxist political economy but from all forms of 'structuralism', using an alleged 'theoretical impasse' to substitute for 'structuralism' (although Marxist class analysis is political as well as structural) a new 'political imaginary' and a postmodern perspective on the development process, namely that all metatheories constructed on the basis of structural analysis, and all associated ideologies and political practices, were no longer relevant. Structuralism in all of its forms, and particularly Marxism, it was argued, was too focused on non-existing (imagined or theorized) structural obstacles to the capacity of individuals to freely construct their own futures, and was unable to grasp the essential subjectivity and openendedness of social life. From this perspective a focus on the dynamics generated by a society's mode of production is misplaced and irrelevant.

This postmodernist perspective not only affected the form that analysis took (in many cases the abandonment of class analysis and 'structuralism' in all of its forms) but it led to political demobilization, undermining as it did the need for the working classes to resist and respond strategically to the forces of capitalist development operating on them. Again, it was Petras among the all too few others who held the line on Marxism and class analysis, exposing the fallacies, idealism and the intellectual and political immobilizing and demobilizing effects of this postmodernist perspective and form of analysis.

As Petras has elaborated in various writings, postmodernism was one of two major intellectual responses to the demand for revolutionary change in the 1970s. The other took the form of a conservative counterrevolution in development theory, manifest in a turn towards a neoclassical theory of economic development that privileged the free market as the engine of growth and justified neoliberal policy reforms by reference to globalization as a process that was desirable and irresistible, the price to be paid for admission into the new world order (Veltmeyer and Petras, 1997, 2000).

The global production crisis brought to an end the golden age of capitalism and with it the post-war labour-capital accord based on an equitable sharing of productivity gains in the capitalist production process. As already mentioned, it also brought about a rather desperate search for a way out of systemic crisis that included a direct assault on labour, the opening gambit in a long class war played out subsequently in diverse theatres on the world stage—a war that by some accounts (Petras', for example) is by no means over but that has engaged many a battle, most of which organised labour seems to have lost, passing on as a result the leadership of the popular movement to the peasantry, rural landless workers and the indigenous communities (Petras, 2007; Petras and Veltmeyer, 2005, 2007). In the Latin American streets and countryside; in the neighbourhoods, communities and workplaces where Petras has conducted and continues to conduct so much of his relentlessly 'political' class analysis of diverse issues, the class war assumed particular forms that brought together as protagonists of revolutionary change an insurgent working class and rural landless peasants.

On the other side of this class war could be found (and Petras indeed did find) the 'State' in its double functionality as (i) a repressive apparatus, an agency for national security (used to repress the insurgency in the form of armies for national liberation aka Cuba); and (ii) an agency of development, representing the 'human' face of US imperialism (disguised as 'international cooperation for development')—the velvet glove to the iron fist of armed military force (Petras, 2003, 2005).

As for the dynamics of these developments over the course of the decade one can do no better than turn to the writings of James Petras who captured the gist of these developments with unparalleled acuity and empirically solid class analysis.

In 1972 Petras took up a teaching position in sociology at the Binghamton campus of SUNY but he returned to Latin America regularly year after year to engage in a series of analytical probes that constitute and remain after more than three decades a model of radical—insurgent or critical—sociological analysis. The essays collected in this book pay homage to some of these contributions, as do Petras' own extensive record of publications, which can be partly accessed via the website of *Rebelión*.

As noted, the 1980s presented another sea change in economic and political developments, change associated with the initial call for and then the installation of a 'new world order' in which the nation-state, once the dominant agency of national development in a context of class war, retreated from its responsibilities for social welfare and development, liberating the 'forces of economic and political freedom' from the regulatory constraints of the welfare-development state. The installation of the 'new' world order of neoliberal globalization, and the dynamics of associated developments, were traced out by Petras and his collaborators in a series of book-length publications over the past two decades (see, in particular, Veltmeyer and Petras, 1997, 2000; Petras and Veltmeyer, 2001, 2005, 2007).

Many academics at the time (in the 1980s, that is) either abandoned the field (leaving an analysis of the economics and politics of social change and development to political scientists and economists in the liberal tradition) or put aside the tools of structural-political class analysis that had been sharpened with several decades of practice. As the State was forced to retreat from its self-assumed and theoretically defined responsibility for welfare and development, many intellectuals retreated from the task of providing theoretically informed sociopolitical analysis, turning instead towards a non-class/post-structuralist form of postmodern discourse (on this see Brass, 2000 as well as Petras).

Petras was among the few who stayed the course and held to the line of theoretically informed and politically relevant class analysis. His writings at the time on political and economic developments—over 20 books and hundreds of scholarly articles and political commentaries over the course of the 1980s and 1990s—provided a behind-the-lines class analysis of the dynamics of the ongoing and as yet unfinished class war, not only in Latin America but elsewhere.

Petras' Sociological and Political Writings in Perspective

The postcolonial era of capitalist development can be periodized as two phases: a period of state-led capitalist development (1945–80) characterised by rapid systemwide growth, and what has been dubbed the 'neoliberal era'—a period of market-friendly or led capitalist development in the form of neoliberal globalization (1981–2002), which, according to many is in decline if not dead in its original form. But overall, this evolution of capitalist development is but the latest phase in a long-term process of productive and social transformation that could be theoretically reconstructed in terms of three alternative 'metanarratives': that of *modernization, industrialization and capitalism* (on this see Petras and Veltmeyer, 2008).

In the mainstream of liberal bourgeois analysis this multidimensional process of change and development implies the transformation of a traditional, precapitalist and agrarian form of society into a modern industrial capitalist one, a process that according to some sociologists came to an end in the 1960s and 1970s, giving way to a new postdevelopment dynamic and the emergence of a post-modern, post-industrial and post-capitalist form of society (Best and Kellner, 1997; Harvey, 1989; Jameson, 1991; Lyotard, 1984).

Petras himself views the dynamics of this capitalist development process in rather different terms: not as transition from modernity to postmodernity (Harvey, 1989) but from a Marxist political economy perspective, and with the lens of class analysis. Araghi and McMichael i(2009) in their proposed contribution to this *festschrift* explore the various permutations of capitalist development over the past two decades and a half in what Petras and others have termed neoliberalism but which from their 'world-historical' perspective they view as 'postmodern'. Notwithstanding their acknowledged debt to Petras' insistence on a theoretically informed, empirically grounded and politically relevant class analysis, and Petras' trenchant critique of postmodernism as a theoretical perspective and form of analysis (on this also see Callinicos, 1990; and Brass, 2000) theoretically reconstruct recent worldwide developments in terms of the notion of 'postmodernity'. However, like Harvey and Jameson they do so not from a postmodernist and poststructuralist (non-Marxist) perspective but in an analysis of 'postmodernity' as a condition of 'late capitalism' that, arguably, is compatible with if not Marxist in form. In fact Araghi and McMichael provide a 'world-historical' contextualized analysis of this condition in terms that Petras, whose intellectual contributions they acknowledge in their own work, might not disagree with or object to. Indeed, they present their essay as a critique of world systems theory and in honour of Petras' substantive and theoretical contributions over the years a well as his concerns as a revolutionary and anti-imperialist. Unfortunately, we were unable to include this essay in this *festschrift*.

As noted, Petras himself prefers to explore the dynamics of social change and development from a Marxist political economy and class perspective. His analysis can be viewed as a nuanced form of class analysis based on a clearly articulated Marxist perspective as well as Marx's general theory of the dynamics of capitalist development— what we refer to in the title of this book as the 'essential verities of capitalism'. In this connection, one of Petras' major contributions to revolutionary social science has been an analysis of the global divide in wealth, and the structural and political dynamics of this divide. Petras has explored these dynamics in both theoretical and political terms, with reference to the class responses to these dynamics, and always on the basis of solid empirical research and data. This research and empirical analysis can be traced out in a host of collaborative book-length studies and several articles over the past decade (for example, Veltmeyer and Petras, 1997, 2000; Petras and Veltmeyer, 2001, 2002, 2003, 2005, 2008).

The 1990s provided another turn in worldwide economic and political developments that can also be traced out in Petras' writings. At the macro and micro-levels it was increasingly evident that neoliberalism and the 'pro-growth' policies under the Washington Consensus were economically dysfunctional and unsustainable. For one thing it tended to generate forces of resistance that were all too readily mobilized against the class and state power of the dominant capitalist class (Veltmeyer and Petras, 1997, 2000; Petras and Veltmeyer, 2001). The dynamics of this resistance were traced out in a series of articles and books on the new wave of social movements in the region—insurgent movements that for the most part had their social basis and agency in landless rural workers, and indigenous communities and diverse organizations of peasant producers. On these forces of resistance see Petras and Veltmeyer (2005, 2009).

Foster and Holleman in their contribution to this volume conceptualize a propensity of capitalism towards crisis, which they trace back to the 1970s but see as endemic to capitalism. Similarly, Petras, like Walden Bello (2009), contextualizes his own analysis of the current crisis in terms of the capitalist production crisis in the early 1970s that gave rise to diverse efforts to restructure and renovate the capitalist system. As for the structural source and developmental dynamics of this crisis, Petras left its analysis to others—notably Lipietz (1987) from a regulationist perspective, Magdoff and Sweezy (1988) from a more strictly Marxist (monopoly capital) perspective, Marglin and Schor (1990) from a profit-crunch or 'political' (viz. the power of organised labour) perspective, and Frank (1980, 1981) as well as Amin, Arrighi and Wallerstein (1982) from a 'world-system' perspective.

To Frank's chagrin his two-volume study on *Crisis Theory* (1980, 1981) was almost totally ignored by other scholars on the Left, not so much for lack of relevance as the lack of resonance in various academic disciplines, especially sociology, that at the time were tuned to emerging postmodern imaginaries or to a globalization discourse that, like the then fashionable postmodernist discourse, drew many sociologists away from an analysis of the real world. However, in part due to Petras' trenchant critique of postmodernist discourse (viz. its

politically demobilizing effects) and the general retreat of so many academics in the 1980s and 1990s from all sorts of 'structuralisms' and
associated politics and class analysis, the postmodern pivot of social
and development thought appears to have seriously waned in recent
years, disappearing into the cracks that emerged in the foundations of
the world capitalist system.

As the postmodern infection of class analysis and capitalist development theory waned (in the late 1990s), radical political economy and
critical sociology came back into their own—but not without the work
of critical scholars and Marxists like Petras who continued to hoe the
line of class analysis in the vacuum of postmodernist thought. Even
so, Marxist class analysis was reconstituted to take into account not
just the 'structural' economic dynamics emphasized by more orthodox
or traditional Marxists but also the political, social, cultural and environmental dimensions of the capitalist development process (on this
see Petras and Veltmeyer, 2009, as well as Bellamy Foster and other
contributors to this volume).

The onset of the current global financial crisis has led to a major
debate as to the propensity of the capitalism towards crisis and its
fundamental dynamics. Much of the bourgeois business press and
most analysts supportive of capitalism—which is to say, most analysts—agree with Petras and other Marxists that crisis is endemic to
the system but they view it as cyclical, and in its current manifestation
as a purely financial or monetary issue, a matter of excessive deregula-
tion and relaxation of capital controls, leading to or allowing, if not
promoting, excessively wild speculative activity and untrammelled
greed, generating problems that are correctible and that can be cor-
rected by a balanced mix of anti-cyclical fiscal and monetary policies.
However, Foster and Magdoff (2009) and Walden Bello (2009)—and
Foster and Holloman in this volume—like Petras, see the global crisis
as essentially a crisis of overproduction, a crisis that reaches deeply
into the structure of the real economy and that has not only begun
to assume global proportions but is taking increasingly diverse and
virulent forms. The multiple dimensions of systemic crisis, which are
explored by various contributors to this volume is evident in the conversion of what initially appeared as a crisis of overproduction in the
1970s into a systemwide or global financial crisis, and the intersection
of this crisis with an incipient global food crisis and a deeply rooted
systemwide ecological crisis (on this see Bello, 2009; McMichael, 2009;
Petras and Veltmeyer, 2009).

As the capitalist system is pushed towards its economic, political and ecological limits it continues to generate forces of resistance. As Petras sees it and has argued in diverse contexts over the years an intellectual and political response to this problematic, and the unification of these forces of resistance, is the most serious challenge confronted by the academic and political Left, who have the responsibility of meeting this challenge rather than retreating from it as so many did at the outset of the capitalist world order of neoliberal globalization.

In this call for a new sociology and political economy of crisis (new in the sense that sociology, unlike economics, has failed to problematize the dynamics of crisis), and for a reconstituted form of class analysis (in terms of its diverse social, cultural and political dynamics) that is adequate to the task of understanding capitalism in its current form and system-wide dynamics, Petras once more is in the forefront of a Marxist class analysis of capitalist development and its dynamics, pointing to the way forward and helping to reshape it in a critical direction of revolutionary change. The various contributions to this volume of essays illustrate the various forms that such an analysis should take—and indeed is taking.

Fernando Leiva's contribution and that of Morris Morley not only take us back to James Petras' entry point into critical sociology in its contemporary form (as it took shape in the 1960s) but provide a useful framework of ideas derived from Marx but elaborated by Petras, for grasping from a critical perspective the connection between the social structure and politics—the initial area of Petras' sociological analysis (1968, 1969, 1970)—as well as the role of the state and the class struggle between capital and labour in the capitalist development process.

The connection between the social structure and politics, as argued by Petras in different contexts and elaborated by Morris Morley in a brilliant exposition (here following Petras, an erstwhile collaborator in various studies and publications) of US intervention in Chile (to topple the socialist regime of Salvador Allende and install a military dictatorship), can be found in the capital-labour relation. Morley's reconstruction of this problematic (the role of US imperialism in the politics of capitalist development) in the case of Chile returns to the object of Petras' analysis in his doctoral dissertation but he goes beyond this analysis to provide a contemporary perspective on the response of the US state to socialist rule in the context of its regional and global imperatives. This analysis provides a useful framework of ideas for understanding the dilemma of US imperialism in an era of declining power and influence, and its possible responses to the advent of 'the socialism of the 21dt century' in the form advanced by Hugo Chávez in Venezuela.

Tom Brass, in his contribution, also focuses on the capital-labour relation in the capitalist development process, but he looks at it from a different angle and from a more theoretical Marxist perspective. In this process a long-standing and as yet unsettled debate has surrounded the assumption that capitalism is predicated on free labour—on the capacity of workers freely to exchange their labour power against capital. But this very 'freedom' has allowed the apologists of capitalism to construct an ideological cover for the exploitation of labour by capital—in effect creating what Marx termed the 'inner secret of capitalism': that the 'appearance' of free exchange disguises the exploitative character of the wage relation.

Brass in his contribution to this volume takes issue with this presumption that capitalism requires and can only function under conditions of 'free labour' (see also Brass, 1999). Going back to Marx's concept of class struggle, Brass argues with considerable evidence and support (not least from Marx himself) that current capitalist production is perfectly compatible with diverse forms of unfree labour, and indeed in different contexts either introduces, reintroduces or reproduces it. In this argument Brass advances, if not settles, an ongoing debate among Marxists and non-Marxists alike. His review of the various debates that have surrounded studies on this question from diverse theoretical perspectives (liberal, neoliberal and varieties of Marxism) provides the most systematic theoretical analysis of the capital-labour relation available. It is squarely in the Marxist tradition of theoretically informed empirical analysis represented by Petras.

Raul Delgado Wise in his contribution picks up on another dimension of the capital-labour relation, namely the 'dialectic of migration and development'. In his analysis of the dynamics of this dialectic he turns towards and leans heavily on Petras' writings in this area and his Marxist perspective on an analysis of these dynamics: a matter of 'forced migration and imperialism'.

In his preamble to his contribution to this volume, Delgado Wise marks the following appreciation of Petras' contributions in the area of 'migration and development'—an appreciation that we could well extend to Petras' contributions to critical sociology and critical development studies (on this see Veltmeyer, 2009) more generally:

James Petras is a prolific writer whose monumental work has always been and continues to be linked to a mordant critique of contemporary capitalism, particularly as it relates to US imperialism. His writings, always polemical, covers a broad gamut of themes but is always closely linked to the interests and struggles of the popular oppressed classes. Although his specific contributions in the area of migration have been sporadic they nevertheless provide vital elements for a Marxist critique of labour migration in the current context of global capitalist development and US imperialism. In many ways his writings have been a fundamental source of inspiration for my own reflections and work in this area.[3]

Delgado Wise's contribution to this volume takes as its point of departure Petras' conception of 'forced migration' as 'imperialism' to engage in a critical analysis of an issue that has captured the attention [if not the imagination] of most analysts today of the labour migration phenomenon: the dialectical relationship of 'migration' to 'development'.

The contributions of Morley, Delgado Wise, Kumbamu, Berberoglu, Lendman and Parenti point towards 'US imperialism' as a fundamental concern and leitmotif, a key point of reference, in Petras' writings over the years, which has often focused on the dynamics of *capitalist development as imperialism*: the use of state power or military force in one context, the discourse on 'globalization' and 'development' in others. The aim of much of Petras' writing in this connection has been to draw attention to the multifaceted dynamics of US imperialism—the projection of ideological, military, economic and political power to serve the geopolitical and economic interests of the US empire.

On this issue, *Ashok Kumbamu* revisits an important theoretical debate between Lenin and Kautsky and amongst other Marxist scholars in the early twentieth century—an important reference point for what we might term the sociology and political economy of imperialism as it unfolded, and was studied, in the second half of the twentieth century: *Pax Americana*. In this connection—and with reference to recent Marxist reformulations of the concept (by Petras and others) and the recent history of US imperialism—he argues that the concept of imperialism is fundamental to a Marxist understanding of the dynamics of

---

[3] The editor notes that the writings of Delgado Wise in this area are second to none and constitute the best available from a critical Marxist perspective, an indispensable source of reference for a critical analysis of the migration-development problematic.

capitalist development. In this he follows Petras in launching a critique of Michael Hardt and Antonio's acclaimed (by postmodernists and the liberal bourgeois business press) study of 'Empire'. On Petras' critique see his *Empire with Imperialism* (Petras and Veltmeyer, 2003).

As for Berberoglu he picks up on a theme dealt with systematically by Petras in his 2001 study *Unmasking Globalization*, namely the projection of ideological power in the idea of globalization, using it as a ideological cover to justify and legitimate neoliberal policies of structural adjustment to the requirements of the 'new world order'. Berberoglu here follows Petras to argue that contemporary neoliberal globalization is the specific form taken by late twentieth century capitalist imperialism. Exposing the class character of neoliberal capitalist globalization as a mechanism of ideological hegemony, a means of advancing the domination and expansion of capitalist class power on a world scale, Berberoglu highlights the inherent contradictions of the neoliberal globalization project in the era of modern imperialism. Focusing on the class contradictions of this process, he draws into the discussion the heavy hand of the imperial state as the leading arm of the transnational monopolies, serving as their protector and guarantor of global political-economic rule in an age of heightened crisis and conflict. Thus, he drives home the point made so convincingly by Petras regarding the centrality of political power and the pivotal role of the imperial state in the global class struggle between labour and capital—a struggle that in the end is a struggle for maintaining or capturing state power. Hence the state becomes the centrepiece of popular struggles that carry the potential for social revolution and societal transformation.

While Berberoglu focuses on the class contradictions of neoliberal globalization, Parenti and Lendman pick up on another major theme of Petras' recent work: *the politics of imperialism* in the form of US foreign policy. Parenti, in this connection, focuses on the 'rational destruction of Yugoslavia' by the forces of US imperialism the US national Security State, to be precise (as Parenti is in his detailed and penetrating account, which has the hallmarks of Petras' combination of analytical and political acuity, solid research and careful empirical analysis).

As for Lendman, he expands on a critical theme of Petras' most recent writings on the US imperial state, namely the projection of US state power in the Middle East and US foreign policy regarding the

Israeli state, Zionism and the Palestine Question. Petras' trenchant critique of Zionism has attracted much opprobrium, even from leftists in the US who have studiously avoided criticizing the state of Israel in this respect. A central concern and the focal point of Petras' recent writings has been the power of the Israeli lobby over US foreign policy, an issue that virtually all American sociologists, even some Marxists, for one reason or the other have totally and inexplicably ignored, notwithstanding its omnipresence and political import.

Lendman's contribution to this volume draws heavily on Petras' writings in this area. There is a sociological tradition in which both the foreign and domestic policies of the capitalist state are analyzed in ethnic as opposed to class terms. However, in regard to Israel virtually all critics apart from Petras fail to differentiate between opposition to a particular ethnic group (which would be problematic) and opposition to a specific nationalist discourse and politics (which is perfectly acceptable). In becoming a nation-state, Israel passed from the former identity to the latter, notwithstanding the frequent efforts to conflate the two positions. This is in fact what Petras has argued, linking the current power of the US lobby and the diaspora in the US to its ability to stigmatize in ethnic terms all criticism of the political actions of the state of Israel. But if the premise of this defence were conceded, it would be impossible to criticize any nation-state for its policies.

The study of imperialism is a field to which Petras has made crucially important contributions. The political economy of capitalist development is another. In this area Foster and Holleman in their contribution draw our attention to a critical feature of capitalist development studied by Petras, namely the propensity of capitalism towards crisis, and the multiple and global dimensions of this crisis. Of course, at the moment there scarcely exists a sociology of *crisis* just as there is no defined sociology of *imperialism* or very little beyond the many writings of Petras in this area (some 20 book-length studies and publications since 1978 and at least 14 since 2000). The dynamics of crisis and imperialism, major focal points of Petras' writings and class analysis—on the need for a sociology and political economy of crisis see Petras (1984)—are generally subsumed (and displaced from the centre of analysis, or entirely) within academic sociology by a concern with, and theoretical discourses on *development* and *globalization*. Thus, today there is a well-defined, albeit changing, field of sociological study subsumed under the rubric of the 'development', and in recent years Sklair (1995), Robinson (2003) and others (Araghi and McMichae, for example)—proponents of a 'world systems (as opposed to a strictly class analysis) approach' to capitalist development—have constructed what we might well term a 'sociology of globalization', which has effectively displaced the sociology of development of earlier years. However, the value of Petras' work in this and other areas is precisely to shift the focus of critical sociology and Marxism away from globalization and development towards imperialism, the 'inner secret' we might say (paraphrasing Marx in regard to capitalism) or the underlying reality of both development and globalization.

The importance of this *festschrift* is that besides paying homage to a major Marxist scholar of the twentieth century it points to the way forward for both Marxism and what has been termed 'critical development studies' (Veltmeyer, 2009)—a critical 'political economy' approach to a class analysis of the dynamics of an epochal shift in global capitalism—what some (e.g. Robinson, 2004; Sassen, 2007) term the 'sociology of globalization' and others, in more conventional terms, 'current world affairs'. This broad field of studies, no matter how labelled, needs to be reconstructed in Marxist terms and directed towards the study of: (1) the social dynamics and contradictions of labour and the class struggle in diverse national contexts; (2) the power dynamics of imperialism and the imperial state set up to advance the capital accumulation process and secure the class interests as well as the system behind it; and (3) the global, national and local dynamics of capitalist development and systemic crisis in its multiple forms.

Again, and to conclude, it is James Petras who has helped us to see the way forward, which is not to abandon but rather to return to and sharpen the tools of class analysis—to reverse the 'postmodern turn' in social analysis identified by Best and Kelner (1997) and to turn back towards a reconstituted Marxist class analysis exemplified by James Petras.

CHAPTER TWO

JAMES PETRAS AND THAT 'LONG PETAL OF WINE,
SEA AND SNOW'

Fernando I. Leiva

The first time I met Salvador Allende was in 1965 in the bar of the US
Senate building. At that time he was a senator, and I was a graduate
student writing my doctoral dissertation and was deeply involved in the
anti-Vietnam War movement in the US. Before leaving San Francisco
for Chile, the organizers of an upcoming demonstration had asked me
to tape an interview with Senator Allende expressing his support for the
anti-war movement in the US. Allende's support was particularly important for the struggle in the US because the mass base of our movement
was basically composed of students, middle-class professionals and very
few workers. We felt it would be important for morale to have the international support of a leftist presidential candidate who received over a
million votes, mainly from the working class, peasants, and the trade
unions.

(Petras, 1998)

Although the work of James Petras has encompassed many different
countries, it is not farfetched to claim that Chile has decisively shaped
both his insights about social processes and commitment to popular
struggles; indeed for more than four decades, that 'long petal of wine,
sea and snow'[1] called Chile has been at the centre of his formation and
maturation as a revolutionary intellectual.

His numerous contributions to our understanding about the interconnected dynamics of capitalist development and class struggles
which over the past half century have shaped Chilean society are
impressive. However equally admirable is that while engaging in
analysis of the highest scholarly and political caliber, Petras has also
consistently displayed three traits worthy of emulation, particularly
at the present moment. Witnessed at first from afar as a mere student and later observed directly as one of his long-list of collaborators and co-authors, perhaps more than any other living intellectual

---

[1] Pablo Neruda, "Cuando de Chile."

James Petras has embodied these three qualities that define activist
scholarship:

1. the unfailing courage to submit to ruthless criticism 'everything
   under the sun' even if it means going against the grain of the cher-
   ished myths of the ruling elites, mainstream academia and even the
   Left itself;[2]
2. a genuine commitment to hear grassroots activists and militants not
   as 'data' but incorporating them into an on-going dialogue as a way
   of 'naming the moment' and defining effective lines of action;
3. a permanent concern with locating specific events transpiring in concrete social formations within the broader development of capitalism
   on a world scale and the struggle against imperialism, and to do so
   without reductionism, teleological thinking or loss of finely grained
   uniqueness of the phenomena studied.

This chapter sketches how these traits have been embedded throughout Chile's sharply different historical periods into his analysis of
the changing interaction among structural transformations, politics,
mass mobilizations and class consciousness.[3] With different degrees
of saliency, one can spot these traits coalescing in his initial study in
the late 1960s of the factors behind the crisis of Chile's old import-
substitution industrialization corporatist model of domination and
the resulting the emergence of class conscious peasants, urban and
rural workers and urban squatters. They are present when examining the election of Salvador Allende and transformative aspirations
under the brief Popular Unity government of the early 1970s as well as
his work on the bloody closure of a pre-revolutionary period through
imperialist intervention and state-terror enthusiastically endorsed by
Chile's dominant classes. Later, they re-emerge and are renewed in his
writings covering Chile's long, brutal counter-revolution that laid the
foundations for capitalist transformation under the seventeen year-
long military dictatorship of General Pinochet (1973–1989). They are

---

[2] In his "Letter to Ruge," written in 1843 when he was only 25 years old, Marx
expresses a conviction which was to orient his life, a conviction that James has also
lived though his work. Marx's letter states: "But, if constructing the future and set-
tling everything for all times are not our affair, it is all the more clear what we have
to accomplish at present: I am referring to *ruthless criticism* of all that exists, ruthless
both in the sense of not being afraid of the results it arrives at and in the sense of being
just as little afraid of conflict with the powers that be."

[3] This is a preliminary approximation based on a re-reading of a limited selection of
his writings on Chile. A fuller account would entail interviews with James and asking
him to reflect on his own personal and intellectual trajectory.

deeply set into the fabric of his work on the negotiated transition to a civilian elected regime that established what has turned out to be a two-decade long series of Concertación administration promising "growth with equity" but delivering the consolidation of transnational capital's hegemony over Chilean society.

The Vaunted Pre-1970 Model of Democracy

Setting out from San Francisco in the early 1960s to begin work on a dissertation focused on studying the class consciousness of the Chilean working class, it soon became apparent, as Petras himself acknowledged that, 'working-class political behaviour could best be understood by examining the working class's relationship to other classes, namely the peasantry, the landowners, and the middle class' (Petras, 1969, vii). Broadening his scope was imperative because such relations were defined to a great extent through political conflicts rooted in existing social conditions and social forces and, in turn, "these conflicts were mediated through changing political mechanisms that frequently shaped the form and even the content of social development" (Petras, 1969: vii). Thus being in Chile of the last 1960s, brought about an important shift in his gaze: "[m]y research interests increasingly turned toward an investigation of the role of political parties and elites, and the bureaucracy, in shaping Chilean development" (Petras, 1969: vii).

Published in this expanded form with the title *Politics and Social Forces in Chilean Development*, his dissertation grappled with one of the great debates at the time: Why, if sharing so many of the similar problems of other countries in Latin America, did Chile enjoy such widespread political stability? This was a particularly confounding question, as along with such stability Chile was *also* a country with a relatively powerful class conscious labour movement and electorally powerful Socialist and Communist Parties, all of them committed in their political programs and every day rhetoric to capitalism's overthrow. Yet since the late 1930s, Chile had experienced a long period of relatively sustained political stability. Despite the appearance of new reformist political forces like the Christian Democratic Party, the existence of a classist labour movement and two avowedly Marxist parties, the power of the ruling elites had remained mostly unchanged. In providing an answer to this apparent conundrum, Petras challenged self-serving myths among mainstream scholars, Chile's elites as well as the Left. As one reviewer summed it up: "Mr. Petras finds that the much admired democratic forms in Chile conceal an essentially exploitative substance; that parliamentary politics has served mainly the interests of party elites; that political coalitions of the working and middle classes have operated to the advantage of the middle class; and that the bureaucracy has reinforced elite rule."[4]

Petras carefully traces how the State and the political system[5] during the 1938–1969 period, played a double role being both 'the cause and consequence of a fusion of modern and traditional values in Chilean society', a blend enabling it ultimately to perform "the dual functions of representing new and traditional groups and serving as a broker for their conflicting demands" (Petras, 1969: 1). This fusion of continuity and change at the political level without substantive modifications in the existing constellation of class power would remain a central theme running though his work on Chile in the following four decades. He first brings it to our attention in the 1960s, capturing the distinctive feature of the Chilean social formation as it engaged in Alliance for Progress-sanctioned 'Revolution in Liberty', the US-endorsed alternative to the Cuban revolution: "The synthesis of modern desires for development and a hierarchical social structure *has produced a corporatist style of politics*. The Christian Democrat's attempts *to increase welfare without replacing dominant groups* reflect the ambiguity associated with corporate-populist politics" (Petras, 1969: 3–4 [emphasis added]). More than just a structural characteristic defining a relatively long period of Chilean history, this contradiction also deeply marked that particular conjuncture: "Political drama is found in the conflicts that unfold when this new elite, committed to altering the past and yet linked by experience to it, attempts to apply its programs for development and reform to an electorate that is disenchanted with past failures. A policy step in any direction (or none at all) may antagonize one or another of the groups that make up the multiclass coalition" (Petras, 1969: 3–4).

By probing the implications of this lack of correspondence between rhetorical and substantive change, Petras sought to bare the inner con-

---

[4] Back cover of Petras (1969).
[5] In a language perhaps still too tinged by mainstream sociology, he calls the State and political system, 'the bureaucracy'.

tradictions of Chilean society at the time: "I intend to examine the friction between the traditional coalition and bargaining methods of governing, and compare the old methods to the new mobilization style of politics rapidly taking hold of the polity" (Petras, 1969: 2). Such examination would provide the key for answering questions such as: 'Why are the middle strata oriented toward *stability* and unconcerned with basic social change? What forces militate against other social groups (peasants, miners) to produce an emergent radical political culture? How has recent economic and social development affected the difference in political orientation between the middle strata and the peasantry? What has produced the dramatic upsurge of Christian Democracy? What are its political appeals?' (Petras, 1969: 2).

Buried under the specifics one finds his work addressing the central question posed by the historical conditions of the time—Reform or Revolution?—a question that was quickly acquiring urgency in Chile and one that profoundly influenced Petras: "The synthesis of modern desires for development and a hierarchical social structure has produced a corporatist style of politics. The Christian Democrat's attempts to increase welfare without replacing dominant groups reflect the ambiguity associated with corporate-populist politics. Political drama is found in the conflicts that unfold when this new elite, committed to altering the past and yet linked by experience to it, attempts to apply its programs for development and reform to an electorate that is disenchanted with past failures. A policy step in any direction (or none at all) may antagonize one or another of the groups that make up the multiclass coalition" (Petras, 1969: 3–4).

Intensifying conflicts within the elites in addition to the radicalization of those involved in reformist 'popular promotion' programs encouraged by the carefully Christian-Democratic choreographed organization of peasants, *pobladores* and women posed two conflicting paths forward which Petras registers and examines: "Mobilization politics manifests two alternative approaches to reorganizing society: *the corporatist approach*, whereby the government controls and directs lower-class associations and links them with existing economic elites in an attempt to encourage collaboration for national development; and *the collectivist approach*, whereby class-conscious political actors *communicate a radical political culture among lower-class individuals* in order to mobilize their support and to undermine the existing elites as the first phase towards the creation of a collectivist society" (Petras, 1969: 5 [emphasis added]).

The 'Politics of Opposition': A Coopted Left along with Emerging New Consciousness

The outcome of such conflict between 'corporatist' and 'radical' mobilization politics was also shaping the Left's 'politics of opposition' as well as the nature of the political consciousness being formed among newly emergent social sectors in the cities and the countryside. Petras examines in great detail both of these elements during this period, making valuable contribution to understanding the dynamics of this historical period.

In a sharp break with the existing thinking at the time, Petras shows how Chile's political system has been able to successfully co-opt the traditional Left parties. His detailed analysis of the Chilean case shows the extent to which, "The working class parties have also been co-opted, on a different scale, with the result that *the Left has adopted the middle—class parliamentary style of politics*. Unable to gain a popular majority, the left-wing parties have turned to parliamentary bargaining, the trading of votes and support for influence on short-run issues" (Petras 1969: 160 [emphasis added]). Thus instead of promoting working class protagonism, endorsement of parliamentary democracy politics has served to domesticate the Left. This penetrating critique, devastating for the Left's self-image and crucial for understanding its real and not perceived historical role, was not argued on the basis of pre-existing doctrinal or ideological bias. Rather, it was solidly anchored on the 'concrete analysis of the concrete', that is on the study of the specific mechanisms through which Left office holding became a vehicle for social mobility and domestication. Thus, based on the compilation of data on the careers of 87 senators and deputies of the Socialist Party obtained from Clodomiro Almeyda, then secretary of organization for the Socialist Party's Santiago regional structure, Petras documents how "[t]wo thirds of the Socialist politicians elected before 1965 rose in social position through their office either because they held office or because the fact of holding office bettered their subsequent employment. Three-quarters of those who held office prior to 1961 rose socially, again for the same reasons" (Petras, 1969: 161).

Among other elements, such analysis opened up a totally different entry point on debates about the relevance of Latin America's revolutionary left. Beyond discussions about the nature of capitalist development in Latin America and the 'anti-feudal' versus 'proletarian' character of the Latin American revolution, the existence or not of a national bourgeoisie, or armed versus peaceful roads, Petras' analysis of the Chilean situation posed a new angle from which to evaluate the role of the emergent revolutionary left: the requisite to preserve significant levels of autonomy from the capitalist state. More than lofty declarations and rhetorical flourishes a practice that preserved real autonomy from the state and the hegemonic political system, became imperative for revolutionary politics at that historical juncture.

In addition to examining the Chilean Left's relation to the State and the political system, Petras was also carrying a detailed analysis of the development of workers and peasants' class consciousness working alternatively with Hugo Zemelman, Maurice Zeitlin, Andy Zimbalist and others. In a couple of articles "Agrarian Radicalism" and "Miners and Agrarian Radicalism" published in Spanish under the suggestive title of *El radicalismo político de la clase trabajadora chilena*, Petras carefully examined how subjective and objective conditions were mutually influencing one another at that particular moment in Chilean history.[6]

Through his carefully researched case studies both in the countryside and the cities, the notion that participation in political struggles could be transformative of each participant's world view emerged with force: "The theoretical issue that cropped up was that conscious participation in social processes by different political actors could become the nexus (intervening variable) between the objective conditions of existence of sectors like the peasantry and the subjective response to such conditions in the form of leftist political behavior and development of their political consciousness" (Petras and Zeitlin, 1969a, 45–46).

Based on extended interviews at the Culiprán fundo in Chile's Central Valley with peasants who recount in their own terms their political evolution over a crucial six-year period, Petras challenged the oft-accepted assumption that peasants represent a passive, traditional, downtrodden group, capable only of following urban-based elites

---

[6] In chapter 5 of *Politics and Social Forces in Chilean Development*, Petras offers the following historical periodization in the development of the working class movement: (1) The mutual aid period 1850–1890; (2) The syndicalist period 1890–1920; (3) The reformist period 1920–1937; (4) The Popular Front period, 1938–1950 and, (5) The resurgence of reformism and growth of the FRAP 1956–to the present. Periodization has been an important tool in the Petras's tool chest.

(Petras and Zemelman, 1972). The book *Peasants in Revolt: A Chilean Case Study, 1965–1971* is divided in two parts. The first presents the authors' analysis, but the second half contains the testimonies of the peasants themselves, who in their own voices, recount their own political evolution as participants in the struggle for land and social rights. The combination of structural analysis with oral history, forcefully evidences how the emergence of revolutionary political consciousness is the result of cumulative experiences and the breakdown of traditional institutions of control as violent land takeovers are increasingly perceived as legitimate forms of struggles by the peasants themselves. But importantly, this very detailed field work, allows Petras to underscore that such consciousness is not fixed, but rather that there is an ebb and flow: "The original dynamism and radicalism that appeared in the initial stages of the land occupation, however, where largely transitory...the once insurgent peasant turned entrepreneurs exploiting labour and accumulating property and capital at the expense of their former compañeros" (p. xii). For the peasantry or any other social strata, in the factories, farms or *poblaciones* studied, the development of political consciousness was the result of this dynamic interplay between objective and subjective conditions, not something automatically predetermined by a structural location in the social division of labour or only by participation in political struggles.

The study of the forms of consciousness and radicalization of peasants, urban squatters and miners in late 1960s Chile is at the source of another major theme will run through his work in the following decades: the tension between institutionalized politics and grassroots mobilizations, a dynamic that can lead both to radicalization as well as cooptation. A rigorous analysis of specific situations which centrally incorporates the actors' voices and perceptions is methodologically essential to assess how such a contradiction is resolved in each different juncture.

The Popular Unity and the Overthrow of Allende

The mobilizations and development in political consciousness studied by Petras as a graduate student led to the opening up of a new historical period in Chilean history: the election of a popular government and the increased political awareness and self organization of vast sectors of the working class and popular sectors. The net outcome of these dynamics would be a unique historical conjuncture during which the working class, the Left and popular movement would achieve their highest level of influence in Chilean history. As in other pre-revolutionary situations in history, under the Allende government and through their struggles of 1970–1973, the Chilean masses were to learn in days and weeks, what under other historical conditions would take decades. In the end, such process would pose the inevitable practical question between the forces of revolution and counter-revolution, the question of power.

From this very succinct review of his pre-1973 work on Chile, a number of themes clearly emerge: (a) the uneven development of Chilean capitalism; (b) how class struggles can erode existing structures of authority and give rise to new forms of political action and consciousness; (c) social mobilizations and social actors going far beyond what political leaders encased by institutional politics, imagined or desired; and (d) the dialectical relationship between national political conjuncture, local struggles and the development of political consciousness. At the same time, during this entire period Petras resorts to a wide range of methodological approaches: structural analysis interlinked but not reduced to the study of the political behaviour of social sectors; a full acknowledgement of the importance of listening to the voice of the actors themselves so as to better unravel realignments unfolding with growing scope and intensity; and the use of periodization to discern how qualitative and quantitative changes lead to shifts in the correlation of forces. Forged in what we could call the first stage of his career, these approaches were to be applied later in Chile and other countries.

Petras closes *Political Forces and Social Development in Chile* with an chillingly exact assessment of the stance of the Chilean ruling class and upper strata of the middle classes under its influence: "The upper class and many middle-class individuals profoundly reject the idea of a strong collectivist government with a populist orientation. Whatever national sentiments they hold, these strata of Chilean society would not be adverse to collaborating with the United States in overthrowing a popularly elected socialist government" (Petras, 1969: 354–355). Such a violent *denouement* would come in 1973 with the US-supported overthrow of Allende.

Bringing the Imperial State Back In

After the September 1973 military coup, Petras became an important voice denouncing the repression of the Junta, serving from 1973 to

1976 as a member of the Bertrand Russell Tribunal, demystifying the
rhetoric of military Junta and its civilian allies known as the Chicago
boys, and carefully detailing the logic behind US intervention.

In 1975, Petras and Morris Morley published *The United States
and Chile: Imperialism and the Overthrow of the Allende Government.*
Based on a systematic analysis of the US government's planning
behind Allende's overthrow, Petras draws a theoretically and politically
important lesson: 'Despite the far-flung and diffuse interests that the
multinationals possess, and despite the enormous economic resources
at their disposal, they do not posses the military, financial, ideological and administrative apparatuses that define the imperial state. *The
growth, expansion, and survival of the multinationals is in large part
dependent on the action of the imperial state*' (Petras and Morley, 1975:
viii). The analysis of the coup in Chile and of the historical role of the
imperial state would undergird some of the debates posed a quarter
of a century later by Hardt and Negri and the theorists of 'empire
without imperialism'. As Petras and Morley point out for the Chilean
case (as the US invasion of Iraq underscores), "Without the military
power or the administrative and ideological infrastructure developed
by the imperial state, it is impossible to conceive of the multinational
corporations establishing roots throughout the world. Moreover, the
expansion of the multinational requires constant injections of *aid* to
subsidize accomodating national states, and develop their infrastructure" (Petras and Morley, 1975: viii).

Replicating early 20th century debates about the nature of imperialism and also of the 1960s about what would constitute successful
strategies for societal transformation, Petras and Morley underscore
that what operated in the overthrow of Allende was not the expression
of *rogue policy* run amok within the US administration, but rather *the
product of systemic reality of imperialism.* As they point out, "Public
lies, covert subversion, the destruction of democracy, and the support
for a military dictatorship *all have their root in imperial capitalism's
need for a regime that opens the country to exploitation.* US policy
makers devised a strategy designed to destroy the democratic-socialist government of Chile and return the country to its former client-
state position within the US sphere of influence" (Petras and Morley,
1975: xvii [emphasis added]). Of equal relevance to struggles unfolding today in Bolivia and Venezuela, Petras and Morley, conclude that,
"The major lesson to be learned by the Third World from the Chilean
experience is that societies intent on revolution must follow the

Cuban example—close all channels to external subversion and extend democracy only to those who abide by the process" (Petras and Morley, 1975: vii).

Conflicts within the Pinochet Regime

Chile's failed attempt at revolution did not sever the links of Petras with Chile. Under a very new historical period, that of neoliberal-led global restructuring of capitalism, Petras remained intimately engaged with examining the policies of the dictatorship and the struggles for democracy, becoming one of the most informed and insightful analysts of the Pinochet regime. During the decade immediately following the military coup, Petras publishes books and journal articles but also begins to regularly publish in the popular press. Just like Marx's writings for *The New York Daily Tribune*, these popular press articles examining specific events under Pinochet's Chile, provide a valuable insight into the power of a sharply honed skills and intimate knowledge of the Chilean situation.

In 1975 for example, *The Nation* published 'The Junta Besieged: Generals without Bankers' reminding us that class conflicts exist not only on a 'vertical' axis between those at the bottom and those at the top, but unfold also on a 'horizontal' level within the bloc in power. Thus, Petras alerts us that "[t]he bankers of New York, the earliest and strongest supporters of the Chilean junta, have begun to doubt the wisdom of sending more good money after bad. The money-men are not troubled by any questions of human rights or political repression. For the First National City executives and their associates the problem is the disintegrating state of the Chilean economy the frightening spectacle of a 400 per cent inflation rate" (Petras, 1975a: 784).

The posterior evolution of this conflict would bring a significant realignment within the military Junta, leading to the exit of Air Force Chief General Gustavo Leigh, Pinochet's consolidation as *primus inter pares* and the predominance of the Chicago Boys over policy making, all factors that were to make Chile the pioneer in neoliberal led capitalist restructuring. At the same time, that these realignments within the bloc in power are explained, Petras highlights the persistence of one of the Chilean bourgeoisie's defining characteristic: its preference for quick and easy profits from financial speculation rather

than productive investment. Thus, Petras suggests that the productive versus speculative circuits for the self-valorization of capital are
an important issue to consider for explaining the renegotiation of the
relationship between empire and client: "Business officials here point
out that the Chilean industrialists have yet to show the entrepreneurial
capacity to invest and save on a scale necessary to promote national
development". As one former Anaconda executive told Petras, "They
[the Chilean industrialists] have a seignorial mentality; they're only
sixty years off the hacienda". In this connection Petras (1975a: 785)
notes that: "[t]he performance of the industrial sector over the past
year hardly refutes that appraisal: inflation has encouraged speculative
investments over production, while reductions in protective legislation
and government credits have pushed the private sector in the same
direction, further feeding the flames of inflation" (ibid.). Further, he
adds: "these economic circumstances and government policies have
led to—sharper criticism of the junta from some Chilean industrial
sectors and from petit-bourgeois commercial groups, who look back to
the pre-Allende days when a government-protected and—subsidized
'private enterprise' flourished under the guise of national development
(Petras, 1975a: 785).

The uncontested predominance of the Chicago Boys, the dogmati-
cally faithful disciples of Milton Friedman was to be short-lived. In
another article published in 1983 also in *The Nation* ('The Chicago
Boys Flunk Out in Chile'), he examines the magnitude of the 1982
economic crisis and how it brought an end to dogmatic neoliberalism
and the unquestioned influence of the Chicago Boys within the military
regime. In Petras' words: "The marked economic decline threw the-
Friedmanites into disarray, resulting in a rapid turnover in the top ech-
elon of economic advisers. Three different teams were sent in to stem
the downward slide in 1982, and each one failed. Economic realities
and political pressures forced the Friedmanites to abandon their free-
market ideology and resort to governmental intervention" (1983: 210).

Petras continues: "Last fall a massive bailout operation was launched
to save the banks. Overdue or unrecoverable bank loans totaled more
than $1 billion half the banking system's capital and reserves-and the
state stepped in, buying up the banks' bad debts and letting the debt-
ors go under". In return for absorbing the bad debts, Petras notes,
"the government assumed control over profits and dividend payments,
and will monitor all lending to prevent conflicts of interest between
corporations and banks". In this context, "[t]he free market ideologues

knew that without state supervision, financiers would channel credit to companies in which they had a financial interest" (Petras, 1983: 210).

In this same vein, with Steve Vieux, Petras would later explore the illusory more than real nature of the so-called Chilean economic miracle (Petras and Vieux, 1990). The deep economic crisis of 1982 would not only bring the decline of the Friedmanite Chicago Boys but it would also place in motion all the social classes and sectors of Chilean society, leading to a crisis of the military regime.

Popular Resistance, Reorganization and Dictatorial Response

The deepening crisis, elite discontent and growing protests, would generate massive and country wide mobilizations during the 1983–1989 period, bringing about a significant ramp up in anti-dictatorial struggles. Again Petras examines the inter-action between economic, political and ideological factors behind the growing number of anti-dictatorial protests. At the root of these protests is the new class basis of Chilean politics, that is the restructuring of Chilean capitalism and the emergence of new natural resource capitalist-intensive export sectors based on the superexploitation of labour (agroexports, mining, forestry, fishing) (Petras, 1988b). As in the 1960s, these structural transformations in Chilean society were bringing the emergence of new social actors, forms of struggles and consciousness, all of which could be radicalized when sifted through the on-going struggles against superexploitation and the historical memory of previous popular power experiences under the Allende government (Leiva and Petras, 1986; Leiva and Petras, 1987).

Along with rising popular resistance and mobilizations, the military regime initiated a series of attempts to prolong its existence. In the mid 1980s, Petras obtained a copy of an internal document from the military regime showing how it was planning to ensure Pinochet's triumph in the 1988 plebiscite and legitimize his rule as President for another decade. Petras analyzed this strategy (Pinochet's "New Order") and explained how it was based on combining decentralization and municipalization of state action, new administrative mechanisms for targeting social policy along with the establishment of new clientelistic relationships based on political interventions at the municipal and local level. All of Pinochet's plans, however, could not stem the overwhelming forces aligning against him. As Petras pointed out, Chile was entering that complex time when it would become necessary to 'sacrifice dictators in order to save the regime'.

After Pinochet's defeat in the 1988 plebiscite, illusions about the imminent return to genuine democracy exploded. Petras sought to bring some clarity to what was transpiring and do so by bringing a class analytic perspective to the new situation. His essay 'The New Class Basis of Chilean Politics' represents a synthesis of his previous studies about the nature of the Greek and Spanish 'transitions to democracy' with his now almost two decade long involvement with Chile. Cutting like a hot knife through butter, his analysis provided the basic points of orientation for understanding the new situation:

> For the new power bloc, however, comprising the armed forces, the capitalist class, bankers and technocrats, the primary concern has been not the plebiscite as such but the need to safeguard the accumulation regime established over the past fifteen years. The Pinochet regime served a number of invaluable historical purposes: destruction of the Popular Unity government and of the socialist movements; consolidation of the military and civilian bureaucracies; integration of Chile into international financial, commercial and agricultural circuits; relocation of political debate on the terrain of private market discourse; and the elimination of most anti-imperialist intellectual currents. In the process of realizing these aims, however, the dictatorship incurred numerous enemies, provoked large-scale, sustained opposition, and eventually became an obstacle to the reproduction and legitimation of the new economic and institutional order. Fifteen years of terror and free market exploitation are not an appropriate basis for winning plebiscites. And the opposition political class, with a critical discourse, is capable of eliciting popular support and subordinating the mass of the population to a political pact with the power bloc-although this bloc itself is demanding stiff terms and setting very narrow margins for mainly legal-political reform (Petras, 1988b).

The issues delineated above were to become the topic of a lengthier and detailed analysis of the forces and interests involved in Chile's negotiated transition (Petras and Leiva, 1988, Petras and Leiva, 1994).

The Negotiated Transition to a Civilian Elected Regime

At the end of the 1980s, Petras again visits Chile and interacts *in situ* with grassroots leaders, activists and left militants. Each visit involves extended conversations and public fora in shantytowns, churches, and trade union halls. Many of the themes of a quarter of a century of work on Chile outlined above, reemerge transformed by the new conditions but retaining more than just family resemblances with the past. It is during this period that the three traits described above—courage to submit everything to ruthless criticism, genuine valuation of the knowledge of grassroots leaders and militants, and linking local phenomena within broader trends—became more sharply constitutive of his analysis of the Chilean case. It is a period in which in meetings with workers, women, farm workers, rank-an file militants, and community organizers, Petras becomes both a researcher as well as an active protagonist in the ideological rearming of Chile's popular movements; Petras both educated and was educated as to the dynamics unfolding.[7]

His prior work on the Greek and Spanish transition to democracy gave him a unique understanding of the nature of the negotiated transition unfolding in Chile and Latin America, an understanding that found great affinity with grassroots activists, but was sorely lacking among the leaders of the left-wing Socialists, the Communist Party and the MIR. While one sector of the left engaged in the 'socialist renovation' process, denounced Marxism and celebrated the purportedly universal value of liberal bourgeois democreacy (la *democracia sin apellidos*), the other Left found itself rudderless and with fraying links with a social base.

In *Democracy and Poverty in Chile: The Limits of Electoral Politics* written by Petras, and Leiva with Veltmeyer, we countered much of the self-serving rhetoric with an approach that emphasized bringing attention to the "intricate interaction of ideological and political, as well as structural and strategic factors that shaped the changes experienced in Chilean society between 1973 and 1992" (Petras and Leiva, 1994: 1–2). In my view, *Democracy and Poverty in Chile: The Limits to Electoral Politics* made four important contributions to debates about understanding the nature of the negotiated transition. First, it analytically separated the categories of 'state', 'regime' and 'government', an

---

[7] This role requires further examination that lies beyond the scope of this article. Three significant elements could be studied: (a) his participation in numerous local assemblies in the urban shantytowns and local trade unionists; (b) publication of his articles in the theoretical journals of the Left, like the MIR's *Debate y Cambio*; and the 1991 publication of his analysis of the transition to democracy as a special 40-page supplement in the left-wing weekly *Punto Final.*

essential step for clearly discerning form from substance when discussing the State and political system, as well as for clearly comprehending the nature of class interests and power relations involved in transition processes. Second, it underscored that the blending of *political change* with the *socioeconomic continuities of class power* constituted an essential entry-point for understanding the nature of transition processes, particularly in the Chilean case. While these first two points have also characterized other transitions, perhaps what distinguished the Chilean transition was the extent and swiftness of the ideological conversion of 'critics into converts'. As one reviewer points out "The authors' claim that the conversion of opposition leaders to neoliberalism and their acceptance of the 'rules of the game' imposed by the authoritarian regime were motivated by the "influence of impersonal institutional powers, and private social ambition" (Castillo, 1995: 92). "The rebels and dissidents of yesterday are the conformist managers and promoters of foreign capital today" (p. 95). They then characterize the Chilean transition as "one from a closed, repressive, centralized military regime to an open, authoritarian, elected civilian regime" (Castillo, 1995: 722–23).

The fourth and final contribution of *Democracy and Poverty in Chile*, draws on a thread picked up by Petras decades before, namely that Chilean development has always been propelled forward by two souls: the bureaucratic, institutionalized conservative one of the elites and its political servants, and the profoundly democratic aspirations of the grassroots and local social movements. Thus, "If official Chilean politics has largely been a series of compromises between a domesticated Left and entrenched privileged classes, where democracy is subordinated to property, then unofficial politics, the politics of the social movements, has been a search by a cumulative set of democratic grassroots organizations hoping to create a political system in which property privileges are subordinated to democracy, in the broadest social, economic, and cultural sense" (Petras and Leiva, 1994: 6).

The Concertacion's Failed Promise

A former textile woman worker who remembers the Allende years told me a couple of years ago Allende was a socialist for the poor; these deputies are socialists for the rich (Petras, 1998).

Towards the end of the 1990s, as it became evident that these demo-cratic grassroots movement had been defeated, the Left fragmented and the hegemony of transnational capital imposed upon Chilean society, Petras shifted his focus to other countries. As his interest on social movements and the potential for societal transformation drew his attention to Brazil, Bolivia and Ecuador, his interest on Chile declined, but have not disappeared. Thus in 2006, four decades after his interview of Salvador Allende in the bar of the US Senate building, Petras once again discussed Chile's latest socialist president, Michelle Bachelet. Forty years of struggles, capitalist restructuring and ideologi-cal realignments had produced however a very different type of social-ist, very alien to the anti-imperialist and revolutionary stance even if through peaceful and institutional means of Salvador Allende. As Petras pointed out again: "Bachelet's rise to power demonstrates that political power is stronger than kinship ties, class allegiance are more powerful than identity politics, that past leftist affiliation are no hin-drance to becoming Washington's best ally in its defense of empire" (Petras, 2006). In a way this indicates that—at least methodologically—Petras analysis has come back full circle. The political orientation of the new socialists has to be understood just like class consciousness of the working class which he set out to study in the mid 1960s, not in isolation, but in relation to other classes and mediated by political conflicts. His analysis of the metamorphosis of Latin American intel-lectuals (Petras, 1990) and of the Concertación-led transition and con-solidation of capitalist restructuring, suggests the value of an approach that is capable of dialectically linking structural transformation, politi-cal conflict, new social actors and consciousness.

New problems loom in the horizon for the Chilean working class and popular sectors, as the working, environmental, and social quality of life is threatened by the continued expansion of transnational capi-tal and the hegemony over the society and polity of a transnationalized capitalist class. As Petras has shown, most of the basic institutions established by the dictatorship remain unchanged, acting as formi-dable barriers to any resurge of transformative social movements. The long-term effects of the authoritarian period are found not only in the state institutions bust also in the social structure, social rela-tions, and economic institutions established during the reign of terror. Democratizing Chilean society will require profound transformations that link institutional with socioeconomic change. Developing the ability to effectively defend workers' interests will demand the critical eye, the revolutionary spirit, the trust in the intellectual and political ability of the grassroots cadre, and the systematic analysis of new historical conditions that has marked both the intellectual production as well as praxis of James Petras.

An Enduring Contribution

With a consistently lucid gaze and trenchant analysis, Petras has examined the origins and crisis of Chile's pre-1973 'old order' as well as the class dynamics and consolidation of the new regime of accumulation under conditions of the new 'neoliberal' historical period.

It is symbolic that Petras himself identifies as a memorable springboard for his intellectual and political journey that in 1965 first brought him to Chile to begin his doctoral was his meeting with Salvador Allende. Even then as a graduate student, Petras intuited that struggles in the 'North' and 'South' were interconnected. For almost half a century, his work on Chile characterized by insightfulness, clarity and intellectual heft has shown the extent to which such struggles have become indeed inextricably connected.

Probably more tongue-in-cheek than historical accuracy, Petras once told me the story of how the son of a Greek immigrant raised in Massachusetts had ended up going to college and graduate school, the gateway that led him on a path that—repeatedly passing through Chile—would transform him into a 'revolutionary and anti-imperialist' as he accurately describes himself. The story is as follows: While helping out in the family store, his father grudgingly came to realize that the youngster sorely lacked the basic skills for gutting and filleting fish. Despite repeated attempts to bring him to basic competence, the father realized that such skills would not be forthcoming. In addition, encouraging any further manipulation of the sharp-edged instruments used in the fishsellers' trade would only result in certain bodily harm, not only to young Petras but to customers unfortunate enough to be around him. Grudgingly, his father concluded: 'This boy would do better going off to college'.

Whether fictional or not, many generations of students, intellectuals, activists, and members of popular movements from throughout the Americas—and especially Chile—must be thankful for this pivotal parental 'aha moment' that transformed him into one of the sharpest analysts of Chilean politics and social development.

James Petras has left a solid legacy contained in the many books and articles on Chile, but also in equal measure, in what we could denominate the ethics of a revolutionary intellectual—fearless commitment to ruthless criticism, a genuine valuing of the knowledge and capacity of grassroots leaders and social organizations both in processes of social transformation but in production of knowledge itself, and always linking the 'local' with the global, exploring how specific struggles within the broader context of capitalist development as a world system. Along with his lucid work on Chile, this modelling of what it means to be a revolutionary intellectual today, is an equally important part of his legacy, one that we can only hope he will continue expanding and enriching for the many years and struggles that lie ahead.

CAPITALISM AND MARXIST THEORY

CHAPTER THREE

TROTSKY AND LATIN AMERICAN DEVELOPMENT THEORY

Ronald H. Chilcote[1]

As we celebrate James Petras and his lifetime of activism and academic accomplishments, I return to a theme that has been of deep interest to me since our years as graduate students during the early 1960s. Our interest evolved through reading and understanding revolutions and contact with progressives throughout Latin America. The Cuban Revolution particularly influenced us. Unlike many of our professors we travelled often, shared concerns and became sensitive to the issues and problems of Latin America. The region's causes became ours as we frequently spoke out against US policy. Over the years Jim [Petras] has written many dozens of books and hundreds of articles and has laid a foundation for understanding Latin America and its relationship to the outside world. While our views may have differed at times, fundamentally we have shared in our criticism of US policy and our desire for radical change in Latin America. Our collaboration is evident in the bimonthly journal *Latin American Perspectives* with our editorial effort since its beginnings in 1974; in a book *Latin America: The Struggle with Dependency and Beyond* (1974) that sold tens of thousands of copies and was widely used in university classrooms; and in a volume on transitions in Southern Europe (1992).

In my travels I met many left intellectuals who represented an array of progressive perspectives. Some of their thinking was influenced by Cuba as they turned against ideas that had emanated from the Soviet Union and the Third International and were prominent within the communist parties throughout Latin America. Authoritarian regimes prevailed throughout most of the region where suppression and censorship made it difficult for intellectuals to speak and write, and many

[1] Thanks to Timothy Harding, Michael Löwy, and Adam Morton for comments and suggestions on my manuscript and to Jennifer Dugan Abbassi, Stan Mallison, and Jerry Riposa for research assistance.

of them sought expression through the communist parties. In 1953 the death of Stalin and the rise of a revolutionary movement in Cuba under Fidel Castro and Ernesto 'Che' Guevara opened intellectual life to new ideas, formation of new parties and social movements, diverse radical tendencies within organized labour and a challenge to the traditional communist parties. A younger generation of intellectuals moved toward diverse political groups on the left, while many older intellectuals confronted an orthodoxy of ideas within their parties and some joined the dialogue on the new left.

I visited Havana during September 1958, a few months before the Revolution consolidated power, and I returned ten years later when Fidel condemned the Soviet invasion of Czechoslovakia and students and intellectuals were questioning the aggression. Throughout Latin America attention turned toward Havana and away from Moscow, and new ideas and thinking began to challenge Soviet intransigence that backwardness was attributable to semi-feudalism and that the rise of a national bourgeoisie would ensure the development of the means of production under capitalism and eventually a transition to socialism. During my travels throughout the 1960s it was clear that the new thinking had opened up debates and intense interest in how imperialism had impacted Latin American development or underde-velopment, and that understanding of dependency on the advanced capitalist world and especially the US was essential in new theoreti-cal formulations. Some of the new thinking was attributable to ideas of Leon Trotsky, who spent the later years of his life in Mexico and incorporated Latin America into his thinking about the world. I came to know some intellectuals who were influenced by Trotsky. I was influenced by the early writings of Silvio Frondizi (1947, 1957, 1960) in Argentina, Guilhermo Lora (1977) in Bolivia and Luis Vitale (1968) in Chile. Over twenty years I corresponded with Lora who shared his writings with me, and occasionally Luis Vitale and I were in touch (I sent him Isaac Deutscher's trilogy (1954–1963) on Trotsky after he had sent me his book indicting the Frei administration that landed him in prison.

This brief background helps to understand my motivation to explore more deeply the influences of Trotsky on Latin American thinking about development, underdevelopment and dependency.

Trotsky and Theory on Underdevelopment and Dependency

The thought of Leon Trotsky (1879–1940) draws heavily from his revolutionary experiences in Russia and its revolution,[2] but also after expulsion from Russia in 1929. His exile in Mexico in 1937 until his death allowed him to reflect on his theoretical ideas as related to Latin America (1961).[3] My study concerns his elaboration of four concepts useful in understanding developmental theory and their relevance to theories of capitalist development, underdevelopment, and dependency, as prominently manifested in Latin America during the last half of the twentieth century.[4]

Backwardness and Delayed Capitalist Development

Less-developed countries do not necessarily follow the path of advanced nations, and their condition may be a consequence of advancing capitalism elsewhere. 'Backwardness' may be described as delayed capitalist development (a term frequently found in the literature on

---

[2] Born in a Jewish farmer's family in the Ukraine, Trotsky evolved from a circle of Norodniks to a Marxist Bolshevik and leader in the St Petersburg Council of Workers' Delegates (the first Soviet in history) in the 1905–1907 revolution and a leader of the 1917 revolution. He was a co-founder with Lenin of the Third International. He organized opposition to Stalin in 1926 and was deported to France in 1929 where he called for a Fourth International. Among the major sympathetic accounts of Trotsky's life are studies by Avenas (1975), Deutscher (1954–1963), and Mandel (1979) and hostile critical portrayals by Mavrakis (1976) and Volkogonov (1996), while Baruch (1979) and Howe (1976) offer useful, critical, but scholarly overviews. Wilson (1972) provides a sympathetic introductory portrait within the European radical tradition. See also Tariq Ali and Phil Evans (1982).

[3] Appraisals of Trotskyism in Latin America include sympathetic details by Campos (1981). Hodges (1974), Mandel (1979), and Munck (1984) along with a comprehensive history by Alexander (1973) that lacks in the detailed analyses of political ideas and ideological divisions within the Trotskyist movement elaborated in Hodges and Munck.

[4] It is not my intent to exaggerate the importance of Trotskyism. Alan Wald suggests that US Trotskyism, established in 1928, has become exhausted but that as Stalinism fades, a revision may be a possibility. He mentions authors such as Paul Buhl, Mike Davis, and Staughton Lynd who may at one time been influenced by Trotskyism (1994–1995: Pt 2, 34). He criticizes Alex Callinicos (1990) for analysis seen through the prism of a particular line of thinking such as the British Socialist Workers Party. Callinicos argues that Trotskyism 'has generally been intellectually resistant to the themes of Western Marxism' that Perry Anderson and others have emphasized in their intellectual history of Marxism (3). Callinicos (1990: 86–87) provides a useful chart on the organization of Trotskyism, especially the American and British strains.

underdevelopment) brought about by ways different than the advanced capitalist countries. Trotsky frequently used the term to describe Russia, and the revolution he envisaged, as a revolution of backwardness. He described this condition in his *The Russian Revolution*: 'The fundamental and most stable feature of Russian history is the slow tempo of her development, with the economic backwardness, primitiveness of social forms and low level of culture resulting from it' (1959: 1).

Although the backward country 'assimilates the material and intellectual conquests of the advanced countries', it 'does not take things in the same order.... The privilege of historic backwardness...permits... skipping a whole series of intermediate stages.... The possibility of skipping over intermediate steps is of course by no means absolute. Its degree is determined in the long run by the economic and cultural capacities of the country. The backward nation, moreover, not infrequently debases the achievements borrowed in the process of adapting them to its own more primitive culture' (2–3).

Trotsky's constant reference to backwardness is similar to the emphasis of Paul Baran whose *Political Economy of Growth* was a bestseller throughout Latin America. He wrote: 'The backward world has always represented the indispensable hinterland of the highly developed capitalist West' (1960: 12). He argued that this region could not achieve accumulation as the advanced countries had or overcome the obstacles of monopoly capitalism and imperialism.

André Gunder Frank studied under conservative economists at the University of Chicago but he was influenced by Paul Baran, a renowned Marxist economist at Stanford University. The Brazilian economist, Guido Mantega, believes that both Trotsky and Rosa Luxemburg may have influenced Frank. He notes that the position of Luxemburg on relations between advanced capitalist and colonial precapitalist countries was similar to the hypothesis of Trotsky on the tendency of the capitalist world to stagnate during the early decades of the twentieth century. Luxemburg and Trotsky noted that capitalist accumulation would lead to a polarization of classes on a worldscale.[5] Trotsky believed that imperialism would impede the advance of the productive forces in less developed countries. These ideas tend to support the

---

[5] Geras believes that Rosa Luxemburg was one of the main architects of the theory of permanent revolution (4). Further, she was close to Trotsky's thinking and despite some differences 'she did adopt a perspective essentially identical with Trotsky's theory of permanent revolution' (1975: 4–5).

notion of capitalist development of underdevelopment that evolved in the work of Frank (1966) and others (Mantega, 1982: 229–230).[6]

Combined and Uneven Development

Trotsky speaks of two laws related to backwardness and delayed capitalist development. 'Unevenness, the most general law of the historic process, reveals itself most sharply and complexly in the destiny of the backward countries. Under the whip of external necessity their backward culture is compelled to make leaps. From the universal law of unevenness thus derives another law which, for the lack of a better name, we may call the law of *combined development*—by which we mean a drawing together of the different stages of the journey, a combining of separate steps, an amalgam of archaic and more contemporary forms' (1959: 4). He notes that combined development is evident in the case of Russia: peasant cultivation of the land remained archaic, while industry reflected technology at the level of or even superior to advanced countries. The rise of the Soviet state was the result of combined development in the form of a mixture of backward elements and modern tendencies coming together: 'a peasant war—that is, a movement characteristic of the dawn of bourgeois development—and a proletarian insurrection, the movement signalizing its decline. That is the essence of 1917' (48).

This passage suggests a characterization of these laws as uneven and combined development, yet Trotskyist analysis generally refers to them as combined and uneven development. Murray Smith considers Trotsky's laws as 'perhaps his greatest single theoretical contribution' (1981: 46–47), and although not fully worked out in the writings of Marx on the Russian peasant commune, he feels that Marx would have embraced the laws of combined and uneven development as essential to historical materialist theory. Michael Löwy, who lived his early life in Brazil and has devoted attention to Latin America, wrote an important book, *The Politics of Combined and Uneven Development* (1981) that includes an analysis of Mexico and Bolivia as well as the Cuban Revolution.

---

[6] Howard and King (1989:223) quote Marx, 'The country that is more developed industrially only shows, to the less developed, the image of its own future', a proposition adhered to by both Plekhanov and Lenin, but not so by Trotsky in his theory of the Russian revolutionary process, first set forth in 1904–1906, which they argue approximates his later views.

Other writers, less sympathetic to Trotsky, focus on uneven and combined development. Howard and King argue that this idea was not introduced solely by Trotsky. They believe that it is found in Marx's *Capital* where historical materialism is implicitly understood as involving a process of uneven and combined development: 'Epochs of transition are those in which two modes of production are combined in a single social formation. Their uneven development, whereby the progressive mode forges ahead and the other stagnates, ultimately brings a crisis that can be solved only through social revolution (Howard and King, 1989: 230). They identify aspects of these ideas in both Plekhanov and Lenin whose perspectives differed from Trotsky. While Lenin, for example in his *Development of Capitalism in Russia* (1899), sought to show both the extent and underdeveloped nature of Russian capitalism, Trotsky instead emphasized its concentrated and advanced form in a context of precapitalist agriculture. Lenin based the alliance of the proletariat and peasantry on a shared condition of backwardness, Trotsky understood the opposite as true. Howard and King suggest that Tugan-Baranovsky seems to have influenced Trotsky, although there is no citation in Trotksy, arguing that it was inconceivable that Trotsky had not read *The Russian Factory* in which these ideas appeared (228).

Trotsky's extension of these ideas thus moves beyond the determinist view, in Marx and Engels' *Communist Manifesto* (1848), of successive stages from primitive forms through capitalism, socialism, and eventually communism. 'For him Russian modernization was an unbalanced process. Some sectors not only leaped ahead of others, they did so by absorbing the most advanced attributes...The core of his argument is that a belatedly modernizing Russia develops economic structures which are simultaneously the most modern and the most retarded in Europe. And it is this unbalanced form from which provides the clue to its history and future' (228).

The economist, James O'Connor, who has written an important book on the impact of monopoly capital on Cuba prior to its revolution in 1959 (1970), has also applied uneven and combined development to the contemporary ecological crisis. He defines uneven development 'as the historically produced, uneven, spatial distribution of industry, banking, commerce, wealth, consumption, labour relations, political configurations and so on' (1989: 1). He refers to some writers who distinguish between development and underdeveloped categories or rich and poor countries. He goes on to suggest that at a more theoretical level, uneven development is the exploitative relationship between dichotomies of town and country, centre and periphery, developed and underdeveloped nations that serve as the basis for the reproduction of global capitalism (2). He defines combined development as combinations of economic, social, and political forms found in developed regions as contrasted with those in underdeveloped regions that allows capital to maximize profits, advance technology, organize industry, and ensure a division of labour. He alludes to Marx as first setting forth the idea of uneven development, but there is no reference to Marx or Trotsky in his discussion of combined development.

Drawing on Marx and Trotsky, Adam Morton (2009) looks at uneven development in Mexico. He takes seriously Novack's assertion that uneven and combined development 'is indispensable for understanding the development of Latin America over the past four centuries' (1976: 103).[7] Both Novak and Löwy (1975) rebut Romagnolo's characterization of 'uneven and combined development' as 'fragmentary and undeveloped' (1975: 8). While concerned with precapitalist and capitalist relations in Mexico, Morton also notes the relevance of the term in the global capitalist world: 'The uneven tendencies of capitalist development have thus unfolded within the framework of an already existing world market and international states-system', and he identifies recent literature to support his assertion. In particular, he notes that Trotsky's attention to the unevenness of historical development was adopted by Adolfo Gilly 'to insert the combination of the nationally specific development of capitalism in Mexico within its uneven mode of insertion into the world market' (5-7).

The Permanent Revolution

Trotsky in his *Permanent Revolution* (1932) argued that the socialist revolution begins on a national level but inevitably extends to other countries, especially in the advanced industrial world: 'A national revolution is not a self-contained whole; it is only a link in the international chain' (Trotsky, 1964a: 65). Trotsky opposed efforts to establish and maintain the reformist democratic stage, arguing that the

---

[7] Morton (personal communication to Chilcote, February 5, 2009) notes that George Novack (1972: 98) looks at the unevenness of development as preceding aspects of its combination and that this emphasis is taken up in J. Rosenberg (2005: 68–69, note 28).

democratic stage is simply transitory and only the socialist transformation of society leads to 'a permanent state of revolutionary development'
(Trotsky, 1964a: 63–64; 1964b). Trotsky also set forth a conception of
development and underdevelopment in his law of uneven and combined development. In *History of the Russian Revolution* he argued that
backward countries do not necessarily follow the path of the advanced
capitalist countries. Their path is not predetermined, he believed, and
they could pass over stages en route to socialism: 'Their development
as a whole acquires a planless, complex, combined character' (Trotsky,
1959: 3). Unevenness is evident especially in 'backward' countries.
Combined development implies different stages drawing together so
that an amalgam of archaic with more contemporary forms might
ensue. Trotsky argued that socialism depends largely on the outcome
of world revolution. Proletarian revolution must spread to backward
areas. Although backward countries may be the first to establish a proletarian revolution, they may be the last to reach socialism. Backward
countries, however, need to develop the forces of production in the
struggle to reach socialism. These notions of development were coun-
terposed to Stalin's stage theory of revolution and his assumption of
a democratic revolution in backward countries independent of a proletarian revolution (Chilcote, 1984: 20).[8]

Ernest Mandel attempts to clarify the central issue around the theory of permanent revolution by distinguishing among several positions. The Mensheviks argued that because the tasks of the revolution
are bourgeois democratic, only a bourgeois government and bourgeois
state can achieve them; efforts by the working class to take power
would result in a revolutionary setback. Trotsky countered that the
bourgeoisie would support the counterrevolution and, further, that
if the bourgeoisie were to maintain its hegemony within the revolution, the revolution would collapse. Only the proletariat could lead the
revolutionary process, allied with the poor peasantry, by destroying
the bourgeois state and taking over the government. Prior to 1917
Lenin held an intermediate position, rejecting the proposition that the
bourgeoisie could carry out the tasks of the national democratic revolution in Russia, but he did not argue that an immediate destruction of

---

[8] Michael Löwy believes that the Cuban Revolution influenced intellectuals since
it exemplifies Trotsky's argument that only a socialist revolution can liberate semicolonial countries from imperialism (Löwy, personal communication to Chilcote,
February 11, 2009).

the bourgeois state was essential in the revolutionary process. Mandel states that Lenin followed a line of 'bourgeois-democratic republic; development of capitalism in Russia; shift of the workers party into the opposition as soon as the democratic revolution triumphed' (1983: 451). Until 1916 Lenin accepted the possibility of peasant political parties independent of both the bourgeoisie and proletariat, a thesis rejected by Trotsky.[9]

Socialist Transition and Revolution

Theories of development generally emphasize capitalist develop-ment, while theories of underdevelopment and dependency stress the exploitation of capitalism upon backward countries. Marx and Engels advocated development of the forces and means of production, from feudalism through capitalism and on to socialism. Generally it was assumed that a national or domestic bourgeoisie should evolve to bring about capitalist development, as in the case of England and the US. Without the democratic bourgeois stage, the forces of production must be developed in backward countries in order to reach socialism. Trotsky believed that the task would rest with the proletariat together with the poor peasantry. He examined paths to revolution. First, con-spiracy 'as the deliberate undertaking of a minority to a spontaneous movement of the majority' and which usually results in the replace-ment of one clique of the same ruling class by another clique. In every society, he argued, there are 'sufficient contractions so that a conspiracy can take root in its cracks', and the historical experience is illustrated in Spain or Portugal or South America. Second, mass insur-rection that results in the victory of one social regime over another, yet popular insurrection and conspiracy are not in all circumstances mutually exclusive: 'An element of conspiracy almost always enters to some degree into any insurrection. Being historically conditioned

---

[9] Howard and King believe that Trotsky's view is the 'most radical statement of rev-olutionary socialism hitherto to be found in Russian Marxism' (1989: 223). Democratic tasks, they argued, cannot be achieved through a bourgeois republic, but only through a socialist revolution. They argue that permanent revolution 'is in consequence locked into a contradiction which can be transcended only if the revolution extends beyond national boundaries and becomes uninterrupted or 'permanent' in the international sphere' (225). Thus, no socialist revolution would succeed in isolation but only would be possible if international capital were weakened by the spread of revolution to other parts of the world (233). The socialist revolution could begin in individual countries but could only be achieved on a world scale (Callinicos, 1990: 11).

by a certain stage in the growth of a revolution, a mass insurrection
is never purely spontaneous.... But a mass insurrection can be fore-
seen and prepared. It can be organized in advance. In this case the
conspiracy is subordinate to the insurrection, serves it, smooths its
path, hastens its victory. The higher the political level of a revolutionary movement and the more serious its leadership, the greater will
be the place occupied by conspiracy in a popular insurrection. It is
very necessary to understand the relations between insurrection and
conspiracy, both as they oppose and as they supplement each other.'
History, he suggests, that in certain conditions a popular insurrection
can be victorious even without a conspiracy: 'Arising *spontaneously*
out of the universal indignation, the scattered protests, demonstrations, strikes, street fights, an insurrection can draw in a part of the
army, paralyze the forces of the enemy, and overthrow the old power.
To a certain degree this is what happened in February 1917 in Russia'
(1959: 304–305). He goes on to contrast the role of the bourgeoisie and
the proletariat in revolution: 'The bourgeoisie may win the power in a
revolution not because it is revolutionary, but because it is bourgeois.
It has in its possession property, education, the press, a network of
strategic positions, a hierarchy of institutions. Quite otherwise with
the proletariat. Deprived in the nature of things of all social advantages, an insurrectionary proletariat can count only on its numbers,
its solidarity, its cadres, its official staff' (306).[10]

At its founding congress in 1938, the Fourth International set
forth a revolutionary program for the transition to socialism, which
emphasized socialism rather than a bourgeois democratic program
(Frank, 1979). Trotsky observed that the capitalist world faced fascism or socialism, which left the proletariat with no other alternative
than a turn to socialism and the socialist revolution. In the revolutionary program Trotsky further developed the idea of combined and
unequal development in backward countries, arguing that the proletariat would elaborate policies that combined the elementary struggles

---

[10] Jon Elster sets out to examine the question, raised by Trotsky that 'the coming
transition from capitalism to communism was crucially dependent on...an advanced
centre and a backward periphery' (1986: 55). He does not believe that the theory of
uneven and combined development explains any particular transition. Further, that
Trotsky failed in his assumption that advance could be attained through the revolutionary potential of the backward countries combining with the highly developed
technology of the advanced countries.

of national independence and bourgeois democracy with the socialist struggle against world imperialism. Thus the democratic revolution would evolve through the rule of the proletariat. He argued that bourgeois liberalism was possible in privileged capitalist countries. He recognized but did not elaborate on the proposition that the survival of capitalism in the dominant metropoles depended not only on profit at home but on the higher rate of surplus value possible through exploitation in the colonies.

Trotskyist Influence in Latin America

Trotsky challenged orthodox ideas about development in Russia and Europe, but he was also concerned with Latin America, especially after reaching Mexico in 1937. In a collection of essays entitled *Por los estados unidos socialistas de América Latina* (1961). Trotsky outlines his strategy for socialism in Latin America, including attention to particular countries. He argues that in Latin America the best way to fight fascism is to struggle against imperialism and to implement an agrarian revolution, and he points to Mexico as an example of a 'semicolonial' country that was able 'to break its servile dependency, give land to the peasants, and elevate the Indians to 'the highest level of civilization' (1961: 13). The principal task of backward countries, he argues, is to struggle against foreign capital and to recognize that industrialization depends less on the bourgeoisie than on the proletariat. The role of the state is to work with the working class to resist imperialism (15). In the backward areas, he argued, the proletariat must have the collaboration of the proletariat of the metropolitan centres and of the working class of the whole world (31).

The problems of the agrarian revolution are connected to the antiimperialist struggle against both England and the US. He delves into a brief analysis of the 'semifascist' regime of Getúlio Vargas in Brazil, suggesting that its nationalist sentiment may serve the antiimperialist struggle. He looks at the role of peasants in Bolivia and advocates their retaining their small individual parcels while also organizing into collective farms carved out of the large latifundios (39).

We may ask to what extent were Trotsky's ideas of importance to Latin American thinking that challenged orthodox ideas about capitalist development? Munck ((1984: 11) believes that the Peruvian independent Marxist, José Carlos Mariátegui, was 'close to Trotsky's conception of permanent revolution' in that his analysis emphasized autonomy from the Stalinist conception of a national-bourgeois and democratic party. He argues that there is widespread consensus in Latin America over the question of the combined and uneven nature of Latin American development, due principally to the popularity of dependency theory that 'owes a lot to the Trotskyist analysis' (114).

Latin American writers have searched for autonomy and a way to develop without being dependent on the advanced capitalist nations, especially the US. The thrust of their understanding often appeared in tandem with some of the Trotsky outlook, but in reality most of them probably were unfamiliar with his ideas. References to Trotsky do not appear in their writings; and Marx is rarely cited. One such example was Raúl Prebisch, the Argentine economist who in response to frustration over the inability of capitalism to modernize Latin America offered a structuralist approach by distinguishing the advanced capitalist centres from the backward periphery. He was concerned with import substitution and imposing tariffs within Latin America so that a capitalist infrastructure could evolve autonomously and a national bourgeoisie could lead national development. Undoubtedly this formulation was of interest to André Gunder Frank, who during the early 1960s travelled to Latin America, Brazil in particular, and soon thereafter crafted his notion of capitalist development of underdevelopment (1966). His dichotomy involved capitalist centres called metropoles and backward peripheries called satellites. Undoubtedly, the ideas of backwardness and surplus in Baran's work influenced his formulation, and although he did not attribute any influence of Trotsky to his thinking, it has been suggested by Guido Mantega (1982: 157) that propositions set forth by Trotsky (above) were explained in more detail by Frank and the Brazilian political economist Ruy Mauro Marini. Marini (1973 and 1978) offered a variant of combined and uneven development with the elaboration of the theory of superexploitation of peripheral workers, wherein he also presented his thesis of subimperialism whereby the development of the Brazilian forces of production are tied to surplus extraction from neighboring countries. These ideas were similar to the conceptions of Leon Trotsky, reproduced in the theses of the Fourth International.

Mantega also shows the similarity of ideas in Theotônio dos Santos and others who advocate a theory of dependency to fundamental Trotskyist assumptions. Dos Santos (1970) identified historical forms of dependency, emphasizing the new dependency, as an explanation for Latin American backwardness.[11] The Mexican anthropologist, Rodolfo Stavenhagen (1968), challenged prevailing notions of backwardness, while sociologist Pablo González Casanova ((1970) adopted the concept of internal colonialism to explain the dichotomy between metropoles and satellites. These thinkers do not explicitly cite Marx, Lenin or Trotsky in their writings, but in a common search for an explanation to the backwardness of their countries, they imply that development of backward nations is not predetermined, stages can be skipped en route to socialism, that development may be uneven, even without planning, complex and combined in character, and that at least by implication a socialist revolution is attainable.

Trotskyist movements in Latin America have been evident since about 1929 when Trotsky went into exile, and opposition to the emerging Communist parties appeared. In 1931 a split within the Chilean Communist Party resulted in the formation of the Izquierda Comunista that organized as a workers party and advanced the cause of peasants and Indians but dissolved a few years later as its Trotskyist leaders joined the Chilean Socialist Party. The principal lines of early Trotskyism revolved around Juan Posadas, Jorge Abelardo Ramos, and Nahuel Moreno in Argentina, Mário Pedrosa in Brazil, Luis Vitale in Chile, Sandino Junco in Cuba, and Guilhermo Lora in Bolivia. A central issue of Trotskyism related to national liberation, a line supported by Ramos whose movement constituted a left wing of Peronism, which it envisaged as an anti-imperialist front. A proletarian tendency, however, opposed any alliance with nationalist movements unless hegemony of the proletariat were assured.

These and other political positions divided Trotskyists not only in Argentina but elsewhere during the 1950s.[12] In 1953 the Partido Obrero Revolucionario (POR) of Bolivia, for instance, divided into two factions, one led by Hugo González Moscoso, became the official line and supported Michel Raptis (1974) or Pablo, and the other, led by Lora, emphasized the need to organize a proletarian party before fomenting an insurrection and seizing power. In 1963 Trotskyists joined with the

---

[11] Dos Santos would insist that fundamentally he does not agree with Trotsky assumptions. In practice, he was influenced by the possibility of democratic socialism and the idea that a national bourgeoisie would be instrumental in building the forces of production en route to socialism in Brazil.

[12] Michael Löwy analyzes these divisions in an undated and unpublished paper in his personal archive that he shared with me, entitled "La quatriéme internationale en Amerique Latine: Les années 50."

MR-13 in Guatemala to proclaim the socialist nature of revolution and to build a workers' party from the guerrilla movement. In Peru two Trotskyist tendencies appeared in 1960, one led by Ismael Frias who sought association with the reformist APRA and the other involving Hugo Blanco (1972) and the organization of militant peasant unions in the La Convención area of the Andes. Although both movements eventually were repressed, Peruvian Trotskyists demonstrated that peasant militias could be closely linked to the needs of the masses, in contrast to the confrontational strategy of guerrilla warfare modeled on the experience of the Cuban Revolution (see Munck, 1984: 79–117 for an extensive discussion of these currents and also Chilcote, 1993: 173–174 which covers the above).

Influenced by the resolution of the Tricontinental or Organización Latinoamericana de Solidaridad (OLAS) and the Castroist revolutionary current, in 1969, the Fourth International uncritically adopted a line of prolonged civil war through guerrilla warfare. This led to the formation of the Partido Revolucionario de Trabajadores or Revolutionary Workers Party (PRT) and its armed wing, the Ejército Revolucionario del Pueblo (ERP) in Argentina although this movement exited from the Fourth International in 1973. A rival group, the Partido Socialista de Trabajadores or Socialist Workers' Party (PST), led by Moreno (1974), participated in the 1973 elections, obtaining 150,000 votes. Although these contrasting perspectives (armed struggle versus electoral participation) divided the Trotskyist movement, both organizations collapsed in the face of brutal repression generated by the 1976 coup. In Chile, Vitale urged Trotskyists to work with the Socialist Party under the UP rather than form an independent revolutionary party. A small group of Trotskyists, however, formed the Liga Comunista de Chile or Communist League of Chile (LCC), which was active in the resistance after the September 1973 coup. In 1975 a coalition of Trotskyist groups, including the Partido Obrero Revolucionario or Revolutionary Workers Party (POR) of Lora reaffirmed his orthodox positions on the nature of the anti-imperialist struggle and attacked mainstream Trotskyist currents in Latin America that had advocated 'focist adventurism'. In Mexico, the PRT evolved out of the student struggles in 1968 and achieved prominence as a revolutionary group of several thousand members to the left of the communist party. Munck characterized the PRT as 'carrying out a Marxist orientation which is principled yet inflexible, orthodox yet creative…without falling into the false activism of ultra-leftism' (1984: 110).

Clearly one of the important advances of Trotskyism in Latin America was its break from Stalinist and orthodox emphasis on a theory of stages, as represented in the revolutionary program called the Theses of Pulacayo that combined a revolutionary Marxist program with emphasis on an evolving Bolivian proletariat that was approved by the POR in 1964. Munck (1984: 86–87) calls it 'one of the most remarkable documents in the history of the working-class movement in Latin America' and he quotes from Lora (1977: 246–247) a passage from its founding document: 'Bolivia is a backward capitalist country.... Bolivia is only another link in the world capitalist chain' and the proletariat 'constitutes the revolutionary class'. Today in Bolivia with the rise of a leftist president, Evo Morales, the POR remains active with frequent position statements, criticism, and analyses by César Uscamayta and his *Prensa Obrera* in La Paz (see http://amr-bolivia. blogspot.com).

The Argentines

Major lines of Trotskyist thinking have prevailed in Argentina, manifested through intellectuals, academics, and students, usually in small parties and labour movements, often obscured by national politics, but at times of crisis conspicuous for ideas and analysis (Caggiola, 1983; Peñalosa, 1983; Valle, 1981). The ensuing discussion focuses on several important personalities. Silvio Frondizi, an Argentina Marxist opposed to intransigent policies of Argentine Communists, drew upon Trotsky's writings and focused on questions of underdevelopment and dependency. His early thinking appeared in an essay on world integration and capitalism (Frondizi, 1947), in which he emphasized the contradictions in British commercial imperialism and in US industrial imperialism. He also examined the ties between imperialism and the national bourgeoisie in colonial and semi-colonial countries, which led to his criticism of the national bourgeoisie and the thesis of dual society advocated by the Communist parties in Latin America. Donald Hodges (1974: 98–99) has suggested that Frondizi was the first to advocate the idea of a new dependency, later to appear in the writings of Brazilian social scientist, Theotônio dos Santos. Frondizi was a leader of a small intellectual current, Praxis, together with Trotskyists Milcíades Peña and Nahuel Moreno (Hugo Bressano). Peña and Moreno had also emphasized the significance of British commercial imperialism and US industrial imperialism in Argentina. Within *Praxis* they contested

the Stalinist line of the Partido Comunista Argentino, and their ideas
had much in common with Trotskyism, although one of Frondizi's
close associates, Marcos Kaplan, insists that Frondizi never formally
associated with the Fourth International (Interview with Chilcote, Rio
de Janeiro, August 14, 1982).

Frondizi's essay on world integration was a response to Argentine
Communist leader, Rodolfo Ghioldi, who had responded to an earlier
version in the Communist daily, *La Hora* (March 16, 1947). Frondizi
argued that early capitalism, based on free competition, could only
survive in backward countries with unlimited expansion of production. This form of capitalism was constrained not only by the low level
of productive forces and technology but also by its own capitalist form.
He also described a more advanced period of capitalism, represented
by the formation of national imperialist systems and the substitution
of monopolies for individual producers. Finally, a third period was
evident after the Second World War in which world capitalism became
dominate, and the US assumed leadership of the capitalist world and
dominance over subjugated nations.

In the elaboration of his thinking, Frondizi in *La realidad argentina*
demonstrated the inadequacy of the Argentine bourgeoisie to the task
of carrying out the bourgeois democratic revolution because of their
direct dependency on international monopoly capitalism (Frondizi,
1957, 1: 333). He believed that the semicolonial and colonial nations
of the periphery did not benefit from the bourgeois-democratic revolution because of their economic and political dependence. These
nations suffered 'a tremendous deforming impact, economically and
politically' (Frondizi, 1957, 1: 27).

Frondizi elaborated a theory of the relationship of dependent,
peripheral, and underdeveloped nations to dominant, central, and
advanced ones by showing how monopoly capital and imperialism
cause the disintegration of national capital. He believed that intervention by the state, subsidization and reformist policies were useless so
that the only solution lay in the path to socialism. He set forth the
requirements for a transition to socialism, including identification of
the conditions for revolution, the seizure of power by the proletariat
(Frondizi, 1957: Vol. 2).

Luis Vitale, born in Argentina in 1927, was involved in several
movements affiliated with the Fourth International, and later became
a naturalized citizen of Chile where he wrote an impressive six-volume

history of Chile (1967). He was particularly influential with an essay (1968) that examined a number of premises about backwardness in Latin America. He argued against the prevailing premise that feudalism was transplanted from medieval Spain to the New World and that a feudal aristocracy had ruled in Latin America and continued to rule until the twentieth century, thus obstructing capitalism and the rise of a national bourgeoisie. He believed that a primitive capitalism had existed since the fifteenth century, that the conquest of the Americas was associated with exploitation and commercialization of precious metals, and that Spanish America was ruled, not by feudal lords, but by a commercial bourgeoisie whose source of wealth was exports. Since independence this ruling bourgeoisie had remained dependent on the world market and this in turn contributed to the backwardness of the continent. A struggle against the bourgeoisie would lead to a break with imperialism: 'Agrarian reform and the expulsion of imperialism is, and will always be, against the bourgeoisie rather than in its favour...' (1968: 42).

The renowned Argentine revolutionary, Ernesto 'Che' Guevara, wrote on socialist man, set forth a manual on guerrilla warfare, but embodied in practice the struggle against imperialism and the possibility of insurrection as a means of building socialism in many places. His success alongside Fidel Castro brought their revolution to power in Cuba in 1959, although in 1967 he died fighting to bring about revolution in Bolivia. Michael Löwy (who spent his early years in Brazil) shows parallels in the thinking of Trotsky and Guevara. Critical of the national bourgeoisie, Che believed in a socialist revolution that Löwy describes as 'in line with... Trotsky's theory of the permanent revolution' (1984: 83). In line with the idea that the socialist revolution may begin on a national level but ultimately spreads to other countries, Che's overall strategy in a war against imperialism involved the creation of 'two, three, several Vietnams, in order to compel imperialism to disperse its forces' (110). One of Che's biographers, Jon Lee Anderson, reminds us that in the depths of the Bolivian rain forest in a skirmish with pursuers, Che lost a volume by Trotsky he had been reading (1997: 721). Although Che never referred to himself as a Trotskyist, another of his biographers, Carlos Castañeda, mentions his contact with Trotskyists in Argentina during January 1964 (1997: 248) and refers to an interview with Che's aide Benigno, who recalls in 1965 that Che was accused of being a Trotskyist: 'The one they call

Trotsky, and they said to Che that he was a Trotskyist.... Raúl was the one who said he was a Trotskyist, that his ideas made it clear that he was a Trotskyist' (296).[13]

With the fall of the Berlin wall and the Soviet Union and Eastern Europe, a Cuban Marxist, Célia Hart Santamaría discovered Trotsky and until her tragic death late in 2008 opened a dialogue on the role of Trotsky in the Latin American revolution, and she related Trotsky to Che: 'I don't think there is a more convincing practical application of permanent revolution than that carried out by this great revolutionary and hero of the youth of the twentieth century.... It was clear to Che that a true revolution and true socialism were not exclusive to the borders of my country or my continent. The flag of this legend charged with romanticism, and purity was interpreted from all angles. It promoted Latin Americanism and anti-imperialism' (2004). Hart considered the Bolivarian Revolution of Hugo Chávez in Venezuela as a basis for Latin American unity as long as it does not compromise with imperialism. She reminds us that Trotsky also dreamed of this unity while in Mexico and that although Stalinism had silenced him, his ideas would be in revolutions that will arise sooner or later: 'We will take him up from this silence and make him be seen, without considering him a terrorist. A strange thing that the imperialists and the Stalinists were in agreement in calling him a terrorist. A point in our favour'. In her reading of Trotsky she found his writings familiar along the same lines of Che Guevara's works. She felt that their ideas had been distorted, and that it was essential to discern concepts that she had grasped from Che Guevara about the permanent revolution, the combined and uneven development of backward capitalist countries, internationalism, or his attacks on Soviet bureaucracy. One should recognize 'his sense of internationalism as a pressing need to continue the revolutionary struggle, a militant internationalism committed in every aspect'. Hart (2007) also criticized the Trotskyist left, especially in Argentina,[14] for viewing Che only as a martyr or hero without recognizing his contributions to revolutionary theory. She argued that

---

[13] Publishing houses influenced by Trotsky, such as Pathfinder Press and Ocean Press, have emphasized the thought and writing of Guevara through translation and reprinting of his work and works about him by others. During a 1987 conference in Havana, I noted similarities in Guevara's outlook and Trotsky's view of permanent revolution, only to be vehemently rebutted by a hard-line Cuban Communist.

[14] In the late 1970s Adolfo Gilly, another Argentine once of Trotskyist persuasion, had criticized Trotskyist intervention in Guatemala, identifying subjective, vanguardist, sectarian, and bureaucratic errors (Munck, 1984:94).

both Che and Trotsky defended the right of the exploited to violence against the exploiters: 'I come from the Cuban Revolution and high-light Trotsky without being a member of any Trotskyist party. I'm just pointing out that my Trotskyist comrades should see in Che Guevara a comrade-in-arms, read his works and realize that no two ways of thinking are more similar than theirs. Even their contradictions reveal they follow a single road and offer similar solutions to the same prob-lems, each in his own day. And the same goes to Che Guevara's fol-lowers: get to know Leon Trotsky a little beyond your parties instead of rejecting him *per se*.... We should coin a term to refer to all those Marxists who strayed from Moscow's official line and kept swimming against the tide despite their Communist orthodoxy. In fact, the push-ers of the official line accused Che, Mella, and many others of being Trotskyist? Could it be that they were right?'

The Brazilians

Trotsky does not hold a major presence among Brazilian intellectuals and workers, but his followers were active since the founding of the Partido Comunista Brasileiro (PCB) in 1922. Cândido Filho (1982) identifies Brazilian intellectuals as major figures in the Trotskyist movement. Most of them broke from the PCB in 1928 (1982: 163–165): Aristides Lobo, Lívio Xavier, Patricia Galvão, Geraldo Ferraz, Plínio Melo, Mário Pedrosa, Edmundo Moniz (1980), Febus Gikovate; and labour leaders such as João da Costa Pimenta, Joaquim Barbosa and Hilcar Leite. In 1937–1938 another schism involved Hermínio Sacchetta, who had headed the PCB in São Paulo, but left the party to organize the Partido Socialista Revolucionário that Mário Pedrosa considered as a splinter group of the Brazilian Trotskyist movement.[15] Sachetta accepted the position that unconditional support should be given to the defense of the Soviet Union, while Pedrosa and Moniz differed in their belief that the state bureaucracy there would become a governing class which would interfere with the realization of a workers or socialist state (Dulles, 1983: 167–168).

Details of Trotskyist activity in Brazil are elaborated in Gorender (1987) who identifies an orthodox current, the Partido Socialista Revolucionário (Trotskista), the PSR(T) which aggregated students

[15] Pedrosa who represented 'the continuity of the revolution' in *Em Tempo* No 140 (November 12 to December 2, 1981) was a member of the first executive committee of the Fourth International in 1938.

and intellectuals associated with the Fourth International, but it disbanded in 1953. Two years later Sachetta, together with Paul Singer, Michael Lówy, and others founded the Liga Socialista Independente of Luxumburguist orientation. Orthodox Trotskyists formed the Partido Operário Revolucionário (POR), which published Frente Operário and was oriented to the line of Juan Posadas and the third world perspective of world revolution, inspired by the Cuban Revolution. About 1962 an independent current also appeared, inspired by Rosa Luxemburg, Bukharin and others and led by intellectuals from Rio de Janeiro, São Paulo, and Minas Gerais who in reaction to the reformist theses of the Brazilian Communist Party founded the Organização Revolucionária Marxista (ORM) and a periodical (initially a newspaper and later a magazine) called *Política Operária*. The full name of this group thus was Organização Revolucionária Marxista Política Operária, but it was generally known by the name of Política Operária (POLOP), included young intellectuals Vânia Bambira, Moniz Bandeira (1978), Juárez Guimarães de Brito, Michael Löwy, Ruy Mauro Marini, Eder Sader, Emir Sader, and Theotônio dos Santos. Eric Sachs, a dissident communist of German origin and living in Brazil with the pseudonym, Ernesto Martins, was influential. The ORM-POLOP held three conferences (1961, 1963 and 1964). It concentrated on a critique of reformism and nationalism, yet according to Gorender (1987: 36), it was unable to elaborate a viable alternative and tended to isolate itself.

In recounting these past moments Emir Sader has noted outside Trotskyist influence in the POLOP movement. Moniz Bandeira was the principal Trotskyist figure at that time. Sader was active as both Leninist and Trotskyist and explains the incorporation of Trotsky and Gramsci and others because their thinking tended to reinforce criticisms of the Soviet Union and the orthodox communist parties. The Posadistas did not enter into this movement, but there was a current in Brazil. Ruy Mauro worked to organize a propaganda arm (*foco militarista*) to mobilize military people, especially in Rio. He was imprisoned in 1964, and a year later he left the country. Theotonio had already left (Interview with Emir Sader, Rio de Janeiro, July 29, 1991).

Confirming that Trotskyist influence was evident within POLOP, Marini has argued it was not a dominant influence. He himself was more Leninist at the time, and there was the great influence of Erich Sachs. Trotsky's criticism was used to attack the PCB. The permanent revolution was not so important, but the idea of combined and uneven development was. This came from Trotsky, but Lenin also used this idea in his works after Luxemburg (Moniz, 1980), and later Trotsky employed the concept. Marini translated some of the texts of Trotsky and Lenin on imperialism. He believes that POLOP was important in the formation of the idea of dependency. Theoretical interest at the time focused more on the ideas of Baran and Paul Sweezy than those of Trotsky, because of their contemporary analysis of the capitalist system. When Frank arrived in 1963, he was very influenced by Baran, and he learned from and was deeply influenced by the Rio intellectuals. He drew from the ideas of POLOP, Lenin, and other authors. His early writing appeared in *Revista Brasiliense*, edited by the renowned historian, Caio Prado Jr., a Communist whose ideas (1966) clashed with the line of his party and was influential. So too was another Communist, Nelson Werneck Sodré, who was a major figure within the Instituto Superior de Estudos Brasileiros or Superior Institute of Brazilian Studies (ISEB), a Rio thinktank noted for its mission of formulating an ideology of developmental nationalism in Brazil. Marini felt it necessary to reformulate analysis of what capitalism is in Brazil, to devise a strategy and a program; he believed that this is what POLOP gave to the left and to the possibility of socialism in Brazil. Marini mentions that the Argentinian magazine, *Praxis*, was important prior to the formation of POLOP and that one of its participants, Marcos Kaplan, had attended the first congress of POLOP in January 1961: 'This was the beginning of our outreach internationally. The work of Silvio Frondizi was also important for us and for the theory of dependency together with the ideas of ECLA and ISEB' (Interview, Ruy Mauro Marini, Rio de Janeiro, July 30, 1991). Marini elaborated his ideas on subimperialism before seeking exile in Mexico in 1965. Theotônio began to write in 1966 on the new dependency: 'We took these ideas abroad in the search of a new theory of dependency. The theory of dependency was never an academic theory. It was a political endeavor. An attempt to develop a non-communist revolutionary theory'. He remained in Mexico until 1969 and then moved to Chile to work with Dos Santos until Salvador Allende was deposed in late 1973.

The dean of Brazilian sociology, Florestán Fernandes, referred to his early affiliation with Trotskyism in an interview with various Brazilian intellectuals (1981a: 18–23) as well as in his interview with me (São Paulo, September 26, 1983), and there is a reference to Trotsky in his *A revolução burguesa no Brasil* (1981b). In a discussion of his early years he explains the interest in the PCB and its renowned leader Luiz Carlos Prestes. The PCB did not attract the radical youth of that

period. After the Estado Novo the PCB moved toward groups supporting Getúlio Vargas: 'I joined an extreme left Trotskyist group during
that time, called Coligiação Democrática Radical and remained with
it until about 1940. I always maintained contact with other groups,
for example the anarchists, the socialists and the old militants who
were not of my generation. I circulated with left people, except for the
PCB...but I was known for my Trotskyist orientation' (1981a: 18).
He explained that few of his fellow activist students knew anything
of Marxism during his intellectual activities during the 1950s. Once
he withdrew from Trotskyism, he became marginalized from political
activities. He had wanted to join the PCB but felt that their positions
were often negative, and he remained outside the party: 'I discussed
this dilemma frequently with António Candido, initially when I joined
the Trotskyist group. His preference was for revolutionary socialism.
After I abandoned Trotskyism, we talked again, and he encouraged
me to carry on with my intellectual work and dedicate myself to my
academic career' (19). In response to a question summarizing his position that the political parties did not offer solutions, he was asked why
the intellectual was unable to fill this space, and he responded that the
intellectual could not do so nor could he form his own movement in
a society of classes in which the worker could not politically mature
and develop as an independent class (23).

Final Thoughts

First, there appears to be a relationship between the theory of permanent revolution and the model of capitalist development of underdevelopment, which reflects one major strand of dependency theory,
particularly evident in the thought of Frank and Marini. Trotsky
departed from the idea of a world capitalist system constituting a total-
ity subject to unequal and combined development where the advanced
countries would continue to develop at the expense of the exploitation
of the colonies and backward semicolonial areas. This is similar to the
metropolis-satellite conception in Frank's thesis on capitalist development of underdevelopment (1967) where the metropolis exploits the
surplus of the satellites that in turn become underdeveloped.

Second, inherent in the theory of the permanent revolution is the
belief that the colonial and semicolonial bourgeoisie is incapable of
leading the revolutionary process in the sense of the bourgeoisie fulfill-

ing its principal historical task of carrying out a bourgeois democratic revolution. Given this circumstance, Mantega argues that Trotsky, Frank, and Marini all emphasize the role of the proletariat in bringing about the necessary transformation through a socialist revolution, thereby liberating the productive forces from capitalism. Yet Marco Aurélio Garcia insists that Marini sought to distinguish himself from Trotskyism by making an unfavourable criticism of the theory of permanent revolution as economistic, although he notes that Marini used the idea of antagonistic cooperation in a form parallel to the theory of combined and uneven development to characterize the relations between the Brazilian bourgeoisie and capitalism. Garcia also affirmed that Trotskyist influence on dependency theory was greater than that of Lenin because 'Lenin dealt with dependency in very general terms, while Trotsky attempted to study dependency more concretely by describing its internal mechanisms' (Interview with Chilcote, Campinas, Brazil, September 12, 1984).[16]

Third, near the end of his life and just prior to the Second World War, Trotsky noted a profound crisis in that the democratic regimes of the centre had to continue to exploit the periphery whose surplus would allow for mitigation of the class struggle in the periphery. The left needed to fight against fascism as well as imperialism (Trotsky, 1961: 13) because the bourgeoisies in some advanced countries such as Germany and Italy (which had lost their colonies) had to turn from democracy to fascism in order to continue with exploitation of the periphery. Likewise, in peripheral countries like Argentina and Brazil the bourgeoisies turned to fascism, a thesis developed by Dos Santos (1973). Thus, fascism allowed for the development of conditions of superexploitation, as elaborated by Trotsky, Dos Santos and Marini who noted similarly that the human productive forces had ceased to grow and that an alternative was necessary.

Fourth, Trotsky's notion of a permanent worldwide revolution was tied to the strategic role of countries in the underdeveloped periphery that broke their ties with the metropoles and precipitated a collapse

[16] Garcia, an astute political observer and essential organizer of the Partido dos Trabalhadores (PT); for Trotskyist influences within the PT, see Santos and Vidal, 1982. Garcia also helped organized the Arquivo Edgard Leunroth, Centro de Documentação e Pesquisa em História Social, Universidade Estadual de Campinas (UNICAMP), which holds important documentation of the Brazilian left and has published *Cadernos de Arquivo Edgard Leuenroth* (No. 1 dated July 1983).

of imperialism. Marini stressed socialist revolution in the peripheral countries, arguing that this would lead to world revolution and bring about socialist revolution in backward countries (Mantega, 1982: 227). Mantega also notes that Trotsky's theory of permanent revolution projected an immediate transition to socialism without the bourgeois transformations suggested by Lenin, a proposition that divided the Brazilian left (1982: 136).

Dos Santos accepted the Marxist theory of the expansion of imperialist centres and their domination over the world economy but also looked for a theory that addressed the laws of internal development in countries affected by that expansion: 'The relation of interdependence between two or more economies, and between these and world trade, assumes the form of dependence when some countries (the dominant ones) can expand and can be self-sustaining while other countries (the dependent ones) can do this only as a reflection of that expansion, which can have either a positive or negative effect on their immediate development' (Dos Santos, 1970: 231). Instead of emphasizing capitalism in the image of the advanced countries as a means for overcoming backwardness, he stressed the unequal nature of development, evident in Trotskyist writing, although he has denied in a personal conversation any Trotskyist influence upon his thinking (Interview with Chilcote, Rio de Janeiro, July 7, 1995). Marco Aurélio Garcia, agrees that Dos Santos, having emanated from the youth movement of the Partido Trabalhista Brasileiro (PTB) was not influenced by Trotskyism and eventually became anti-Trotskyist (Interview with Chilcote, Campinas, September 12, 1984). Garcia offers an historical overview of Trotskyism in Brazil, noting its strength in the 1930s and the 1980s. In the latter period several currents prevailed, including the Alicerce da Juventude Socialista, linked internationally with Nahuel Moreno; the *Causa Operária* and its journal of the same name; and Democracia Socialista, linked to the publication *Em Tempo*.

All these ideas on underdevelopment were part of an attack by independent left intellectuals on the intransigent positions of the PCB, particularly on the questions of semifeudalism as a basis for backwardness and the promise of the national bourgeoisie fulfilling its historical role in the capitalist transformation. Mantega maintains that these ideas were largely inspired by the thought of Trotsky that the proletariat under certain conditions could rise to power prior to the proletariat of advanced countries, a thesis defended by Trotsky in 1906 where he argued that Russian backwardness was not an obstacle to the socialist revolution. He believed that under certain circumstances the low level of capitalist development in Russia could lead to a rapid rise to power of the proletariat. Trotsky (like Lenin) argued that despite its backwardness Russia had indeed developed some industrialization along capitalist lines in the last decades of the nineteenth century, especially in Moscow and St. Petersburg where a large proletariat had developed along with a weak bourgeoisie, and industrialization was largely implanted by foreign capital aided by the state. Thus the bourgeoisie could not eliminate feudal remnants because it was weak at the time. This gave the proletariat the opportunity to bring about revolutionary change. In the *Permanent Revolution*, Trotsky elaborated this idea by arguing that the delayed bourgeois revolution in Russia could be advanced through the proletariat, specifically its objectives would be the achievement of the agrarian reform and the democratic reconstruction of the state. Agrarian reform implied the nationalization of property and elimination of income differences. These different patterns of progress illustrate the idea of combined and uneven capitalist development on a world scale, where the colonies and former colonies feed the accumulation of the imperialist metropoles at their own expense so that peripheral capitalism remains weak, precluding the bourgeoisie from fulfilling the tasks of a democratic revolution. Mantega claims that Trotsky 'interprets capitalism in its imperialist phase as an international system articulated by ties of domination and dependency' (1982: 143), and he shows the impossibility of a democratic national revolutionary full democracy in the backward countries.

CHAPTER FOUR

CAPITALISM, PRIMITIVE ACCUMULATION AND UNFREE LABOUR

Tom Brass

Introduction

Anyone writing about the shape of a 21st century labour regime is faced with a rather obvious contradiction. On the one hand, much political economy insists that to operate efficiently, a 'fully functioning' capitalist enterprise needs workers who are free. On the other, there are numerous instances of 'fully functioning' capitalist enterprises the world over that introduce, reintroduce or reproduce labour relations that are unfree.

Among the many examples, not just in areas of capitalist agriculture, but also in some industrial urban contexts are the following: debt bondage in India and Latin America; the continuing use of peonage, sweatshops and convict labour in the United States; the offshore programme in Canada (migrants from the Caribbean); contract migrant labour in white South African mining and industry and the sunbelt states in the USA; a resurgent gangmaster system in UK agribusiness; unfree plantation workers in West Africa; and the existence of unfree industrial labour both in the brick kilns of Pakistan and in the export processing zones of China.[1]

To talk about a capitalist labour régime in the twenty-first century as entailing an increase in the incidence of worker unfreedom remains controversial, given the degree to which this kind of development is opposed by non-Marxist and Marxist political economy. Both the latter, so the argument goes, adamantly dispute the acceptability to

---

[1] These are well documented case studies, referred to both by me—in Brass (1999) as well as in previous and subsequent texts, many of them published in *The Journal of Peasant Studies*—and by many others (e.g., Lichtenstein, 1996; Krissman, 1997; Martins, 1997; Ross, 1997; Bonnet, 2000; Assies, 2003; Ercelawn and Nauman, 2004; Lawrence, 2004; Bedoya Garland and Bedoya Silva-Santisteban, 2005a, 2005b; Manzo, 2005).

capitalist producers of unfree labour, maintaining much rather that a 'fully functioning' accumulation process cannot operate efficiently—let alone profitably—without workers who are free. Whilst this may be true of the way non-Marxist theory perceives the link between capitalism and unfreedom, that it applies similarly to the most important—let alone all—Marxist political economy is disputed here.

Generally speaking, both non-Marxist and (some) Marxist theory subscribe to three positions about the link between unfree labour and capitalism. First, that capitalist development is in a general sense incompatible with production relations that are unfree. Second, that current approaches which do connect unfree labour and capitalism may indeed be right empirically, but in theoretical terms cannot be said to be Marxist. And third, faced with the dissonance between what is said to be Marxist theory and the acceptability of unfree labour to capitalist enterprises, purportedly Marxist approaches take refuge in the concept of primitive accumulation.

Against these three positions, I shall deploy the following arguments. First, that although it is important to distinguish theoretical approaches on the part of non-Marxist and certain kinds of Marxist analysis to the link between capitalism and unfree labour, they nevertheless share a number of assumptions about the capitalism/unfreedom link. Second, and following on from this, there are two distinct and occasionally contradictory Marxist approaches to the capitalism/unfreedom link. For this reason, a distinction exists between the Marxist analysis of unfree labour employed here and a number of other analyses by Marxists of the same relation.

The presentation is divided into six sections, of which the first two examine the impact of Smithian assumptions about the capitalism/ unfreedom link, and the objections to them. Current and past approaches on the part of Marxist theory to the same question are considered in sections three and four, while sections five and six look at the difficulties in confining unfree labour to the pre-history of capitalism (= primitive accumulation), and thus delinking it from a 'fully functioning' capitalist system.

The Smithian Inheritance

Significantly, perhaps, the most ardent historical exponents of the argument that unfree labour was economically inefficient were non-Marxists: Adam Smith in the late eighteenth century; John Stuart Mill and John Bright in the mid-nineteenth century; and Max Weber over the late nineteenth and early twentieth century. Equally significant is the fact that most of the latter were economic liberals, and forerunners of neo-classical economic theory. For all of them, therefore, productivity was equated with the capacity of the individual worker to exercise 'choice' in the context of the labour process, to 'choose' to work hard because he/she individually benefited from this.

Smith, Mill, Bright and Weber all questioned the compatibility between capitalism and unfree labour, mainly on the grounds that this kind of working arrangement was too costly and/or inefficient. More recently, neo-classical economic historians of unfreedom—such as Fogel and Engerman—espouse the same argument but invert its logic: because the antebellum plantation was in their view economically efficient, its workforce must in some sense have been uncoerced, and remained on the plantation voluntarily, attracted by the good pay and conditions on offer there.[2] In the end, these non-Marxists adhere to the same epistemology: as in their view unfree labour is economically inefficient, workers employed by a capitalist enterprise that in economic terms is efficient are—and can only ever be—free.

Adam Smith on Unfree Labour

The importance of Adam Smith's contribution to the debate about unfree labour is simply put: it was the first major theoretical attempt to understand the dynamic of capital accumulation, to link labour to the creation of value, and to characterize labour in terms of a wider political economy. Even those who disagreed with him on fundamental aspects of these questions, such as Mill, nevertheless accepted much of what he had to say about the systemic dissonance of unfreedom and its negative economic role in the accumulation process. Epistemologically, therefore, Smiths assumptions about the capitalism/unfreedom link permeate both non-Marxist and—as will be seen below—semi-feudal Marxist political economy.[3]

---

[2] See Brass (1999: Chapter 5) for the epistemology informing the arguments advanced by Fogel and Engerman.

[3] When Adam Smith contrasts unfree labour with sharecropping, therefore, the inference is that the latter is a free relation of production, a view which overlooks the fact that in India, sharecropping relations involve poor peasants who are themselves bonded by debt, i.e. unfree labour. In contrast to Smith, therefore, sharecropping is not on a relational continuum at the beginning of which stands unfree labour and at the end of which is freedom. Much rather, sharecroppers who begin as free

It is equally clear that Smithian teleology concerning the economic inefficiency of unfree labour, and hence its high cost when compared to free labour, can itself be traced back to two of the central theoretical emplacements informing his analytical framework: his view of labour as the source of value and thus of national wealth, and the distinction between productive and unproductive labour. In contrast to the French physiocrats, for whom land/Nature was the sole repository of economic value, Smith allocated this same role to labour, on the productivity of which rested industrialization and with it the capacity to augment national wealth.[4]

The enhancement of labour productivity, however, depended in turn on the installation of advanced technical inputs and machinery, both of which required capital investment and neither of which were in his opinion compatible with the employment of a workforce that was unfree. The presence of the latter was accordingly a twofold obstacle to accumulation: not only was unfree labour itself incapable of operating advanced productive forces, but capital would not invest in a labour process where workers deemed by Smith to be unproductive—that is, slaves and other forms of unfree labour—were employed.

Although he does not explicitly include slavery within the category of unproductive labour, this linkage (slaves = idle = unproductive) is nevertheless inferred. 'Wherever capital predominates,' Smith observes, 'industry prevails: wherever revenue, idleness'.[5] The presence of the latter characteristic is attributed in turn to the absence where slaves are concerned of an incentive on their part to work hard or well, a situation which he contrasts with that of labour which is free, and which for this reason not only responds positively to economic incentives but also works hard and efficiently. Thus, for example, the economically backward character of large feudal estates in England was attributed by Smith to the employment of a work force that was unfree, in his opinion the most costly form of labour-power because—unlike a free worker—one who is unfree has no incentive to work well.[6]

workers gradually lose this economic identity, as they become increasingly indebted to employers.
[4] For the French physiocrats see Beer (1939).
[5] See Smith (1812, II: 12).
[6] See Smith (1812, II: 87–88), where the following oft-quoted passage is to be found: 'But if great improvements are seldom to be expected from great proprietors, they are least of all to be expected when they employ slaves for their workmen. The experience of all ages and nations, I believe, demonstrates that the work done by slaves, though it

Extending this argument, Smith also claimed that—again unlike free workers—'slaves...are very seldom inventive', as a consequence of which 'all the most important improvements, either in machinery, or in the arrangement and distribution of work, which facilitate and abridge labour, have been the discoveries of freedmen'.[7] He then insisted, rather oddly, that: 'Should a slave propose any improvement of this kind, his master would be very apt to consider the proposal as the suggestion of laziness, and of a desire to save his own labour at the master's expense. The poor slave, instead of reward, would probably meet with much abuse, perhaps with some punishment'. This bizarre argument verges on the nonsensical: even staying within the confines of the logic adopted by Smith, a completely different outcome is in order. Not only would a master not reject an improvement simply because it was suggested by his slave, therefore, but the former would regard it—like the subject who made the original suggestion—as his own property.

From all this Smith concluded that the employment of slaves was the least productive and thus the most costly form of working arrangement. This argument, variations on which are a constant refrain in most of the texts about political economy which follow his, was elaborated by him in the following manner. Accepting that employers preferred slave labour to that of free workers, he argued that whereas cash crops such as sugar and tobacco 'can afford the expense of slave cultivation, corn cannot, and is therefore grown by free labour'.[8] Since tobacco and sugar were sufficiently profitable to justify cultivation with expensive forms of labour, they—and only they—could be grown using workers that were unfree.[9]

Contrasting the *metayer* system of cultivation using tenant labour with that based on slaves, Smith argued similarly that because share-cropping tenants were free, and thus able both to acquire property

---

appears to cost only their maintenance, is in the end the dearest of any.' For the same argument, see also Smith (1812, III: 37–8).

[7] On this point, see Smith (1812, III: 37).

[8] See Smith (1812, II: 89–90).

[9] Elsewhere Smith (1812, III: 38) maintains that the high price of luxury items produced in antiquity was due mainly to the fact that these goods were the product of slave labour. A similar theme informed the argument about capitalism and slavery advanced at the beginning of the twentieth century by Sombart (1967: 125–7, 142–5), who maintained that slaves were employed on large colonial plantations mainly in order to produce the luxuries for bourgeois consumption in Europe.

and to benefit from the application of their own labour-power, they had an incentive to work harder and were thus more productive than slaves, who were unfree.[10] It was to this difference in productivity that he attributed the decline of servitude in European history, although he accepts that 'slavery continued to take place almost universally for several centuries afterwards', until it was abolished 'from above'. Because Adam Smith (and others) attribute the eradication of unfreedom simply to 'from above' agency, no mention is made of the role of class struggle waged 'from below' in the demise of unfree labour.

Mill and Bright on Unfree Labour

Following the line of argument laid down by Adam Smith, John Stuart Mill similarly dismissed the possibility that production carried out with unfree workers was—or could ever be—economically efficient. 'It is a truism to assert,' he maintained, 'that labour extorted by fear of punishment is inefficient and unproductive... [a]ll processes carried on by slave labour are conducted in the rudest and most unimproved manner'.[11] Confusing technical skills which enhance production (and profitability), which he agreed slaves possessed, and an understandable reluctance on their part to work as hard as possible, which slaves will not do unless threatened with physical coercion, Mill concluded that slavery and other forms of unfreedom (serfdom) were an obstacle both to the utilization of modern technique and to profitability generated by the application of the latter.[12] For this reason, output by free workers was perceived as superior, and always exceeds in quantity

---

[10] Hence the view (Smith, 1812, II: 90–1) that: 'Such tenants, being freemen, are capable of acquiring property, and having a certain proportion of the produce of land, they have a plain interest that the whole produce should be as great as possible, in order that their own proportion may be so. A slave, on the contrary, who can acquire nothing but his maintenance, consults his own ease by making the land produce as little as possible over and above that maintenance.'

[11] Mill (1849a: 305, 306). For a different view, see Mill (1849a: 589; 1849b: 226), where he accepts that the employment by planters in the antebellum American south of slaves conferred cost advantages on commodities they produced for and sold in international markets that would be eliminated in the event of their having been produced by a workforce that was free.

[12] See Mill (1849a: 306–7), who regarded the quantitative/qualitative gap in output produced by free and unfree labour as unbridgeable, given even the better control and (by inference) the threats of physical coercion exercised over workers who are not free: 'What is wanting in the quality of labour itself, is not made up by any excellence in the direction and superintendence'.

CAPITALISM, PRIMITIVE ACCUMULATION AND UNFREE LABOUR

and quality that of those who are unfree: items produced by the latter are consequently regarded not only as inferior but also as dearer than those made when employing free labour.

As with most other non-Marxists, Mill's views about the disjuncture between unfree labour and capitalism were grounded in the defence of the latter, and had little to do with humanitarian considerations. Like Smith, he regarded ancient slavery as generally benign.[13] And, like Bright, Mill also perceived the main economic problem with unfree labour to be its inability to reproduce itself demographically: because of this, it was incapable of providing producers with an assured/continuous supply of workers. When examining the conditions favouring the employment of unfree workers over free ones, therefore, Mill—like Bright—identified the supply of unfree workers as crucial. His coldly pragmatic argument was that, if these kinds of worker could indeed be procured without hindrance, landholders would no longer have to worry about the biological reproduction of the slave population (i.e., accommodate the economically unproductive members of the slave family). In such circumstances, therefore, they could simply work the unfree labourers in their employ 'to death', in the knowledge that such resources of labour-power were both guaranteed and inexhaustible.[14]

In a similar vein, the abolitionist views expressed by Bright in the mid-1860s were linked to his conviction that the continued existence of plantation slavery in the antebellum South was an obstacle to capitalist economic efficiency.[15] At a time when both the market and the demand for cotton were expanding, an increase in the output of this commodity depended on augmenting the supply of labour-power employed in its cultivation. A capitalist whose investment was all in

---

[13] See Mill (1849a: 304).

[14] Hence the view (Mill, 1849a: 303) that: 'If full-grown able-bodied slaves can be procured in sufficient numbers, and imported at a moderate expense, enlightened self-interest will recommend working the slaves to death, and replacing them by importation, in preference to the slow and expensive process of breeding them. Nor are the slave-owners generally backward in learning this lesson.'

[15] For this argument, see, for example, the speeches made by Bright (1865: 194ff., 235–9) in London during 1863. In the United States during the nineteenth century, the view about the inefficiency of unfree labour was a commonplace amongst bourgeois economists. Thus, for example, a widely used economics text book (Walker, 1888: 54) of that era advocating 'full and free competition' also observed that, as 'the production of wealth (depended on) the maximum of effect, and the minimum of waste', the main obstacle to this was 'most conspicuously seen in the wastefulness and inefficiency of slave labour.'

the Lancashire cotton mills, Bright argued strongly that, since the natural demographic growth of the slave population was low, and as only
a quarter of all slaves were anyway engaged in cotton production, an
increase in the output of this cash crop depended either on resuming
the slave trade or persuading free workers in the North voluntarily to
migrate southwards and complement the supply of labour employed
in cultivating cotton. Since the Union government would not permit
the resumption of the slave trade, and free workers in the northern
states would not migrate to the cotton south for fear that they, too,
would become unfree, the problem of low output linked to an inad-
equate labour supply would persist for as long as slavery continued,
and it was for this (pragmatic rather than humanitarian) reason that
Bright advocated the ending of unfreedom in America.[16]

Max Weber on Unfree Labour

A different set of arguments were advanced by Max Weber in support
of the same claim, that unfree labour was organizationally 'irrational', expensive, economically inefficient, and thus incompatible with
modern capital accumulation.[17] Not only did the purchase of slaves
tie up capital, burden owners with additional costs of maintaining the
unproductive labour of the slave family, and involve political risks in
the form of potential abolition, therefore, but fluctuations in the availability and cost of such unfree workers also precluded both supply
and price stability, as well as the installation of advanced productive

[16] That it was an increase in cotton production, which depended on ending slavery, rather than just the latter, which interested Bright most, is evident from what
he himself wrote and said during the early and mid-1860s. As Bright (1865: 213–14)
himself admitted, 'I am speaking now as a matter of business. I am glad when matters of business go straight with matters of high sentiment and morality...from this
platform I declare my solemn conviction that there is no greater enemy to Lancashire,
to its capital and to its labour, than the man who wishes the cotton agriculture of the
Southern States to be continued under slave labour'.
[17] Unsurprisingly, and like most other commentators on the connection between
capitalism and slavery, Weber's arguments are somewhat contradictory. Having
accepted that slaves were employed in production that was highly profitable, and
further that this 'profitableness of slave labour depended upon strict plantation discipline, ruthless driving of the slave, and perpetual importation...and finally exploitative agriculture', he nevertheless denies it any (let alone an initial) economic role
in contributing to the origins of modern capitalism: 'This accumulation of wealth
brought about through colonial trade,' he notes (Weber, 1927: 300), 'has been of little
significance for the development of modern capitalism'.

technique.[18] The latter was attributed by Weber in turn to the absence under slavery of two conditions that contribute to economic efficiency: first, the fact that the latter required a worker to exercise care/responsibility in the labour process (particularly where costly machines/equipment were concerned); and second, to the fact that the intensity of labour was determined by the element of worker self-interest, neither of which in his view were features of unfree production relations.[19]

According to Weberian sociological theory, however, the most important obstacle posed by the presence of unfreedom to the process of economic rationalization on which capitalist development depends was the consequent inability of employers to recruit/dismiss workers in keeping with business requirements. For this and the above reasons, Weber maintained that it was possible to employ unfree labour only when the following three conditions were met: where slaves could be maintained cheaply, where a large and continuous supply of such workers was assured, and in large-scale agricultural enterprises (e.g., plantations) or technologically underdeveloped (= 'simple') industrial labour processes.[20] Because of the accruing 'advantages to industrial profitability and efficiency', he argued, unfree relations invariably disappeared once free workers became available. From the viewpoint of the producer, Weber concluded, these advantages took the form of a decline in capital investment/risk, the capacity to shift the cost of family subsistence/maintenance onto the labourer himself, and—crucially—a capacity to hire/fire; that is, both to select suitable workers and to dismiss unsuitable ones, thereby maximizing a worker's self-interest in efficient capitalist production.[21] The latter is, of course, the same argument as that advanced by Adam Smith (see above).

---

[18] For these arguments, see Weber (1947: 253–4).

[19] Weber (1947: 254).

[20] On this last point, Weber (1947: 215) observes that, where domestic slaves or serfs are employed, '(t)he appropriation of returns of labour may be used by the owner...as a means of profit. In that case the dependent may be obligated to contribute goods or to work on raw materials provided by the owner. The owner will then sell the product. This is unfree domestic industry. He may, finally, be used as a labourer in an organized shop—a slave or a serf workshop.' Although he does consider the case of the antebellum American south, instances of plantations worked with unfree labour are confined by Weber (1927: 80–1, 125ff.; 1976) largely to antiquity.

[21] On the importance for economic rationality/efficiency of 'the worker's own interest in maximizing...production', see Weber (1947: 218). In the context of a market economy, he notes (Weber, 1947: 240–1), a wage incentive 'appeals immensely more strongly to the worker's self-interest', and '(i)n this sense it has a higher degree of formal rationality, from the point of view of technical considerations, than any

Objections to the Smithian Inheritance

Let us consider the main reasons given by Smith, Mill, Bright, Weber, and others, for the incompatibility between capitalism and unfree production relations, and evaluate them in terms of their current applicability. These include the argument that unfree labour is inefficient, cannot undertake skilled tasks and cannot be combined with advanced productive forces, is too costly, hinders market expansion, and the supply of such workers is anyway not assured. All these claims are to a large degree interlinked epistemologically: thus the argument that unfree labour is economically inefficient is itself part of the claim that it is incompatible with an increased level of productive forces that characterize a 'fully functioning' capitalism.

To begin with, it is self-evidently the case that many of the objections raised with regard to the employment by capital of labour-power that is unfree apply with equal (if not more) force to the employment by capital of workers who are free. The latter, for example, are not all skilled, neither do they always respond to incentives to work hard, nor is a regular supply of free labour-power always assured. Weber's argument that, together with the unavailability of unfree workers, fluctuating slave prices undermines accounting stability, overlooks the fact that both these conditions operate in situations where workers are free; hence the availability or unavailability of free labour-power is—as in the case of unfree equivalents—reflected in the widespread price fluctuations of this commodity experienced by prospective buyers who are capitalist producers.[22]

The carelessness and inefficiency which many observers attributed to unfree workers, and invoked as a reason why employers always preferred labour that was not unfree, was a characteristic of free

---

kind of direct compulsion to work'. It should be pointed out, however, that—unlike neo-classical economic historiography—Weber did not equate slave emancipation in the American south with the ending of unfree production relations in that context, much rather the contrary: '(t)he negroes are share tenants bound by debt,' he observed (Weber, 1927:84), 'and their freedom of movement exists only on paper'.

[22] Perhaps because he was trapped by the epistemological rigidities of his analyses of economic rationality generally, whereby historical forms of unfree labour were uniformly cast as organizationally 'irrational', financially expensive, and thus economically inefficient, Weber was unable to comprehend the extent to which Polish migrant workers employed in Prussian agriculture at the turn of the nineteenth century were not only unfree, but also how the presence of the latter relation contributed to (and was therefore compatible) with modern capital accumulation in Germany.

labour as well.[23] As the occurrence of sabotage undertaken by workers employed in factories operating in industrial capitalism attests, deliberate acts of carelessness/inefficiency (= 'the conscious withdrawal of the workers' industrial efficiency') have been and are resorted to by free labour as part of the class struggle.[24] Conversely, there are numerous instances historically of commercial enterprises which employed skilled workers—those manual labourers exhibiting precisely technical accomplishments in relation to tasks done, and thus not categorized as careless/inefficient—who were not free. In the case of the commercially important American whaling industry during the nineteenth century, for example, crews were composed of highly skilled workers; the latter were nevertheless recruited/controlled by means of debt bondage relations initiated/reproduced by means of two familiar mechanisms: cash advances and purchases from the ship's store.[25]

---

[23] About migrant agricultural workers employed on commercial farms in England during the 1890s, a spokesperson (Rew, 1913: 76) for agricultural producers commented as follows: 'The carelessness and lack of interest in their work of many farm labourers are a common cause of complaint (by employers), and no doubt also a source of annual waste and loss. If it were possible to devise some practical means by which the labourer could be financially interested in the success of the year's operations, no one, probably, would dispute its desirability.'

[24] On the incidence and impact of sabotage as a weapon used by free workers in industrial capitalist enterprises, see among many others Kornbluh (1968: 51–53), Beynon (1973: 129ff.), and Dubois (1976). According to Elizabeth Gurley Flynn (1916), industrial sabotage was a crucial part of the class struggle, whereby members of the industrial proletariat engaged in 'putting the machine on strike'. In the words of one member of the Industrial Workers of the World uttered during 1911, '(h)ere we come to the real point on the question of sabotage: it is a *war measure*, made necessary by the nature of the class struggle' (Kornbluh, 1968: 52, original emphasis).

[25] This emerges clearly from the analysis by Hohman (1928: 14), who states that 'the legal status of whalemen at sea, like that of seamen in general, was strongly reminiscent of medieval serfdom...this unfree status resulted from...political weakness on the part of seamen as a class, which made it difficult to secure protective legislation and to enforce those laws which were on the statute books.' Debts incurred as a result of high prices charged by the ship's store, plus cash advances made to crew members, meant that, after having worked for between two and four years, seamen in debt to agents of the vessel were then 'induced...to embark upon another voyage for the same firm' (Hohman, 1928: 234–5). Whaling companies made 100% profit on items obtained from the ship's store, and most of the crewmen who re-enlisted did so because of debts owed (Hohman, 1928: 219, 228, 245ff.). According to Hohman (1928: 238), this was because 'a large proportion of a man's earnings was required to pay for outfit and (ship's store) articles, and to meet heavy interest charges upon (cash) advances', with the result that at the end of the voyage crewmen not only had no payment coming but actually owed their employer money. In order to clear this debt, a crewman was required to sign up with the same employer for the next voyage. The central role played in reproducing this form of unfreedom was a combination of on the one hand withholding payment due, and on the other high prices charged for

Perhaps because of its epistemological roots in a liberal political
economy, the claim that workers who are unfree lack an incentive to
work hard, and are for this reason inefficient, misses the point entirely.
The dynamic is wholly different: tasks are undertaken and completed
by a worker who is unfree not in response to the presence of incentives, in form of reward (cash/kind payment), but rather in order to
avoid punishment in the event of non-compliance (violence, coercion).
Historically, therefore, slaves, serfs and bonded labourers have indeed
worked hard, the absence of positive incentives notwithstanding, for
the simple reason that such workers are compelled to do so by the
threat (or actualization) of violence/coercion. Indeed, avoidance of the
latter can be seen as a 'rational outcome' corresponding to Weber's
notion of 'worker self-interest'. Accordingly, a labourer who is unfree
works as hard as (or harder than) one who is free for a different reason: namely, because of the fear of the consequences if he/she fails to
do this.[26]

Unfreedom and Deskilling

Characterizing unfree labour as inefficient economically also overlooks
the contemporary impact of mechanization and technology in deskilling labour-power.[27] The debate about work organization and 'scientific

---

items consumed. About this the same source observes (Hohman, 1928: 258): 'If annual
or semi-annual settlements had allowed the whalemen to receive a part of the earnings actually due them, it would have been unnecessary, in many instances for them
to ask for cash advances.' The outcome is equally familiar. Due in part to the high
prices charged by ship's stores and interest charged on cash advances, notes Hohman
(1928: 229, 233, 234–35), average wages declined over the nineteenth century and the
earnings gap between officers and men widened.

[26] This point has long been recognized. Why slaves on the cotton plantation in the
antebellum south worked hard is explained thus by Sutch (1975: 342): 'The frequency
with which a punishment is administered is a poor measure of its effectiveness... It is
the *fear* of eventual punishment which motivates behaviour... A slave need never have
felt the lash to know the consequences of disobedience' (original emphasis). Much
the same point was made by Roger Casement in his report about the coercive labour
régime the Putumayo region of Peru at the start of the twentieth century. On this he
commented as follows (Singleton-Gates and Girodias, 1959: 290): 'Wholesale murder
and torture endure... and the wonder is that any Indians were left in the district at
all to continue the tale of rubber working on to 1910. This aspect of such continuous
criminality is pointed to by those who, not having encountered the demoralisation
that attends the methods described, happily infrequent, assert that no man will deliberately kill the goose that lays the golden eggs...(The freebooter on the Putumayo)
hunted, killed, and tortured today in order to terrify fresh victims for tomorrow.'

[27] The concept 'deskilling' is associated principally with the analytical approach

management' over the latter part of the twentieth century has been concerned mainly with the way technology and machinery undermine traditional craft skills, and the corresponding impact of this on the industrial working class.[28] Whilst important, the focus of discussion has nevertheless tended to be on changes affecting the labour aristocracy in metropolitan contexts, and how such manual workers who are employed in industry on a permanent basis have been replaced by a combination of machines and temporary labour. However, little attention was paid to the fact that the installation of machinery also permits employers to replace skilled labour-power with non-skilled equivalents, and even less attention was paid to the implication of this for the kind of relational shift licensed by such restructuring. It is, in short, a transformation that, in a global work régime, simultaneously

---

of Braverman (1974). Although an important corrective to those who have predicated capitalist development on the skilled worker, this approach has two particular shortcomings. First, a tendency to idealize non-capitalist work organization, and especially traditional farming practices (= 'the natural mode of life of the family') as conducted by self-sufficient independent proprietors, an interpretation similar to that of Chayanov where the peasant family farm is concerned. Hence the view (Braverman, 1974: 272–73): 'So long as the bulk of the population lived on farms or in small towns, commodity production confronted a barrier that limited its expansion. On the United States farm, for example, much of the construction work (apart from basic framing, as a rule) was accomplished without recourse to the market, as was a good deal of house furnishing. Food production, including the raising of crops and livestock and the processing of these products for table use was of course the daily activity of the farm family, and in a large measure so also was the home production of clothing. The farmer and his wife and their children divided among them such tasks as making brooms, mattresses, and soap, carpentry and small smith work, tanning, brewing and distilling, harness making, churning and cheese making, pressing and boiling sorghum for molasses, cutting posts and splitting rails for fencing, baking and preserving, and sometimes even spinning and weaving. Many of these farm activities continued as the natural mode of life of the family even after the beginnings of urbanization and the transfer of employment from the farm to the factory or other city job.' And second, deskilling is equated unproblematically with proletarianization (Braverman, 1974: 377ff.), whereas—as is argued here—it can just as easily give rise to social relations of production that are unfree: deproletarianization, in other words.
[28] It is important to note the two different ways in which deskilling is effected: one involves a skilled worker employed in tasks for which these skills are unnecessary; the other entails allocating such tasks to workers who are themselves non-skilled. According to Braverman (1974: 113, original emphasis), the object of deskilling is 'the *dissociation of the labour process from the skills of the workers*. The labour process is to be rendered independent of craft, tradition, and the workers' knowledge. Henceforth it is to depend not at all upon the abilities of workers, but entirely upon the practices of management.' Predictably, the critique of capitalist management techniques by Braverman has itself been challenged by those antagonistic to Marxism, for an example of which see the contributions to the volume edited by Giddens and Mackenzie (1982).

enables the insertion (or re-insertion) of unfree production relations
into a capitalist labour process.

One of the main planks in the argument of those who maintained
that unfree labour-power was incompatible with a 'fully functioning'
accumulation process stemmed from the assumption that, as capitalism developed, it would require the employment of an increasingly
skilled workforce.[29] It is clear, however, that the opposite is the case: a
consequence of increasing the level of the productive forces through
the installation of machinery and the application of technology, therefore, results in the *de*skilling of the workforce.[30] This in turn enables
capitalists to employ those from rural backgrounds who—in terms
of the agribusiness and/or industrial labour process—usually possess the least skills, and it is this particular segment of the workforce
that is most vulnerable to relational arrangements (debt, coercion)
that are unfree.

[29] This argument, decoupling unfree labour and economic development on account
of a dissonance between an employer's requirement for workers who were skilled and
the absence of such labour-power among the unfree, has been made with regard to
the antebellum South. Hence the following assertion (Farnam, 1938: 177): 'Viewed
in its broadest economic and social aspects, the slavery question involved a contest
between the ideals of a static and those of a dynamic society. Slavery was not incompatible with culture, refinement, kindliness, and religion on the part of individual slave
owners, and the Southerners could quote good authority in the writings of the Greek
philosophers for thinking that a free commonwealth should be based on slavery. But,
disregarding entirely the abuses of slavery, and considering it only at its best, it is clear
that it is inconsistent with economic progress, certainly with the kind of economic
progress which has characterized the nineteenth century. That progress implies a constant increase in wealth by means of the application of science, (and) of mechanical
appliances...to the processes of production. This, however, implies a skilled, intelligent, responsible, and, above all, and adapting labouring class.'

[30] This antinomy is neatly captured by Braverman (1974: 3–4): 'On the one hand, it
is emphasized that modern work, as a result of the scientific-technical revolution and
"automation," requires ever higher levels of education, training, the greater exercise
of intelligence and mental effort in general. At the same time, a mounting dissatisfac-
tion with the conditions of industrial and office labour appears to contradict this view.
For it is also said—sometimes by the same people who at other times support the
first view—that work has become increasingly subdivided into petty operations that
fail to sustain the interest or engage the capacities of humans with current levels of
education; that these petty operations demand ever less skill and training; and that the
modern trend of work by its "mindlessness" and "bureaucratization" is "alienating"
ever larger sections of the working population. As generalizations, these two views
cannot easily be harmonized.'

Unfreedom and the Reserve Army of Labour

Current forms and pace of deskilling also make possible the activation of hitherto unutilized elements belonging to the industrial reserve army of labour.[31] Although the latter encompasses those thrown out of work as a result of mechanization and technification, members of the reserve army can be incorporated by capital into its labour process for two distinct reasons. The first refers to a reserve to be drawn on when market demand expands, and capitalists need further amounts of labour-power. By contrast, the second refers to those who—as a mass of unemployed also part of the reserve army—are drawn on by capitalists not so much to increase production but rather as a weapon in their struggle against those still in work.[32]

---

[31] About the perception by bourgeois economists of the connection between the reserve army of labour and capitalism, Marx (1976a: 786) noted: 'Modern industry's whole form of motion therefore depends on the constant transformation of a part of the working population into unemployed or semi-employed "hands". The superficiality of political economy shows itself in the fact that it views the expansion and contraction of credit as the cause of periodic alternations in the industrial cycle, whereas it is a mere symptom of them...When this periodicity has once become consolidated, even political economy sees that the production of a relative surplus population—i.e. a population surplus in relation to capital's average requirements for valorization—is a necessary condition for modern industry.' Against the tendency of bourgeois economics to interpret declining wages and living standards in a national context as an effect simply of demographic growth, he commented (*Marx*, 1976a: 788, 790): 'Capitalist production can by no means content itself with the quantity of disposable labour-power which the natural increase of population yields. It requires for its unrestricted activity an industrial reserve army which is independent of these natural limits. (...) Taking them as a whole, the general movements of wages are exclusively regulated by the expansion and contraction of the industrial reserve army, and this in turn corresponds to the periodic alternations of the industrial cycle. They are not therefore determined by the variations of the absolute numbers of the working population, but by the varying proportions in which the working class is divided into an active army and a reserve army, by the increase or diminution in the relative amount of the surplus population, by the extent to which it is alternately absorbed and set free...It would be utterly absurd, in place of this, to lay down a law according to which the movement of capital depended simply on the movement of the population. Yet this is the dogma of economists.'

[32] Sweezy (1946: 99, emphasis added) recognized the importance of this distinction, observing that 'the increasing use of machinery, which in itself means a higher organic composition of capital, sets free workers and thus creates "relative overpopulation" or the reserve army. Marx stresses the point that the existence of unemployed labourers is conducive to the setting up of new industries with a relatively low organic composition of capital and hence a relatively high rate of profit...*It would seem, however, that a more important effect of the reserve army is...through competition on the labour market with the active labour force, to depress the rate of wages and in this way to elevate the rate of surplus value.*'

In this second role, members of the reserve army are no longer used simply in addition to an existing workforce but now instead of the latter.[33] Replacing skilled, more costly and/or better organized workers already established in the capitalist labour process with less skilled, cheaper, and/or unorganized ones, enables producers to exert a downward pressure on the pay, conditions and living standards of the proletariat generally, not just in particular national contexts.[34] As is now very clear, such restructuring, based on an enhanced ability to draw on what is a *de facto* global reserve army in order to decompose/recompose the capitalist labour process worldwide, has followed the implementation in the Third World of the Green Revolution programme during the 1960s and *laissez faire* policies in the 1980s.

It is also in this second role—the reserve army composed of deskilled workers drawn into the labour process so as to undermine the bargaining power of free workers in secure employment, with the object of reducing their pay and conditions, and thus maintaining or augmenting profitability—that capitalism finds a use for workers who are not free.[35] According to Marx, the reserve army comes into its

---

[33] The assumption that those expelled from the labour force by the application of machinery and technology would—after a brief sojourn in the reserve army—find alternative employment, is both pervasive and misplaced. It is linked to the notion that such workers would be employed as a result of investment in new enterprises by capitalists whose enhanced profits derived from the original labour-displacing strategy. This view is problematic, since it applies only when capital and labour are national in scope, and not international. Where the latter is the case, capital is able to do two things: either to invest elsewhere, in contexts where labour-power is available and even cheaper; or to employ (perhaps even to import) migrants who meet the same requirements. Whichever the instance, the outcome is the same: any new jobs created do not necessarily go to those expelled from the labour process because of technification/mechanization of production. The obviousness of this outcome notwithstanding, it is unfortunately still possible to hear—even from some on the left—the mantra that workers displaced in this manner will automatically find employment in new industries created by capital.

[34] The realization of this particular effect—the deployment of the reserve army in the class struggle between labour and capital—was linked by Marx (1976a: 786, note) in turn to the internationalization of the market. He did not, as some insist, confine the impact of the reserve army to national contexts and economies. It goes without saying that, insofar as the reserve army becomes global in scope, such a development licenses racist ideology among the proletariat in a given country, thereby splitting workers along national/ethnic lines. Equally unsurprising is that capital not only benefits from this but also encourages this kind of consciousness, in the process shifting the latter from the sameness of class to the difference of cultural 'otherness'.

[35] Both the existence and the importance of a connection between on the one hand deploying labour-power that is unfree, and the processes of deskilling, trade uionization, reproducing the reserve army, capitalist restructuring and the profitability of

own once the early stage of capitalism—that generally associated with primitive accumulation—has been left behind.[36] Both it and its relational forms—among them the unfree ones which provide employers with a method of controlling the workforce crucial to the success of the whole accumulation process—are thus not confined merely to the initial development of the capitalist mode of production.

---

accumulation are made clear by Marx (1976a: 788, 793, 795) in the following way: 'We have seen that the capitalist buys with the same capital a greater mass of labour-power, as he progressively replaces skilled workers by less skilled, mature labour-power by immature, male by female, that of adults by that of young persons or children. (…) The movement of the law of supply and demand of labour on this basis completes the despotism of capital. Thus as soon as the workers learn the secret of why it happens that the more they work, the more alien wealth they produce, and that the more the productivity of their labour increases, the more their very function as a means for the valorization of capital becomes precarious; as soon as they discover that the degree of intensity of the competition among themselves depends wholly on the pressure of the relative surplus population; as soon as, by setting up trade unions, etc., they try to organize planned co-operation between the employed and the unemployed in order to obviate or weaken the ruinous effects of this natural law of capitalist production on their class, so soon does capital and its sycophant, political economy, cry out at the infringement of the "eternal" and so to speak "sacred" law of supply and demand. (…) Capital demands more youthful workers, fewer adults.' The role of unfree labour in age- and gender-related capitalist restructuring is noted subsequently (Marx, 1976a: 850): 'A temporary and local shortage of labour does not bring about a rise in wages, but rather forces the women and children into the fields, and constantly lowers the age at which exploitation begins. As soon as the exploitation of women and children takes place on a large scale, it becomes in turn a new means of making the male agricultural labourer "redundant" and keeping down his wage. The finest fruit of this vicious circle thrives in the east of England—this is the so-called gang-system…'. As is evident below, Marx regarded female and child workers as unfree.

[36] Marx (1976a: 784–85) emphasizes thus the central economic role played by the industrial reserve army in the capitalist mode of production: 'But if a surplus population of workers is a necessary product of accumulation or of the development of wealth on a capitalist basis, this surplus population also becomes, conversely, the lever of capitalist accumulation, indeed becomes a condition for the existence of the capitalist mode of production. It forms a disposable industrial reserve army, which belongs to capital just as absolutely as if the latter had bred it at its own cost. Independently of the limits of the actual increase of population, it creates a mass of human material always ready for exploitation by capital in the interests of capital's own changing valorization requirements. With accumulation, and the development of the productivity of labour that accompanies it, capital's power of sudden expansion also grows;…The path characteristically described by modern industry, which takes the form of a decennial cycle (interrupted by smaller oscillations) of periods of average activity, production at high pressure, crisis, and stagnation, depends on the constant formation, the greater or less absorption, and the re-formation of the industrial reserve army or surplus population.' Of particular interest is what he says next (Marx, 1976a: 785): 'This particular cycle of modern industry, which occurs in no earlier period of human history, was also impossible when capitalist production was in its infancy.'

Unfreedom and Advanced Productive Forces

Turning to the issue of a supposed incompatibility between unfree
labour and the presence of advanced productive forces, it is necessary first to distinguish between two particular situations. Thus it may
indeed be true that the existence of unfree labour inhibits the *development* of the productive forces. However, once established, there is no
intrinsic reason why capital should not employ unfree workers in con-
junction with advanced productive forces. As has been noted above,
this is especially the case where advanced productive forces results in
deskilling, which in turn enables capitalists to draw from an expanded
industrial reserve army, amongst which is to be found workers who
are unfree.

Among those who pointed out that farms where labour was unfree
were highly efficient economically, not least because such workers
were employed alongside advanced productive forces, was Edward
Gibbon Wakefield, whose analysis of colonial agriculture was com-
mended by Marx.[37] Comparing large commercial farms in Tasmania
with those in British colonies elsewhere, he contrasted the economic
efficiency of the former with the relative backwardness of the latter,
noting simultaneously that those in Tasmania were operated using the
unfree labour of convicts, while the less efficient farms of a similar size
in other colonies employed workers who were free.[38] That the employ-

---

[37] Although critical of Wakefield, Marx nevertheless attributed to him insights
regarding the kind of labour regime desired by an agrarian capitalist. The generally
positive view held by Marx (1976a: 932, original emphasis) about Wakefield is evident
from the following: 'It is the great merit of E.G. Wakefield to have discovered, not
something new *about* the colonies, but, *in* the colonies, the truth about capitalist relations in the mother country.'
[38] In Tasmania, notes Wakefield (1849: 176–78) 'there are farms, being single
properties, consisting of seven or eight hundred acres each, under cultivation, besides
extensive sheep and cattle runs, the farming of which is not inferior to that of Norfolk
and the Lothians. A description of one of these farms is before me. The eight hundred
acres are divided into fields of from thirty to fifty acres each. The fences are as good
as can be. The land is kept thoroughly clear of weeds; a strict course of husbandry is
pursued; and the crops, especially of turnips, are very large. The garden and orchards
are extensive, kept in apple-pie order, and very productive. The house is of stone, large
and commodious. The farm buildings are ample in extent, and built of stone with
solid roofs. The implements are all of the best kinds, and kept in perfect order. The
live stock, for the most part bred upon the spot, is visited as a show on account of its
excellence, and would be admired in the best-farmed parts of England: it consist of
30 cart horses, 50 working bullocks, 100 pigs, 20 brood mares, 1000 head of horned
cattle, and 25,000 fine-wooled sheep. On this single establishment, by one master, seventy labourers have been employed at the same time. They were nearly all convicts. By

ment of unfree workers could be economically efficient was an argument accepted even by some conservatives: those of them who were ardent Catholics objected on the grounds that the spread of liberalism and capitalism which undermined religious belief also destroyed what they regarded as an eternal and 'natural' (= 'God-given') hierarchy that bound societies together.[39]

In part, the view about the incompatibility between unfree labour on the one hand, and more advanced productive forces necessitated by capitalist technical rationalization on the other, may have its epistemological roots in long-discredited racist ideology which accompanied and justified nineteenth century colonial and imperial rule. Thus, for example, Weberian claims regarding the supposed inability of unfree workers to operate modern technical inputs are themselves based on the view that '[i]f the labour force was dear' on the antebellum southern

---

convict labour, and that alone, this fine establishment was founded and maintained. Nothing of the sort could have existed in the island if convicts had not been transmitted thither, and assigned upon their landing to settlers authorized to make slaves of them. In this small island, of which the whole population is under 50,000, there have been at one time fifty establishments much resembling that which I have described.' Comparing this situation with the United States, where capitalist producers employed Irish immigrant workers who were free, the same source concludes: 'In British North America, there is not one (large commercial farming establishment) that bears the slightest resemblance to it, in point of scale, perfection of management, or productiveness in proportion to the capital or labour employed: for the slavish Irish labour of a colony is less easily combined, and less surely retained, than convict slave-labour. I doubt whether in all Canada, though many a first-rate English and Scotch farmer have emigrated thither, there is even one farm of 500 acres, the management of which would not be deemed very slovenly in Scotland or England, or of which the produce in proportion to capital and labour amounts to half that of a Tasmanian farm.'

[39] Thus, for example, Belloc (1924: 99–100, original emphasis) observed: 'One often hears it said that slave labour is less productive than free labour, that is, labour working at a wage under Capitalism. People sometimes point to modern examples of this contrast, saying that places like the Southern States of America, where slave labour was used a lifetime ago, were less productive than the Northern States, where labour was free. But though this is true of particular moments in history, it is not generally true. Free labour working at a wage under the first institution of capitalism—when, for instance, a body of capitalists are beginning to develop a new country with hired free men to work for them—will be full of energy and highly productive. But when what is called "free labour"—that is, men without property working by contract for a wage—gets into routine and habit, it is doubtful whether it is more productive than slave labour. It is accompanied by a great deal of ill-will. There is perpetual interruption by strikes, and lock-outs, and the process of production cannot be as minutely and absolutely directed by the small and leisured class as can slave labour. *There is no reason why a free man working for another's profit should do his best.* On the contrary, he has every reason to work as little as possible, while the slave can be compelled to work hard.' Unlike Marxists, however, Belloc mounted an attack on capitalism from the political right, so as to defend Catholicism and its socio-economic hierarchy.

plantation, it was because 'the negroes could not be trusted with modern implements and used only the most primitive tools'.[40] To some
degree, the same could also be said of the observation by John Stuart
Mill that 'it remains certain that slavery is incompatible with...any
real efficiency of labour. For all products which require much skill,
slave countries are always dependent on foreigners'.[41]

Significantly, Thomas Nelson Page and Ulrich Bonnell Phillips, both
apologists for the slave labour régime on the antebellum Southern plantation, regarded the inefficiency of labour-power that was unfree—its
incompatibility with the requirements of skilled tasks and careful use
of agricultural implements—as an innate characteristic of racial difference.[42] Equally significantly, it was to combat this view of plantation

---

[40] For this argument, see Weber (1927: 82–3). Elsewhere he appears to suggest ('the
specifically occidental form of the organization of labour') that the dichotomy between
free and unfree labour was overlaid by an additional polarity between 'Western self'
and 'Eastern other' (Weber, 1927: 300).

[41] See Mill (1849a: 306, 309), who extended this view (slaves = primitive subjects =
technologically backward, therefore slaves ≠ operators of modern techniques, implements, consequently unfree labour = economically inefficient) to 'the Slavonic nations,
who have not yet advanced beyond a state of civilization corresponding to the age of
villeinage in western Europe, and can only be expected to emerge from it in the same
gradual manner (as "Negro-slaves"), however much accelerated by the salutary influence of the ideas of more advanced countries'.

[42] In the opinion of Thomas Nelson Page (1919: 313, 314, 320, original emphasis),
therefore, '(s)cientifically, historically, congenitally, the white race and the negro race
differ...What of value to the human race has the negro mind as yet produced? In art,
in mechanical development, in literature, in mental and moral science, in all the range
of mental action, no notable work has up until this time come from a negro...(T)he
negroes *as a race* have never exhibited any capacity to advance;...as a race they are
inferior.' He concluded (*Page*, 1919: 338–39): 'They do not appear to possess the fac-
ulties which are essential to conduct any business in which reason has to be applied
beyond the immediate act in hand,' adding that a 'great strike occurred last year in
one of the large iron-works of the city of Richmond. The president of the company
told me afterwards that, although the places at the machines were filled later on by vol-
unteers, and although there were many negroes employed in the works who did not
strike, it never occurred to either the management or to the negroes that they could
work at the machines, and not one had ever suggested it.' This lack of ability and skill
in turn underwrote his argument (*Page*, 1919: 277ff.) that, following emancipation,
blacks who had no 'civilization', and could not be 'civilized,' should not be included
in the franchise. Ulrich Bonnell Phillips similarly maintained that slave inefficiency
in the antebellum South was an attribute of—and proof for—the 'backwardness'/
'primitiveness' of workers who were black In his view, therefore, (*Phillips*, 1918: 339),
'negroes furnished inertly obeying minds and muscles...But in the work of a plantation squad no delicate implements could be employed, for they would be broken;
and no discriminating care in the handling of crops could be had except at a cost of
supervision which was generally prohibitive. The whole establishment would work
with success only when management fully recognized and allowed for the crudity

slaves as innately inferior and unskilled that a subsequent revisionist interpretation emerged: the influential neo-classical economic historiography (= cliometrics) associated with the work of Robert Fogel and Stanley Engerman.[43] Ironically, however, portraying black unfree workers in the antebellum South as empowered led neo-classical historians to depict the plantation régime as essentially an harmonious system containing 'choice-making' subjects, a view not so dissimilar ideologically from the one they had initially set out to challenge.[44]

The Costs of Unfree Labour

Because unfree labour is classified as fixed capital, it is perceived as too costly when compared with free labour. This is because an employer is

---

of labour. The planters faced this fact with mingled resolution and resignation. The sluggishness of the bulk of their slaves they took as a racial trait to be conquered by discipline, even though their ineptitude was not to be eradicated...'

[43] Cliometric approaches to unfree labour include not just Fogel and Engerman (1974) but also and earlier Conrad and Meyer (1965: 43ff.), Coats and Robertson (1969), Andreano (1970), Parker (1970) and Temin (1973: 337ff.). It should be noted that until the cliometric intervention in the debate about American slavery began to exercise influence on other fields, the focus of discussion concerning unfreedom—see, for example, the contributions to collections edited by Herskovits and Harwitz (1964), Tuden and Plotnicov (1970), and Bowker and Carrier (1976)—tended to be not so much on its connection with economic development (let alone capitalism) as on the problem of ethnic stratification and plural society. Even though one may disagree strongly with cliometric epistemology, therefore, it nevertheless reoriented the debate in an important way, bringing it back within the domain of political economy.

[44] In a Preface to one edited volume (Engerman and Genovese, 1975) on slavery, Fogel (1975: vii) observed that '(d)uring the late 1960s there were raging debates as to whether black studies and black history had a legitimate place in the university curriculum,' adding that 'now we have this volume which shows that black history has become the leading arena in the effort to apply quantitative methods to historical research.' That the racism of Phillips was the target of much cliometric analysis is evident from Engerman (1973), who counterposes to the view of the former—equating slavery with inefficient black workers, the 'Sambo' sterotype—the findings from his new economic historiography: namely, that slaves were much rather hard workers who responded rationally and efficiently to 'pecuniary incentives'. In this way, the plantation slave was declared empowered and recuperated for neoclassical economic analysis; the coercive nature of the labour régime was correspondingly denied or downplayed, and the plantation declared to be the epitome of a capitalist firm employing what was in effect no different from the free workers used in manufacturing occupations elsewhere. Although such an approach dispelled a central emplacement of racism—that blacks were economically inefficient workers incapable of undertaking agricultural tasks without the supervision of or direction by white planters—it replaced this with an alternative stereotype. Namely, of an unquestioning black worker colluding with planters in his or her own subjection. This, it scarcely needs pointing out, is very different from the view advanced here: that although the plantation was indeed capitalist, its workforce was coerced, an effect of class struggle, and thus not empowered.

unable to get rid of these kinds of workers when there is nothing for
them to do, and consequently there are long periods when they are not
employed productively (= efficiently). The assumption is that unfree
workers—like machinery—have to be paid for during periods when
they are not producing commodities, and thus the whole cost is borne
by the capitalist. However, the argument about the expense of using
workers that are not free is faced with three rather obvious problems.

To begin with, the objection advanced by Weber about the high
cost to the owner of maintaining slave family is valid only where the
members of the slave family do not themselves work in the fields, or
cannot be sold, neither of which considerations applied historically to
the antebellum plantation régime.[45] More importantly, if unfree labour
is so costly in comparison to its free equivalent, why then do commercial producers keep on recruiting and retaining such workers where/
when possible? And why, if it was so costly, did European capitalists at
the start of the twentieth century insist that their competitors should
not employ unfree workers to produce commodities destined for the
international market?

In these contexts capitalist opposition to the employment of unfree
labour had less to do with upholding humanitarian principle and more
to do with countering and negating the cost advantages that such practices conferred on economic rivals.[46] Unfree labour is indeed profit-

---

[45] As is well known, the objection about the cost to an employer of maintaining
kinfolk of unfree workers does not apply to India, where family members of a bonded
labourer frequently toil alongside the latter in the fields or in the household of the
employer.

[46] This element of inter-imperial commercial rivalry emerged at the start of the
twentieth century in the case of the campaign by British cocoa manufacturers against
the labour régime on cocoa plantations in the islands of St. Thomé and Principe, both
of which were Portuguese colonial possessions. The latter provided cocoa for capitalist enterprises selling to the American market, and the use of unfree labour (serviçal)
from Angola gave US companies a competitive edge. It was this as much as anything
that informed the both opposition to unfree labour voiced by British cocoa manufacturers (Cadbury, 1909; Anti-Slavery and Aborigines Protection Society, 1913) and the
refusal by American firms to join them in denouncing the plantation work régime.
As noted by a representative of the British cocoa manufacturers (Cadbury, 1909: 3–4),
'A large American firm approached did not, much to our regret, see their way at that
time to interest themselves in the subject'. Much of the debate between rival imperialist powers concerned the incidence and causes of mortality rates among plantation
workers, the object of those who employed unfree labour being to decouple mortality
from the work régime on commercial enterprises. In keeping with the practice of
either denying the high incidence of mortality among unfree workers or else blaming
this on 'natural' factors unconnected with their pay and conditions, for example, the
last governor of German East Africa (Schnee, 1926: 138–39) at first disavowed a link

able, not only intrinsically—because workers who are unfree are not able to negotiate over the price of their labour-power or sell it freely on the open market—but also because it drags down the price of free labour, which in cases where the latter is more costly the former either cheapens or displaces. Once again, evidence confirming this can be sought from the most advanced form of capitalism: the United States during the nineteenth and twentieth centuries.

That the object of restructuring was to replace more expensive free labour with workers who, because they were unfree, were also cheaper to employ, was a point conceded even by supporters of the slave labour régime as it existed on the Southern plantation. According to one such—Ulrich Bonnell Phillips—this kind of workforce recomposition was driven mainly by considerations of cost and control. Unfree labour-power was preferred because a capacity of free workers to go on strike at harvest time amounted to 'an overindulgence by the labourers in the privileges of liberty [that] might bring ruin to the employers'.[47] The perceived economic inefficiency of unfree labour-power was accordingly offset by its cheapness and governability.

During the late 1860s convict leasing in Mississipi was advocated not by an economically backward (= 'feudal') landowning class that had been defeated in the Civil war but rather by an economically dynamic capitalist class composed of commercial farmers, rich industrialists and businessmen, all of whom wanted to see black prisoners 'serve their sentences in the coal mines, sawmills, railroad camps, and cotton

---

between forced labour and an indigenous population decline. He then accepted that the death-rate among plantation workers was 'at times regrettably high'; however, this was attributed by him not to working conditions but to 'natural' occurrences, such as climate, epidemics and fevers.

[47] Writing about the labour régime on antebellum Southern plantations, Ulrich Bonnell Phillips—a prominent defender of slavery—used the following example to illustrate why employers opted for a workforce that was unfree: 'Free workingmen in general, whether farmers, artisans or unskilled wage earners, merely filled the interstices in and about the slave plantations,' he noted (Phillips, 1918: 337), and proceeded to explain why. 'One year in the eighteen-forties a planter near New Orleans, attempting to dispense with slave labour, assembled a force of about a hundred Irish and German immigrants for his crop routine. Things went smoothly until the midst of the grinding season, when with one accord the gang struck for double pay. Rejecting the demand the planter was unable to proceed with his harvest and lost some ten thousand dollars worth of his crop. The generality of the planters realized, without such a demonstration, that each year must bring its crop crisis during which an overindulgence by the labourers in the privileges of liberty might bring ruin to the employers. To secure immunity from this they were more fully reconciled to the limitations of their peculiar labour supply.'

fields of the emerging New South'.[48] That the employment preference
of those owning means of production was for workers who were unfree
and not free ones is underlined by the fact that in the mid-1870s the
number of offences carrying a prison sentence was extended by the
state, precisely in order to increase the number of unfree workers
made available to capital through the convict lease system.[49] Capitalist
firms in the post-bellum South either employed prisoners directly,
on their own cotton plantations, coal mines and textile mills, or else
leased them to other employers, such as railroad construction companies, who hired unfree labour thus obtained in preference to the free
workers (migrants from Europe) already available for hire.[50] Convicts
deployed in this manner were used in the production of cheap iron,
lumber, turpentine, sugar, and tobacco, among other commodities.[51]

Convict labour is in one important sense a misnomer: used in a
general sense, the term conveys the ostensibly neutral activity of work
carried out by inmates, a perception that translates easily into the
concept of prison work as a form of occupational therapy. The role
discharged by incarceration in contexts such as the New South (and
South Africa), however, possessed a different logic: it was not a case
of an already existing inmate population being put to work, therefore,
as of a free workforce being turned into a prison population with the
object of converting its subjects into labour that was no longer free.
This commercial leasing of prison labour has continued to fuel the
'fully functioning' accumulation process in the United States.

A consequence of the expansion in the numbers of inmates and the
privatization of prison operations is that incarcerated subjects in the

[48] See Oshinsky (1997: 35–6).
[49] See Oshinsky (1997: 40–41), who comments: 'As the legislature increased the
penalties for minor property crimes, the local courts moved to weaken the protections
only recently afforded black defendants'.
[50] Hence the view (Oshinsky, 1997: 58) that, in the aftermath of the Civil war '(t)he
advantages of convict labour were quickly perceived. When the Cincinnati Southern
Railroad decided to run a trunk line over the Cumberland mountains to Chattanooga,
it first hired gangs of Irish, Italian, and black workers at wages ranging from $1.25 to
$3.50 a day. But free labour proved hard to manage, on and off the job...so the rail-
road turned to convicts. Four hundred of them were leased...at the daily rate of $1 per
man...The convicts worked 16 hour shifts with a short break for meals. Completed in
a single year, the Cumberland line came in well under budget, and the high quality of
the work led some to call it the "best railroad built in the United States"'.
[51] According to Oshinsky (1997: 44), in Mississipi the employment of unfree
labour was indeed profitable, not least because it does '30 percent more work than
free labourers'.

United States are perceived nowadays by industrial capitalist enterprises as a reliable and cheap source of labour-power.[52] Contrary to the view of Adam Smith and others that the work they produced was of poor quality, and that consequently they were less profitable and more costly to employ, and in economic terms generally less efficient, therefore, unfree labourers in the United States completed the tasks to which they were allocated by capital not only more cheaply, more profitably, and quicker than free labour, but the work itself was also of a higher quality.[53] This is even more so the case today.

Markets and Unfreedom

The argument that unfree labour inhibits the expansion of a home market for the commodities produced by capitalism holds only where the market outlet for such output remains domestic, and consumers are themselves unfree. Where products made by unfree labour are exported to other (international) markets, the consumers of which are free, the market expansion argument does not hold. There is accordingly no obstacle to employment by capitalist producers of workers who are unfree in situations where a fundamental break occurs between producer and consumer, a characteristic that obtains where accumulation is global in scope.[54]

---

[52] According to a recent account, in the United States 'the number of privately-operated prisons has jumped from five to 100 in the past decade alone, and is still growing...the private use of prison labour is legal in 37 states and has been enthusiastically embraced by dozens of household-name firms, including IBM, Boeing, Microsoft and AT&T.' The same account continues: '(T)he scale of US prison labour makes it a first-choice source of reliable, pliant workers who can be paid less than the minimum wage and cannot strike. That's deemed unfair on the prisoners but more so on local non-prison workers, because it drives down wages and conditions. Prisoners are increasingly taking on the kind of low-skilled farmwork done until recently by immigrant labour. There are also reports in the US press of "maquiladora" operations—US firms that exploit cheap labour in Mexico—shifting factories back north of the border to take advantage of US prisoners.' See 'Free markets, unfree labour', *MoneyWeek*, 15 April, 2008.

[53] Not only did coal production in Alabama increase from 67,000 to 8.4 million tons over the 1875–1900 period, therefore, but 'convict leasing was essential to this growth' (Oshinsky, 1997: 76).

[54] Where no capitalism exists, the presence of cheap unfree workers may indeed act as a break to economic growth, but not for the reason given: namely that unfreedom is inherently incompatible with technology. Where unfreedom exists, therefore, capital will not invest because workers possess little purchasing power, and consequently there is no market for its commodities. By contrast, where markets exist elsewhere,

As long as capital accumulation depends on the continued consuming power of workers producing the commodities, it will be in the interests of capital to ensure that wages paid its labourers either retain or increase their purchasing power, a situation which does not favour the employment of cheap unfree labour. This was the logic behind the agrarian reform programmes in Latin America and elsewhere during the 'development decade' of the 1960s, which envisaged that among other things land redistribution would create or enlarge a market—composed of peasant smallholders—for commodities produced by domestic capital. However, once capital no longer has to rely on the purchasing power of its own workers, it can solve crises of profitability by recourse to recomposition/restructuring that entails the displacement of free with unfree labour force.

The emphasis of current *laissez faire* policy on a low cost export agriculture contrasts with that of the 1960s 'development decade', when the implementation of Keynesian demand management policies was premissed on providing a nascent capitalist class with a domestic market capable of buying the commodities it produced. In Third World nations at that conjuncture this involved creating a mass market composed of peasants and agricultural workers newly endowed with purchasing power as a result of agrarian reform programmes. Central to this economic strategy was a process of institutional reform: by the mid-1970s, even the World Bank had not only incorporated within its own analytical framework the critique of feudal landownership as an obstacle to economic development, but was also using the concept 'feudalism' itself in its own policy documents.[55]

The assumption was that rising income levels in rural areas would generate the consumer demand that would in turn fuel economic development in what had hitherto been underdeveloped nations. Given the latter objective, it is hardly surprising that one of the main reasons for expropriating large landowners was to eradicate the control they exercised over poor peasants and workers via the debt bondage mechanism designed to keep rural wages low. Clearly, an effect of the continued presence of unfree labour in rural areas would have

---

capital is no longer dependent on local workers for consuming commodities, and it can accordingly deploy unfree relations in its labour process.

[55] See World Bank (1975: 16ff.) for evidence of the fact that, by the mid-1970s, the concept 'feudalism' had become part of the accepted terminology in its policy framework when analyzing development strategy.

been incompatible with the desire to create a mass market in such underdeveloped contexts.

Where a mass market already exists, as is the case in metropolitan capitalist nations—the employment of workers who are unfree confers a different kind of economic advantage. In such contexts this relation also enables agribusiness enterprises to keep down the cost of labour-power, particularly when this is provided by immigrant workers, thereby lowering the cost to domestic capital of foodstuffs—and through this the bundle of wage goods—consumed by industrial labour in the context in question.

In the current global market, therefore, capitalists can get round this difficulty by supplying commodities produced by unfree labour to the international market, and not the home market. This avoids the contradiction of employers having to pay their own workers more to consume the items produced by capitalism. Once capital is no longer exclusively national, this particular problem is no longer a central consideration. Much the same cause—the internationalization of the market, but this time for workers—is the reason why there are not difficulties with the supply of labour that is unfree.

The argument that capitalists eschew unfree labour because it is in short supply is also open to a number of objections. As with other claims about the incompatibility between unfreedom and accumulation, this objection could as easily apply to free labour. Most significantly, this objection is informed by a subtext which, in effect, undermines it: hence the argument that it is the uncertainty of supply which prevents the reproduction of slavery and other forms of unfree relation admits the premises that, in the event of the supply being assured, there would be no reason why such production relations might not continue, a view found even in the framework of some Marxists.[56]

In contrast to the argument that, from the point of view of a prospective capitalist employer, a major problem with using workers who are unfree is the non-assured or unreliable nature of the supply, in contexts where such production relations have been—and are—reproduced institutionally (e.g., the United States, South Africa under the

---

[56] Thus, for example, in his analysis of the reasons why slavery was replaced by serfdom in ancient India, Dange (1949: 176) observes that '(r)eplenishing the worn-out or the lost slave was becoming difficult'.

apartheid system) they constitute an assured and dependable source of labour-power precisely because its subjects are not free.[57]

For both Weber and Mill, the inability to guarantee employers of unfree labour with continued access to plentiful supplies of such workers constituted an important obstacle to production based on their use: were such workers to be available in the amounts and at a (low) cost acceptable to producers, they could be 'worked to death', thereby obviating for any supposed shortcomings in the quantity/quality of commodities produced by them. It is these very conditions that are in fact met by modern forms of unfree labour, linked as they are to the global expansion of the industrial reserve army of labour during the post-1945 era.

Semi-Feudalism versus Deproletarianization

Turning to the way Marxism currently interprets the capitalism/ unfreedom link, here one is confronted with two antithetical interpretations. On the one hand, therefore, the semi-feudal thesis insists that capitalism and unfree labour are incompatible. It regards unfree labour as a precapitalist relation, destined to be replaced by a workforce that is free as capitalism spreads throughout the agrarian sector of Third World nations.

---

[57] 'From a business standpoint,' notes Oshinsky (1997: 44), 'the subleasing (of convict labour in Mississipi during the latter half of the nineteenth century) was ideal. It plugged the major weakness of the old system: the high fixed cost of labour. Under the sublease, an employer was not stuck with a set number of prisoners over a long period of time. He did not have to feed, clothe, and guard them when there was little work to be done. He could now lease convicts according to his specific, or seasonal needs.' For the regular and dependable nature of the supply of unfree black labour to commercial farmers in South Africa during the apartheid era, see Ainslie (1977) and Cook (1982). As the report into forced labour by United Nations and International Labour Office (1953: 77) confirms, in South Africa 'prison labour is hired out to railways, harbours local authorities, certain gold mines, farmers and other private persons.' The same source (United Nations and International Labour Office, 1953: 78) noted further that commercial farmers themselves formed associations to secure such unfree workers from the state, noting that '(t)he districts where these prisons are are situated include the country's highest food-producing centres, where labour is extremely short.' On the dependability of the supply of prison labour in the United States, see Oshinsky (1997: 80–81), who notes: Convicts did not skip work for picnics, holidays, funerals, and excursions. Nor did they…leave town in search of better wages, or go out on strike. "Convict labour is desirable by firms or corporations for the reason that it can be depended on—always ready for work," boasted one prison official. "Contracts for the output can be made with the knowledge that the goods can be delivered.'

Like much of the non-Marxist theory considered above, the semi-feudal variant of Marxism views unfree labour as incompatible not just with capitalism but also with advanced productive forces, economic efficiency, skilled workers, and market expansion.[58] Most crucially, the epistemological importance of the claim, by Marxists who are exponents of the semi-feudal thesis and non-Marxists alike, that unfree labour is always and everywhere an economically inefficient relational form, is its corollary. Namely, that capital is seen as opposed to using unfree labour, and in contexts where the latter relational form is found, invariably strives to replace it with free labour-power.

On the other hand, an alternative Marxist interpretation based on the concept deproletarianization maintains that unfree labour is not merely compatible with capitalism but in particular circumstances its relation of choice. This is because deproletarianization of the rural workforce (= decomposition/recomposition of the working class by means of restructuring) is a crucial part of the class struggle involving capital and labour. As such it enables capitalist producers to depoliticize/cheapen/discipline their workforce.

Until the 1980s, the most common argument made with regard to agrarian transformation in India and elsewhere was that of the semi-feudal thesis, exponents of which insisted that capitalists would replace unfree labour with free workers, a view that still informs much of the discussion about rural transition and the agrarian question.[59] According to this view, all social relations of production in Third World agriculture will gradually metamorphose into those that characterize agriculture in metropolitan capitalist countries. Since in the semi-feudal framework unfree relations are regarded as precapitalist, their presence in any context invariably signals either the absence or incompleteness of a transition to capitalism.

The proponents of the semi-feudal thesis argue, even now, for the necessity of boosting agricultural performance, so that the ever elusive agrarian capitalist—the absent 'other' of this framework—may finally emerge onto the historical stage and begin to provide a surplus for

---

[58] Among other things, the focus by both non-Marxist theory and exponents of the semi-feudal thesis on technical improvements as the motor of economic transformation—allocating primacy to the forces of production, in other words—opens the door to the position that it is possible to increase output *without* altering social relations.

[59] On the claims made by and the persistence of the semi-feudal thesis, see Brass (1994; 1995; 1999: 154ff.; 2002).

what in their view is an as-yet insufficiently realized drive to industrialization. This, it seems will continue to be their view as long as the
production relations they regard as capitalist—'pure' wage labour that
is free, in other words—are not encountered in agriculture.[60]

This interpretation licenses in turn a specific politics. Equating
unfree labour with the absence of capitalism, exponents of the semi-
feudal thesis maintain that systemic transformation entails a transition
not to socialism but much rather to capitalism. For this reason, their
political agenda consists of furthering the following strategic objectives: bourgeois democracy, to be realized by means of an all-embrac-
ing alliance between workers, peasants and a 'progressive' national
bourgeoisie in order to install a purportedly absent or an as-yet not
'fully functioning' capitalism.

In the semi-feudal framework, therefore, the class struggle takes a
specific form. It is located between on the one hand the progressive
social forces, consisting not just of workers and poor peasants but also
of a national bourgeoisie (= as yet not 'fully functioning' capitalists),
and on the other international capital and its feudal representatives
within the nation. Both the latter constitute an obstacle to the installation of a 'fully functioning' capitalism', for which reason all the former are ranged against them, with the object of setting in motion the
accumulation process.

Because their focus is on the coming of capitalism, therefore, exponents of the 'semi-feudal' thesis tend also to focus on unfreedom as an
obstacle to capitalist development. By its very nature, such an approach
postpones and thus precludes the necessity of having to focus on the
coming of socialism; accordingly, exponents of the 'semi-feudal' thesis

---

[60] The palpable fact of unfree labour employed by agrarian capitalists has led to
an equally palpable discomfiture on the part of exponents of the semi-feudal thesis.
An example is the way in which Byres (1999) attempts to sidestep the persistence of
bonded labour in the highly commercialized agriculture of the most advanced regions
in India. In the states of Haryana, Punjab, Uttar Pradesh, and Andhra Pradesh, therefore, he is unable to deny that the 'dominant classes'—for really rather obvious reasons,
he cannot bring himself to write 'agrarian capitalists'—do indeed utilize 'various tied
labour arrangements'. However, he then goes on to describe as 'contradictions' in the
emancipatory process (unfree → free) the fact that in Andhra Pradesh the incidence
of female attached labour has increased, and qualifies it yet further by casting doubt
on this being a widespread a phenomenon (*Byres*, 1999: 18–19). Symptomatically,
therefore, he fails to question the extent to which such developments in the capitalist
labour process (free → unfree) are typical, categorizing them as 'anomalies' (= 'contradictions') instead of asking whether in fact they *are* anomalies.

also miss the fact that unfreedom is now used in the class struggle—
and increasingly so—not by feudal landlords in a context where capitalism has yet to develop but by agrarian capitalists (farmers, rich
peasants) in situations where capitalism has already developed, in
order to pre-empt/prevent conditions that are favourable to the coming of socialism.

By contrast, another variant of Marxism analyses the same capital-
ism/unfreedom link in a very different way. It insists on the centrality to the accumulation process of unfree production relations, a view
embodied in the concept deproletarianization. The latter involves the
reproduction, the introduction (or reintroduction) of unfree labour,
and corresponds to a form of workforce decomposition/recomposition
frequently resorted to by employers in their struggle with labour.[61] In
contexts/periods where/when further accumulation is blocked by overproduction, therefore, economic crisis may force capital to restructure
its labour process in one of two ways: either by replacing free workers
with unfree equivalents, or by converting the former into the latter.

Both these kinds of transformation correspond to deproletariniza-
tion, or the economic and politico-ideological decommodification of
labour power.[62] The economic advantage of such restructuring is that
it enables landholders/planters first to lower the cost of local workers
by importing unfree, more easily regulated, and thus cheaper outside
labour, and then to lower the cost of the latter if/when the original

---

[61] Details about the interrelationship between on the one hand the decommodification of labour-power, the employment of unfree labour, capitalist restructuring, and
workforce decomposition/recomposition, and on the other the process of deproletarianization are outlined in Brass (1999). The latter outlines also the many examples of
strong worker opposition to restructuring, and equally forthright attempts by employers to proceed with this, in order to cut production costs. Numerous contextually and
historically-specific instances exist of the central role played by unfree labour in the
process of capitalist restructuring, a procedure whereby employers used it to replace
free workers bargaining over pay and conditions or engaged in strike action. Over the
past two decades, Marxist theory about deproletarianization has been defended from
critiques emanating largely from (mainly) anti-Marxist frameworks. The latter include
not only neo-classical economic historiography (Steinfeld, Shlomowitz, Fogel and
Engerman,), postmodernism (Prakash, Taussig) and exercises in eclecticism (Banaji),
but also interpretations linked to the semi-feudal thesis (Byres, Patnaik, Breman).

[62] Labour-power is free by virtue of its owner being able to commodify and recommodify it unconditionally: that is, to be free in the sense understood by Marx and
Marxism a worker must be able personally to sell his/her own labour-power on a
continuous basis. That such a worker does not actually do this does not prevent the
capacity to do this—should the owner of labour-power so wish—defining any and
every production relation as free.

external/local wage differential has been eroded. In this way it is possible for commercial producers either to maintain wages at existing
(low) levels or even to decrease pay and conditions of each component
of the workforce, thereby restoring/enhancing profitability within the
capitalist labour process.[63]

Deproletarianization as a concept is based on Marxist theory about
labour power as the personal property of the worker, indeed his/her
only one. It is clear that when Marx talks of labour power being
'free', he is simply contrasting the feudal serf with the capitalist wage
labourer. Whereas the former was still not separated either from means
of production (land) or from the control of its owner (feudal lord), the
latter is now compelled to provide the capitalist with labour-power.
As described by Marx, this transition did not necessarily generate a
workforce that is free.[64]

Trotsky clearly regarded agrarian relations identified as 'semifeudal'
and reproduced by a declining landlord class as in fact capitalist, and
thus reproduced by a rural bourgeoisie. This is my view, and accords
precisely with my interpretation of unfree labour as deproletarianization undertaken by capital.[65] During the 1970s, a number of commen-

---

[63] This is the reason why the capitalist state is frequently called upon to ensure that
those separated from their means of production are not just available to employers but
also remain so. Hence the battery of legislative ordinances (peonage, pass laws, master
and servant laws, vagrancy laws) designed to keep those without the means of labour
in employment that may not be either of their choosing or to their liking. Whereas
making those separated from their means of production sell their labour-power on
the market is compatible with free work relations, requiring them to stay within such
employment once entered into is not.

[64] About this Marx (1976a: 875) noted: 'The starting point of the development that
gave rise both to the wage labourer and to the capitalist was the enslavement of the
worker. The advance made consisted in a change in the form of this servitude, in the
transformation of feudal exploitation into capitalist exploitation...' Elsewhere, however, it is not labour-power but rather labourers themselves who are categorized as
by Marx and Engels as commodities under capitalism, a view which suggests that
they perceived little relational distinctiveness between slaves and workers employed
by capital. Hence the statement (Marx and Engels, 1976: 490) to the effect that '(i)n
proportion as the bourgeoisie, i.e., capital, is developed, in the same proportion is the
proletariat, the modern working class, developed—a class of labourers, who live only
so long as they find work, and who find work only so long as their labour increases
capital. These labourers, who must sell themselves piecemeal, are a commodity, like
every other article of commerce, and are consequently exposed to all the vicissitudes
of competition, to all the fluctuations of the market.'

[65] Writing in 1931 about the agrarian question in Spain, Trotsky (1973: 77) observed:
'The relationships in the Spanish countryside present a picture of semifeudal exploitation. The poverty of the peasants... the oppression by the landowners, authorities, and
village chiefs have already more than once driven the agricultural workers and the

tators took issue with Deutscher's view that Trotsky was a Marxist internationalist who, because his interest was in world revolution, possessed an outlook that extended beyond Russia.[66]

For these commentators, therefore, Trotskyism was essentially about how Marxist theory coped (or failed to cope with) the conditions generated by economic backwardness: hence the view that 'far from being mired in internationalist concerns, [Trotsky] was throughout his life preoccupied with the problem of the relationship and applicability of Marxism to Russia, or, more generally, to backward, non-capitalist societies, and the idea of "world revolution" was an *aspect of this*, not *vice versa*'.[67]

By contrast, the argument here is that Trotsky was not interested simply in the Marxist theory about backwardness, much rather the opposite: precisely because his political objective involved world revolution, and his analytical focus was correspondingly on how capitalism operated and reproduced itself as a (world) system, Trotsky insisted that any meaningful examination of the latter process required an understanding of the way in which accumulation occurred *both* in advanced *and* in backward societies simultaneously, as part of the same systemic unity. In short, his argument was not about economic backwardness *per se*, as claimed, but rather about the contradictions generated by economic *forwardness*, or how what happens in seemingly backward societies where apparently non-capitalist (= 'feudal'

---

peasant poor to the door of open mutiny. Does this mean, however, that even during a revolution bourgeois relations can be purged of feudalism? No. It only means that under the current conditions in Spain, capitalism must use feudal means to exploit the peasantry. To aim the weapon of the revolution against the remnants of the Spanish Middle Ages means to aim it against the very roots of bourgeois rule.' Five year later, in 1937, Trotsky (1973: 307) notes: 'According to (the Stalinists), the Spanish revolution was called upon to solve only its "democratic" tasks, for which a united front with the "democratic" bourgeoisie was indispensable…Fascism, however, is not a feudal but a bourgeois reaction'. Trotsky then goes on to state that the attempt not to 'transgress the bounds of bourgeois democracy' is made in ignorance of the fact that 'the landowners are intimately bound up with the commercial, industrial and banking bourgeoisie, and the bourgeois intelligentsia that depends on them.' He concludes (*Trotsky*, 1973: 307–8) that 'The agrarian revolution could have been accomplished only *against* the bourgeoisie, and therefore only through measures of the dictatorship of the proletariat. There is no third, intermediate regime.'

[66] Among those who subscribed to this kind of critique of Trotskyism were Day (1973), Hodgson (1975), and Knei-Paz (1977). On Trotsky's internationalism, see the justly celebrated trilogy by Deutscher (1954; 1959; 1963).

[67] This is the view of Knei-Paz (1977: 67, emphasis added), who goes on to categorize Trotsky's theory of 'permanent revolution' as the 'revolution of backwardness'.

or 'semi-feudal') relations are supposedly dominant, is actually determined by the unrecognized presence there of advanced capitalist
elements.

It is certainly true that there exists a strand of Marxism (= semi-feudal thesis) which associates the presence/absence of capitalism exclusively with a corresponding presence/absence of labour-power that
is relationally free.[68] Equally true, however, is that such a view overlooks or downplays an alternative Marxist interpretation (= deproletarianization) of the potential/actual role of unfreedom, which links
its reproduction to the class struggle between workers and employers once capitalism is well established. Given the current divergence
in interpretation, therefore, it is necessary to ask the following question. Is there much support in Marxist theory on the subject of the
capitalism/unfreedom link for the claim made here: namely that deproletarianization and class struggle offer better explanations than the
semi-feudal thesis of what a capitalist labour régime in the twenty-first
century might look like?

What Marx and Other Marxists Really Said

The attempt to decouple Marxist theory about the capitalism/unfree-
dom link from the concept deproletarianization raises a number of
rather obvious problems. If the notion of free labour-power being crucial to a 'fully-functioning' capitalism is so central to Marxist theory,
as is claimed, why then do so many Marxists maintain the opposite?
Why do not just Marx, Engels, Kautsky, Lenin and Trotsky but also
Mandel, Dobb, Kuczynski and Guérin all accept that accumulation
does not necessarily require free labour-power, and can indeed do
without this?

Marx and Engels on Unfree Labour

Contrary to received wisdom, the resort by capital to production relations that are unfree does find support in the views of Marx, both about
the specific historical instances—child labour in Britain and plantation

---

[68] The existence of a considerable epistemological overlap between on the one hand
the non-Marxist interpretations considered above (Adam Smith, John Stuart Mill,
John Bright), and on the other the semi-feudal thesis, ought to signal caution where
claims to Marxist 'authenticity' are concerned.

slavery in the antebellum American South—and more generally about the centrality to the accumulation process of class struggle.[69] Indeed, in describing the impact of the reserve army of labour, and the importance of its role in the reproduction of capitalism, Marx observes that '[a]accumulation of wealth at one pole is, therefore, at the same time accumulation of misery, the torment of labour, slavery, ignorance, brutalization and moral degradation at the opposite pole, i.e., on the side of the class that produces its own product as capital.'[70]

That child workers employed in the factories of mid-nineteenth century Britain were for Marx a form of unfree labour is clear from two things: not just from the fact that their personal labour-power was sold by others, but also from the comparison he makes between such workers and plantation slaves.[71] Furthermore, he noted that wages paid to such workers were held down by the operation of the truck

---

[69] Not the least of the many ironies is that the approach of Marx to the role of child labour in the capitalist economy of Britain during the nineteenth century is very similar to that used by organizations such as the UN and the ILO in their critiques of child labour in India and other developing countries. Acknowledging that many child workers are unfree, a report by the UN Special Rapporteur (Bouhdiba, 1982: 23) noted: 'As has often been stressed, child labour brings down wages and therefore keeps adults in a highly insecure employment position...It is only in appearance that it helps families to survive. Far from improving the household income, child labour helps to reduce it.' This is also the view in a report about child labour published in India itself (Government of India, 1979: 8) some three decades ago: 'Child labour is as much the cause as the consequence of adult unemployment and under-employment. It at once supplements and depresses the family income. Child labour is not only a subsidy to industry but a direct inducement to the payment of low wages to adult workers. The entrance of children into the labour market reduces the volume of employment for the adult and lowers the bargaining power of adult workers.' Such critiques, indicting as they do the economic structures of the capitalist system, are very different from the kind of approach noted above, that seeks merely to verify whether or not such relational forms are prohibited in law.

[70] See Marx (1976a: 799). Anticipating the account by Lenin of Russia (see below), Marx (1976a: 821, 830, 849) refers to miners in nineteenth century England as 'bound' workers—bonded to their capitalist employers for a twelve month period, like attached labourers in India—and endorses the description of agricultural workers as the 'white slaves' of farmers.

[71] About this Marx (1976a: 519) wrote as follows: 'But now the capitalist buys children and young persons. Previously the worker sold his own labour-power, which he disposed of as a free agent...Now he sells wife and child. He has become a slave-dealer. Notices of demand for children's labour often resemble in form the inquiries for Negro slaves that were formerly to be read among the advertisements in American journals.' He went on to observe (Marx, 1976a: 922) that 'the transformation of manufacturing production into factory production and the establishment of the true relation between capital and labour-power' entails among other things 'child-slavery'.

system, a classic debt bondage mechanism.[72] Most significantly, Marx emphasized that the employment of child labour was made possible by the introduction of machinery, where children worked alongside older female and male labourers.[73] As is well known, the current prevalence of bonded child labour in agribusiness enterprises throughout India is a matter of record.[74]

[72] 'Wages', argues Marx (1976a: 599), 'miserable as they are (the maximum wages of a child in the straw-plait schools rising in rare cases to 3 shillings), are reduced far below their nominal amount by the prevalence of the truck system everywhere, but especially in the lace districts.'

[73] 'The labour of women and children was therefore the first result of the capitalist application of machinery...If machinery is the most powerful means of raising the productivity of labour, i.e., of shortening the working time needed to produce a commodity, it is also, as a repository of capital, the most powerful means of lengthening the working day beyond all natural limits in those industries first directly seized on by it', noted Marx (1976a: 517, 526–7). He continued (Marx, 1976a: 590): 'In contrast with the period of manufacture, the division of labour is now based, wherever possible, on the employment of women, of children of all ages and of unskilled workers, in short of "cheap labour", as the English typically describe it.' In the *Communist Manifesto*, Marx and Engels (1976: 491) made much the same point: 'The less the skill and exertion of strength implied in manual labour....the more modern industry becomes developed, the more is the labour of men superseded by that of women (and children).'

[74] There are, unfortunately, still those—for example, Lieten (2003: 227ff.)—who take an idealized and largely uncritical view of child labour in India. The link between on the one hand capitalist competition and maintaining/enhancing profitability, and securing higher output by employing the unfree labour of child workers emerged clearly from evidence presented to the 1931 Royal Commission on Labour in India. The exchanges contained in the latter about the kind of production relations used, and the reasons for this, are remarkable in terms of their frankness (Government of India, 1931: 104–106, B-1367, B-1370, B-1171, B-1172, B-1374, B-1375, B-1376). Because rival producers were undercutting them ('Persia is producing carpets considerably cheaper than we can produce here'), capitalist enterprises in India operating an outwork system to make carpets for the international market extracted greater quantities of surplus labour from their debt bonded child workers ('Until the money is paid back the boy has to work for me'). Master weavers who operated this outwork system made no secret either of the coercive methods used, or that this was the way in which higher output was obtained ('we see to it that the boy is made to work a little more than he ought to work; if it is one rupee's amount of work we see that we get 17 annas out of the boy'). In response to the question 'if the children are playful, and not quick in learning (to work) or do not diligently do their work, how does the weaver get work from them?', a master weaver answered: 'By punishing them.' To the next question, 'What sort of punishment?', the reply was: 'A slight beating'. When asked 'if a boy does not turn out efficient work how do you get him to do it?', the master weaver replied with remarkable candour: 'Beat him, hit him on the face, hit him with the fist and whatever we have handy at the time such as a stick.' Unsurprisingly, the subsequent query concerned the reaction to such maltreatment, the answer revealing the extent to which such debt bondage relations were enforced by kin: 'Does the boy sometimes

When accurately translated, it is clear that Marx himself subscribed to the view that owners of American slave plantations were capitalists, thereby confirming that in his view accumulation could occur on the basis of unfree labour.[75] Writing about the conflict in America between the Northern and Southern states at the outbreak of the Civil War, he characterized this not just as a struggle between slavery and free labour, nor as a defensive war to ensure that the South could continue to employ labour that was unfree, but rather as a conflict to extend the latter to the North and throughout the whole of North American society.[76]

In short, were the South to be victorious in this struggle, Northern capitalism in the United States would—in the words of Marx—be the subject of 'a reorganization on the basis of slavery'.[77] That is, a process of restructuring whereby workers who were free would be replaced by labour that was unfree ('a war of conquest for the spread and perpetuation of slavery').[78] A more succinct definition of struggle involving

---

run away?—Yes. When he runs away how is he brought back to work?—Very few run away; when they do run away we go after them or send the parents after them.'

[75] For this point, see Mintz (1977: 268–69, note 32). That Marx regarded plantation-owners in America as capitalists is evident from the following observation (Marx, 1986: 436, original emphasis): 'That we now not only describe the plantation-owners as capitalists, but that they *are* capitalists...'.

[76] On this, Marx (1984: 44, original emphasis) writes as follows: 'A large part of the territory thus claimed is still in the possession of the Union and would first have to be conquered from it. None of the so-called border states, however, not even those in the possession of the Confederacy, were ever *actual slave states*. Rather, they constitute an area of the United States in which the system of slavery and the system of free labour exist side by side and contend for mastery, the actual field of battle between South and North, between slavery and freedom. The war of the Southern Confederacy is, therefore, not a war of defence, but a war of conquest, a war of conquest for the spread and perpetuation of slavery.' Lest there be any doubt about it, this is repeated subsequently (*Marx*, 1984: 49): 'One sees, therefore, that the war of the Southern Confederacy is in the true sense of the word a war of conquest for the spread and perpetuation of slavery.'

[77] Hence the view (Marx, 1984: 50, original emphasis): 'What would have taken place would be not a dissolution of the Union, but a *reorganization* of it, a *reorganization on the basis of slavery*, under the recognized control of the slaveholding oligarchy.... The slave system would infect the whole Union. In the Northern states, where Negro slavery is in practice impossible, the white working class would gradually be forced down to the level of helotry... The present struggle between the South and the North is, therefore, nothing but a struggle between two social systems, the system of slavery and the system of free labour. The struggle has broken out because the two systems can no longer live peacefully side by side on the North American continent. It can only be ended by the victory of one system or the other.'

[78] In a review of *Capital*, Engels drew attention to the fact that capitalist production on the basis of slavery was accompanied by the intensification of labour. Hence the

workforce restructuring—a conflict over decomposition/recomposi-
tion of the labour process in terms of free/unfree workers, or what I
term deproletarianization—is difficult to imagine.[79]
    Since other Marxists have made much the same point about the
antebellum plantation economy, it is hard to see quite in what way
this view can still be considered 'non-Marxist'.[80] Thus the situation
is the opposite of what it is usually presented as being: rather than
regarding the slave plantation in nineteenth century southern US as
pre- or non-capitalist, therefore, what Marx actually said—when not
mistranslated—was that the slave plantation was a capitalist unit.[81]

---

following (Engels, 1985: 252): 'But wherever a nation whose production is carried on
in the more rudimentary forms of slavery or serfage, lives in the midst of a universal
market dominated by capitalist production, and where therefore the sale of its products for exports forms its chief purpose—there to the barbarous infamies of slavery or
serfdom are superadded the civilized infamies of over-working. Thus in the Southern
States of America slave-labour preserved a moderate and patriarchal character while
production was directed to immediate domestic consumption chiefly. But in the same
measure as the export of cotton became a vital interest to those states, the over-working of the negro, in some instances even the wearing-out of his life in seven working
years, became an element in a calculated and calculating system....'. The same point
was made subsequently by Guérin (see below).
    [79] That Marx himself saw the dangers of and was opposed to workforce restructur-
ing is evident from the following (Marx, 1985: 186): 'To counteract the intrigues of
capitalists always ready, in cases of strikes and lockouts, to misuse the foreign workman as a tool against the native workman, is one of the particular functions which
our Society has hitherto performed with success. It is one of the great purposes of the
(International Working Men's) Association to make the workmen of different countries not only feel but act as bretheren and comrades in the army of emancipation.'
    [80] According to Daniel Guérin (1956) in his Marxist analysis of the race question in
the United States, unfree labour was compatible not just with capitalist production but
also with advanced productive forces. Hence the view (Guérin, 1956: 29–30, emphasis
added) that '...a technological revolution resuscitated the slave system and gave it a
new lease on life: that is, the invention of the mechanical cotton gin by Eli Whitney in
1794...(in) the mid-19th century, slavery was not, as one might think, a rather shame-
ful residue, an anachronistic vestige of the past, on the verge of disappearing. On the
contrary, it reached its height in the years 1820 to 1860, the period when Cotton was
King. It was not a feudal but a capitalist institution...Moreover, the steadily declining
price which the planters received for their cotton in the markets of New England and
Europe narrowed their margin of profit and induced them to redouble their exploitation of the slaves. The institution of slavery, far from being mitigated, became ever
more vile, ferocious and inhuman when modern capitalism revived it and worked it to
the fullest.' According to Ingram (1895: 285), following the invention of the cotton
gin, exports from the United States of cotton rose from 138,328 pounds to 38,118,041
pounds in 1804 and to 127,860,152 pounds in 1820.
    [81] Noting the fact that Marx classified planters as capitalists and/or plantation
agriculture as capitalist, some exponents of the semi-feudal thesis then simply deny
this as being the case. Thus, for example, having asserted that for Marx slavery was
incompatible with capitalism, Byres (1996: 253, 279 note 40, original emphasis) then

Hence the argument that unfree labour was perfectly acceptable to producers who were capitalist is not inconsistent with the theoretical framework of Marx himself.[82]

This is especially so when the dynamic role of conflict is considered, and how the relative economic importance of free and unfree labour is structured by the dialectic. Not only did Marx himself point out that no social form vanishes until all its uses have been exhausted, but Engels (as well as Marx: see above) saw the role of class struggle as central to in the reproduction of capitalism, determining the way in which its production relations are constituted.[83] In a similar vein, Engels chronicled historical reversals, whereby in the course of class struggle production relations that were initially free can indeed give way to those that are unfree.[84]

Marx himself hinted at the same possibility when observing that in historical instances where conquest occurs, and plunder entails the enslavement of the defeated population, 'a mode of production appropriate to slave labour must be established'.[85] This could apply just as easily to flows of migrant labour from present-day contexts either that

---

accepts that '(t)here is a problem here.... (t)his is Marx's apparent categorization...of plantation owners (slaveholders) as *capitalists*...slavery clearly cannot be viewed as capitalism and must be seen as quite distinct from it.'

[82] Observing that '(s)lavery is an economic category like any other', Marx (1976b: 167) continued: 'Direct slavery is just as much the pivot of bourgeois industry as machinery, credits, etc. Without slavery you have no cotton; without cotton you have no modern industry. It is slavery that gave the colonies their value; it is the colonies that created world trade, and it is world trade that is the precondition of large-scale industry. Thus slavery is an economic category of the greatest importance. Without slavery North America, the most progressive of countries, would be transformed into a patriarchal country. Wipe North America off the map of the world, and you will have anarchy—the complete decay of modern commerce and civilization.'

[83] Hence the observation in the 1859 Preface by Marx (1913: 12), and the following observation by Engels (Marx and Engels, 1957: 257): 'In modern history at least it is, therefore, proved that all political struggles are class struggles, and all class struggles for emancipation, despite their necessarily political form—for every class struggle is a political struggle—turn ultimately on the question of *economic* emancipation.'

[84] The historical reversal of emancipation—from free to unfree relations of production—as the outcome of class struggle is noted by Engels in his introduction to the English edition of *Socialism: Utopian and Scientific* (1892). There he (Marx and Engels, 1957: 298) wrote as follows: 'The Lutheran Reformation produced a new creed, indeed a religion adapted to absolute monarchy. No sooner were the peasants of North East Germany converted to Lutheranism than they were from freemen reduced to serfs.'

[85] See Marx (1986: 35), who was referring to the plantation agriculture in the antebellum South. This was a view echoed by Plekhanov in the 1890s. 'Slavery in the European colonies is also, at first glance,' he wrote (Plekhanov, 1976: 175, original emphasis), 'a paradoxical example of capitalist development. This phenomenon...

neoliberalism has penetrated economically, or which imperialism has literally conquered. In both cases, the incorporation of such workers into the labour process of the victorious social formation entails changes to—but is not incompatible with—the existing mode of production (capitalism).

Kautsky and Lenin on Unfree Labour

Although Kautsky appears to belong to the ranks of those who classify unfree labour as economically inefficient, he nevertheless accepted that, where and when large enterprises had access to such production relations, they were able to maintain or enhance their profitability.[86] He also recognized, as did Lenin (see below), that the real economic significance of the small-scale rural 'enterprise' lay in its role as a source of outworkers—composed for the most part of female and child labour—on which large-scale agribusiness and industrial capitalists depended in order to boost profitability.

That he did not believe a capitalist agriculture would automatically replace unfree workers with free equivalents was clear from what Kautsky wrote during the 1890s: both in the Erfurt programme, and in *The Agrarian Question*.[87] Not only did he maintain that, with the introduction into the accumulation process of machinery, capital would increasingly replace the labour-power of men with that of women and children, but he also saw depriving workers of their freedom as being the logical outcome of capitalist development.[88] Central to all these

---

cannot be explained by the logic of economic life in the countries it was to be met in. The explanation is to be sought in *international economic relations.*'

[86] Despite associating 'the exercise of care' (= economic efficiency in the sense he understood the term) n the labour process with workers only when employed on large farms, Kautsky noted that the conditions licensing such a situation—good pay, good food and good treatment—were not only absent from the majority of capitalist agribusiness enterprises but would also not be introduced voluntarily by these employers. About this he wrote (Kautsky, 1988: 118, emphasis added): 'If the position of most small farmers is inimicable to the exercise of care, conversely the large farm is eminently capable of getting careful work out of its wage labourers. Good pay, good food, and good treatment have a considerable effect...Well-paid and well-fed, and hence intelligent, workers are an indispensable prerequisite for rational large-scale farming. *This precondition is still undoubtedly lacking in the majority of instances, and it would be naïve to expect any improvement from the "enlightened despotism" of large-scale farmers.*'

[87] For translations into English of the 1891 Erfurt Programme and the 1899 Agrarian Question, see Kautsky (1910; 1988).

[88] Like other Marxists, Kautsky (1910: 24–25) argued that, as capitalism developed,

processes, Kautsky argued, was the element of class struggle linked to the formation, expansion and reproduction of an industrial reserve army of labour.[89]

The latter took a form that is familiar to all those who study the pattern of agrarian capitalist development in the so-called Third World. Kautsky effects a contrast between on the one hand the big peasant, who works alongside and supervises his labourers, and on the other the small peasant, who is required to overwork his kinfolk/family, making them 'slaves without a will of their own'.[90] A peasant smallholding is able to reproduce itself not because it is inherently efficient economically, let alone able to compete successfully with capitalist units, as populists maintained, but rather because it constituted a labour reserve on which large commercial farms drew for the purpose of accumulation.[91]

the labour-power of males would be replaced by that of women and children: 'There was a time when skill and strength were requisites for the working-man...Now, however, the progress made in the division of labour and the introduction of machinery render skill and strength superfluous; they make it possible to substitute unskilled and cheap workmen for skilled ones; and, consequently, to put...women and even children in the place of men. In the early stages of manufacturing this tendency is already perceptible; but not until machinery is introduced into production do we find the wholesale exploitation of women and children—the most helpless among the helpless.... The labour of women and children, moreover, affords the additional advantage that these are less capable of resistance than men.' On the erosion by capital of freedom, his comments are as follows (Kautsky, 1910: 86–87): 'Private ownership in the implements of labour has long ceased to secure to each producer the product of his labour and to guarantee him freedom. Today, on the contrary, society is rapidly drifting to the point where the whole population of capitalist nations will be deprived of both property and freedom.'

[89] 'We have seen that the introduction of female and child-labour in industry is one of the most powerful means whereby capitalists reduce the wages of working-men,' notes Kautsky (1910: 29, 32, 34), adding that: 'To the capitalist this reserve army is invaluable. It places in his hands a powerful weapon with which to curb the army of the employed. After excessive work on the part of some has produced lack of work for others, then the idleness of these is used as a means to keep up, and even increase, the excessive work of the former...unemployment becomes greater the harder and the longer the workman toils; he brings enforced idleness upon himself through his own labour.'

[90] For this description, see Kautsky (1984: 25). Elsewhere Kautsky (1988: 110, 111) writes: 'The small peasants not only flog themselves into this drudgery: their families are not spared either. Since the running of the household and the farm are intimately linked together in agriculture, children—the most submissive of all labour—are always at hand!...Opportunities for the more intensive use of child-labour also work in the same direction (= intensification of labour, lengthening of the working day).'

[91] As Kautsky (1988: 111, 112) notes: 'It takes a very obdurate admirer of smallscale landownership to see the advantages derived from forcing small cultivators down to the level of beasts of burden, into a life occupied by nothing other than work—apart

This meant, Kautsky pointed out, that the large commercial unit had 'at its disposal very cheap forced labour. If the source of this *cheap forced labour* dried up the large-scale enterprise became unprofitable and was replaced by the small one.'[92] This was the central thesis of his argument concerning the seemingly irrational survival of peasant cultivators in an agriculture that is capitalist: namely, that because smallholdings are a source of labour-power, they are never wholly displaced by large farms.[93] This, and not their economic efficiency, is the reason why peasant economy survives.

This labour-power was provided, Kautsky pointed out, on a casual, seasonal or permanent basis by members of the peasant family farm, and controlled by large capitalist producers through the debt mechanism.[94] By itself, however, the creation or reproduction of peasant

from time set aside for sleeping and eating...The overwork of the small independent farmers and their families is therefore not a factor which should be numbered amongst the advantages of the small farm even from a purely economic standpoint, leaving aside any ethical or other conditions.'

[92] See Kautsky (1984: 14). The dynamic structuring this seemingly 'autonomous' peasant economy is made clear in the following manner (Kautsky, 1984: 19, original emphasis): 'The capitalists favour this settlement of their workers on the land because they can make sure of their labour-power in this way, and make make the workers more dependent on them...Thus the number of dwarf-enterprises can grow under certain circumstances within the capitalist mode of production, alongside the latter, and as part of the latter's growth, of the growth of the large-scale enterprise, of the growth of the proletariat. The dwarf-enterprise does not draw its vital force from its *ability to compete* but from *the worker's wage.*'

[93] See Kautsky (1988: 163), where he writes as follows: 'The best conditions for bringing up a plentiful supply of able-bodied labour are found among the owners (or tenants) of small farms on which an independent household is linked with independent farming. Not only does this group supply labour-power for itself, but also turns out a surplus (in the form of) workers via their children, for whom there is no room on the family farm, and who can therefore be taken on as house-servants or day-labourers by large farms.'

[94] Observing that historically 'the large-scale agricultural enterprise became impossible to keep up, and peasant and tenant farms took the place of the plantations,' Kautsky (1984: 14–15) adds: 'This is also one of the reasons for the phenomenon that on the continent of Europe it is precisely in the most economically and politically developed states, states which were the first to suppress compulsory feudal labour services, that peasant economy is most strongly entrenched'. Elsewhere in Europe the large-scale unit continues to be commercially viable precisely because 'since the abolition of forced labour (this has rested) first and foremost on a new kind of slavery, *the slavery of indebtedness*' (original emphasis). Such a view was prevalent right across the political spectrum at that conjuncture, as is evident from what A.J. Balfour, the British Conservative Member of Parliament, stated in an address to the Industrial Remuneration Conference in 1885. On this subject, he wrote as follows (Dilke, 1968: 342–43): 'This view which, with very great reluctance I am compelled to accept, asserts that a peasant proprietary may, and in all old countries where it extensively prevails actually does, co-exist with great poverty in the large towns, with low wages and some-

economy by large commercial farms so as to retain a labour reserve is insufficient to prevent such workers from seeking better-paid employment in industry, and for this reason coercion is necessary to keep them on large enterprises.[95] Kautsky makes clear not only the unfree nature of the workforce retained/employed in agriculture at this conjuncture, but also how this is achieved: state compulsion, punishing breach of contract, enforcing the Masters and Servants Ordinance ('to ensure that farmers can keep their servants'), and preventing the 'free movement' of migrants (= foreign workers).[96]

In other words, a large farm had also to prevent the workers forming the labour reserve it had created from personally commodifying or recommodifying their own labour-power in the manner of a proletariat; that is, it was necessary to deproletarianize them. His twofold conclusion is significant. First, that what populists misinterpreted as the 'blossoming' of peasant economy—its seeming capacity to reproduce itself in the face of capitalism—was much rather a sign of its distress, one characteristic of which was that 'feudal forms of labour contract are re-emerging.'[97] And second, the latter underlined the extent to

---

times with harsh treatment of the labourer in the country districts. That while peasant proprietors are hard masters, and, where they have the chance, hard landlords, they themselves are too frequently subjected to a condition of dependence more cruel than that of any tenant or any landlord, or any labourer or any employer—the dependence, namely of a small debtor on a professional moneylender.' Balfour went on seemingly to commend the work of Marx on this subject (Dilke, 1968: 344), saying that—although he himself was no socialist—in his view it possessed 'intellectual force,' 'consistency,' and 'economic reasoning'.

[95] Hence the observation (Kautsky, 1988: 225) that 'large-scale landownership set about the artificial creation of small farms wherever the land has been cleared of them. And the stronger the pull of the town, the more landowners will try to bind the workers they need to the land. But often the mere creation of small peasant plots is not sufficient to overcome the attraction of industry: legal compulsion also has to be used to keep workers on the large estates.'

[96] Where flight from the land continues, observes Kautsky (1988: 231), 'state compulsion steps in to assist. Tightening up the Servants Ordinance, punishing breach of contract...are all meant to ensure that the farmers can keep their servants. The elimination or obstruction of free movement by banning (internal) migration, measures making it more difficult for migrants to settle in towns...and similar moves, are meant to keep migrants at home.' That is, economically immobile, on the land. This, Kautsky agrees, 'will merely make rural life even more unbearable for the servants and contract workers (and) would rob numerous small peasants of the only opportunity they have for supplementary employment and throw them into acute poverty.'

[97] Empirical data suggesting that peasant economy was reproducing itself economically, argued Kautsky (1988: 233), 'warm the hearts of all good citizens who see the peasantry as the sturdiest bulwark of the existing order. Look, they exclaim, there is no movement—in agriculture that is: Marx's dogma does not apply *here*... The peasantry (in the 1880s) appears to be blossoming anew—to the detriment of all those socialist

which agrarian capitalist development in Germany during the 1880s
was being accompanied by the intensification, not the elimination, of
unfree labour.[98]

Lenin, too, understood the connection between on the one hand the
presence of debt bondage and on the other the centrality of class struggle leading to the restructuring the capitalist labour process, using outworkers composed of unfree labour drawn form the industrial reserve
army. About restructuring he notes that the outwork system which
takes the form of domestic industry 'by no means eliminates the concept of capitalist manufacture, but on the contrary, is sometimes even
a sign of its further development'.[99] The importance of these small
establishments is that they are connected with big ones to form what
he calls 'a single system of industry', an arrangement described as typical of capitalist manufacture.[100] Many of those who became 'master-
industrialists', observed Lenin, were in fact better-off peasants.[101]

tendencies produced by industry. But this blossom has its roots in a swamp. It is not
a product of the *well-being* of the peasantry, but of the *distress* of the whole of agriculture...feudal forms of labour contract are re-emerging' (original emphasis).

[98] The continued significance of unfree labour at this conjuncture is evident from
the fact that it is enshrined in German legislative ordinances. Thus the 1891 Industrial
Code Amendment Bill (Germany) contains the following clauses (Schäffle, 1893: 232,
233): 'If the apprentice quits his instruction...without consent of his master...the
police magistrate may, on application of the master, oblige the apprentice to remain
under instruction so long as apprentice relations are declared by judicial ruling to be
still undissolved...In case of refusal (by the worker), the police magistrate may cause
the apprentice to be taken back by force, or he may compel him to return under pain
of a fine, to the amount of fifty marks, or detention for five days...The apprentice
shall not be employed in the same trade by another employer, without consent of
the former master, within nine months after such dissolution of apprentice relations'
(Clauses §130 and §132).

[99] See Lenin (1964a: 413). Opposing the Narodnik view that domestic industry
was an autonomous economic form of production unconnected with capitalism,
Lenin (1964: 450, 452) argued that outworkers wrongly classified as part of 'handicraft industry' should more realistically be categorized as 'capitalistically employed
workers'—that is, as part of a specifically capitalist system of production, and its social
relations consequently seen as desired and reproduced by it. His conclusion (Lenin,
1964a: 541) is equally emphatic: 'The facts utterly refute the view widespread here
in Russia that "factory" and "handicraft" are isolated from each other. On the contrary, such a division is purely artificial. The connection and continuity between the
forms...is of the most direct and intimate kind.'

[100] See Lenin (1964a: 414, 438). Criticizing the Russian populists for missing this
connection ('The fundamental error of Narodnik economics is that it ignores, or
glosses over, the connection between the big and the small establishments...'), he goes
on to point out that (Lenin, 1964a: 441) 'capitalist domestic industry is met with at
all stages of the development of capitalism in industry, but it is most characteristic of
manufacture'.

[101] 'We have seen,' notes Lenin (1964a: 446), 'that the big master-industrialists, the

In late nineteenth century Russia, the sweating system not merely
drew in but depended upon the unfree and thus cheap labour-power
of women and children, a phenomenon Marx had earlier identified
in the case of Britain.[102] And again like Marx, Lenin noted the prevalence of unfree production relations (bonded labour, the truck system)
accompanying this process of capitalist restructuring.[103] Observing that
the latter gives rise to a worker who is 'not only a wage-slave, but also
a debt-slave', Lenin confirms thereby that in his opinion accumulation
results in labour-power that is paid and simultaneously unfree.[104]

In line with almost all other Marxists, Lenin was aware of not only
the importance of class struggle as waged by capital so as to cheapen/
discipline labour, but also the resort by an employer to unfreedom
when his (or 'his') workers attempt personally to commodify/recom-
modify their own labour-power and sell it to the highest bidder.[105]

---

buyers-up, work-room owners and subcontractors are at the same time well-to-do
agriculturalists.' In the construction industry, the labour contractor is described as the
one who becomes 'a real capitalist' (Lenin, 1964a: 530ff.). The same kind of phenomenon was noted earlier by Marx in relation to the gang system in nineteenth century
English agriculture, where the labour contractor was a gangmaster who recruited and
controlled groups of workers. 'Some gangmasters,' he observed (Marx, 1976a: 851
note 10), 'have worked up to a position of farmers of 500 acres, or proprietors of
whole rows of houses.'

[102] Referring to manufacturing apprenticeship, Lenin (1964a: 427–28) argues that it
'is well known that under general conditions of commodity economy and capitalism
this (apprenticeship) gives rise to the worst form of dependence and exploitation'.
He then compares the practice of apprenticeship to the conditions structuring the
employment of child labour in manufacturing industry. Children continue to work,
Lenin notes, even with 'the advent of large-scale industry', concurring with the analysis
by Marx himself of this same trend in British industry some three decades earlier.

[103] 'Alongside the sweating system, and perhaps as one of its forms, should be
placed the truck system,' which, Lenin (1964a: 443) accepts, is commonplace in outwork arrangements, adding that the 'drawing of women and children of the tenderest
age into production is nearly always observed in domestic industry.'

[104] Hence the following (Lenin, 1964a: 445): 'The isolation of the home workers and
the abundance of middlemen naturally leads to widespread bondage...which usually
accompany "patriarchal" relationships in remote rural districts. Workers' indebtedness to employers is extremely widespread in the "handicraft" industries in general,
and in domestic industry in particular. Usually the worker is not only a Lohnsklave
(wage-slave) but also a Schuldsklave (debt-slave).' Having described the squirrel-fur
industry as 'a typical example of capitalist manufacture', Lenin (1964a: 408–9) accepts
that 'relations between masters and workers are "patriarchal"', an employment situation where 'masters knock them (labourers) about'. The same is true of relations in
the button industry (Lenin, 1964a: 411).

[105] Lenin (1964a: 440) accepts that even the development of industrial capitalism—as distinct from merchant capital—does not lead to the eradication of bonded
labour ('The mass of peasants...are in a similar state of bondage. Can one, under such
circumstances, rejoice over the slight development of industrial capital?').

Accordingly, those categorized by Lenin as capitalist wage labourers
are also described as being subordinated by all the mechanisms famil-
iarly associated with unfree production relations: employer collusion,
retaining workers passports, and prohibiting farmers from employing
'absconding' agricultural labourers.[106] The employment of child labour
in agriculture is perceived as a way in which peasant compete with
capitalism, and in industry—specifically, the outwork system—it is
seen as a way in which enables some capitalist enterprises to compete
with other capitalist ones.[107]

Nor was it the case that constraints on outmigration posed by the
existence in rural areas of unfree relations prevented the access by
capital to an industrial reserve army of labour.[108] In cases where rural

---

[106] Lenin (1964a: 246) cites the following example from the Kuban region: 'The
Cossack resorts to every possible method to force down the price of labour, acting
either individually or through the community...cutting down the food, increasing the
work quota, docking the pay, retaining workers' passports, adopting public resolutions
prohibiting specific farmers from employing workers, on pain of a fine, at above a
definite rate, etc.'

[107] On the employment of child labour in Russian agriculture, see Lenin (1963:
209–13). Significantly, even when he differentiates backward forms of capitalism from
more advanced kinds, it is clear that unfree labour is common to both. Thus, for
example, the mining industry in the Urals is characterized as a 'backward' form of
capitalism where bonded labour persists, whereas mining in the South is described
as a 'purely capitalist industry' (Lenin, 1964a: 488ff.). He then goes on to accept that
unfree relations *do* exist even in the South, which earlier he held up as the epitome of
'advanced capitalism', stating (Lenin, 1964a: 495): 'Can one be surprised, for instance,
at Southern mine owners being eager to tie the workers down and to secure the legislative prohibition of competition by small establishments, when in the other mining
area (i.e., the 'backward' Urals) such tying down and such prohibitions have existed
for ages, and exist to this day, and when in another area the iron-masters, by using
more primitive methods and employing cheaper and more docile labour, get a profit
on their pig-iron, without effort...?'

[108] About the lumber and building industries, Lenin (1964a: 525ff.) asks 'How is
this industry organized?', and answers 'On purely capitalistic lines'. He goes on to
delineate the relational forms characterizing such capitalist enterprises: 'Lumbering
is one of the worst paid occupations...Left to toil in the remote forest depths, these
workers are in a totally defenceless position, and in this branch of industry bondage,
the truck system, and such-like concomitants of the "patriachal" peasant industries
prevail...Moscow statisticians mention the "compulsory purchase of provisions,"
which usually reduces to a marked degree the lumber workers' earnings.' Further on
he (Lenin, 1964a: 528–29, original emphasis) notes that the 'peasants are in "perpetual bondage" to the lumber industrialists', and goes on to observe that lumbermen
'represent that form of the reserve army (or relative surplus-population in capitalist
society) which (Marxist) theory describes as *latent*; a certain (and, as we have seen,
quite large) section of the rural population must always be ready to undertake such
work, must always be in need of it. That is a condition for the existence and development of capitalism.'

inhabitants were unable to leave their communities, therefore, factories were sited in the villages. This, as Lenin observed, meant that '[w]hile the erection of factories in the countryside involves quite a few inconveniences, it does, however, guarantee a supply of cheap labour. The muzhik is not allowed to go to the factory, so the factory goes to the muzhik.'[109] The contemporary resonance of this kind of capitalist relocation, plus the reason for undertaking it, and the working arrangements licensed thereby, are too obvious to need much elaboration.[110]

Trotsky and Other Marxists on Unfree Labour

Where issues of systemic and relational transition are involved, the work of Trotsky also provides a useful guide to a Marxist understanding of the apparently contradictory way in which capital deploys/reproduces both free and unfree labour-power in the course of agrarian transformation. That Trotsky himself subscribed to the view that capitalism strives to replace free wage labour with unfree production relations is clear from a number of things. From the fact of his opposition to the conceptual apparatus structuring the concept 'semi-feudal' and 'feudal', from his belief that the agrarian question would be resolved not by the bourgeoisie under capitalism but by the proletariat under socialism, and—most importantly—from what he wrote in 1925 about the way in which accumulation made it necessary for advanced capitalist production to negate the very conditions of its own existence. On the latter point, therefore, Trotsky observed that advanced capital undermined not only competition (or the free market) but also 'the freedom of labour'.[111]

---

[109] See Lenin (1964a: 524), where the reason for this is explained as follows: 'The muzhik lacks complete freedom (thanks to the collective-responsibility system and the obstacles to his leaving the community) to seek an employer who gives the greatest advantage; but the employer has a perfect way of seeking out the cheapest worker.'

[110] This pattern of relocation in search of ever-cheaper and more easily subordinated forms of labour-power—an industrial reserve army that is global in scope, in other words—corresponds to what currently takes the form of the new international division of labour (Fröbel, Heinrichs and Kreye, 1980). It corresponds closely to the dynamic identified a century ago by Lenin (1964a: 525, original emphasis): 'By converting the backwoodsman-muzhik into a factory worker *at one stroke*, the factory may for a time ensure for itself a supply of the cheapest, least developed and least exacting "hands"'.

[111] His observation about this is as follows (Trotsky, 1976: 49, emphasis added): 'Standardization is socialization carried into the technical side of production. We see how in this direction technical science in the leading capitalist countries is tearing

Much the same point was made subsequently by a number of historians who were also Marxists, among whom were Jürgen Kuczynski, Maurice Dobb, Daniel Guérin and Ernest Mandel. Each recognized that, even in an advanced capitalist economy, unfree labour could be an outcome of class struggle. All of them accepted that capital did not always try to eliminate unfreedom and replace it with free labour, nor indeed did accumulation necessarily depend on this kind of trans-formation.[112] In fact, Dobb—like Mandel—had no difficulty in recognizing that, even in metropolitan contexts, capital imposed unfreedom on labour when market conditions favoured workers and not employers.[113]

through the cover of private property, and embarking on what is, in essence, *a negation of the principle of competition, "the freedom of labour" and everything connected with it.*'

[112] 'The freedom of mobility has been taken away from labour to a degree which makes one question whether one can really still speak of a proletariat such as we have known since the Industrial Revolution', noted Kuczynski (1939: 42), adding that '(o)ne can speak of the German worker only in a very limited sense as a "free-wage worker", free to sell his labour where he gets the least lowly price for it.' Dobb made much the same kind of point. Designed 'to lessen the "labour turnover" and to tie a worker to a particular firm', restrictions on economic freedom include a lack of information about alternative employment, tied and company housing, and the truck system (Dobb, 1946: 13–15). In a similar vein, Guérin (1956: 27) maintained that the acceptability to capitalism of unfree labour should be understood with reference to the fact that '(s)lavery flourished as long as it was *profitable*' (original emphasis).

[113] Talking about war-time Britain, Dobb (1940: 332) observes: 'The crucial limit seems to be...full employment in the labour market to raise wages to such an extent as to precipitate a sharp shrinkage of surplus value, and consequently to change the value both of existing capital and of new investment. So abhorrent and unnatural does such a situation appear as to cause exceptional measures to be taken to clip the wings of labour—even...*to curtail the normal working of competitive forces*—whenever labour scarcity shows signs of becoming an enduring condition of the labour market' (emphasis added). Talking about war-time Germany, Mandel (1975: 162) observes in a similar vein: '(E)ven under conditions where the working class is completely atomized, the laws of the market which determine short-term fluctuations in the price of the commodity labour-power do not disappear. As soon as the industrial reserve army contracted in the Third Reich, workers were able to try, by means of rapid job mobility—for instance into the spheres of heavy industry and armaments which paid higher wage-rates and overtime—to achieve at least a modest improvement in their wages, even without trade union action. Only a violent intervention by the Nazi state to sustain the rate of surplus-value and the rate of profit, in the form of the legal *prohibition* of job changes, and the *compulsory tying* of workers to their job, was able to prevent the working class from utilizing more propitious conditions on the labour market. This abolition of freedom of movement of the German proletariat was one of the most striking demonstrations of the capitalist class nature of the Nationalist Socialist State' (original emphasis).

Similarly, in the 1960s Mandel contrasted two extreme forms of capitalism; whereas the object of public expenditure under the then dominant welfare state was 'improving the position of low-income families and to purposes of public utility', under the recently defeated fascism the same economic activity had been designed to reduce living standards of workers in order to maintain or boost capitalist profitability.[114] Central to the latter, he argued, is the replacement of free labour with workers that are unfree, the object being to lower the cost of labour-power by depressing yet further the subsistence minimum, so as to enhance the level of surplus extracted in the course of the accumulation process.[115] This is not to say that the resort by capital to unfree labour-power either prefigures fascism or is evidence for the presence of the latter, only to recognize that in periods of acute class struggle with labour, where its own survival may be at stake, capital does not rule out any option available to it. And deproletarianization is just such an option.

Unfree Labour and Primitive Accumulation

Although the implausibility of continuing to deny the existence of deproletarianization is now evident, the Marxist argument about the capitalism/unfreedom link has shifted of late. Some of those who earlier questioned the acceptability to capital of unfree labour have relativized their position, and these days claim one of two things. Either that the use by employers of unfree labour in the midst of capitalism amounts to 'primitive accumulation', or that capital uses—but does not actually seek out or reproduce—this kind of relation. Hence the problem remains: whether or not unfreedom constitutes a central aspect of

---

[114] Hence the view (Mandel, 1968: 537): 'The significance of this policy is clear—to bring about a recovery in the rate of profit at the expense of the working class, which is deprived of its political and trade-union means of defence...In the extreme form which it assumed, above all in Germany, during the Second World War, fascism goes beyond the militarisation of labour, to the abolition of free labour in the strict sense of the word, to a return to slave labour on an ever larger scale.'

[115] 'What is characteristic of forced labour,' Mandel (1968: 537, third footnote) points out, is 'precisely that the mere idea of a necessary product, of a subsistence minimum, is completely deprived of meaning. The "payment" of labour is lowered so as not merely no longer to ensure survival in good health but even to imply certain death within a brief period of time.'

a 'fully functioning' capitalist system, as distinct from merely its
'pre-history'.

According to Marx, primitive accumulation not only 'precedes capitalist accumulation' but is also 'an accumulation which is not the result
of the capitalist mode of production but its point of departure'.[116] Such
accumulation is labelled 'primitive' because, in his words, '[i]t forms
the pre-history of capital, and of the mode of production corresponding to capital'.[117] In the opinion of Marx, therefore, '[i]n Western
Europe, the homeland of political economy, the process of primitive
accumulation has more or less been accomplished.[118] That the process
of primitive accumulation was confined to the 'pre-history of capital'
is a view supported also by Lenin, Kautsky and Dobb in their commentaries on Marx's ideas.[119]

[116] See Marx (1976a: 873). As is well known, the concept 'primitive accumulation'
was designed to undermine the prevailing view held by economists about the origins
of capitalism. According to the latter, capitalism emerged as a result of virtuous and/
or industrious thrift, enabling some to save and prosper. Those who did not prosper
were the ones that did not work hard and save, a morality tale which blames the victim, who is deemed responsible for his/her own economic plight. Against this idealized view, Marx (1976a: Chapter 26) showed that accumulation was the result, much
rather, of expropriation combined with appropriation of surplus labour, a process
built on the separation of some from the means of production and its simultaneous
consolidation by others.

[117] See Marx (1976a: 874–75), where he makes the following observation: 'So-called
primitive accumulation, therefore, is nothing else than the historical process of divorc-
ing the producer from the means of production. It appears as "primitive" because it
forms the pre-history of capital, and of the mode of production corresponding to
capital. The economic structure of capitalist society has grown out of the economic
structure of feudal society. The dissolution of the latter set free the elements of the
former.' Although he noted the existence of continuities between primitive accumulation and the capitalist mode of production, Marx (1972: 272) nevertheless emphasized
the prefiguring role of the former. He regarded capitalism as the 'normalization' of
primitive accumulation: conditions and processes which seem anomalous historically
in the case of primitive accumulation emerge as central to the reproduction of capitalism proper. Seen thus, unfree relations of production that characterize primitive
accumulation can therefore be said to become 'normal' under capitalism.

[118] See Marx (1976a: 931).

[119] See, for example, Lenin (1964b) and Kautsky (1936: Ch. VI). The latter even
entitles his Chapter on primitive accumulation 'The Dawn of the Capitalist Mode of
Production'. Much the same point was made by Dobb (1946: 178, 209), who states
unambiguously that '(i)f any sense is to be made…of the notion of "primitive accumulation" (in Marx's sense of the term) *prior in time* to the full flowering of capitalist
production…(…) In short, the Mercantile System was a system of State-regulated
trade which played a highly important rôle in the adolescence of capitalist industry:
it was essentially the economic policy of an age of primitive accumulation' (original
emphasis). The close of the nineteenth century in English history is described by Dobb

For Marx, therefore, primitive accumulation is distinctive in two specific ways: in terms of historical conjuncture, and the use of force. It occurred at 'the dawn of capitalism', and was characterized by the forcible separation of the direct producer from his/her means of production, a process of dispossession which—as he made clear—could only be achieved by considerable violence.[120] As is well known, the problem of decoupling the capitalist mode of production from the conditions and context associated with primitive accumulation was identified originally by Luxemburg.[121] Although recognizing the importance

---

(1946: 273) as a period when 'the epoch of "primitive accumulation" (had) long since passed'.

[120] As Marx (1976a: 875, 876) points out, 'this history, the history of their expropriation, is written in the annals of mankind in letters of fire and blood…The expropriation of the agricultural producer, of the peasant, from the soil is the basis of the whole process.' In certain respects, this view associating unfreedom with expropriation at 'the dawn of capitalism' (= 'primitive accumulation') is not so different from that of Nierboer (1910), whose argument is that unfreedom is necessary only as long as resources are open: that is to say land is available to those wishing to become smallholders. A producer has to compel labourers to work for him, by using coercion to prevent them becoming producers in their own right: namely, selling the product of labour rather than labour-power itself. Once all land has been acquired, however, and this economic resource is accordingly no longer available, then the owners of labour-power—no longer having an alternative—are forced to sell this for a living, and work for other. According to Nierboer, therefore, the end of open resources also marks the end of the need for employers to resort to unfree relations of production. The difficulty with this interpretation is that whilst Nierboer explains the presence of unfreedom in a non-capitalist agriculture, it cannot account for the continuation of such relations once capitalist development established itself. It is precisely the latter situation that is explained by the class struggle argument, based on deproletarianization of labour-power.

[121] Anticipating some of the theoretical problems that arise from associating primitive accumulation with the 'pre-history of capital', Luxemburg (1951: 364–65) notes that 'Marx dealt in detail with the process of appropriating non-capitalist means of production as well as with the transformation of the peasants into a capitalist proletariat… Yet we must bear in mind that all this is treated solely with a view to so-called primitive accumulation. For Marx, these processes are incidental, illustrating merely the genesis of capital, its first appearance in the world; they are, as it were, travails by which the capitalist mode of production emerges from a feudal society. As soon as he comes to analyse the capitalist process of production and circulation, he reaffirms the universal and exclusive domination of capitalist production.' The central difficulty is identified by her (Luxemburg, 1951: 365, emphasis added) as follows: 'Yet…capitalism *in its full maturity* depends in all respects on non-capitalist strata and social organizations existing side by side with it. It is not merely a question of a market for the additional product, as Sismondi and the later critics and doubters of capitalist accumulation would have it. The interrelations of accumulating capital and non-capitalist forms of production extend over values as well as over material conditions, for constant capital, variable capital and surplus value alike. The non-capitalist mode of production is the given historical setting for this process…Capital needs the

of what she then understandably categorized as non-capitalist social
formations and production relations to the reproduction of 'capitalism
in its full maturity', nowadays it is difficult to see either of the former
as in any way external to the latter.[122]

The recognition, initially by Luxemburg and subsequently by others,
of contexts/relations that are ostensibly anomalous where the capitalist
mode of production is concerned, however, has facilitated an discur-
sive slide on the part of those now studying present developments in
the agrarian sector of so-called Third World nations. It is easy to see
how, associated as it is with the forcible expropriation of the peasant
smallholder, primitive accumulation can be extended temporally and
conceptually to account for the existence of other kinds of coercion
in the present. That is, when applied currently to explain the continuing presence in a global capitalist system of relational forms—such as
bonded labour—that have hitherto been classified as anomalous precapitalist work arrangements.

Relocating Primitive Accumulation

The main theoretical relocation of the concept 'primitive accumulation', and its resulting extension from an historical point at the inception of capitalism to an aspect of capitalism proper, occurred during

means of production and the labour power of the whole globe for untrammelled accumulation; it cannot manage without the natural resources and the labour power of all
territories... And in fact, primitive conditions allow of a greater drive and of far more
ruthless measures than could be tolerated under purely capitalist social conditions.'
On the nature of the capitalism/non-capitalism link, and how this renders problematic
the whole concept of an historically-specific process of primitive accumulation that is
common to all social formations, Luxemburg (1951: 366) concludes: 'Whatever the
theoretical aspects, the accumulation of capital, as an historical process, depends in
every respect upon non-capitalist social strata and forms of social organization... The
solution envisaged by Marx lies in the dialectical conflict that capitalism needs non-
capitalist social organizations as the setting for its development, that it proceeds by
assimilating the very conditions which alone can ensure its own existence.'
[122] The point about 'primitive accumulation' in Third World agrarian contexts was
made most succinctly by Gunder Frank (1977: 88–89): 'If "pre"-capitalist means previous to capitalist, then, by definition it is also "non"-capitalist. If "pre"-capitalist means
the beginning of capitalist, then it is part capitalist, part non-capitalist. But in either
event, "non"-capitalist need not be "pre"-capitalist, since it can also be simultaneous
with, or even post-capitalist. Thus, insofar as "primitive" accumulation refers to accumulation on the basis of production with non-capitalist relations relations of production, it need not be prior to, but can also be contemporary with capitalist production
and accumulation.'

and after the 'development decade' of the 1960s.[123] Because of the centrality at that conjuncture to debates about development of economic growth in Third World agriculture, therefore, whether or not capitalism was present in the latter context, and—if so—did it amount to 'primitive accumulation', became paramount considerations. Of late, the concept 'primitive accumulation' has crept back into analyses of neoliberal economic development, in the course of which it has been repositioned in relation to the history of capitalism.

For advocates of the semi-feudal thesis who have been wrong-footed over claims that capital always and everywhere seeks to replace unfree workers with free equivalents, therefore, 'primitive accumulation' in the midst of neoliberal capitalism has become a theoretical refuge.[124] Unable any longer to deny that unfree workers are acceptable to commercial producers, they nevertheless still assert that unfree labour belongs to a pre- or non-capitalist (= 'primitive') stage. For them, therefore, because primitive accumulation precedes an as-yet unrealized

---

[123] Among those who have subsequently questioned the conjunctural specificity of primitive accumulation, and the its anchoring in the 'pre-history' of the capitalist mode of production, are Althusser and Balibar (1970: 276ff.). Categorizing as the 'second great discovery' made by Marx the 'incredible means used to achieve "primitive accumulation"', Althusser (1971: 85, original emphasis) went on more cautiously to observe that it was 'thanks to which capitalism was "born" and grew in Western societies, helped also by the existence of a mass of "free labourers" (i.e. labourers stripped of means of labour) and technical discoveries. This means the most brutal violence: the thefts and massacres which cleared capitalism's royal road into human history. This last chapter contains a prodigious wealth which has not yet been exploited: in particular the thesis (which we shall have to develop) that capitalism has always used and, in the "margins" of its metropolitan existence—i.e. in the colonial and ex-colonial countries—is still using well into the twentieth century, *the most brutally violent means*.' Like Luxemburg, therefore, Althusser and Balibar recognized that the characteristics ascribed to 'primitive accumulation' continued unabated even when capitalism proper had been established.

[124] A case in point is Byres who, in the face of substantial evidence to the contrary, has long insisted on the unacceptability to capitalism of workers who are unfree—a central theoretical emplacement of the semi-feudal thesis. Now he maintains (Byres, 2005: 85, 89) both that '(f)or as long as the conditions for capitalist accumulation had not been established, domestic primitive accumulation would be necessary', and that primitive accumulation 'has been a necessary condition for successful capitalist transition and its accompanying structural transformation (and) has never been more than a preliminary to them.' The capitalism-needs-a-proletariat argument is made (*Byres*, 2005: 87) with regard to rural Latin America, where 'communities are dispossessed by extra-economic means and there is clear proletarianisation'. This was his view a decade ago, when he informed this writer that 'free wage labour (free in the double sense) is crucial to a fully functioning capitalism' (personal communication, 11 September 1998).

blossoming of the accumulation process (= 'a fully functioning capitalism'), unfree relations consequently remain a prefiguring relational
form as distinct from one compatible with capitalism 'proper'. A link
between advanced capitalism and unfree labour is accordingly in effect
denied.

Those who have recently accepted or currently do recognize the
existence of just such a link take a seemingly different position. For
world-systems theorists such as Wallerstein, therefore, unfree labour is
acceptable to capital, but only on the periphery of the global economy
where this relational form is encountered.[125] In the core metropolitan
capitalist countries the workforce is free, whilst unfree labour-power
remains external to capitalism proper.[126] On the basis of a dualistic
modes of production framework, Miles comes to a similar conclusion:
due to a combination of uneven capitalist expansion and the persistence of peasant smallholding in peripheral contexts, labour shortages
there prevent the emergence of free wage labour on which capitalism depends.[127] In both cases, therefore, capitalism is said to require
labour-power that free, and to draw on unfree equivalents solely when-
ever/wherever its preferred variant is unavailable.

---

[125] Hence the view (Wallerstein, 1979: 148) that associates a declining incidence
of unfreedom with workers on the periphery, still attached to the land, and who are
not paid: 'Over time, it has steadily become less profitable to use non-wage modes of
remuneration. But they still continue to be used in part.' Wallerstein (1979: 149, original emphasis) is correct to note that 'it is the *combination* of free and "unfree" labor
and land that characterizes the capitalist world-economy', but misses two crucial facts.
First, that such a combination does not correspond to a dichotomy whereby core =
free/periphery = unfree: the free/unfree combination can operate not only within the
capitalist core but also on the periphery. And second, because unfreedom is confined
to the periphery, epistemologically it is associated largely with tying labour to land:
again, the fact that unfree relations are found also in the core economies means that
unfree relations can just as easily apply to workers who are landless.
[126] Hence the following view (*Wolf*, 1982: 316): 'Yet the shift from slave labor to
other forms of labor control within the British orbit must be understood not only in
terms of internal British development but also in terms of the changing international
system of which Britain formed a part. Under the rising hegemony of industrial capitalism, there was a growing preference for the use of free labor over slavery. It must
be noted, however, that slavery continued in the United States, and it even intensified
in Brazil and Cuba in the course of the nineteenth century... The end of slave trading
and slave labor in one part of the world led to its continuation and even intensification
in another part. One of the areas that continued to use slave labor was the American
Cotton South, now the major producer of the strategic raw material for the expanding
capitalism in Britain. The rise of industrial capitalism thus rested on the maintenance
of slavery in another part of the world, even though that slavery was no longer dependent on the continuation of the slave trade.'
[127] See Miles (1987).

Dispossession by (Primitive) Accumulation

The same is true of a recent and influential analysis by Harvey of what he terms the 'new' imperialism.[128] Although he mentions all the forms of and processes involved in what he terms 'dispossession by accumulation', Harvey has next to nothing to say about how and why this affects the relations whereby labour-power is reproduced. Whilst correct to note that '[a]ll features of primitive accumulation that Marx mentions have remained powerfully present within [capitalism] up until now', Harvey nevertheless equates coercion with proletarianization.[129] For him, therefore, the continued presence of debt peonage amounts to 'a trace of precapitalist social relations in working class formation', and the labour regime of the 'new' imperialism is a 'new' proletariat'.[130]

There is an irony here, in that Harvey fails to spot the space unfreedom might occupy in his theoretical framework. Why should unfree relations of production not be seen also as a case of 'dispossession by accumulation' (to use the term preferred by Harvey) where owners of labour-power are concerned? That is, literally 'dispossessing' workers ultimately of a capacity personally to commodify or recommodify their only commodity. This, surely, is a logical final step in the class struggle waged by capital, one that would ensure that workers are deprived of the sole remaining weapon in their conflict with owners of the means of production: making or not making available their labour-power, according to the conditions stipulated by the market.

Much current development theory that uses the concept 'primitive accumulation', therefore, tends to categorize the continuing

---

[128] See Harvey (2003) which, although of interest, does not in theoretical terms go beyond earlier analyses of the capitalist system, not just by Bukharin (c. 1930) and Luxemburg (1951) during the first half of the twentieth century, but also by Amin (1974), Gunder Frank (1977, 1978), Wallerstein (1974, 1979), Fröbel, Heinrichs and Kreye (1980), Wolf (1982) and Mintz (1985) in the second half. What was then classified simply as imperialism that would necessarily extend the reach of a hitherto regional (Europe, North America) capitalism throughout the world is now doubly recategorized: as a process of 'globalization' that is 'new'.

[129] See Harvey (2003: 145–6), where he maintains that the 'process of proletarianization...entails a mix of coercions and of appropriations of precapitalist skills...on the part of those being proletarianized. Kinship structures, familial and household arrangements, gender and authority relations (including those exercised through religion and its institutions) all have their part to play.' The latter, he fails to note, are deployed in order to enforce production relations that are unfree, not free.

[130] See Harvey (2003: 147, 164).

employment of unfree workers as an instance of this process. Unfree labour is perceived as acceptable to, but not actually reproduced by, capitalism proper. This differs from the semi-feudal thesis in terms of emphasis only: advanced capitalism is not regarded as being in a fundamental sense incompatible with bonded labour, but accumulation does not actively seek out and reproduce a workforce that is unfree.

Within a capitalism that is 'fully functioning', therefore, it would correspond to a situation whereby most or all the advantages that have accrued to workers as a result of class struggle waged by them have been stripped away, including the all-important ability to sell their own labour-power to employers. Having become a proletariat (a class-in-itself), and acted consciously as such (a class-for-itself) even in the midst of a well-established accumulation process to wrest better pay and conditions from capital.

Unfree Labour as Primitive Accumulation?

For a number of reasons, there are obvious difficulties with all these views. Where primitive accumulation is concerned, the theoretical problem lies in a frequent conflation of two distinct situations: between primitive accumulation as *creating the conditions* for capitalist accumulation proper, and its *actually being a form* of capital accumulation.[131] In earlier Marxist theory, primitive accumulation corresponded

---

[131] Rightly eschewing the tendency of apologists for capitalism to separate 'domestic industry' from 'factory work', Hobsbawm (1964: 105ff.) nevertheless associates outwork—a characteristic of primitive accumulation—with what he calls 'capitalist industrialization in its early phases'. Hence the following observation (Hobsbawm, 1964: 116, original emphasis): 'The almost universal argument of the optimists is that cottage-workers and outworkers before the industrial revolution were exploited as harshly as the factory proletariat, while their pay and material conditions were worse. But this is an artificial contrast. The early industrial period was not one which *replaced* domestic workers by factory workers, except in a very few trades...on the contrary: it multiplied them. That it later starved them to death, like the handloom weavers, or drove them elsewhere, is another matter, in itself relevant to the problem of social conditions under early capitalism; but the point is, that the handloom weavers and other who were starved out were not simply "survivals from the middle ages", but a class multiplied, and largely created *as part of capitalist industrialization in its early phases* just as factory workers were. The armies of seamstresses sewing cotton shirts in the garrets for 2s.6d. or 3s. 6d. a week belong to the history of the rise of the cotton industry just as much as the mule-spinners in the mills, or for that matter the Negro slaves who increased by leaps and bounds in the Southern States of America in response to the insatiable demand of Lancashire for raw cotton. It is as unrealistic to leave the non-factory workers of the early industrial period out of the picture, as

to the pre-history of capitalism. As used by many analyses of current development, by contrast, primitive accumulation is simply a form of 'savage capitalism' located within and emblematic of a neoliberal accumulation project.[132]

Because they reify the wage, however, many who regard themselves as Marxist confuse the fact of payment made to a worker (= wage labour) with labour-power that is free.[133] The two aspects are, of course, distinct: one has to do with the kind of production relation linking a worker to his/her employer, while the other concerns the form taken by the remuneration for labour expended. The epistemological problem generated by conflating payment of a wage with labour-power that is free is obvious. Throughout history many different kinds of worker who were relationally unfree nevertheless received payment whilst in the employ of another. That they were paid did not of itself signal the presence of labour-power that was free, as many examples of payments made to workers who were also chattel slaves, indentured labourers, debt peons and attached or bonded, all attest.

As important is the fact that, if unfree labour is a characteristic not simply of 'the dawn of capitalism'—and is thus confined to primitive accumulation—but of capitalism *per se*, then this epistemology in effect concedes the point about the acceptability to capitalist enterprises of work arrangements that are not free. It thereby deprivileges the cliché that a 'fully functioning' accumulation process ultimately depends on the generalized presence of labour-power that is free. If it is the case that primitive accumulation was long ago accomplished in Europe, as Marx himself insisted, how then is it possible to categorize

---

it would be to confine the discussion of the social effects of the introduction of the typewriter to the wages and grading of workers in the mass-production engineering factories which make them, and leave out the typists.' His opinion, therefore, is that outwork must be considered as part of capitalism, but only in its initial stage. In mitigation of the latter qualification—which is clearly incorrect—it should be noted that Hobsbawm wrote this in 1958, before the outsourcing/downsizing of production that became a common aspect of 'fully functioning' capitalist development from the 1980s onwards.

[132] Yet others have used the term 'savage capitalism' to describe the violent struggle not between capital and labour but rather between rival commercial enterprises. Thus Andrade (1982: 179) uses the term to describe the way the Brazilian state became 'aloof' from competition among large capitalist enterprises for government favour during the era of the Brazilian 'miracle' (1968–73).

[133] See, for example, Banaji (2003), whose interpretation has been criticized by me (*Brass*, 2003; 2005).

the employment currently by gangmasters of unfree migrant workers in UK agriculture as an instance of primitive accumulation?[134]

Similarly, how can primitive accumulation come long after capitalist development established itself in specific national contexts outside Europe, such as Russia and China, to the degree that accumulation was said by Marxists there to be ripe for the socialism which supplanted it?[135] The fault lies not with Marx, who was clear about the fact that in every social formation primitive accumulation occurred at 'the dawn of capitalism', but with those who now apply this same concept in an a-historical manner, to contexts where capitalism is already established or has developed at an earlier conjuncture.

What Marx and other Marxists attributed to the process of primitive accumulation was a twofold transformation: separating the direct producer from the means of production—land—so as to make his/her labour power available to capitalists engaged in accumulation. Although the kind of production relation that would result after the direct producer had been dispossessed of his/her means of production and then offered his/her labour-power for sale to capital, was of interest, the central issue was dispossession (or 'de-peasantization').[136] Making workers available for the accumulation process was, in short, the main consideration, and in this Marx and other Marxists were right.

The assumption was, and remains still, that any subsequent working arrangement would be free in the double sense understood by Marx: a

---

[134] On the role of gangmasters in UK agriculture, plus the unfree nature of the labour régime involving the recruitment and control by them of migrant workers, see House of Commons Environment, Food and Rural Affairs Committee (2003) and Brass (2004).

[135] That capitalism was already present in the Russian countryside towards the end of the nineteenth century was a central point made by Lenin (1964a) in his debate with populists, who maintained by contrast that villages were characterized not by capitalism but by peasant economy. As well as Latin America, post-socialist Russia and China are the two instances of neoliberal primitive accumulation cited by Byres (2005: 88–89). There is a delightful irony in Byres' advocacy of primitive accumulation in the present-day rural Russia, since to do this he has in effect to align himself not with Lenin (for whom rural capitalism was present) but rather with the view of the countryside a century ago held by the populists (who maintained capitalism was absent). Hitherto, Byres has always insisted that populists were wrong and Lenin was right; it will be necessary for Byres to reverse this interpretation if he wishes to sustain his claim about primitive accumulation in Russia.

[136] Since dispossession coincided with a transition from a feudal to a capitalist mode of production, the epistemological centrality of separation of the direct producer from the land s/he cultivated is in an important sense unsurprising.

worker would be free both of the means of labour and of the control exercised by a particular employer. As such, dispossessed peasants were transformed into—and remained thereafter—a proletariat, in that they were henceforth able personally to sell their only commodity, labour-power. Marx was right, therefore, to identify as the object of dispossession—an object realized at the very moment of dispossession—the provision of the commodity labour-power to capital.[137] Again as is well known, this transformation corresponded to a process of class formation, whereby buyers and sellers of a particular commodity—labour power—faced one another in the market place.

Class Formation and/as Class Struggle

At that particular moment, however, and following the initial process of class *formation*, the transaction between capital and labour gave

---

[137] The importance of the moment dispossession on those providing capital with their labour-power, and its impact on all that follows, can be illustrated with reference to 1990s Russia. As is well known, the end of the Soviet Union was characterized by three developments: the replacement of the centrally-planned economy by the market; the privatization of state-owned resources; and the distribution of shares to employees in state-owned companies. Less well known are the events leading to and licensing the subsequent consolidation of share ownership. Levy and Scott-Clark (2004: 14–26) set out to answer two interconnected questions: '(H)ow did (an oligarch) make so much money in such a short amount of time? How did one man come to control a reported £5.3bn stake in Sibneft, a state energy provider that only 10 years ago was bequeathed to Russia's citizens, predominantly the tens of thousands of Soviet oil workers and managers who built the industry?' Their conclusion is significant, revealing that—in a manner reminiscent of the truck system, where consumption is restricted to stores owned/operated by the employer—workers to whom the Russian government had issued shares in the oil company were compelled to part with them cheaply to the new owners, not least because the latter withheld their wages. Following the post-communist adoption of *laissez faire* policies, decontrolled prices led to mass impoverishment throughout Russia. This was compounded when oil companies stopped paying workers for months at a time ('our wages were held back', as one oil worker described it). However, oil companies then announced that they would purchase the shares that had been distributed to the workers. Company shops sprung up to facilitate this transaction, providing consumer items in exchange not for cash but for shares. Having no wages, oil workers were compelled to exchange the shares they had received, shares which enabled Russian oligarchs to exercise control over hugely valuable resources. This method of gaining control in order to extract surplus or appropriate resources was used by plantation and estate owners to force their workers into debt. It consists of holding back wages due, thereby compelling them to borrow and go into debt in order to survive. Owners of privatized oil companies did much the same thing to their workers: by holding back wages due the latter, workers were forced to part with their shares in the oilfields (which the owners then offered to 'buy'). The company store facilitated this procedure, offering workers consumer goods on condition they surrendered their shares.

rise to an additional process: class *struggle*.[138] The capacity of workers—once free—not just to combine and organize in furtherance of
their class interests but also to withdraw their labour power, either
absolutely by going on strike, or relatively by selling their commodity to the highest bidder, posed a fundamental challenge to capitalist
discipline and profitability. It is hardly surprising, therefore, to find
limiting or curbing the ability of workers to commodify/recommodify
labour power among the weapons deployed by capital in its struggle
with a proletariat seeking to improve pay and conditions.

Accordingly, it was this need to maintain or enhance profitability in
the face of 'from below' class struggle that, dialectically, triggered an
antithetical 'from above' response by employers interested in disciplin-
ing and cheapening the cost of their labour-power: either converting
free workers into unfree equivalents, or replacing the former with the
latter. Hence the acceptability of unfree labour to capital: it is the process of class struggle subsequent to class formation which results in
proletarianization giving rise to its opposite, deproletarianization.

This capacity on the part of capital currently to employ workers
that are unfree is in turn facilitated by two conditions that are both
currently a feature of neoliberal capitalism. The first is that in many
contexts of the Third World, agricultural production is for export. This
means that one of the usual objections to employing unfree labour—
that driving down the wages of a domestic workforce simultaneously
deprives agrarian capitalists of consumers, thereby negating the economic advantages of using bonded labour—no longer holds. And second, a consequence of seemingly limitless global migration patterns is
that rural producers in many contexts—metropolitan capitalist nations
no less that developing countries—now possess an ability to drawn
upon a large industrial reserve army of labour.

Since each of these conditions was either unmet or unrecognized at
an earlier conjuncture, however, some Marxists questioned whether it
was possible for capital to continue employing a workforce that was

---

[138] Among the Marxists who recognized that unfree labour could be an outcome of
class struggle was Ernest Mandel. Having noted that in an advanced capitalist nation
the object of unfreedom was 'to bring about a recovery in the rate of profit at the
expense of the working class, which is deprived of its political and trade-union means
of defence', he (Mandel, 1968: 537) then observed: 'In the extreme form which (the
capitalist labour regime) assumed, above all in Germany, during the Second World
war, fascism goes beyond the militarization of labour, to the abolition of free labour in
the strict sense of the word, to a return to slave labour on an ever larger scale.'

unfree.[139] For this reason, they persisted in regarding unfree labour simply as 'other', a relational anomaly somehow located within—but not actually part of, let alone actively reproduced by employers in—the wider capitalist system.[140] What they missed thereby was the way in which unfree labour currently fits into an employment matrix forming an optimal combination where agribusiness enterprises are concerned.

Where a worker employed by capital is also a migrant whose labour power is unfree for the duration of the agricultural peak season, therefore, the wage payment remains low when labour costs are high. In such circumstances, a worker who is free would be able to sell his/her labour power to the highest bidder, which a worker who is unfree cannot do. Such a combination (waged migrant who is unfree) is doubly advantageous: it permits an employer not only to pay less for labour power than s/he would otherwise have to, but also to avoid the kind of costs associated historically with maintaining a permanent workforce—composed of chattel slaves or attached labour—during the off-peak season. In short, capital gets the best of all worlds: a workforce that has neither the cost disadvantages of being employed on a permanent basis, nor the organizational advantages of being a modern proletariat.

Conclusion

Labour-power is neither always and everywhere free, nor is it always and everywhere unfree. What has to be understood is that historically there is a dynamic interaction between labour-power that is free and forms which are unfree, a dialectic informed by class struggle. Hence the latter process cannot but structure the prevalence in the trend of each form, the kind of social relation dominant at a given conjuncture

---

[139] A case in point was Ernest Mandel, who confessed that he was uncomfortable with the view that unfree labour was acceptable to capital because this enabled employers in effect to do away with the idea of a subsistence minimum. 'The "payment" of labour is lowered so as not merely no longer to ensure survival in good health,' he observed (Mandel, 1968: 537, note), 'but even to imply certain death within a brief period of time.' Whilst it may have been inconceivable at that time, even to a Marxist of Mandel's intellectual calibre, the global expansion of the industrial reserve army of labour licensing a rapid use-up of the workforce are processes that no longer surprise.

[140] Among them Corrigan (1977), Miles (1987) and Cohen (1987).

being determined by the respective power—economic, political and ideological—exercised by those who either own or are separated from the means of production.

In non-Marxist political economy which eschews class struggle—that of Adam Smith, John Stuart Mill, John Bright and Max Weber—the idea that unfree labour might be acceptable to capitalists was dismissed on the grounds that such workers would necessarily be inefficient, unskilled, costly, and scarce. Because it was an obstacle both to market formation and expansion, and to the installation of advanced productive forces, these non-Marxists argued, unfree labour-power was incompatible with a dynamic process of accumulation within particular national contexts. This interpretation currently informs the theoretical approach not just of neo-classical political economy but also the semi-feudal thesis, notwithstanding the fact that in the present global capitalist system none of these objections continue to hold.

Those who insist that free labour is the *sine qua non* of a 'fully functioning' capitalism, and invoke Marx in support of this position, are confounded by the fact that Marx's views about the historical centrality of class struggle to the shaping of the accumulation process lead to the opposite conclusion. Labour-power is unfree not because capitalism is at its beginning—that is to say, where accumulation is in its early or 'primitive' stage—but much rather because it is mature. Where accumulation has a global reach, as it does currently, it could be argued capital now has the confidence and the power to dispense with the compromise with labour it has had to make in the past. Put bluntly, because they can draw upon what is now a global industrial reserve army of labour, employers no longer have to accommodate the wishes and interests of their workers.

Claims about the acceptability to capitalist producers of bonded labour—an unfree production relation that is prevalent in the agrarian sector of many countries, not just those in the so-called Third World—are grounded in Marxist theory, an insistence to the contrary notwithstanding. This concerns in particular Marxist views about the interrelationship between the separation of the direct producer from his/her means of labour, the reproduction of the industrial reserve army, the process of workforce restructuring, and—most importantly—the conflict between labour and capital. Only in the undialectical framework used both by neoclassical economists and by adherents of the semi-feudal thesis (a species of Whig historiography) is there a failure to recognize such a dynamic.

As has been noted on many previous occasions, adherents of the semi-feudal thesis share with neoclassical economists a touching faith in the emergence and continued reproduction of a benign (= 'kind', 'caring') form of capitalism, one that will voluntarily do away with oppressive and exploitative relations such as unfree labour. Only then will there be a 'fully functioning' accumulation process, under the benevolent eye of selfless capitalists who are gentle, sweet and good. Not only was this never going to happen, but the developments in the world economy from the 1980s onwards, when capitalism went global and competition and class struggle became correspondingly more acute and international in scope, have effectively rebutted this conservative—not to say naïve—interpretation.

Many of those on the left, who subscribed to a unilinear epistemology, thought that—once implemented—a socialist programme was irreversible. Because it ignores the fact and the impact of class struggle, however, such a view is mistaken, in that it counts without the capacity of those whose property has been expropriated to continue to campaign for its return (= class struggle 'from above'). Hence the current attempts on the part of families whose holdings were confiscated by revolutionary governments (for example, Russia in 1917) to secure either a return of the same, or compensation payments from the state following the end of actually existing socialism in 1989.

For this reason, class struggle waged 'from above' does not end with expropriation; it merely continues in a different form (legal agitation for restitution or compensation). Unless an equivalent form of class struggle is also waged 'from below', ceaselessly defending gains made—however modest, and however limited in scope—in the course of implementing a socialist programme, the latter will therefore be overturned in what is an unending process of socio-economic conflict. This applies as much to property rights exercised by workers over their sole commodity, labour-power, as it does to property rights enjoyed by owners of means of production (land and other resources).

Analysing a twenty-first century capitalism though the lens of class struggle therefore undermines the hitherto prevalent approach to ways of conceptualizing the labour régime. Today unfree workers are more profitable to employ but no less efficient than their counterparts who are free. Moreover, deskilling combined with a reserve army that is global in scope makes it possible for capitalist producers to use many different kinds of worker, many of whom are unfree (convicts, debt peons, bonded labourers). Instead of the emancipational linearity which structures the semi-feudal thesis, whereby capitalist producers automatically replace unfree labour with free equivalents, the concept of deproletarianization includes the possibility of historical reversals, understood not in a chronological but rather in an emancipatory sense.

Because it is informed by the dynamic of class struggle, deproletarianization accepts that such a process (conflict) is waged 'from above' as well as 'from below'. Consequently, just as unfree relations can be—and have been—eliminated by 'from below' class agency, so they can be—and on occasion are—reinstated or introduced by 'from above' class agency. This is the dynamic that is missing from those who interpret history as an unproblematic and irreversible progression from unfree labour that is unpaid and employed on a permanent basis to free labour in receipt of a wage and hired on a daily, seasonal or casual basis.

Unlike the semi-feudal thesis and neoclassical economics, most Marxist theory accepts that gains made in the course of class struggle can just as easily be reversed, the 'from below' relational emancipation (plus the advantages this confers) unravelling as a consequence of class struggle waged 'from above'. This is especially true of the way global capitalist regimes have been transformed over the past quarter of a century, a period dominated by *laissez faire* development policies. In such circumstances, economic and ideological benefits secured by workers and poor peasants in the course of conflict with employers and the capitalist state can be—and have been—watered down or cancelled by the reintroduction of unfreedom.

In short, proletarianization can be—and on occasion has been—displaced by its 'other', deproletarianization. An inability to recognize this, however, has led to frequent claims about the requirement or non-completion of a capitalist transition in Indian agriculture, which have as a result tended to conflate systemic change (which has been effected) with relational transformation (which is not always necessary). There is—or ought to be—no mystery about this apparent contradiction (the employment of unfree workers in the accumulation process), not least given current opposition by capital everywhere to a reduction in labour market 'flexibility', to improving legislative protection, pay and conditions.

All the latter are characterized by employers as unwarranted attempts to 'undermine competitiveness'. Capital is able to sustain this opposition to improvements in the pay/conditions of its workforce by drawing on a seemingly inexhaustible supply of labour-power. Following the Green Revolution, and particularly in the era of neoliberal policies, the industrial reserve army of labour has expanded to the degree that that imposing (or re-imposing) unfreedom is an economic option now available to and used by commercial producers.

The resulting decomposition/recomposition of the labour process is a relational (not systemic) change that involves either the replacement of free labour by unfree equivalents, or the conversion of the former into the latter. This kind of agrarian transformation is a form of capitalist restructuring that corresponds to deproletarianization, a concept which refers not just to permanent and/or local debt bondage relations but also to ones that extend to include migrant, seasonal and casual workers. In the course of restructuring the labour process, therefore, capitalist producers have not only replaced permanent labour with temporary workers but also shifted the element of unfreedom, from long-term employment to casual/migrant jobs.

CHAPTER FIVE

FAREWELL TO IMPERIALISM?
A CRITICAL SOCIOLOGICAL STUDY OF EMPIRE

*Ashok Kumbamu**

Michael Hardt and Antonio Negri's *Empire* has generated a vibrant discussion in left-wing circles as well as the corporate media about the nature and dynamics of the neoliberal global order. The book has been acclaimed and promoted as a revised and updated version of the *Communist Manifesto* in the 'internet age' of postmodern globalization (Žižek, 2001).[1] The major, and much disputed claim made by Hardt and Negri is that the concept of 'imperialism' in a classical Marxist or Leninist sense has no relevance for understanding the contemporary capitalist world system. Imperialism is dead because a centered and territorialized and state-based national sovereignty has been replaced with a decentered and deterritorialized form of sovereignty with "a new logic and structure of rule". The geopolitical division of an 'inside' (the capitalist world) and 'outside' (the non-capitalist world) is destroyed because "at a certain point the boundaries created by imperialist practices obstruct capitalist development and the full realization of its world market" (Hardt and Negri, 2000: 234). They name the new global sovereign power 'Empire', which has "no territorial centre of power and does not rely on fixed boundaries or barriers" (Hardt and Negri, 2000: xii).

According to Hardt and Negri, the new Empire is different from historical empires in its conception, structure and *modus operandi*. The unique characteristics of the new Empire are:

---

* I would like to thank Henry Veltmeyer, Gordon Laxer, Michael Gismondi and Sourayan Mookerjea for their helpful comments and suggestions. I am also grateful to Satoshi Ikeda for several fruitful discussions about these and related issues.
[1] For a discussion on whether Hardt and Negri's *Empire* bears any resemblance to the *Communist Manifesto*, see Turchetto (2003: 23–24); Fotopoulos and Gezerlis (2002).

1. Empire has *no territorial boundaries* to exercise its power and to expand its sphere of influence, because its power 'is both everywhere and nowhere' (Hardt and Negri, 2000: 190).
2. Empire has *no temporal boundaries* because it is not a historical regime, or a particular stage, in an historical imperial project that born out of conflicts and conquests. Rather, it is an eternal 'state of affairs' that rejects the teleological views of historical stages in sociopolitical transitions (such as Lenin's conceptualization of imperialism as the highest stage of capitalism) (Hardt and Negri, 2000: xiv).
3. Empire embodies *'biopower'*—"a form of power that regulates social life from its interior, following it, interpreting it, absorbing it, and rearticulating it" (Hardt and Negri, 2000: 24). The primary task of biopower is to produce, reproduce, and administer all aspects of life itself.
4. Empire wages *'just wars'* using both military as well as ethical instruments in order to build the new imperial (rather than imperialist) global order, and maintain it as the 'permanent, eternal, and necessary' system across universal space and time (Hardt and Negri, 2000: 10–11).

The concept of 'just wars' is traditional to an ancient imperial order, based on the premise that: "[w]hen a state finds itself confronted with a threat of aggression that can endanger its territorial integrity or political independence, it has a *jus ad bellum* [right to make war]" (Hardt and Negri, 2000: 12). Since Empire has no specific territory or place it wages a new form of 'just wars' at various fronts across space and time not only with lethal force but also ethical and judicial instruments in the form of the operations of international institutions such as corporate media, religious organizations, non-governmental organizations, international financial institutions etc. The moral and legal intervention of 'just wars' constitutes a 'new tradition of Empire' and it 'often serves as the first act that prepares the stage for military intervention' (Hardt and Negri, 2000: 37), as well, Empire tries to build consensuses cross the globe in order to legitimize military aggressions in the name of 'humanitarian intervention', 'peacebuilding', 'conflict resolution', 'democratization' and 'liberation'.

For Hardt and Negri, the communication and information technology revolution, and the globalized network of production, circulation and consumption have created a "smooth world—a world defined by new and complex regimes of differentiation and homogenization, deterritorialization and reterritorialization" (Hardt and Negri, 2000: xiii). In such a new world, "it is no longer possible to demarcate large geographical zones as center and periphery, North and South" (Hardt and Negri, 2000: 335). For example, they argue that today the global North and South "clearly infuse one another, distributing inequalities and barriers along multiple and fractured lines...between them are no differences of nature, only differences of degree" (Hardt and Negri, 2000: 335).

While criticizing aspects of Empire, Hardt and Negri (2000: 43) welcome its appearance, seeing it as a better system than the old imperialism "in the same way that Marx insists that capitalism is better than the form of society and modes of production that came before". About a century ago, German social democrat Heinrich Cunow made a similar assertion in his debate with Karl Kautsky: "Imperialism is present-day capitalism; the development of capitalism is inevitable and progressive; therefore imperialism is progressive; we should grovel before it and glorify it!" (Lenin, 1965: 111). But in Lenin's view such an understanding of imperialism was absurd—a reactionary utopia.

In their review of such classical theories of imperialism, Hardt and Negri conduct a cursory review of the Lenin-Kautsky debate about imperialism in the early twentieth century, but they elude many issues raised in this debate, in order to advance their post-imperialist thesis. In this paper, I argue that their position is neo-Kautskian, and that their discussion of theories of imperialism mainly centres on Rosa Luxemburg's theory of underconsumption. Most reviewers of *Empire* have made little or no reference to the Lenin-Kautsky debate. For example, Petras and Veltmeyer (2003, 2005) prefer to focus on the book's deficiencies in grasping the current dynamics of capitalist development and imperialism, and the lack of any empirical data and analysis. Notwithstanding their hard hitting and effective critique of Hardt and Negri's thesis (that it is constructed on the basis of deductions from philosophical premises rather than empirical analysis of the real world), I propose in this paper to return to the Lenin-Kautsky debate in a deconstructive critique of Hardt and Negri's post-imperialist thesis in *Empire*, to assess the validity and relevance of their arguments.

136

Farewell to Imperialism and Welcome to Empire

Although Hardt and Negri depart from a 'traditional' Marxist political line, they followed Rosa Luxemburg's theory of realization of capital in their conceptualization of Empire. Luxemburg, in her major theoretical work, *The Accumulation of Capital*, offered a complementary explanation to Karl Marx's scheme of reproduction and accumulation of capital. Marx divides total social production into two major departments: Department I, comprising the production of means of production, or the production of 'machine goods'; Department II, comprising the production of means of consumption, or the production of both 'wage goods'/the 'necessary means of consumption' and 'luxury goods/luxury means of consumption'. Marx assumed that, in simple reproduction, all of the surplus value created in Department I is consumed by capitalists and workers in Department II without any scope for accumulation. Whereas in expanded reproduction, which is always intended for the accumulation of capital, capitalists have to invest a portion of surplus value to purchase variable and constant capital in order to enhance the scale of production and the rate of profits.

But the change in the forces of production (i.e. technology) increases labour productivity and overall production on the one hand, and decreases real wages as well as the rate of absorption of wage labourers into workforce on the other. This undermines the purchasing power of wage labourer as a consumer, and consequently generates a disproportion between production (supply) and consumption (demand) (Marx, 1992).

Generally, capitalists unproductively consume a portion of supply, but not to the extent of filling the gap because their consuming power is "restricted by the tendency to accumulate, the greed for an expansion of capital and a production of surplus value on an enlarged scale" (Luxemburg, 1963: 344). Consequently, underconsumption diminishes the rate and mass of profits, and thereby, the rate of future accumulation of capital. Thus, a decrease in the capitalization of surplus value and accumulation of capital gradually creates a crisis in the capitalist system. Capitalists can manage this crisis by raising the rate of relative surplus value; by increasing labour productivity or the rate of absolute surplus value (increasing the hours of work); or by the deployment of labour from non-capitalist sectors (Desai, 2000: 552).

As Luxemburg understands it, Marx believed that "there was no need for a continual extension of the market beyond the consumption of capitalists and workers" (Luxemburg, 1963: 346). Luxemburg questions this assumption, arguing that when the forces of production are revolutionized, production increases and results in an overaccumulation of commodities. This eventually leads to a crisis of underconsumption because the capitalist system cannot distribute or absorb the total surplus value. For Luxemburg, the only way the capitalist system can resolve the contradiction between the 'capacity to produce' and the 'capacity to consume', (between the forces of production and the relations of production) is by constantly expanding into the non-capitalist world to acquire additional means of production and to search for the new markets, and by establishing the 'exclusive world rule of capitalist production' (Luxemburg, 1972: 145).

Luxemburg also warns that when the capitalist system brings all corners of the globe under its 'sphere of influence' leaving no place untouched, and exploiting them at an ever faster rate, capitalism ceases to develop further (Luxemburg, 1972: 145–6). Therefore, the capitalist system eventually collapses either by the erosion of new avenues to occupy for further expansion of the market, or by the assault from the non-capitalist world. Luxemburg anticipates that when the capitalist system reaches the collapsing point, the working classes in the capitalist world "will join with their respective capitalist classes to beat back the revolt of the 'third' world" (Tarbuck, 1972: 32). But, this argument is often interpreted as 'political fatalism' and "as displaying a boundless faith in the spontaneity of the masses" of first world workers to be reactionary (Geras, 2000: 328).

Although Hardt and Negri acknowledge the limitations of the underconsumption thesis, they reiterate it in their book without critical comment. But unlike Luxemburg they believe that the contradictions of imperialism are resolved 'peacefully' when the non-capitalist world is completely encroached by the capitalist world, a situation in which there are no new frontiers to occupy and exploit. Incorporating the 'outside' into the 'inside', Hardt and Negri (2000: 189) declare that the contemporary capitalist world system has reached a stage where "the history of imperialist, inter-imperialist, and anti-imperialist wars is over…enter[ing] the era of minor and internal conflicts" (Hardt and Negri, 2000: 189). This characterization of the world system in terms of an idea rather than any empirical analysis (as Petras and Veltmeyer critique), resonates with Karl Kautsky's notion of 'peaceful' ultra-imperialism rather than Lenin's more useful concept of 'inter-imperialist rivalry'. For a limited but yet useful application of the later concept in an analysis of the contemporary of US-led imperialism see Petras and Veltmeyer (2005: 127–160). At issue here—but not in Hardt and Negri's abstracted philosophical discourse on 'Empire'—is Lenin's assumption that inter-imperialist rivalry will inevitably lead to an inter-imperialist war or, as Petras argues, as anti-imperialist war.

For Lenin, imperialism was an extension of capitalism in its historical trajectory, indeed, the highest stage of capitalism, where a few monopoly capitalists dominate the entire world economy. As theorized and elaborated by Paul Sweezy and Harry Magdoff among others at the *Monthly Review*, monopoly capital grows out of, and comes to dominate, the 'free competition' among capitalists, "the fundamental characteristic of capitalism and of commodity production generally" (Lenin, 1965: 105). Lenin adds that imperialists also compete and divide the globe for the export of financial capital (as opposed to the export of commodities, as per Luxemburg) in order to realize super profits. In the process of dividing up and dominating the world, the imperialist states (to serve the best interests of their respective national bourgeoisie) finally enter into an inter-imperialist war (Lenin, 1965: 106).

Against Lenin, Karl Kautsky argued that the monopolization of capital obliterates free market competition promoting the formation of cartels among the strongest monopolies. This eventually diminishes a militarized inter-imperialist rivalry facilitating a 'holy alliance of the imperialists' (Kautsky, 1983: 88–9). Kautsky terms this imperialist policy as 'ultra-imperialism', a situation in which capitalists cooperate rather than compete with each other, and divide the world 'peacefully' among themselves for mutual gains, even though the share of the gains is uneven. This is the reason why 'every far-sighted capitalist', as Kautsky put it, 'must call to his comrades: Capitalists of the world, unite!' (Kautsky, 1983: 86).

From a neo-Kautskian perspective, Hardt and Negri (2000: 233) misinterpret Lenin to argue that "he emphasized the fact…that competition, essential for the functioning and expansion of capital, declines necessarily in the imperialist phase in the proportion to the growth of monopolies". Therefore, in the phase of monopoly capitalism free competition totally disappears and 'peaceful' cooperation among the capitalists begins. To the contrary Lenin asserts: "The monopolies, which have grown out of free competition, do not eliminate the later, but exist over it and alongside of it, and thereby give rise to a number of very acute, intense antagonisms, frictions and conflicts" (Lenin, 1965: 105).

For Lenin (1965: 113), as for Petras and Veltmeyer in their critique of Hardt and Negri, Kautsky's characterization of ultra-imperialism was 'utterly meaningless' and a 'lifeless abstraction' because Kautsky failed to understand the 'concrete reality' of world economy—the sharpening inter-imperialist contradictions. Questioning the possibilities of peaceful alliances among capitalist in conditions prevailing at the time, Lenin argues: "Peaceful alliances prepare the ground for wars, and in their turn grow out of wars; the one conditions the other, giving rise to alternative forms of peaceful and non-peaceful struggle out of *one and the same* basis of imperialist connections and relations within world economics and world politics" (Lenin, 1965: 144–5, emphasis original).

Commenting on whether the formation of a 'universal cartel' of capitalists and the development of a 'single world trust' would lead to a new phase of capitalism, i.e. 'ultra-imperialism', Lenin further writes: "In the abstract one can think of such a phase. In practice, however, he who denies the sharp tasks of today in the name of dreams about soft tasks of the future becomes opportunist. Theoretically it means to fail to base oneself on the developments now going on in real life, to detach oneself from them in the name of dreams" (Lenin, 1972: 13–14).

Rudolf Hilferding in his pioneering work *Financial Capital*, and Nikolai Bukharin in his influential book *Imperialism and World Economy*, had expressed similar views regarding the possibility of achieving and sustaining ultra-imperialism. Bukharin asserted that Kautsky's ultra-imperialism was a utopian project, which considers "imperialism not as an inevitable accompaniment of capitalist development but as…one of the *dark sides* of capitalist development… [and] wishes to eliminate *dark* imperialism leaving intact the *sunny* sides of the capitalist order" (Bukharin, 1972: 135, 142–3). In a similar way, "while excoriating its destructive aspects, Hardt and Negri welcome globalization as the dawn of a new era full of promise for the realization of the desires of the wretched of the earth" (Arrighi, 2002: 3).

As it turned out, the outbreak of the First and Second World Wars and the struggles among the imperialist states in the interwar and cold war periods supported Lenin's critique of ultra-imperialism. But in fact, in the post-cold war period, under the leadership of the US, there has been a growing tendency of cooperation, mergers, and collaboration amongst capitalists. This phenomenon provides some reasonable support to Kautsky's ultra-imperialism. However, this does not mean that the inter-imperialist contradictions are totally dissolved. See

Petras and Veltmeyer (2005: 127–160) for some detail and an analysis
on the 'dynamics of inter-imperialist rivalry' in the post-war period.
In this connection it has been argued in the literature that "Kautsky's
world had been achieved by Leninist means" (Bromley, 2003: 30).

According to Perry Anderson, ultra-imperialism was not achieved
until the end of the Cold War because of the absence of potential
"superordinate power capable of imposing discipline on the system as
a whole in the common interest of all parties" (Anderson, 2002: 20–21)
and of coordinating the monopoly capitalists through 'persuasion'[2] to
form a federation. But, since the end of cold war the US has emerged
as a single superpower and the centre of the new world order because
it "has acquired absolute military dominance over every other state
or combination of states on the entire planet, a development without
precedent in world history" (Gowan, 2001: 81). These developments,
as Gowan observes, helped the US attain the position of super-impe-
rialist as opposed to ultra-imperialist.[3]

Leo Panitch and Sam Gindin (2003) contend that unlike the British
state in its empire, the US emerged as an informal empire in the post-
World War II era by incorporating other imperialist states into 'free
trade imperialism' through economic and cultural penetration, and
political and military coordination. However, multiple economic crises
in the 1970s diminished the economic domination of the US (Arrighi,
2005; Sutcliffe, 2006). And since then the American empire has been
"increasingly turning to military force to consolidate its hegemony and
the economic advantage that come with it—for instance with control
of oil" (Wood, 2003: 160) But to the contrary, and somewhat frivo-
lously, Hardt and Negri (2000: 384) assert that: "The idea of American
Empire as the redemption of utopia is completely illusory. First of all,

---

[2] The 'imposition of discipline', as Anderson argues, 'cannot be a product of brutal
force. It must also correspond to a genuine capacity of persuasion—ideally, a form of
leadership that can offer the most advanced model of production and culture of its
day, as target of imitation for all others' (Anderson, 2002: 21).
[3] Both ultra-imperialism and super-imperialism refer to cooperative relations
among the strongest imperialist powers. In the case of ultra-imperialism, "cooperation
results from co-ordination to mutual advantage" (Bromley, 2003: 33, emphasis added).
But this can only be possible by gathering 'collective power'—'the notion of power
implicit in the idea that states have common interests that can be advanced by forms
of cooperation' (Bromley, 2004: 160). In the case of super-imperialism, 'cooperation
is enforced by the super power of one state' (Bromley, 2003: 33, emphasis added). This
is only possible by imposing 'distributive power'—'the capacity of one party to get
another to comply with its goal by imposing costs' (Bromley, 2004: 159).

the coming of Empire is not American and the United States is not its centre. The fundamental principle of Empire...is that its power has no actual and localizable terrain or centre. Imperial power is distributed in networks, through mobile and articulated mechanism of control."

If we have entered a new era of stateless Empire, then, why do a few dominant states actively initiate and spearhead regional trade organizations such as Association of Southeast Asian Nations, European Union (EU), the North American Free Trade Agreement, Free Trade Area of the Americas etc.? Why does the US always try to exclude EU from the South American market, and why does EU protect its economy from the penetration of US transnational capital? Why do the imperial states use the transnational corporations as the vehicles of capital's global reach? Why does the US coordinate its allies and architect the global war on 'terror' and exclude investments in Iraq from countries 'not of the willing'. Answers to these questions require further analysis of whether we have entered an era of post-imperialist Empire or an informal US Empire (i.e. US imperialism without formal colonies).

Empire without Emperor or the Informal US Empire?

Hardt and Negri, throughout their book, rhythmically repeat that in the "smooth space of Empire, there is no *place* of power—it is everywhere and nowhere. Empire is an *ou-topia*, or really a *non-place*" (2000: 190). But James Petras (2002: 139) in his devastating critique of Hardt and Negri's thesis, contends that the "argument for a state-less empire exaggerates the autonomy of capital vis-à-vis the state, and parrots the false proposition of the free market ideologues who argue that the *world market* is supreme and acceptable politically precisely because it operates independently of specific national interests" (See also Petras and Veltmeyer, 2007: 30–31). In a similar way, Ellen Meiksins Wood in *Empire of Capital* argues that globalist views of stateless imperial sovereignty "not only miss something truly essential in today's global order but leave us powerless to resist the empire of capital"[4] (Wood,

---

[4] This critique reminds us Lenin's rejection of Kautsky's theory of ultra-imperialism as reactionary politics: 'The only objective, i.e., real, social significance Kautsky's theory can have, is: a most reactionary method of consoling the masses with hopes of permanent peace being possible under capitalism, by distracting their attention

2003: 6). She further asserts, "the state is more essential than ever to capital, even, or especially, in its global form".

Wood (2003: 10) argues that the capitalist system is uniquely different from other class societies, such as precapitalism or feudalism, in exercising both economic and extraeconomic power (such as institutional, political, military and judicial power). In noncapitalist societies, economic power often depends on 'extraeconomic' coercion. It is therefore very difficult to differentiate two. For example, feudal lords relied more on extraeconomic coercion (i.e. military power) to extract surplus labour rents from tenant-peasants and to exploit bonded and other forms of 'unfree labour' (see Brass in this volume). As Wood (2003: 12) remarks, even "old colonial empires dominated territory and subject people by means of extraeconomic coercion, by military conquest and often direct political rule".

In capitalist imperialism, economic power dominates the working class very impersonally and indirectly through market mechanisms. Also, it creates structural and institutional conditions under which wage labourers 'voluntarily' participate in the capitalist system of production and sell his or her labour power as commodity. Extraeconomic power helps sustain a social order or structural-institutional environment, which in turn facilitates and guarantees the availability of 'disciplined' cheap labour, and provides the legitimacy of exploitation in the process of the endless accumulation of capital (Wood, 2003: 3–10).

In fact, Kautsky had also made a similar analysis of imperialism and argued that politics (the state apparatus) and economics (the market) function separately. But Lenin accused Kautsky of being 'reformist', 'opportunist' and 'renegade' (Lenin, 1965: 110). In the political-economic context of his period, Lenin's criticism was apt because the aim of imperialism at that time was to colonize and plunder the non-capitalist territories of the world, and, in order to achieve this, imperial powers had to use both economic and extraeconomic powers as a united force. Thus, at that historical moment, the separation of economic and political dimensions of imperialism was certainly reformist.

---

from the sharp antagonisms and acute problems of the present times, and directing it towards illusory prospects of an imaginary ultraimperialism of the future' (Lenin, 1965: 143).

A superficial reading of Wood's argument might suggest that she also falls into the trap of providing an economistic explanation of imperialism. But a careful reading would suggest otherwise. Since the new imperialist project does not aim at direct rule and formal colonization, it does not use both economic and extraeconomic force together. For Wood, the separation of these two logics of power is a particular feature of the 'new' imperialism. However, although they appear like two separate entities, in the end they help each other. As Petras and Veltmeyer (2003: 46) put it succinctly: "empire begins with military and/or political conquest but ultimately rests on the economy". The separation and unity of the two 'spheres of influence' should be seen as *tactical detachment* and *strategic unity* respectively, because imperial powers tactically use them separately to meet immediate needs, and strategically employ them as a united force to realize long-term goals. The general assumption is that tactical separation of these powers allows the market forces to operate 'freely' and 'autonomously' without any extraeconomic constraints. But, it is highly questionable because, in reality, it is not possible for economic power to operate independent of 'extraeconomic' power.

Parallel to Wood, social geographer David Harvey explains the new imperialism in terms of two logics of power: The 'capitalist logic of power' and the 'territorial logic of power'. He remarks that the capitalist logic of power "operates in continuous space and time" and supports capitalist actions of exploitation through the market mechanisms; whereas the territorial logic of power "operates in a territorialized and, at least in democracies, in a temporality dictated by an electoral cycle" (Harvey, 2003: 27; Sutcliffe, 2006: 65). But, imperialist countries, in order to maintain their hegemony, must extend and intensify their 'territorial logic of power' beyond borders, and perpetuate the political hierarchy of nation states (Sutcliffe, 2006: 65). Indeed, the two logics of power always function dialectically rather than mechanically.

Imperial states exercise their 'extraeconomic' power in various ways. They effectively use the supranational institutional mechanisms (such as the Bretton Woods institutions, the United Nations, NATO) to consolidate their political and economic power, and develop a comprador bourgeoisie class and install puppet regimes in the 'Third World' to liquidate any kind of resistance to global capital. This political environment enormously helps the full-fledged exercise of economic power across the globe. Therefore the operation of economic and 'extraeconomic' power depends on the strategies and tactics of the imperial states, and the interests of their allies around the world.

Harvey argues that though the primary motive of imperialism remains the same—the endless accumulation of capital and the imposition of global hegemony—it has adopted the new mechanisms to solve its central problem, i.e. the overaccumulation of capital. The imperial states effectively use the new mechanisms (such as privatization, financialization, the management and manipulation of crises, and state redistribution of public resources and services for private benefit) in the creation of the new avenues for the absorption of capital surpluses across space and time. Adapting Marx's concept of the 'primitive accumulation of capital', Harvey terms this process as 'accumulation by dispossession' (Harvey, 2003, 2007).

Moreover, in the age of neoliberal globalization, although capital, technology and commodities can flow across space and time without any barriers; they certainly need political 'stability' and market 'predictability' in the places where they finally reach (Woods, 2003: 17). A conceivable apparatus or institution that could effectively provide such an environment is the nation state. The nation state provides a legal and institutional framework, keeps social order, protects the private property system, manages financial transactions, enters into international agreements and treaties, acts as a financial crisis manager or savior,[5] and so on (Petras 2003: 43–51; Wood, 2003: 17; Harvey, 2003, 2007). As Petras (2002: 142) argues: "The imperial state operates in synergy with its multinational corporations...the multinational corporations want state participation to guarantee that their capital will not be expropriated, subject to 'discriminatory' taxes or restricted in remitting profits. The state is, to put it bluntly, the enforcer of investment guarantees, a crucial element in corporate investment expansion."

Critiquing the 'globalist' thesis of a "world without nation states", Petras and Veltmeyer (2005: 14) metaphorically write: 'So-called globalization grew out of the barrel of a gun—a gun wielded, pointed and fired by the imperial state'. Thus, in today's globalized economy,

---

[5] There are several instances where the imperial state acts as a financial crisis manager, and saves big corporations from bankruptcy. A study of the top 100 corporations of 1993 *Fortune* list by Winfried Ruigrock and Rob Van Tulder reveals that at least 20 of them would not have survived if their governments had not intervened and bailed them out (Borón, 2005: 46).

the nation state is more relevant than ever before to provide all these "daily regularities or the conditions of accumulation that capital needs" (Wood, 2003: 20). In this context, Hardt and Negri's celebration of the disappearance of the nation state begs the following questions: Who participates in and defines the trade agreements of all kinds (multi-lateral, bilateral, and unilateral)? Who regulates markets for effective functioning or who mediates in market operations for higher rate of returns? Who imposes sanctions on certain countries that are labeled as 'rogue states' (such as Iran, North Korea, Cuba, and Venezuela) or the 'enemies' of imperial order? Who crafts and impose international trade rules and regulations? Who supports transnational corporations (TNCs) in conquering overseas markets? Who protects local market by putting barriers in place? In fact, the nation state does all these things. Petras (2002: 141) contends that the "markets do not transcend the state, but operate within state-defined boundaries". He further argues, "the imperial states, far from being superseded by the overseas expansion of capital, have grown and become essential component of the configuration of the world political economy" (Petras, 2003: 47).

Imperial states place their representatives as the heads of the international financial institutions (IFIs) in order to have more space for their political and economic maneuver. As a continuation of an institutional 'tradition' the US government always appoints an American citizen as the president of the World Bank, and the European Union always appoints the managing director of the International Monitory Fund (IMF). And, the headquarters of both the institutions are located in Washington DC, and the US is the only country that has veto power in the World Bank and IMF.

Moreover, dominant countries of the world provide a major portion of funds for the international financial institutions, and gain more decision-making power, because the proportion of funding determines the vote weightage of a country and its representatives on the executive board of directors. For instance, in the World Bank, of the total 185 members, G8 countries possess 45.7 percent of voting power in the bank's strategic agenda: the US 16.4 percent; Japan 7.9 percent; Germany 4.5 percent; UK 4.3 percent; France 4.3 percent; Canada—2.8 percent; Italy 2.8 percent; and Russia 2.8 percent. The Bank, although rhetorically, emphasizes 'democratic participation' in development projects in the 'Third World', but it does not adhere to the same principle when it comes to decision-making at its headquarters. Moreover, the bank imposes its neoliberal hegemony on all borrowing countries

by exerting its enormous political-economic power, and on all coun-
ties across the globe by creating 'epistemic communities' and establishing a network of institutions through rigorous knowledge-production
activities (Goldman, 2005; Moore, 2007).

Similarly, a few developed countries dominate the International
Monetary Fund as well. Out of 185 member countries, the G8 countries possess 47.2 percent of the voting power in the Fund, the Board
of Governors: the US 16.8 percent; Japan 6.0 percent; Germany 5.9
percent; UK 4.3 percent; France 4.3 percent; Canada 2.8 percent; Italy
2.8 percent, and Russia 2.7 percent. In an unequal weighted voting
system, a few dominant countries get more power in effectively making or blocking global strategic decisions based on their political
and economic interests. Hardt and Negri overestimate the power of
supranational institutions and totally underplay its dependency on
the imperial states, and "ignore its political and social subjective conditions" (Petras and Veltmeyer, 2007: 11). Harvey (2003: 32) argues
that "one of the state's key tasks is to try to preserve…the pattern of
asymmetries in exchange over space that works to its own advantage".
The imperial states keep the 'pattern of asymmetries' by imposing its
domination over the supranational institutions (Magdoff, 2003). In
fact, these institutions have become mere instruments in the hand of
the imperial hegemon, the US, and its allies.

A majority of the headquarters of transnational corporations
(TNCs) are located in the imperial triad (the US, the EU and Japan).
From 1970 to 2006, the total number of TNCs rose from 7,000 to
77,000. And, according to the United Nations Conference on Trade
and Development (UNCTAD), 85 of the top 100 TNCs have their
headquarters in the Triad—25 in the US, 53 in European Union, and
seven in Japan. In 2005, the top 100 TNCs accounted for 10 percent of
foreign assets, 17 percent of sales, and 13 percent of employment of all
TNCs worldwide. And, the total annual income of the top 200 TNCs
is as big as the combined income of poorest 80 percent of the world's
population (Borón, 2005: 46). Although TNCs operate all over the
globe, as Borón (2005: 46) notes that "their property and their owners
have a clear national base". Moreover, "their earnings flow from all
over the world to their headquarters", and if trequired, they could easily get operational loans "by their headquarters in the national banks
at interest rates impossible to find in peripheral capitalisms, thanks to
which they can easily displace their competitors".

The US, as the leader of the new imperialist project, since the end of World War II exercised its both economic and extraeconomic power in the age of developmentalism (from 1945 to 1970) as well as in the subsequent era of neoliberal of globalization (Petras and Veltmeyer, 2001). In the era of developmental state, the US played a major role in creating the institutional framework for governing international relations (the Bretton Woods system) with the objective of ensuring that the national development of all countries, especially those in the 'economically backward' areas of the 'post-colonial' 'third world', would take the capitalist path paved by the advanced capitalist countries in the West (McMichael, 2004: 41; Petras and Veltmeyer, 2005: 177–181). However, the US used "humanitarian" development projects to strengthen its hegemonic power, and "to protect client regimes throughout the world that were supportive of US interests" (Harvey, 2003: 53).

In the era of neoliberal globalization, the US has emerged as a sole superpower and has played a paramount role in restructuring the global production, circulation and exchange on the one hand, and in creating a new imperial order by eroding "the sovereignty and self-determination of other countries" on the other (Laxer, 2003: 136).[6] As Petras and Veltmeyer (2005: 19) argue, "neoliberal imperialism always meant selective openness to selective countries over specified time periods in selective product areas". In a similar way political economist Gordon Laxer contends, "capitalists are the true globalizers, not workers or citizens". If capital, especially in its grossly overextended speculative form, is increasingly mobile across borders, labour is not. National borders also have been tightened since the events of 9/11 (Laxer, 2003: 148).

The borders in the global North have been strictly controlled through different surveillance measures to prevent the 'illegal' entry of the so-called terrorists as well as economically displaced people from the global South. For instance, the US has been constructing real physical borders of fencing along the Mexico-US borders as well as the so-called 'Smart Borders' using information technology, communications and biometric identifications such as fingerprints and facial

---

[6] For a detailed history of US political and military interventions across the globe from 1945 to the present, see Blum (2000) and Chomsky (2001).

recognition. Although the transnational mobility of skilled labourers
gives an impression that borders in the age of neoliberal globalization
are more permeable, the nation states strictly control and monitor the
flow of people by various stringent immigration policies. All these new
developments, in fact invalidate Hardt and Negri's claim that the borders of the nation state have been eroded in the age of Empire.

After 9/11, the US constructed and has attempted to construct a
new social order across the globe by an extension of its national security doctrine, a new war doctrine of preemptive war and the unilateral
projection of its ideological, political and military power beyond its
borders. While the sovereignties of many nation states were undermined and destroyed by the imperial imposition of political and
economic sanction as well as the Washington Consensus on correct
macroeconomic policy, the US continues to strongly defend its own
sovereignty and assiduously protect its national interests (Laxer, 2005).
In this connection, the US has refused to ratify any international convention or treaty that did not take into account the national interests
of the US. The US has continuously opposed or withdrawn from any
UN agency or convention the agenda for which it could not control.
The US has refused to participate in the International War Crime
Tribunal, opposed signing the Kyoto Agreement aimed at reducing
carbon emissions and refused to sign the International Convention on
the Rights of the Child.

Conclusion

Three major contradictions of imperialism, first identified by Lenin
(1965), which reinforce asymmetric international relations on a global
scale, are: *(i)* the relation between capital and labour, or between the
ruling class and the working class; *(ii)* the relation between the imperialist monopolies and the imperial states; *(iii)* contradiction between the
oppressor countries and the oppressed people. For Hardt and Negri,
Empire has 'resolved' all these structural contradictions by eroding the
nation state, the inside-outside division, and place-time constraints.
But in reality they remain intact. Thus, the classical theories of imperialism are still relevant for our understanding of the current global
order.

I have argued in support of the argument of Petras and others that
the nation state in the era of the new imperialism is as functional for

capitalist development than ever before—that, as Petras and Veltmeyer (2005, 2007) have argued so persuasively, the soft side of imperialism, the 'velvet glove' over its 'iron fist' of military force (cooperation for international development, policies of neoliberal globalization) have reproduced and even deepened the North-South development gap, and that Hardt and Negri's concept of a stateless Empire is a grand myth serving to obfuscate and draw attention away from the operative dynamics of state power.[7] Although the US empire-building agenda has suffered major tactical setbacks in recent years, "the strategic goals of US foreign policy remains constant: to enhance US hegemony and its domination of the new world order" (Petras and Veltmeyer, 2007: 6). Considering the role and capacity of the US as the hegemon[8] and leader of "the new political order of globalization", I conclude that we live in an era of an informal US Empire in decline rather than the post-imperialist Empire without imperialism conceived of by Hardt and Negri.

---

[7] Imperial state uses various formal as well as informal mechanisms to impose its hegemony and domination over the people across the globe. In my own work (Kumbamu, 2006) I have analysed how the structural-institutional, technological and legal mechanisms of imperialism have been effectively used to dispossess the peasantry in India from their means as well as conditions of production.

[8] By definition a hegemon should possess unique features and refer to a particular state. "The hegemon must possess superior force of arms, a national attribute that cannot be alienated or shared, as the first condition of its sway" (Anderson, 2002: 22).

CAPITALISM IN THE ERA OF NEOLIBERALISM:
A SYSTEM IN CRISIS

CHAPTER SIX

THE CLASS NATURE OF NEOLIBERAL GLOBALIZATION IN THE AGE OF IMPERIALISM

Berch Berberoglu

There has been a proliferation of literature on globalization and the political economy of global capitalism over the course of the past two decades. Few of these works, however, have attempted to link this process to imperialism or the expansive, predatory practices of advanced capitalism operating on a global scale. Fewer still have focused on the exploitative nature of this process and its destructive course of development that necessitates its transformation. And fewer yet have identified the working class as the leading agent of change and transformation of global capitalism as we move forward in the twenty-first century.

My recent book, *Globalization and Change: The Transformation of Global Capitalism*, published in 2005, attempted to fill this gap in globalization studies by highlighting the nature, dynamics, and contradictions of neoliberal globalization as the highest stage of capitalist imperialism, and sought to convey the underlying fault lines of this process worldwide in order to assist those who are struggling to change it (Berberoglu, 2005). It thus attempted to provide an analysis and a road map to trace global capitalism's course of development and to understand the political work that is necessary to bring about its transformation.

Acknowledging James Petras' immense influence on my thinking about neoliberal globalization, class struggle, and revolution in the age of capitalist imperialism, and dedicating this book to him, I wrote in its 'Preface': "I would especially like to thank James Petras for his inspiring work on imperialism, class struggle, and revolution, as well as his keen understanding of the class nature of the globalization process and its contradictions, which he has conveyed in many of his books over the years, especially in such pioneering work as his *Critical Perspectives on Imperialism and Social Class in the Third World*, as well as *Class, State, and Power in the Third World*, and his path-breaking recent work on globalization, with Henry Veltmeyer, *Globalization Unmasked: Imperialism in the Twentieth Century*, published in 2001. For his tireless lifelong dedication to the struggle against imperialism and global capitalism that has spanned a successful academic career for more than three decades, one that is being emulated by a new generation of revolutionary intellectuals who are carrying on the struggle for a just world, this book is dedicated to my mentor, teacher and friend—James Petras" (Berberoglu, 2005: x).

As a revolutionary intellectual true to his principles, James Petras has succeeded in moving the discussion and debate over globalization along class lines, and doing so with a keen understanding of the dynamics and contradictions of capitalism on a world scale and its development into capitalist imperialism through the so-called neoliberal globalization process (Petras, 1998, 2007).

Globalization and Change: The Transformation of Global Capitalism was the third in a series of a multi-year, multi-level project that I launched a few years ago with the publication in 2002 of a book that I edited titled *Labour and Capital in the Age of Globalization*, which presented a series of case studies on the labour process and labour-capital relations at the point of production under advanced, global capitalism (Berberoglu, 2002). Following this, I published in 2003 a second book that I wrote, titled *Globalization of Capital and the Nation-State: Imperialism, Class Struggle, and the State in the Age of Global Capitalism*, to expose the nature and contradictions of neoliberal globalization, tracing the evolution of capitalism and the capitalist state through its various stages leading to the globalization of capital and capitalist imperialism that the transnational corporations and the imperial state came to represent in this latest and highest stage of capitalist development at the end of the twentieth and the beginning of the twenty-first centuries (Berberoglu, 2003).

Culminating as the third book in the series, *Globalization and Change* complemented the previous two volumes by moving from an analysis of capitalism as a system of production to its class essence and political character in the form of the capitalist state, to its global manifestations through imperialist expansion and domination under the rule of the transnationals and the imperial state, and to the class struggles that are the outcome of this process and are the basis of the struggle against capitalist globalization and transformation of the global capitalist system (Berberoglu, 2005).

Neoliberal globalization, which some have argued represents a qualitative change in the development of capitalism, has been effectively shown by Petras and his colleagues, in particular Henry Veltmeyer, as a continuation of the process of transnational capitalist expansion and domination of rival and subordinate states for purposes of plunder based on the exploitation and oppression of the working class and other classes under the dictates of capital and the capitalist state on a global scale (Petras and Veltmeyer, 2001, 2003, 2007). It is within the framework of this understanding of class relations across the world that Petras has made a major and lasting contribution to the analysis of the global political economy, its contradictions, and sources of its eventual transformation.

In this chapter I examine the relationship between globalization and imperialism, the dynamics, contradictions, and crisis of global capitalism, and its political-military arm the imperial state, the developing and maturing class struggle, and the prospects for social change and transformation of global capitalism. I examine these within the context of the globalization of capital in the twentieth century and map out the political implications of this process for the future course of capitalist development on a world scale.

Globalization and Imperialism

Imperialism is the highest stage of capitalism operating on a world scale, and neoliberal globalization is the highest stage of imperialism that has penetrated every corner of the world. Both are an outgrowth of twentieth-century monopoly capitalism—an inevitable consequence, or manifestation, of monopoly capital that now dominates the world capitalist political economy. Thus, the current wave of globalization is an extension of this process that operates at a more advanced and accelerated level.

A central feature of this current phase of transnational capitalism, besides its speed and intensity, is the increased privatization of various spheres of the economy and society. Under the current wave of globalization, this has especially been the case in areas such as communications, information technology, education, and the cultural sphere, where privatization is becoming increasingly prevalent.

The rate at which these changes have been taking place, and the vigour with which transnational capital has been exercising more

power vis-à-vis the state, has led some to declare globalization a quali-
tatively new stage in the development of world capitalism (Ross and
Trachte, 1990; Burbach and Robinson, 1999). However, I would argue,
as does Petras (2008), that these quantitative, surface manifestations
of contemporary capitalism, no matter how pervasive they are, do *not*
change the fundamental nature of capitalism and capitalist relations,
nor the nature of the capitalist/imperialist state and the class contradictions generated by these relations, which are inherent characteristics of the system itself. They cannot change the nature of capitalism
in any qualitative sense to warrant globalization a distinct status that
these critics have come to assign as something fundamentally different than what Marxist political economists have always argued to be
the 'normal' operation and evolution of global capitalism in the age
of imperialism (Szymanski, 1981; Warren, 1980; Beams, 1998; Foster,
2002; Harvey, 2003; Petras, 2008).

Today, in the early twenty-first century, the dominant institution
that has facilitated global capitalist expansion on behalf of the current
centre of world imperialism since the post-World War II period—the
United States—is the *transnational corporation*. As other capitalist rivals from Europe and the Pacific Basin have recently begun to
emerge on the world scene as serious contenders for global economic
power, they too have developed and unleashed their own transnational
corporate and financial institutions to carve out greater profits, accumulate greater wealth, and thereby dominate the global economy. The
transnational corporations and banks, based in the leading centres of
world capitalism, have thus become the chief instruments of global
capitalist expansion and capital accumulation (Petras and Veltmeyer,
2007; Mittelman and Othman, 2002; Waters, 1995; see also Barnet
and Cavenagh, 1994). It is therefore in the export of capital and its
expanded reproduction abroad to accumulate greater wealth for the
capitalist classes of the advanced capitalist countries that one can find
the motive force of imperialism and neoliberal globalization today.

Neoliberal globalization, much as during earlier stages of capitalism, is driven by the logic of *profit* for the private accumulation of
capital based on the exploitation of labour throughout the world. It
is, in essence, the highest and most pervasive phase of transnational
capitalism operating on a world scale. It is the most widespread and
penetrating manifestation of modern capitalist imperialism in the
age of the Internet—a development that signifies not only the most
thorough economic domination of the world by the biggest capitalist

monopolies, but also increasingly direct military intervention by the chief imperialist state to secure the global economic position of its own corporations.

The relationship between the owners of the transnational corporations—the monopoly capitalist class—and the imperialist state and the role and functions of this state, including the use of military force to advance the interests of the monopoly capitalist class, thus reveals the class nature of the imperialist state and the class logic of imperialism and capitalist globalization (Warren, 1980; Szymanski, 1981; Berberoglu, 1987, 2003, 2005). But this logic is more pervasive and is based on a more fundamental class relation between labour and capital that now operates on a global level—that is, a relation based on exploitation. Thus, in the age of neoliberal globalization (i.e. in the epoch of capitalist imperialism), social classes and class struggles are a product of the logic of the global capitalist system based on the exploitation of labour worldwide (Gerstein, 1977; Petras, 1978; Berberoglu, 1987, 1994, 2003, 2009).

Capitalist expansion on a world scale at this stage of the globalization of capital and capitalist production has brought with it the globalization of the production process and the exploitation of wage labour on a world scale. With the intensified exploitation of the working class at super-low wages in repressive neocolonial societies throughout the Third World, the transnational corporations of the leading capitalist states have come to amass great fortunes that they have used to build up a global empire through the powers of the imperial state, which has not hesitated to use its military power to protect and advance the interests of capital in every corner of the globe. It is in this context that we see the coalescence of the interests of the global economy and empire as manifested in control of cheap labour, new markets, and vital sources of raw materials, such as oil, and the intervention of the imperial state to protect these when their continued supply to the imperial centre are threatened (Petras and Veltmeyer, 2001).

Imperialism has been an enormous source of profit and wealth for the capitalist class of the advanced capitalist countries, who, through the mechanisms of the transnational monopolies and the imperial state, have accumulated great fortunes from the exploitation of labour on a world scale. Given the uneven development of capitalism, however, some countries have grown more rapidly than others, while some previously less developed countries have emerged as new contenders in the global economy. The rivalry between the capitalist classes of the old and newly emergent capitalist states has turned into rivalry among the leading countries within the world capitalist system. This has led to intense competition and conflict between the rising capitalist powers and the declining imperial centres on a world scale, hence leading to shifts in centres of global economic and political power.

Focusing on the US experience, it is clear that in the post World War II period the United States emerged as the dominant power in the capitalist world. In subsequent decades, US-controlled transnational production reached a decisive stage, necessitating the restructuring of the international division of labour, as the export of productive capital brought about a shift in the nature and location of production: the expansion of manufacturing industry on an unprecedented scale into previously precapitalist, peripheral areas of the global capitalist economy. This marked a turning point in the rise of the US economy and the emergence of the US as the leading capitalist/imperialist power in the world (Berberoglu, 2003).

Although the large-scale US postwar global expansion ushered in a period of unquestioned US supremacy over the world economy and polity during the 1950s and 1960s, the economic strength of US capital over foreign markets through investment, production, and trade during the 1970s took on a new significance—one resulting from the restructuring of the international division of labour. US transnational capital, in line with its transfer of large segments of the production process to the periphery, poured massive amounts of capital into select areas of the Third World, as well as into its traditional bases of foreign investment—Canada and Western Europe—and became the leading centre of world capitalism in a new way (that is, by becoming the dominant force in the worldwide production process). Thus not only did overall US direct investment expand immensely during this period, but also a shift in the form of investment in favour of manufacturing came to constitute the new basis of changes in the international division of labour with great impact on the national economies of both the periphery and the centre states, including the US. This process further fueled the contradictions and conflicts inherent in capitalist production and class relations on a global scale, including interimperialist rivalry between the chief capitalist states on the one hand and the exploitation of labour on a global scale on the other, with all the consequences associated with this process—a process that has led to the crisis of global capitalism.

Imperialism, the State, and the Crisis of Global Capitalism

The global expansion of capital over the past one-hundred years has had varied effects on the economy, state, and class relations on a world scale. Figure 1 outlines the origins and development of capitalism and the capitalist state through its various stages—from its early beginnings to the modern global age. It shows that, as capitalism developed from its competitive to monopoly stage, it underwent a major transformation that elevated it from the national to the global level. This was accompanied by a worldwide process of economic expansion as the export of capital replaced the export of goods that was characteristic of the earlier stage of capitalist development. Monopoly rule over the global economy facilitated by the advanced capitalist state, set the stage for imperialism through the internationalization of capital and capitalist relations across the world, and led to the consolidation of capital's grip over the world economy. This provided the political framework for the direct role of the advanced capitalist state in safeguarding the interests of capital and the capitalist class around the world—a role facilitated by the World Bank, the International Monetary Fund, and the World Trade Organization—global institutions designed to advance the worldwide operations of the trans-national corporations as the instruments of global capitalism (Payer, 1974, 1982; Kloby, 2003).

The capitalist state, now controlled by the monopoly fraction of the capitalist class, thus came to serve the long-term interests of global capital and the global capitalist system through its political and military apparatus in service of the transnationals and the transnational capitalist class (Sklair, 2001). Looking at neoliberal globalization in class terms, we see that a complex web of class relations has developed at the global level that is both complementary and contradictory. Thus while the capitalist classes of the dominant imperialist states cooperate in their collective exploitation of labour and plunder of resources at the global level, the underlying contradictions of global competition and conflict among these classes lead at the same time to interimperialist rivalries and confrontation around the world (Hart, 1992). Just as each imperialist power exploits its own as well as its rivals' working classes for global supremacy, so too one observes the potential unity of the working classes of these rival imperialist states as workers come together in forging a protracted struggle against the entire global capitalist system. It is here that the capitalist/imperialist state comes to

play a critical role in facilitating the exploitation of global labour by
transnational capital, but in doing so also risks its demise through the
unfolding contradictions of this very same process that it is increasingly unable to control and regulate (Berberoglu, 2003, 2005).

The problems that the imperial state has come to tackle, at both the
global and national levels, are such that it is no longer able to manage
its affairs with any degree of certainty. At the global level, the imperial
state has been unable to deal with the consequences of ever-growing
superexploitation of labour in Third World sweatshops that has led
to immense poverty and inequality worldwide; nor has it been able
to take measures to reverse the depletion of resources, environmental pollution and other health hazards, a growing national debt tying
many countries to the World Bank, the International Monetary Fund,
and other global financial institutions, and a growing militarization of
society through the institution of brutal military and civilian dictatorships that violate basic human rights.

The domination and control of Third World countries for transnational profits through the instrumentality of the imperial state has at
the same time created various forms of dependence on the centre that
has become a defining characteristic of neoliberal globalization and
imperialism (Amaladoss, 1999; Sklair, 2002).

Domestically, the globalization of capital and imperialist expansion
has had immense dislocations in the national economies of imperialist states. Expansion of manufacturing industry abroad has meant
a decline in local industry, as plant closings in the US and other
advanced capitalist countries has worsened the unemployment situation. The massive expansion of capital abroad has resulted in hundreds
of factory shutdowns with millions of workers losing their jobs, hence
the surge in unemployment in the United States and other imperialist
states (Phillips, 1998; Wagner 2000). This has led to a decline in wages
of workers in the advanced capitalist centers, as low wages abroad
have played a competitive role in keeping wages down in the imperialist heartlands. The drop in incomes among a growing section of the
working class has thus lowered the standard of living in general and
led to a further polarization between labour and capital (Berberoglu,
1992, 2002).

The dialectics of global capitalist expansion, which has caused so
much exploitation, oppression, and misery for the peoples of the
world, both in the Third World and in the imperialist countries themselves, has in turn created the conditions for its own destruction.

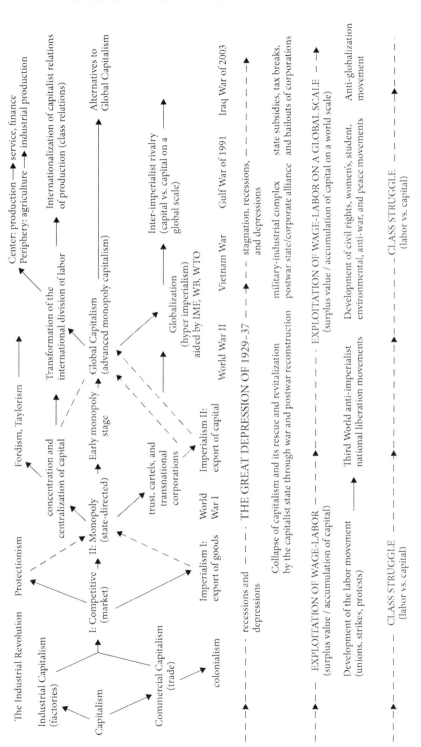

Figure 1   The Origins and Development of Global Capitalism and the Capitalist State Through Its Various Stages

Economically, it has afflicted the system with recessions, depressions, and an associated realization crisis; politically, it has set into motion an imperial interventionist state that through its presence in every corner of the world has incurred an enormous military expenditure to maintain an empire, while gaining the resentment of millions of people across the globe who are engaged in active struggle against it.[1]

The imperial state, acting as the repressive arm of global capital and extending its rule across vast territories, has dwarfed the militaristic adventures of past empires many times over. Moreover, through its political and military supremacy, it has come to exert its control over many countries and facilitate the exploitation of labour on a world scale. As a result, it has reinforced the domination of capital over labour and its rule on behalf of capital. This, in turn, has greatly politicized the struggle between labour and capital and called for the recognition of the importance of political organization that many find it necessary to effect change in order to transform the capitalist-imperialist system.

The global domination of capital and the advanced capitalist/imperial state during the twentieth century did not proceed without a fight, as a protracted struggle of the working class against capital and the capitalist state unfolded throughout this period of capitalist globalization. The labour movement, the anti-imperialist national liberation movements, and the civil rights, women's, student, environmental, anti-war, and peace movements all contributed to the development of the emerging anti-globalization movement in the late twentieth and early twenty-first centuries. These and related contradictions of late-twentieth-century capitalist globalization led to the crisis of the imperial state and the entire globalization project which increasingly came under attack by the mass movements of the global era that came to challenge the rule of capital and the capitalist state throughout the world (Brecher, Costello and Smith, 2000).

---

[1] While one consequence of imperialism and neoliberal globalization has been economic contraction and an associated class polarization, a more costly and dangerous outcome of this process has been increased militarization and intervention abroad, such that the defence of an expanding capitalist empire worldwide has come to require an increasing military presence and a permanent interventionist foreign policy to keep the world economy clear of obstructions that go against the interests of the transnational monopolies. However, such aggressive military posture has created (and continues to create) major problems for the imperialist state and is increasingly threatening its effectiveness and, in the long run, its very existence.

The Crisis of the Imperial State on a Global Scale

The crisis of the imperial state at the global level is a manifestation of the contradictions of the global economy, which in the early twenty-first century has reached a critical stage in its development. The massive flow of US transnational investment throughout the world, especially in Western Europe, Japan, and other advanced capitalist regions, has led to the post World War II reemergence of interimperialist rivalry among the major capitalist powers, while fostering alternate cycles of cooperation and conflict in the scramble for the peripheral regions of the global capitalist system—Latin America, Asia, Africa, and the Middle East (Hart, 1992; Falk, 1999; Halliday, 2001).

With the integration of the economies of Western Europe into the European Union (EU), the postwar emergence of Japan as a powerful economic force, and the more recent rise of China to global prominence, the position of the United States has declined relative to both its own postwar supremacy in the 1940s and 1950s and to other advanced capitalist economies since that time. Despite the fact that US capital continues to control the biggest share of overseas markets and accounts for the largest volume of international investments, its hold on the global economy has recently begun to slip in a manner similar to Britain's in the early twentieth century. This has, in turn, led the US state to take a more aggressive role in foreign policy to protect US transnational interests abroad. Its massive deployment in the Middle East in the early 1990s, which led to the Persian Gulf War of 1991, and most recently its intervention in Afghanistan in 2001 and invasion of Iraq in 2003, has resulted in great military expenditures and translated into an enormous burden on working people of the United States, who have come to shoulder the colossal cost of maintaining a global empire whose vast military machine encompasses the world (Beams, 1998).

In the current phase of the crisis of the US imperial state, the problems it faces are of such magnitude that they threaten the very existence of the global capitalist system. Internal economic and budgetary problems have been compounded by ever-growing military spending propped up by armed intervention in the Third World, while a declining economic base at home manifested in the housing and banking crisis, and a recessionary economy is further complicated by the global rivalry between the major capitalist powers that is not always restricted to the economic field, but has political (and even military) implications that are global in magnitude (Beams, 2005; Panitch and Leys, 2003).

The growing prospects of interimperialist rivalry between the major capitalist powers, backed up by their states, are effecting changes in their relations that render the global political economy an increasingly unstable character. Competition between the United States, Japan, and European imperial states representing the interests of their own respective capitalist classes are leading them on a collision course for world supremacy, manifested in struggles for markets, raw materials, and spheres of influence in geopolitical—as well as economic—terms, which may in fact lead to a new balance of forces, and consequently alliances that will have serious political implications in global power politics. As the continuing economic ascendance of the major capitalist rivals of the United States take their prominent position in the global economy, pressures will build toward the politicization and militarization of these states from within, where the leading class forces bent on dominating the world economy will press forward with the necessary political and military corollary of their growing economic power in the global capitalist system (Hart, 1992; Falk, 1999).

These developments in global economic and geopolitical shifts in the balance of forces among the major capitalist powers will bring to the fore new and yet untested international alliances for world supremacy and domination in the post Cold War era. Such alliances will bring key powers like Russia and China into play in a new and complicated relationship that holds the key for the success or failure of the new rising imperial centres that will emerge as the decisive forces in the global economic, political, and military equation in the early twenty-first century (Halliday, 2001).

The contradictions and conflicts imbedded in relations between the rival states of the major capitalist powers will again surface as an important component of international relations in the years ahead. And these are part and parcel of the restructuring of the international division of labour and the transfer of production to overseas territories in line with the globalization of capital on a worldwide basis—a process that has serious consequences for the economies of both the advanced capitalist and less developed capitalist countries. Economic decline in the imperial centres (manifested in plant closings, unemployment, and recession) and superexploitation of workers in the Third World (maintained by repressive regimes) yield the same combined result that has a singular global logic: the accumulation of transnational profits for the capitalist class of the advanced capitalist states—above all, that of the US, the current centre of global capitalism. It is in this context of the changes that are taking place on a world scale that the imperial state is beginning to confront the current crisis of global capitalism.

Globalization, Class Struggle, and Social Transformation

With the spread of capitalism and capitalist class relations around the world, capital has effected transformations in the class structure of societies with which it has come into contact. As a result, the class contradictions of global capitalism have become the primary source of class conflict and class struggle throughout the world (Berberoglu, 2009).

The development of capitalism over the past hundred years formed and transformed capitalist society on a global scale. This transformation came about through the restructuring of the international division of labour prompted by the export of capital and transfer of production to cheap labour areas abroad. This, in turn, led to the intensification of the exploitation of labour through expanded production and reproduction of surplus value and profits by further accumulation of capital and the reproduction of capitalist relations of production on a world scale. A major consequence of this process is the increased polarization of wealth and income between labour and capital at the national and global levels, and growth in numbers of the poor and marginalized segments of the population throughout the world. These and other related contradictions of global capitalism define the parameters of neoliberal capitalist globalization and provide us the framework of discussion and debate on the nature and dynamics of globalization in the world today (Veltmeyer, 2008).

The widening gap between the accumulated wealth of the capitalist class and the declining incomes of workers has sharpened the class struggle in a new political direction, which has brought the advanced capitalist state to the centre stage of the conflict between labour and capital and revealed its ties to the monopolies. This has undermined the legitimacy of the capitalist state, such that the struggles of the working class and the masses in general are becoming directed not merely against capital, but against the state itself (Beams, 1998). This transformation of the workers' struggle from the economic to the political sphere is bound to set the stage for protracted struggles in the period

ahead—struggles that would facilitate the development of a much
more politicized international labour movement. The globalization of
capital is thus bound to accelerate the politicization of the working
class and lead to the building of a solid foundation for international
solidarity of workers on a world scale that is directed against global
capitalism and the advanced capitalist state on a world scale (Bina and
Davis, 2002; Howard, 2005; Stevis and Boswell, 2008).

The relationship between the owners of the transnational corpora-
tions-the global capitalist class—and the imperial state, and the role and
functions of this state, including the use of military force to advance
the interests of the capitalist class, thus reveals the class nature of the
imperial state and the class logic of neoliberal globalization today
(Warren, 1980; Szymanski, 1981; Berberoglu, 1987, 2001, 2009). But
this logic is more pervasive and is based on a more fundamental class
relation between labour and capital that now operates on a global level
(that is, a relation based on exploitation). Thus, in the age of capitalist globalization, social classes and class struggles are a product of the
logic of the global capitalist system based on the exploitation of labour
worldwide (Petras, 1978; Berberoglu, 1994).

Capitalist expansion on a world scale at this stage of the globalization of capital and capitalist production has brought with it the globalization of the production process and the exploitation of wage labour
on a world scale. With the intensified exploitation of the working class
at super-low wages in repressive neocolonial societies throughout the
world, the transnational corporations of the leading capitalist countries have come to amass great fortunes that they have used to build
up a global empire through the powers of the imperial state, which
has not hesitated to use its military force to protect and advance the
interests of capital in every corner of the globe. It is in this context
that we see the coalescence of the interests of the global economy and
empire as manifested in control of cheap labour, new markets, and
vital sources of raw materials, such as oil, and the intervention of the
capitalist state to protect these when their continued supply to the
imperial centre are threatened.

Lenin, in his book *Imperialism: The Highest Stage of Capitalism*,
pointed out that capitalism in its highest and most mature monopoly
stage has spread to every corner of the world and thus has planted the
seeds of its own contradictions everywhere (Lenin [1917] 1975). It is in
this context of the developing worldwide contradictions of advanced,

monopoly capitalism that Lenin pointed out, '[I]mperialism is the eve of the social revolution of the proletariat...on a worldwide scale' (Lenin [1917] 1975: 640).

In considering the emerging class struggles throughout the globe, the question that one now confronts is thus a *political* one. Given what we know of neoliberal globalization and its class contradictions on a world scale, how will the peoples' movements respond to it *politically* worldwide? What strategy and tactics will be adopted to confront this colossal force? It is important to think about these questions concretely, in a practical way—one that involves careful analysis and organized political action.

Understanding the necessity of mobilizing labour and the importance of political leadership in this struggle, radical labour organizations have in fact taken steps emphasizing the importance for the working class to mobilize its ranks and take united action to wage battle against capitalist globalization (Waterman, 1998; Munck, 2002; Stevis and Boswell, 2008).

Strikes, demonstrations, and mass protests initiated by workers and other popular forces have become frequent in a growing number of countries controlled by the transnationals in recent years. Working people are rising up against the local ruling classes, the state, and the transnational monopolies that have together effected the superexploitation of labour for decades. Various forms of struggle are now underway in many countries under the grip of transnational capital (Polet, 2007; Stevis and Boswell, 2008; Berberoglu, 2009).

The logic of transnational capitalist expansion on a global scale is such that it leads to the emergence and development of forces that are in conflict with this expansion. The working class has been in the forefront of these forces. Armed insurrection, civil war, and revolutionary upheavals are all a response to the repression imposed on working people by global capitalism and its client states throughout the world. Together, these struggles have been effective in frustrating the efforts of global capital to expand and dominate the world, while at the same time building the basis of an international working-class movement that finally overcomes national, ethnic, cultural, and linguistic boundaries that artificially separate the workers in their fight against global capitalism. In this sense, labour internationalism (or the political alliance of workers across national boundaries in their struggle against global capitalism) is increasingly being seen as a political weapon that would serve as a unifying force in labour's frontal attack on capital in the early twenty-first century (Beams, 1998; Fishman, Scott, and Modupe, 2005).[2]

The solidarity achieved through this process has helped expand the strength of the international working class and increased its determination to defeat all vestiges of global capitalism throughout the world, and build a new egalitarian social order that advances the interests of working people and ultimately all of humanity.

Global capitalism today represents a dual, contradictory development whose dialectical resolution will be an outcome of its very nature—a product of its growth and expansion across time and space within the confines of a structure that promotes its own destruction and demise. However, while the process itself is a self-destructing one, it is important to understand that the nature of the class struggle that these contradictions generate is such that the critical factor that tips the balance of class forces in favour of the working class to win state power is *political organization*, the building of *class alliances* among the oppressed and exploited classes, the development of strong and theoretically well-informed *revolutionary leadership* that is organically linked to the working class, and a clear understanding of the forces at work in the class struggle, including especially the *role of the state* and its military and police apparatus—the focal point of the struggle for state power (Szymanski, 1978; Knapp and Spector, 1991; Berberoglu, 2001; Stevis and Boswell, 2008). The success of the working class and its revolutionary leadership in confronting the power of the capitalist state thus becomes the critical element ensuring that once captured, the state can become an instrument that the workers can use to establish their rule and in the process transform society and the state itself to promote labour's interests in line with its vision for a new society free of exploitation and oppression, one based on the rule of the working class and the labouring masses in general.

---

[2] The necessity of the struggle against global capital in an organized political fashion has been emphasized by working-class organizations and this has led to several successful revolutions during the twentieth century. Throughout this period, working class organizations have emphasized the centrality of international working class solidarity (or proletarian internationalism) for any worldwide effort to wage a successful battle against global capitalism.

Conclusion

I have outlined the class contradictions of neoliberal globalization/ imperialism, the crisis of the global economy and the imperial state, the emergent forms of class struggle and the prospects for the transformation of global capitalism in the twenty-first century. I discussed these within the context of the globalization of capital in the twentieth century and mapped out the political implications of this process for the future course of development and transformation of capitalism on a global scale.

Our understanding of the necessity for the transformation of global capitalism, which is political in nature, demands a clear and concise analysis of its contradictions in late twentieth—and early twenty-first-century form, so that this knowledge can be put to use to facilitate the class struggle in a revolutionary direction. In this context, one will want to know not only the extent and depth of global capitalist expansion, but also its base of support, its linkage to the major institutions of capitalist society (above all the state, but also other religious, cultural, and social institutions), the extent of its ideological hegemony and control over mass consciousness, and other aspects of social, economic, political, and ideological domination. Moreover—and this is the most important point—one must study its weaknesses, its problem areas, its vulnerabilities, its weak links, and the various dimensions of its crisis—especially those that affect its continued reproduction and survival. Armed with this knowledge, one would be better equipped to confront capital and the capitalist state in the struggle for the transformation of global capitalism in this century.

CHAPTER SEVEN

THE MIGRATION-DEVELOPMENT NEXUS: A MARXIST CLASS PERSPECTIVE

Raúl Delgado Wise

Led by the World Bank and the Inter-American Development Bank (IDB), most international organizations and governments have been pursuing a political agenda in the area of migration and development. They posit that remittances sent home by migrants can promote local, regional and national development in the countries of origin. By extension, remittances are seen as an indispensable source of foreign exchange that provides macroeconomic stability and alleviates the ravages caused by insidious problems such as poverty. This view is supported by the growing importance of remittances as a source of foreign exchange and subsistence income for many households in underdeveloped countries. The United Nations Development Programmeme has estimated that 500 million people (8% of the world's population) receive remittances (UNDP, 2007). According to World Bank figures, remittances sent home by emigrants from underdeveloped countries rose from 85 billion US dollars in 2000 to 199 billion US dollars in 2006. If unrecorded flows through informal channels are considered, this figure may increase recorded flows by 50% or more (World Bank, 2006). Taking unrecorded flows into account, the overall amount of remittances surpassed foreign direct investment flows and more than doubled official aid received by Third World countries. In many cases remittances have become the largest and less volatile source of foreign exchange earnings.

Although, in a recent document, the World Bank's position vis-à-vis the relationship between remittances and migration has been more cautious (Lapper, 2006), it should be pointed out that the impact of the implementation of structural adjustment programmes as a key element of the neoliberal policy promoted by the World Bank and the International Monetary Fund (IMF) is the root cause of the upsurge in South-North migration and remittances flows. Moreover, far from contributing to the development of migrant-sending countries, structural adjustment programmes have reinforced the dynamics of underde-velopment and transformed many countries in 'people-exporting' countries.

The great paradox of the migration-development agenda is that it leaves the principles that underpin neoliberal globalization—referring to the current phase of US imperialism—intact and does not affect the specific way in which neoliberal policies are applied in migrant-send-ing countries (Delgado Wise and Marquez, 2007; Castles and Delgado Wise, 2007).

This chapter underscores the need for a theoretical approach based on a Marxist critique of the dominant perspectives regarding the migration-development nexus, taking into consideration James Petras' insights and contributions regarding both, the nature of contempo-rary US imperialism and his characterization, in this context, of labour migration as *forced migration* (a concept used by Marx in his analysis of the Irish question). From this perspective special attention is placed on: (a) the relationship between US imperialism and forced migra-tion, and (b) the role of remittances, which are chiefly assessed as a wage component embedded in a complex set of transnational social relations and used for the subsistence of a surplus population that is forced to enter cross-border job markets under conditions of labour precarization and social exclusion.

Most of the studies that address the relationship between migration and development tend to view the relationship from a unidirectional and decontextualized perspective, as if migration were an independent variable and development possibilities were subject to and depended exclusively on the resources and initiatives of migrants. Nevertheless, given the analytical complexity of this relationship it is necessary to come up with an alternative approach that does not centre on the phe-nomenon of migration but focuses on the macro-processes of under-development and development in the broader context of contemporary capitalism or, more specifically, what Petras (2007: 40) characterizes as 'the imperialist-centreed model of capitalist accumulation'.

Departing from the above considerations, this chapter is divided in two main sections and includes a brief section of concluding remarks. The first section offers an analytical framework for understanding the relationship between migration and development rooted in Marxism. The second one shows the interpretive capabilities of the proposed approach when applied to the analysis of Mexico's asymmetrical and subordinated regional integration process with the US.

A Marxist Approach for Analyzing the Development-Migration Nexus

As Petras points out, 'all the orthodox explanations of international migration fail to examine the social structure of the political economy of the 'people-exporting' countries and 'people-importing' countries. To that end, he adds, "it is obligatory to put forth an economic model which encompasses the historical relations between the imperialist nations and semi-colonies of the Third World" (Petras, 2007: 40).

From this perspective and considering some of the basic charac-teristics of contemporary capitalism (the Imperialist-Centred Model of Capitalist accumulation in Petras' terms), it is possible to identify at least four critical aspects of the dialectical process underlying the development-migration relation:

1. *Current capital restructuring-as a manifestation of the dominant imperialist project-operates as a catalyst for forced migration from peripheral to developed countries.* In this context, core-developed countries led by the US-EU employ a geopolitical-imperialist strategy of economic restructuring that internationalizes productive, commer-cial, and financial capital at the same time that it allows the major developed countries and its elites to appropriate the natural resources, economic surplus, and cheap workforce of underdeveloped nations. The relations maintained between 'people-importing' countries and peripheral and postcolonial nations exacerbate the latter's conditions of underdevelopment. Underdeveloped countries find themselves with massive population reserves (and, therefore, a large volume of surplus population, well beyond the conventional formulation of the *reserve army of the unemployed*), members of which are unable to find decent working conditions in their countries of origin for ensuring personal and family reproduction. This is the direct result of reduced accumula-tion processes derived from their asymmetrical relations with devel-oped nations (an unequal exchange that translates into diverse forms of surplus transfer).

Petras refers to this impact in the following terms: "The *destructur-ing* of labour (delinking the development of industry and infrastruc-ture from the local population) and the relocation of profits to the receiving country creates a mass permanent surplus labour population in the dominated country. The imperialist-centreed model of capitalist accumulation (ICMCA) further weakens the employment generating potentialities of the dominated 'people-exporting' countries by cap-turing local savings—they do not 'risk' their own capital. Local banks

prefer to lend to large foreign MNCs because they believe there is less
risk than lending to local manufacturers, farmers or service enterprises.
By 'crowding out' local borrowers from the credit market and forcing them to borrow at higher rates in the informal credit market, the
MNCs increase the local bankruptcy rates among the locally owned,
labour-intensive enterprises' (Petras, 2007: 41).

The above conditions are not socially sustainable and lead to forced
migration, which we understand as population movements occasioned
by the lack of proper living and working conditions, or life-threaten-
ing political or social conflicts. It also implies locating migrants 'at
the bottom of the social and economic class hierarchy in the receiving country', where they are 'exposed to discrimination additional to
that related to poverty—disparagement of their culture and ethnicity…[and moreover] cheated in their salaries, subject to a kind of
perpetual debt peonage, or abuse by employers of the lack of the sender
country protection or local trade union solidarity' (Petras, 2007: 50).

Forced migration can result in substantial population loss for
countries of origin, sometimes even leading to relative or absolute
depopulation. The loss of qualified and unqualified workforce is also
associated with the abandonment of productive activities and the loss
of potential wealth.

2. *Exploitation of migrant labour contributes to socioeconomic dynamism and to the concentration and centralization of capital in core-
developed countries.* Developed-imperialist nations demand large
quantities of qualified and unqualified workforce; in some cases,
this human merchandise is rendered increasingly vulnerable and is
additionally devalued by the regulation of migration imposed by the
imperial country. First, this ongoing demand results from developed
nations' increased accumulation capacity, which is derived from the
transference of resources and surpluses from underdeveloped countries. Secondly, it is the consequence of processes of demographic
transition and an ageing population. Immigrants contribute to an
overall cheapening of the workforce since they tend to be employed
in work-intensive areas of production where they rescue or substitute a national workforce that tends to earn higher wages and benefits.
Although the qualified immigrant workforce belongs to an elite sector
it is still comparatively cheap, as an immigrant's salary is lower than
that of a national citizen employed in the same position. In the case
of both qualified and unqualified migrants the receiving country reaps
substantial benefits, having invested nothing in the formation of the

human capital it now enjoys. In this regard Petras posits that "[t]he imperial state regulates the inflow of and restrictions on labour immigration". For one thing, "it determines the scope (how many immigrants), the timing (when more or less immigrants can enter and when they will be expelled), the 'quality' of the immigrants (skill level and specific categories of professionals) and laws governing the longevity of the immigrants' work permits" (Petras, 2007: 42). For another, "the imperial state decides on the penalties for illegal entry and on repatriation and whether to bring criminal charges. Immigration policies of the imperial state are directly linked to the business cycle, to the tightness of the labour market and to the social strategies of the capitalist class" (ibid.).

Moreover, Petras adds, "[i]mmigration policies have served the capitalist class by creating a reserve army of cheap labour to lower wages, to undermine unionization and to fill 'niches' in the domestic labour market in low-paid, unhealthy work'. Equally significant, 'capitalists hire low wage immigrant workers to replace skilled and semi-skilled workers in higher paying jobs such as nurses, doctors, carpenters, plumbers, plasterers, painters, machinists, cooks, meat cutters and so on'" (ibid.).

Contrary to the argument of many 'progressives', Petras points out that 'immigrant labour is used to downgrade existing high-paying jobs with expensive health and safety protections into low-paying degraded, unsafe and unhealthy work'. Thus the progressive argument that immigrants are mostly 'unskilled' cheap labour engaged in work that the local workers reject is partially false. 'While the 'first and second waves' of immigrants might have fit that profile during the 1950s and 1980s, it is not the story today. Capital now imports skilled labour in information technology, home and office specialty repairs, and medicine-in order to lower the costs to the state, employers and affluent homeowners (Petras, 2007: 43).

Not only do immigrants provide static comparative advantages derived from a reduction in production costs: they also bring comparative dynamic ones through their participation in accelerated innovation processes. Overall, working immigrants and their families internally strengthen the receiving country's market through consumption. Even the so-called 'nostalgia market' entails the creation of consumer demand, which fortifies internal economic activity. On the other hand, immigrants' taxable contributions enrich the country's fiscal fund but do not translate into the kinds of social benefits enjoyed by the national population, which denotes a criterion of social exclusion. Immigrant workers also help pay for the current crisis faced by pension systems due to the massive retirement of the Baby Boomer generation.

Petras notes that the capitalist class imports immigrant labour to pay into the pension system for local retirees, thus keeping state expenditures and thus taxes on the rich very low—counting on the immigrant worker never being able to benefit from his pension contributions. In brief, "an open immigration policy lowers state expenditures, such as pension and health costs, allowing the imperial state to channel resources to subsidize agricultural interests and MNCs" (Petras, 2007: 43–44). Moreover, he adds, "the high rates of profits, derived directly from employing immigrant labour and indirectly from the depressed wages and salaries of local workers, facilitate overseas expansion" (ibid.). Although these contributions counteract some of the effects brought about by the dismantling of the welfare state, they obviously do not constitute a long-term solution.[1]

1. *Migrants help maintain precarious socioeconomic stability in their countries of origin.* Migrants' wage-based remittances contribute to the subsistence of family members in the country of origin.[2] To a lesser extent, remittances also help finance small businesses in the subsistence economy. The participative remittances collected by migrant organizations finance public works and social projects in the places of origin. In some cases this practice has become institutionalized: Mexico's Programme *Tres por Uno* (Three for One) has been replicated in other countries. Migrants with savings or entrepreneurial plans use their money to finance micro-projects in their places of origin. The most important type of remittance is, however, the salary-based one employed for family subsistence, which means that the resources sent by migrants are rarely destined to processes of development and social transformation.

In a macroeconomic context, remittances serve neoliberal governments that, not bothering to come up with actual development alternatives, use them as a source of foreign exchange income that

---

[1] The advance and development of migration dynamics have created a complex social transnational space that engages societies of origin and destination and serves as a dynamic field of economic activity. Economic opportunities in this field are usually seized by the large corporations of developed countries (Guarnizo 2003).

[2] For the different types of remittance see Márquez Covarrubias (2006).

sustains the country's fragile macroeconomic stability. In some cases, remittances have even been used as a guarantee when incurring foreign debt. In the absence of any kind of project, migrants are now portrayed as the 'heroes of development', an utterly cynical move that renders them responsible for the promotion of said development while the state, opting for the conservative stance of minimal participation, is no longer held accountable.

The strategy of market regulation postulated by fundamentalist neoliberals lacks any sort of development plan that involves migrants as well as other social sectors and promotes processes of social transformation. In truth, underdeveloped 'people-exporting' countries fulfill a particular role as workforce reserves and their potential development is obstructed by increasingly reduced national elites, which are subordinated to the interests of governing circles in developed countries and, to a great extent, the interests of US capital.

Petras emphasizes this point by sustaining that "[t]he ICMCA is not simply an 'imposition' from the outside by the IMF and MNCs". It is in large part "a model imposed from the *inside* by imperial *hegemonized economists* whose higher education has been financed by imperial foundations and institutions". Through the 'people-exporting countries', Petras adds, "the local policy elites linked by business interests, bribes and ideology to the imperial countries, impose and implement the ICMCA". Thus, "financial and economic ministers, central bankers, trade and agricultural officials trained by and identified with the ICMCA execute the neoliberal policies that are an integral part of the empire-centreed model" (Petras, 2007: 42).

2. *The promotion of development as social transformation could curtail forced migration.* Globalization depicts migration as inevitable; we must endorse, both in theory and practice, the viability of alternative processes of development and do so on different levels. We must first redefine the asymmetrical terms that developed countries, aided by principles that have by now turned into fetishes (e.g. democracy, liberty, and free trade), used for imperialist domination. This involves an exposé of imperialist practices, which have created oceans of inequality and condemned vast regions of the world to marginalization, poverty, social exclusion, and unfettered migration. Foreign investment (FI) has been a fundamental driving force in this regard. A genuine process of social transformation involving the migrant and non-migrant sectors of society would not only seek to contain the overwhelming flow of forced migration but also revert the ongoing processes of social

degradation that characterize underdevelopment and even pose a threat to human existence (Harvey, 2007; Bello, 2006).

As an alternative to the current phase of imperialist domination, Petras argues in favour of a Worker-Engineer Public Control model (WEPC) based on six main principles: tax revenues versus tax evasions; profit remittances and privileged salaries versus social investment; high reinvestment ratios versus capital flight; long term investment in research and development versus speculative investment; social welfare versus capitalist privileges; and fixed capital/mobile labour versus mobile capital/fixed labour (Petras, 2007: 234–235).

This model provides an alternative approach that maximizes national and working-class interests: 'it has potential drawbacks and internal contradictions, which require constant reflection, deliberation, debate and reforms' (Petras, 2007: 237). Nonetheless, 'the model provides the surest and most direct road to development with democracy, social justice and national independence. The success of the WEPC model, its introduction and sustainability, does not depend merely on its socioeconomic viability but also on appropriate and supporting national security and cultural policies and institutions (Petras, 2007: 237–238).

Following the above considerations, an approach based on a Marxist critique of the World Bank's views regarding the migration-development nexus, would posit that international migration is an element of the current imperialist project led by the US and that the migration phenomenon has to be examined in this context in order to reveal its root causes and effects. In order to approach migration's cause-and-effect relationships with development and examine specific moments in the dialectic interaction between development and migration, the following issues must be addressed:[3]

1. *Strategic practices.* These refer to the confrontation between different projects that espouse diverging class interests, which in turn underlie the structures of contemporary capitalism and its inherent development problems. There are currently two major projects. The hegemonic one is promoted by the large MNCs, the governments of developed countries led by US imperialism, and allied elites in under-

---

[3] For our analytical purposes we adopt Petras and Veltmeyer's (2001) approach for understanding the nature of contemporary capitalism and unmasking the notion of globalization by considering, following Marx's method, two critical and interrelated analytical dimensions: strategic and structural.

developed nations, all under the umbrella of international organizations commanded by the US government, like the IMF and the World
Bank. The project's loss of legitimacy under the aegis of neoliberal globalization means that, nowadays, rather than writing of hegemony we
can use the term 'domination'. The implementation of this imperialist
project is not the result of consensus but rather military force and the
financial imposition of macroeconomic 'structural reform' along the
lines of the Washington—or Post-Washington Consensus.

The second alternative project consists of the sociopolitical actions
of a range of social classes and movements as well as collective subjects and agents, including migrant associations that endorse a political project designed to transform the structural dynamics and political
and institutional environments which bar the implementation of alternative development strategies on the global, regional, national and
local levels.

2. *Structural dynamics.* These refer to the uneven development processes driven by the dynamics of US imperialism on several planes
and levels. This includes the financial, commercial, productive, and
labour market spheres, as well as technological innovation (a strategic form of control) and the use and allotment of natural resources
and environmental impacts. These factors condition the ways in which
(*i*) developed; (*ii*) developed and underdeveloped (including 'people-
importing' and 'people exporting' nations); and (*iii*) underdeveloped,
peripheral or postcolonial countries relate to each other. They also
determine the fields in which interactions between sectors, groups,
movements, and social classes take place, within and across national
borders. All of this entails different—albeit interrelated—dynamics at
the global, regional, national and local levels.

The Dialectic of Development and Migration in Mexico and the US

Since the late 1970s, the US has promoted the implementation of neoliberal structural adjustment policies in Latin American, which have
been carried out by several international organizations in tandem with
the Latin American elites and national governments. In accordance
with new models of regional integration, these policies focused on
exports.

The export-led Mexican economic model and the particular mode
of regional integration determined by the North American Free Trade
Agreement (NAFTA) are the result of strategic policies implemented

by agents of large transnational corporations and the US government under the umbrella of the international organizations at their service: the World Bank and IMF. In fact, as has been amply documented, NAFTA itself was created and implemented by a sector of the US political class allied to the large transnational corporations and their counterparts in Canada and Mexico (Cypher, 1993; Faux, 2006). In the case of the latter, the government and a sector of the Mexican business elite led by the *Consejo Coordinador Empresarial* (Enterpreneurial Council), which is linked to the *Comisión de Organismos Empresariales de Comercio Exterior* (Commission of Entrepreneurial External Commerce Organizations) participated actively in this process (Puga, 2004; Cypher and Delgado Wise, 2007).

Mexico soon became Latin America's major exporter and the world's thirteenth. This 'achievement' was irresponsibly and superficially attributed to the successful implementation of the neoliberal economic reforms (i.e. the structural adjustment programmes). At first glance, 90% of its export platform was comprised of manufactured products, 39.4% of which was classified as 'technical progress-diffusing goods' (CEPAL, 2002). This stance can create an optical illusion, and an examination of the subject becomes necessary: what is it that the country really exports?

The Basis for Mexico's Cheap Labour Export-Led Model

The way in which Mexico entered the orbit of US capitalism under neoliberalism, and particularly in the context of NAFTA, plays a fundamental role in the understanding of the model of 'development' adopted in the country. As has been documented elsewhere and contrary to what Mexico's progress along the secondary-exporting path would indicate (i.e. the establishment of a successful model of manufactured exports), the country's export-led model is based on cheap labour (Delgado Wise and Márquez, 2005; Delgado Wise and Cypher, 2005). This model, which, as a component of its renovated imperialist architecture, is crucial to the US productive restructuring process, comprises three inter-related mechanisms that, taken together, indicate the asymmetrical and subordinated integration of the country's economy into that of the US:

1. *The maquiladora industry*, made up of assembly plants and involving a strategy of productive relocation led by large US corporations in order to take advantage of low labour costs in Mexico. The result is that the nation experiences a very low level of integration with the

domestic economy and, in addition, is subject to a further dismantling of its productive apparatus.

2. *Disguised maquila*, or manufacturing plants with productive processes that are more complex than maquila assembly operations but operate under the same temporary import regime as maquiladoras (e.g. the automobile and electronics sectors).

It should be noted here that maquilla and disguised maquilla share two characteristics: (i) they are practically devoid of productive upstream and downstream links to the rest of the national production apparatus, and (ii) they are subject to intense processes of labour precarization. Maquillas issue wages that are around 1/10 of those in the US, while the difference in disguised maquilla is 1/7. Due to their high levels of imported components (between 80 and 90% of the total export value), their contribution to the Mexican economy is basically restricted to the wage earnings; in other words, the value of the labour incorporated into the exports. This means that the country is engaging in the *indirect exportation of labour*, or a transfer of the workforce that does not require workers to leave the country (Tello, 1996). This is a crucial conceptual element that demystifies the purported success of Mexican manufacture exports and reveals retrograde movement in the export platform.

Although Petras does not use the notion of the indirect exportation of labour he has been aware of the implications of this aspect of the process of industrial restructuring. When discussing the implications of foreign direct investment (FI), he notes that 'since the 1990s, FI has increasingly looked toward *outsourcing* skilled jobs to low-wages/salary regions'. This, he notes, 'requires state promotion of an educated low-paid work force and financing of local business elites to act as recruiters and point men for the FI'. Overseas relocation (both the reality and the threat of it) is a common policy for lowering wages, pensions, health benefits and job security in the imperial countries. Foreign investors, he notes, benefit from both ends: 'exploiting skilled and unskilled labour in assembly plants and manufacturing industries in Latin America while reducing labour costs within the US'. Thus, the MNCs play one against the other and secure labour-related incentives in both. 'The net effect is to increase profitability by squeezing out greater productivity per worker at lower costs, expanding market shares and creating lucrative export platforms to sell back into the *home market*' (Petras, 2007: 216).

3. *Labour migration*, which involves the mass exodus of Mexicans to the US as a result of the constrained size and precarization of the Mexican formal labour market and the process of neoliberal regional integration.

If we add indirect labour exports to the *direct exportation of the workforce* through labour migration, the true makeup of Mexico's exports is revealed. This is why we characterize the current model of export growth as *the cheap labour export-led model.*

The New Migration Dynamics

Under de labour export-led model migration from Mexico to the US has experienced an exponential growth during the past two and a half decades. This growth was accentuated by the implementation of NAFTA, which turned Mexico into the world's major migrant sender to the US. The sheer dimensions of the migration phenomenon speak for themselves: in 2007, the US population of Mexican origin—including Mexican-born documented and undocumented migrants (12 million) as well as US citizens of Mexican ascendancy—was estimated at 30 million people. It is the world's largest diaspora to be established in a single country. According to the UN (2006) estimates, during the 1990–1995 period, Mexico was the country with the largest annual number of emigrants (a total of 400,000 people vis-à-vis 390,000 from China and 280,000 from India). Between 2000 and 2005, the Mexican annual exodus rose to 560,000. The country has consequently experienced an exponential growth in remittances and, along with India, is the world's major recipient (IFAD, 2007). In 2007, the amount of remittances received by Mexico amounted to 24 billion US dollars (Banco de México, 2008).

Practically all of Mexico's territory shows incidence of international migration. In 2000, 96.2% of national municipalities experienced some type of migration-related activity. This territorial expansion has resulted in the emergence of new migration circuits (historical, indigenous-traditional, emerging, etc.) with particular dynamics and problems (Zúñiga, 2004). At the same time, even though the Mexican immigrant population in the US is still concentrated in a handful of states, in the last two decades it has expanded throughout most of the national territory. Migration circuits have also expanded to the eastern and central-northern areas (Zúñiga and Hernández-León, 2005), where some of the most dynamic centres of industrial restructuring are located (Champlin and Hake, 2006).

In 2005, 39% of the population aged 15 years and older born in Mexico and residing in the US had a level of education higher than a basic high-school diploma (Giorguli, Gaspar and Leite, 2007). In contrast, the average figure for Mexico is 33.2%, which means that in general terms and in contrast to what is commonly believed more qualified workers are leaving than remaining in the country. In other words, there is a clear selective trend, in line with the underlying rationale behind international migration. It should also be noted, however, that in comparison to other immigrant groups in the US, the Mexican contingent is the one with the lowest average levels of schooling. That situation does not attenuate the problem; on the contrary, it highlights the serious educational shortcomings that still exist in the country and that have been heightened with the adoption of neoliberal policies (OECD, 2005).

One high-profile form of labour migration that does not fall in with the stereotypes involves Mexican residents in the US with university degrees or postgraduate qualifications. This figure totals slightly more than 590,000 individuals born (CONAPO, 2008), indicating that the 'brain drain' has become a significant problem. Thus, under Mexico's prevailing maquilladora-based model there is very limited demand for qualified workers and practically no demand for scientific and technological knowledge, which leads to a hemorrhaging of highly qualified human resources.

These changes have been accompanied by transformations in the migration patterns, which have moved from circular to established migration and show increased participation on the part of women and complete families (Delgado Wise, Márquez and Rodríguez, 2004). Even though the evolution of migration flows often leads to established migration, in this case the tendency has been accompanied by a unilateral closing of the border that, in contravention of its goals, has not contained the exodus; rather, given the return risks and difficulties, it has encouraged new migrants to prolong their stay indefinitely. These changes and Mexico's decreasing birth rate have resulted in a worrisome and growing tendency toward depopulation: between 2000 and 2005, one in every two municipalities, had a negative growth rate (CONAPO, 2008).

Given the hemispheric extension of the economic political integration promoted by the US government, Mexico has also become a
transit country and must address the concomitant problems. In 2004,
nearly 400 thousand people moved through the Mexican southern
border; most of them were Central American undocumented migrants
(INM, 2005).

The Implications and Paradoxes of Regional Integration under NAFTA

It is evident that the promises made by the promoters of regional integration under NAFTA only benefited a small segment of the Mexican
and US elites, particularly the latter. This reveals the policy's true purpose and explains why its supporters continue to brag about the success
of the restructuring strategy and the regional integration scheme.

The following is a brief summary of the effects this process has
had on the Mexican economy and society, which have been the most
affected:

1. *The generation of disaccumulation processes in the Mexican economy.* The indirect export of labour force via the *maquilla* and *disguised
maquilla* industries implies a *transfer of net profits* to the US economy.
This constitutes a new mode of uneven exchange that is even more
acute that those examined in the structuralist and dependency theories
previously endorsed by the Economic Commission for Latin America
and the Caribbean (ECLAC).

2. *The loss of a labourforce whose formation costs fall on the national
economy.* Mexican labour migration represents a drain of valuable
human resources which, in turn, leads to the neglect of productive
activities, constitutes a waste of resources spent on the formation of
the emigrating labourforce, and, to an extent, the displacement of relatively qualified workforce. It also implies the transference of the reproduction costs of this labour from Mexico to the US, which according
our own estimations—based on official information—amounted 356
billion US dollars considering the population born in Mexico and
residing in the US in 2006.

Regarding this point Petras underlines that "almost all the costs
of raising workers from childhood—educational, training and health
costs—are borne by the *sender* country". This means on average "at
least 25 years investment amounting to billions of dollars in expenditures by sender countries without receiving the benefits of the pro-

ductive years, which take place in the receiver country, and facing the possibility of the return tapped-out workers once their usefulness has been exhausted". In other words, "hundreds of billions of dollars in value added labour accrues to the overseas capitalist class and the state receives the tax revenues. What is remitted by the immigrants to their families is a small percentage of the value produced" (Petras, 2007: 49).

Furthermore, "the overseas migration deprives the nation of its most innovative, skillful and ambitious workers who provide the basis for creating a diversified economy based on industry and services". What remains 'is a client state dependent on agro-mineral exports, tourism and of course immigrant remittance (ibid.).

3. *The dismantling of a substantial part of the Mexican production apparatus.* Economic regional integration and the implementation of the current export model have contributed to the progressive dismantling of the internally-focused production apparatus, which plays an irrelevant role in the neoliberal agenda. There is evidence that at least 40 production chains in the in the small—and medium-sized business sector have been destroyed after the implacable reorientation of the economy toward the external market (Cadena, 2005).

4. *The reduction and precarization of formal employment.* Neoliberal policies have failed to create high quality formal employment; rather, they have destroyed employment sources and increased precarization and flexibilization in the current formal job market. In the absence of benefits such as unemployment insurance, the informal sector is a source of precarious subsistence for large sectors of the population who have been excluded from the formal job market. The informal employment sector comprises a large population that lives at a subsistence level and serves as a labour reserve that further depreciates labour costs both in Mexico and the US. Paradoxically, the informal sector (a sort of safety net for Mexican labour market) and migrant remittances have breathed artificial life into a development model that exacerbates social inequalities and damages the country's productive activities.

To conclude this section, it is worth mentioning that the labour export-led model—as expression of the dialectic relationship between migration and development within the Mexico-US context—involves two paradoxes:

1. *Economic integration under NAFTA does not promote the development convergence between Mexico and the US. Rather, it has contributed to the expansion and deepening of asymmetries between the two
nations.* While, in 1994, the US per capita GDP was 2.6 times higher
than the Mexican one, in 2004 the gap had grown to 2.9. In 1994, US
manufacturing wages were 5.7 times higher than in Mexico; in 2004
the difference was 6.8. Paradoxically, this growing income gap does
not mirror productivity levels, which have declined. In fact, Mexico
has shown more productivity in certain sectors, particularly those
related to the labour export-led model.

2. *Economic integration has not encouraged the creation of job
opportunities in Mexico. Rather, it has become a motor of direct labour
force exporting and increased socioeconomic dependence on remittances.* According to official data, remittance reception in Mexico has
increased thirtyfold. On a macroeconomic level, remittances are the
second source of foreign currency and the one with the most consis-
tent growth rate given the relative loss of importance of other sources
of external financing (e.g. foreign direct investment, or FI, and manufactured exports). On a microeconomic level, remittances support
family consumption and ensure the subsistence of 1.6 million homes
(CONAPO, 2008). To a lesser extent, they serve to fund public works
and productive investments through programmes such as *Tres por
Uno* (Three for One).

Having taken all of this into account, it is possible to assert that
migration operates as crucial cog in the neoliberal machinery, providing it with an appearance of 'stability' and, paradoxically, a 'human
face'. On a macroeconomic level, remittances serve to extend the life
of a development model that is already showing signs of unsustain-
ability. On a microeconomic one, they help ease poverty and marginalization inasmuch as they involve a transfer of resources that lack any
solid ties to savings strategies but improve productive capacity and
economic growth. In other words, "[i]mmigrant remittances help sustain a parasitical oligarchic ruling class which uses the hard currency
remitted to pay illegal foreign debts, luxury imports and corrupt politicians. Without overseas remittances, many of the oligarchic regimes
would collapse or enter into profound crises" (Petras, 2007: 40–50).

Social Resistance and a Tentative Project of Social Transformation

The profound need for change in the structural dynamics and strategic practices at work in the current schemes of regional integration and neoliberal national development have given way to two types of social agents, which can be separated into two groups: those 'from above' and those 'from below'. The current economic project has clearly been implemented 'from above' by the agents of US imperialism in tandem with Mexican allies. They work within a political coalition that seeks to maintain the privileges of neoliberal integration and push them to its very limits. In short, this is an actual class project that promotes economic asymmetries, social inequalities and phenomena such as poverty, unemployment, labour precarization and migration.

In contrast, those 'below'—particularly in Mexico—are mostly unhappy and disenchanted, although they sometimes engage in open acts of opposition, resistance, and rebellion. It is true that there is currently no collective agent that can articulate a project that counters the one being implemented by neoliberal elites. However, we should point out that a number of disperse social alternative movements have willfully, even optimistically, sprung up.

The Mexican agricultural sector, one of the quarters that has been hardest hit by the implementation of NAFTA and is suffering in the productive, commercial, population and environmental areas, has given rise to movements like *El Barzón* (The 'Plow'), *El Campo No Aguanta Más* (The Countryside Can't Take Anymore; Bartra, 2003) and the campaign *Sin Maíz no hay País* (No Corn, no Country). Other denouncers of the neoliberal system include the *Ejército Zapatista de Liberación Nacional* (Zapatista Army of National Liberation, EZLN) and its *Otra Campaña* (Other Campaign), as well as some sectors of the social and electoral left who have converged into the *Coalición por el Bien de Todos* (Coalition for the Good of All) and the *Convención Nacional Democrática* (National Democratic Convention). There are also other more or less important national sociopolitical movements, but what is worth noticing is that the widespread popular discontent (which could even extend to the majority of Mexicans) is not expressed in an organized manner and has not produced yet an alternative development project.

On a binational level, the actions of opposition forces have been even more scattered. Initially, the *Red Mexicana de Acción frente al Libre Comercio* (Mexican Action Network in Opposition of Free Trade) communicated with likeminded organizations in the US and Canada that opposed the signing of NAFTA but since then its actions (which involve agreements between unions and social organizations on both sides of the border) have been few and far between (Brooks and Fox, 2004).

The idea that migrants are agents of development has been promoted for over a decade. This proposal, which is in no way sustainable when applied to large-scale social processes, suggests that migrants should be held responsible for promoting development in their countries of origin. And yet, as Fox (2005) has pointed out, migrant society has produced social actors who operate on three levels: (i) integration into US society (e.g. unions, the media, and religious organizations); (ii) networking and promotion of development in places of origin (i.e., native organizations), and (iii) binational relationships that combine the previous two (i.e. pan-ethnic organizations). For example, Mexican migrant organizations fund public works and social projects in their communities of origin with the aid of the Programme *Tres por Uno*. And during the spring of 2006 US-residing immigrants participated in massive marches in favour their worker's, political, social, and civil rights. As for the latter, Petras (2006) points out that 'between March 25 and May 1, 2006 close to five million migrant workers and their supporters marched through nearly 100 cities of the US'. This, he notes, is the biggest and most sustained workers' demonstration in the history of the US. In its 50-year history, the US trade union confederation, the AFL-CIO has never been capable of mobilizing even a fraction of the workers convoked by the migrant workers movement. The rise and growth of the movement is rooted in the historical experience of the migrant workers (overwhelmingly from Mexico, Central America and the Caribbean), the exploitative and racist experience they confront today in the US and the future in which they face imprisonment, expulsion and dispossession.

Generally speaking, migrants and their organizations affect the political, social, economic, and cultural aspects of sending and receiving countries to varying degrees. However, it would be a theoretical mistake to present migrants themselves as a collective agent of transformation. If we intend to portray them as agents of development, then we had better examine the strategic projects and structural dynamics present on the different planes and levels, as well as the interests that prompt participation 'from above' and 'from below'. This will allow us to understand the role played by migrants. Stating that they cannot be considered agents of development does not entail a pessimistic message advocating immobility. Quite the opposite: this can help us disentangle possible forms of articulation between migrant organizations and social sectors that seek a new type of development agenda, one that can be applied on the global, regional, national, and local levels. Only then will we be able to discuss the configuration of an agent of social transformation that includes migrant participation.

In any case, as Petras (2006), has pointed out, "[t]he emergence of the mass migrant workers' movement opens a new chapter in the working class struggle both in North America, and Central America'. First and foremost it represents the first major upsurge of independent working class struggle in the US after over fifty years of decline, stagnation and retreat by the established trade union confederation.

Final Remarks

The theoretical framework outlined in this chapter for understanding the dialectic relationship between development and migration has four critical components:

1. *A critical approach to neoliberal globalization.* Contrary to the discourse regarding its inevitability (on this see Petras and Veltmeyer, 2000) we posit that the current phase of imperialist domination is historical and can and should be transformed. In this regard, it is fundamental to notice that "[t]he principal factor generating international migration is not globalization but imperialism, which pillages nations and creates conditions for the exploitation of labour in the imperial centre" (Petras, 2007: 51–52).

2. *A critical reconstitution of the field of development studies.* The favouring of a singular mode of analysis based on the belief that free markets work as powerful regulatory mechanisms, efficiently assigning resources and providing patterns of economic convergence among countries and their populations, has clearly resulted in failure. New theoretical and practical alternatives are needed, and we propose a revaluation of development as a process of social transformation through a multidimensional, multi-spatial, and properly contextualized approach, 'using the concept of imperialism as an alternative explanatory framework of international capitalist expansion and the growing inequalities' (Petras and Veltmeyer, 2000). This integral approach requires the consideration of the strategic and structural aspects of

190   RAÚL DELGADO WISE

the dynamic of uneven contemporary capitalism development, which
should be examined at the global, regional, national, and local levels.
For this purpose it is crucial to understand, *inter alia*, a) the central
role placed by foreign investment in the process of neoliberal restructuring of peripheral economies, and b) the new modalities of surplus
transfer characterizing contemporary capitalism.

3. *Constructing an agent of change.* The globalization project led by
the US has ceased to be consensual: it has only benefited capitalist
elites and excluded and damaged an overwhelming number of people
throughout the world. Economic, political, social, cultural and environmental changes are all needed but a transformation of this magnitude is not viable unless diverse movements, classes, and agents
can establish common goals. The construction of an agent of change
requires not only an alternative theory of development but also collective action and horizontal collaboration: the sharing of experiences, the
conciliation of interests and visions, and the construction of alliances
inside the framework of South-South and South-North relations.

4. *A reassessment of migration and development studies.* The current explosion of forced migration is part of the intricate machinery of
contemporary capitalism as an expression of the dominant imperialist
project. In order to understand this process we need to redefine the
boundaries of studies that address migration and development: expand
our field of research and invert the terms of the unidirectional orthodox vision of the migration-development nexus in order to situate the
complex issues of uneven development and imperialist domination at
the centre of an alternative dialectical framework. This entails a new
way of understanding the migration phenomenon.

CHAPTER EIGHT

THE FINANCIALIZATION OF THE CAPITALIST CLASS: MONOPOLY-FINANCE CAPITAL AND THE NEW CONTRADICTORY RELATIONS OF RULING CLASS POWER

John Bellamy Foster and Hannah Holleman

Today the concept of 'financialization' stands for the shift in the centre of gravity of the capitalist economy from production to finance. Although financial speculation has always characterized the peak of the business cycle, a major secular shift toward finance in capitalism as a whole, transcending mere business cycle swings, is unique to the last few decades. Led by the US, a financial explosion first emerged in the 1970s and 1980s and eventually became a globalized phenomenon. Some have suggested that this has significantly altered the structure of ruling class power. Thus Paul Sweezy referred in the late 1990s to the 'Triumph of Financial Capital' (Sweezy, 1994: 1–11). Indeed, the last decades of the previous century and the first decade of the present one witnessed what could be called the 'financialization of the capitalist class' in the sense of a shift in the primary sources of wealth accumulation at the very top of society from production to finance.

An important question that arises from these developments is the extent to which the ruling class has actually changed. Has it metamorphosed from a class that once drew its power primarily from control over the means of production to one that now draws it primarily from control over the means of finance? To be sure, wealth in a developed capitalist economy is always held largely in the form of financial assets, i.e. as financial claims to wealth. Nevertheless, the issue now arises as to whether finance has permanently established itself as the *leading sector* in the amassing of ruling class wealth.

Making matters even more complex, we are now in the midst of the greatest financial and economic crisis since the Great Depression— one that James Petras was the first to refer to as the 'Great Financial Crisis'. This has produced immense losses within the finance sector in particular. It is still unclear, though, how much this has actually diminished the relative power of financial capital. Thus the Obama administration, which is dominated by such interests, is now pouring hundreds of billions, even trillions, of dollars into the coffers of banks and other financial institutions in an effort to stabilize their position at the apex of the system and in an attempt to reflate the speculative balloon (Foster and Magdoff, 2009; Petras, 2007). This has been called a 'quiet coup', whereby financial capital in the US has increasingly resorted to the state to preserve its tenuous economic dominance (Johnson, 2009).

We argue in what follows that the financialization of the US capitalist class is a concrete empirical reality of the last few decades. Yet, neither the continued ascendancy of financial capital nor its future demise can be regarded as certain at this point. Instead, we are presented with a contradictory and crisis-ridden reality; one that can be best characterized as a hybrid phase of monopoly-finance capital (Foster and Magdoff, 2009: 63–76). The system of concentrated capital of today has shown itself to be more and more dependent on a ballooning financial superstructure to compensate for the downward pull of economic stagnation in its underlying productive base. Yet, such financialization has failed to offer a stable solution, while generating new, irreversible sources of crisis in capitalist society.

The Changing Wealth Sectors of the US Ruling Class

This question of the growing influence of financial capital within the capitalist class as a result of the shift of the overall economy from production to finance was addressed almost twenty years ago by James Petras and Christian Davenport (1990: 33–37) in an article for the December 1990 issue of *Monthly Review* entitled 'The Changing Wealth of the US Ruling Class'. Rather than arguing the then popular notion that the US had shifted toward a post-industrial, high-technology, information economy, Petras and Davenport saw this as secondary compared to 'the ascendancy of finance, real estate, and speculative capital', symbolized at that time by the growth of the junk bond market.

In order to test this proposition, insofar as it could be seen as reflected in the US ruling class itself, Petras and Davenport looked at changes in the primary sources of wealth of the so-called "Forbes 400" a compilation of data on 'America's very richest' individuals, over the

Table 1. Distribution of the Primary Sources of Wealth of the Forbes 400:
1983 and 1988 (percentages)

	1983	1988
Finance and Real Estate	25	38
High Tech	3	4
Oil and Gas	16	8
Mass Media	16	18
Manufacturing	26	19
Retail and Other	14	14
Total	100	100

Source: Petras and Davenport (1990: 35; Forbes, October 24, 1988).

short period, 1983–1988, for which this data was then available. Their table on the changes in this period is reproduced as Table 1 above.[1]

The results that they obtained were striking. By 1988 a full 38 percent of the Forbes 400 obtained their wealth from finance and real estate, as opposed to only 25 percent in 1983, while the percentage that derived their primary wealth from manufacturing dropped from 26 to 19 percent, and the percentage gaining primarily from oil and gas fell from 16 to eight percent over the same period. As a result of these findings, they argued that there was "scant evidence to justify the claim that the US has shifted from being an industrial society to being an information society. The proportion of top capitalists with their main wealth in the high-tech sector, which was only 3 percent in 1983, was no more than 4 percent in 1988. The spread between the paper [financial] economy and high-tech actually widened from 22 percentage points in 1983 to 34 percentage points in 1988."

Petras and Davenport went on to conclude: "The data from the Forbes 400 suggest that speculator capitalists have become increasingly dominant in the US ruling class, displacing industrial and petroleum capitalists....Moreover, the speculative basis of US capitalism brings greater risk of instability. The biggest winners in recent years have been the financial and real estate sectors—and the impending recession could exacerbate their weaknesses and bring them down along with the major industrial sectors to which they are linked."

---

[1] As they observed in their piece: "Forbes's estimates are admittedly very rough, and of necessity are patched together from a variety of shaky sources, using arbitrary rules of thumb." Petras and Davenport (1990: 38). The methodology is described in Forbes, October 28, 1985.

There is no doubt that this critique of the growing speculative basis of US capitalism, presented in the late 1980s, showed considerable foresight viewed from the standpoint of today. In commenting on Petras and Davenport's argument *Monthly Review* editors Harry Magdoff and Paul M. Sweezy insisted that the real problem lay in the creeping stagnation, i.e. long-term slowdown, in US capitalism and advanced capitalism generally. The growth of an increasingly overextended financial superstructure of the economy was a countervailing factor, helping the economy to grow despite stagnation in its underlying base. The shift to finance, what we now call financialization, was therefore 'the *result*, not the cause, of the economic malaise' (Magdoff and Sweezy, 1990: 37–38). But the symptom could aggravate the disease, leading to worse problems ahead.

The degree to which financialization had begun to take over the entire political-economic structure of US capitalism manifested itself symbolically a few years after Petras and Davenport wrote their article, when Bill Clinton, shocked by the power that financial capital exerted over his administration's economic policy, queried in spring 1993: "You mean to tell me that the success of the programme and my re-election depends on the Federal Reserve and a bunch of f.…bond traders?" (quoted in Phillips, 2006: 283). This gave rise to the notion, promoted by heterodox economist E. Ray Canterbery (2000), among others, that what had emerged was a new, dominant 'bondholding class'—although the shifting nature of the capitalist class in this period is better seen as the rise to dominance of finance or speculative capital generally.

Financial Capital and Class After a Quarter-Century

When Petras and Davenport presented their thesis that a shift was occurring from production to finance as the primary wealth sector of the US capitalist class they had only five or six years of such data on which to base their observations. How do these same observations stack up almost twenty years later, now that we have a quarter-century of such data, and after a period of extended financialization of the US economy? Direct comparisons of the data with the earlier figures provided by Petras and Davenport are difficult to make due to considerable changes in the overall Forbes series, including categorization. We use the historical data reconstructed by Peter W. Bernstein and Annalyn Swan, who, in consultation with the Forbes 400 team of researchers, and utilizing the Forbes data archives, published in 2007, *All the Money in the World: How the Forbes 400 Make—and Spend— Their Fortunes.* We supplemented this with later research by the same authors published in the October 8, 2007 issue of *Forbes.*

The changing structure of Forbes 400 wealth over the twenty-five year period, from 1982–2007 is shown in Chart 1. The data presented in this more developed series constitutes an attempt to refine the Forbes 400 estimates over time. Not only do the percentages differ considerably from those provided by Petras and Davenport, the 1982 figures also do not include retail as a category, which was then subsumed under the category 'other'. The key categories of manufacturing, oil and gas, finance, and real estate, are, however, clearly shown

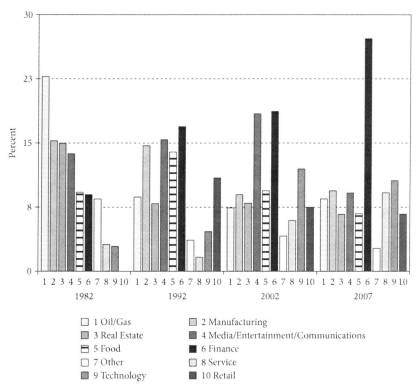

Sources: Bernstein and Swan (2007: 112–13); and "Vast Wealth," *Forbes,* October 8, 2007, 42–44.

Chart 1. Percent of the Forbes 400 Associated with Primary Sources of Wealth for Selected Years.

here, along with other crucial sectors, such as media/entertainment and communications, and technology.

In 1982 oil and gas was the primary source of wealth for 22.8 percent of the Forbes 400, with manufacturing second at 15.3 percent. Finance, in contrast, was the primary wealth sector for only 9 percent (with finance and real estate together representing 24 percent).

Only a decade later, in 1992, finance had surpassed all other areas, representing the primary source of wealth for 17 percent of the Forbes 400 (while finance plus real estate together constituted 25 percent). Oil and gas meanwhile had shrunk to 8.8 percent. Manufacturing, at 14.8 percent, had managed largely to maintain its overall share of Forbes 400 primary wealth sources, though it was now surpassed by finance, as well as a booming media, entertainment and communications sector, which had risen to 15.5 percent.

In 2002, a decade further on, finance led as the primary wealth sector for 18.8 percent of the Forbes 400 (with finance and real estate constituting 26.8 percent) while media/entertainment/communications closely followed finance at 18.5 percent.

A mere five years later, on the brink of The Great Financial Crisis, in 2007, the percentage of the Forbes 400 deriving their main source of wealth from finance had soared to 27.3 percent (while finance plus real estate accounted for about 34 percent). The nearest competitor at this time—technology—accounted for about 10.8 percent of Forbes 400 wealth. Manufacturing had sunk to 9.5 percent, although it now slightly exceeded media/entertainment/communications (9.3 percent). Overall the shift in a quarter-century had been substantial. In 1982 manufacturing had exceeded finance as a primary source of wealth for the Forbes 400 by 6 percentage points. In 2007 finance exceeded manufacturing by 18 percentage points.

How representative is this of trends in the US ruling class as a whole? This is not easy to answer, since comparable data for the entire capitalist class is not available. Of course, the Forbes 400 richest Americans comprise only an infinitesimal proportion of those belonging to the capitalist class, the dimensions of which could be roughly equated with the super rich-often thought of in terms of the top 1 percent (or at most the top 5 percent) of wealth holders. Even so, the Forbes 400, due to their level of wealth dominance, arguably constitute a good indicator of trends within the capitalist class as a whole. The average wealth of those in the Forbes 400, according to *Forbes* (October 6, 2008) was $3.9 billion per person, while their aggregate wealth was a by no means insignificant $1.57 trillion. This constituted 2.4 percent of household wealth (using 2007 figures for the latter). The richest 400 Americans own a very large share—around 7 percent—of the wealth of the top 1 percent of wealth holders in the US, which in 2007 was 33.8 percent of all net worth in the country. Aggregate Forbes 400 wealth is about equal to the GDP of Canada, or more than 10 percent of US national income. The trend in the sector distribution of Forbes 400 wealth is therefore a significant marker of the shift in the direction of the economy itself (*Forbes*, December 25, 2008; *Forbes*, October 6, 2008: 30; Reuters, March 12, 2009; Kennickell, 2004: 4–7; Federal Reserve Board, 2009: 35, Table 4; Domhoff, 2009).

Speculative Bubbles and Financialization

Viewing the last quarter-century as a whole, the overall trend in wealth at the very top of US capitalism, as the Forbes 400 data highlights, has been one of a dramatic shift toward speculative finance as the primary source of wealth, reflecting the overall financialization of the US economy in this period. The causes of the turn to the finance sector recorded by this data are complex. Nevertheless, they can be traced through the theory introduced by such twentieth-century Marxist political economists as Michal Kalecki, Josef Steindl, Paul Baran, Paul Sweezy, and Harry Magdoff, to tendencies toward monopolization and stagnation. In essence, the giant corporations generate more economic surplus than they are able to find profitable investment outlets for—given structural weaknesses in demand caused by insufficient real wage growth and a tendency toward growing idle capacity inhibiting investment. The result is a long-term decline in net investment. The system thus gravitates toward slow growth or stagnation, compensated for by various factors, such as military spending, and more recently financial expansion.

The diversion of surplus investment-seeking capital into speculation on asset prices—and the creation by the financial services industries of seemingly endless new products to absorb this inflow capital while leveraging it upward with ever larger amounts of debt—constituted the new phenomenon of financialization, viewed as a long-term and global process. In the US economy the profits of financial corporations grew from 13 percent of domestic corporate profits in 1965 to 44 percent in 2003 (Council of Economic Advisers, 2008). Average compensation in the financial sector also jumped. As Simon Johnson, professor at MIT's Sloan School of Management, noted, "From 1948 to 1982, average compensation in the financial sector ranged between 99 percent and 108 percent of the average for all domestic private industries. From 1983, it shot upward, reaching 181 percent in 2007" (Johnson, 2009). In fact, economists Thomas Philippon and Ariell Reshef (2008: 3–4) circulated a paper that demonstrated that wages of the financial sector relative to the rest of private industry followed what they call a "U-shaped pattern from 1909 to 2006". In the 1920s relative pay in finance shot up, but this wage premium was lost in the 1930s, before beginning to rise again in the 1980s, reaching the same heights as in the late 1920s (before the 1929 crash) by 2006 (Johnson, 2009; Edmunds, 2006: 118–33). Reflecting this financialization of the system, the wealth of the top tier of the capitalist class, as we have seen, increasingly came from the financial sector. It was the finance king Warren Buffet, even more than the technology king, Bill Gates, who most exemplified the new age of monopoly-finance capital.

Financialization, conceived in these terms, was a long-term response of the system to stagnation or the slowdown in growth of the underlying economy. Under these circumstances FIRE (finance, insurance, and real estate) helped lift the economy, providing new sources of demand. It continued as a long-term process despite the periodic bursting of financial bubbles—such as the stock market crash of 1987, the Savings and Loan crisis of the late 1980s and early 1990s, the Asian financial crisis of the late 1990s, the New Economy crash of 2000—during these same decades. In spite of such periodic severe credit crunches financialization remained a seemingly unstoppable trend, leading to new and greater bubbles—and the expectation each time that this system had freed itself from the real economy of production, creating enhanced asset values endlessly out of the buying and trading of paper claims to wealth.

Perhaps the most fantastic example of such illusions was an article by financial economist John C. Edmunds, entitled, "Securities: The New World Wealth Machine," published in *Foreign Policy* in 1996. Edmunds claimed that securitization or the repackaging and bundling of a myriad of financial claims into "high quality bonds and stocks" constituted "the most powerful engine of wealth creation in today's world economy" and had far surpassed the relatively minute processes of actual production. "Securitization," Edmunds argued, "creates value as it spreads." Governments should, he suggested, no longer

focus on economic growth but on wealth creation through asset inflation, resulting from the magic of securitization. "More and more," he
wrote, "states have the opportunity to benefit from the global increase
in wealth that securitization has brought. We have entered a new economic age" (Edmunds, 1996). A little more than a decade later this
'new economic age' had generated the greatest financial and economic
crisis since the Great Depression of the 1930s. The mortgage-based
securities glorified by Edmunds and others had turned into financial
toxic waste.

The US Economy and the Future of Financial Dominance

If recent decades saw 'the triumph of financial capital', we are now wit-
nessing the greatest financial crisis since the 1929 stock market crash.
Taken together these seem to represent contradictory tendencies.

On one side of the coin, 'big banks', as Johnson observed in the
Atlantic in May 2009, "have only gained political strength since the
crisis began.... With the financial system so fragile, the damage that
a major bank failure could cause—Lehman was small relative to
Citigroup or Bank of America—is much greater than it would be during ordinary times. The banks have been exploiting this fear as they
wring favourable deals out of Washington. Bank of America obtained
its second bailout package (in January) after warning the government
that it might not be able to go through the acquisition of Merrill
Lynch, a prospect that Treasury did not want to consider." Indeed,
as Senate Majority Whip Richard Durbin of Illinois has noted: "The
banks—hard to believe in a time when we're facing a banking crisis
that many of the banks created—are still the most powerful lobby on
Capitol Hill. And they frankly own the place" (Johnson, 2009; Durban,
quoted in Moyers and Winship, 2009; Krugman, 2009).

Yet, on the other side of the coin, just as the domination of finance
within the US ruling class and its centrality to the economy and the
global system as a whole has become crystal clear, its future, given the
arrested state of bank lending and the new era of financial risk avoidance, is in question. The stock market crash of 1929 that ignited the
Great Depression of the 1930s resulted in the US government attempts
to salvage banks. But it also led in the long-term to a decline in the
power and influence of financial capital in relation to industrial capital.
Much tighter regulations were imposed on the former in the decades

that followed. Some economists are arguing that the economy needs to be steered clear of financial dominance.

The approach of the Obama administration with regards to these matters at present seems very straightforward. Treasury Secretary Timothy Geithner and Obama's chief economic adviser Lawrence Summers, director of the White House's National Economic Council, both worked under banker-financier Robert Rubin when the latter was Clinton's first Treasury Secretary (Summers succeeded in the job) and are widely viewed as Rubin's protégées. Rubin was employed for 26 years by Goldman Sachs prior to becoming Clinton's Treasury secretary. After leaving the administration he became a director and senior counselor at Citigroup (resigning in January 2009). Geithner, according to the *New York Times*, has also been particularly close to Sanford Weill, the financial baron who assembled Citigroup. Weill proudly displays in the carpeted hallway of his skyscraper Manhattan office the pen with which President Clinton revoked the Glass-Steagall Act in 1999, thereby removing the main regulatory measures which restricted the growth and concentration of financial institutions by creating firewalls separating commercial and investment banking and stock brokerage (Uchitelle, 2007). Rubin, Summers and Geithner played leading roles (along with Alan Greenspan as chairman of the Federal Reserve, assisted by current Federal Reserve chairman Ben Bernanke who was then a Federal Reserve governor) in the US government's promotion of the financial bubbles of the late 1990s and early 2000s.

Obama's choice of these particular figures to direct economic policy in his administration in the context of the worst financial crisis since the Great Depression was an indication that the goal was not to change, but to stabilize, and if possible restart, the financialization process. There can be little doubt that this reflects the power, as we have seen, of finance within the ruling class, and not simply the economic needs of the country. As of May 2009 the US government had committed $14.9 trillion in the form of capital infusions, loans, and debt guarantees primarily to the financial sector in the context of this crisis. The great bulk of this, according to the *Wall Street Journal* (May 21, 2009), "is designated for propping up areas including money-market mutual funds and commercial-paper markets, and for purchases of asset backed securities." One problem, according to the *Wall Street Journal*, is that government aid appears to be becoming 'entrenched' and won't necessarily go away when the recovery starts.

Some, however, even within the mainstream economic tradition—including Paul Krugman and Joseph Stiglitz (both winners of the Bank of Sweden's Nobel Memorial Prize in Economic Sciences), along with more heterodox economists like James K. Galbraith—argue for nationalization of troubled banks, increased regulation, pulling the economy back from an emphasis on finance, and re-grounding it in production. Krugman wants to see the country go back to what he calls 'the era of boring banking' that succeeded the 1930s, during which finance played a distinctly secondary role in the economy. If restrictions on finance are not imposed, he warns, "the current crisis won't be a one-time event; it will be the shape of things to come" (Krugman, 2009).

Still, these critics are well outside the administration at present, and are bucking the high tide of financial power built up for decades, which is governing the economic rescue effort. As James Petras (2007) noted early in the crisis, this has become a problem for the entire capitalist class: "the risk of letting the bad boys sink is that there are too many of them, working in most of the most powerful investment houses, managing too many funds, for the most powerful financiers." If anything, this has become far clearer as we have gone further into the "Black Hole of the financial crisis" (Petras, 2007).

Indeed, it is highly unlikely that the Obama administration—or, more to the point, a US ruling class increasingly geared to financialization—will take advice to de-financialize the economy seriously, barring a major social revolt from below that changes the power constellation of US society. With the underlying capitalist economy slowing down decade by decade, the only substantial stimulus during this period has come from financial bubbles (Foster and Magdoff, 2009: 11–40). In this sense the system is caught in a trap of its own making with no obvious way out. Although further financialization (if possible) will only worsen the overall problem, no other immediate options present themselves. Financial globalization based on dollar hegemony further limits US options, if the crisis is not to be followed by a crash of the dollar itself, and with it the US economy and empire. From the standpoint of contemporary monopoly-finance capital then there is no visible exit strategy. Indeed, all rational human courses of action point beyond the present system.

CHAPTER NINE

FOOD, WATER AND FUEL:
THE CRISIS OF LIFE UNDER CAPITALISM

Michel Chossudovsky

The sugar-coated bullets of the [free market' are killing our children. The act to kill is unpremeditated. It is instrumented in a detached fashion through computer programme trading on the New York and Chicago mercantile exchanges, where the global prices of rice, wheat and corn are decided upon. Poverty is not solely the result of policy failures at a national level. People in different countries are being impoverished simultaneously as a result of a global market mechanism. A small number of financial institutions and global corporations have the ability to determine, through market manipulation, the standard of living of millions of people around the World.

We are at the crossroads of the most serious economic and social crisis in modern history. The process of global impoverishment unleashed at the outset of the 1980s debt crisis has reached a major turning point, leading to the simultaneous outbreak of famines in all major regions of the developing World. There are many complex features underlying the global economic crisis pertaining to financial markets, the decline in production, the collapse of state institutions and the rapid development of a profit-driven war economy. What is rarely mentioned in this analysis is how this global economic restructuring forcibly impinges on three fundamental necessities of life: food, water and fuel.

The provision of food, water and fuel is a precondition of civilized society. They are necessary factors for the survival of the human species as well as basic human needs. In recent years, the prices of these commodified goods have increased dramatically at the global level, with devastating economic and social consequences (Engdahl, 2007).

These three essential goods or commodities, which in a real sense determine the reproduction of economic and social life on planet earth, are under the control of a small number of global corporations and financial institutions that make up what neoliberals and neoconservatives term 'forces of freedom'—forces that the capitalist state in its diverse forms and current regimes are committed to protect and advance. Both the State as well as the gamut of international organizations—often referred to as the 'international community'—serve the interests of global capitalism be they unfettered as prescribed by the neoliberal model or fettered (regulated) as prescribed by Keynesian and institutional economists (Petras and Veltmeyer, 2001, 2003, 2005). The main intergovernmental bodies, including the United Nations and the original Bretton Woods institutions as well as the then still-born (in 1944) but now reconstituted (50 years later) World Trade Organization, have endorsed the New World Order on behalf of their corporate sponsors. In the name of this new world order—the price of admission, in effect—governments in both developed and developing countries have abandoned their historical role of regulating key economic activities and the markets of the private sector, especially in regard to the financial institutions and capitalist corporations in this sector. As a result they also abrogated their historical responsiblity (in the context of the welfare and development state formed respectively in the wake of the Great Depression and the a post-war decolonization)[1] for ensuring a minimum standard of living and livelihood for their people.

Protest movements directed against the hikes in the prices of food and gasoline have erupted simultaneously in different regions of the World. On this see inter alia several studies by James Petras published in *Rebelion* as well *Global Research* (1). Conditions are particularly critical in Haiti, Nicaragua, Guatemala, India and Bangladesh but the global crisis in the current conjuncture is exacerbating conditions in many other parts of the world as well. Spiraling food and fuel prices in Somalia have precipitated the entire country into a situation of mass starvation, coupled with severe water shortages. A similar and equally serious situation prevails in Ethiopia.

Other countries affected by spiraling food prices include Indonesia, the Philippines, Liberia, Egypt, Sudan, Mozambique, Zimbabwe, Kenya, Eritrea—a long list of impoverished countries not to mention those under foreign military occupation, including Iraq, Afghanistan and Palestine.

---

[1] Please Supply Footnote text.

The Crisis Dynamics of Financial and Market Deregulation

The provision of food, water and fuel are no longer the object of governmental or intergovernmental regulation or intervention, with a view to alleviating poverty or averting the outbreak of famines. The fate of millions of human beings is managed behind closed doors in the corporate boardrooms as part of a profit-driven agenda. And because these powerful economic actors operate through a seemingly neutral and 'invisible' market mechanism, the devastating social impacts of engineered hikes in the prices of food, fuel and water are casually dismissed as the result of supply and demand forces that are beyond control.

The Nature of the Global Economic and Social Crisis

Largely obfuscated by official and media reports, both the 'food crisis' and the 'oil crisis' are the result of the speculative manipulation of market values by powerful economic actors.

We are not dealing with distinct and separate food, fuel and water 'crises' but with a single global process of economic and social restructuring that is designed to shed labour as well as reduce the rate of participation of labour in the global social product. In the context of this 'restructuring', as shown by Walden Bello in his contribution to this festschrift, the dramatic price hikes of these three essential commodities is anything but haphazard or incidental. All three variables, including the prices of basic food staples, water for production and consumption, and fuel are the object of deliberate and simultaneous market manipulation.

At the heart of the food crisis is the rising price of food staples coupled with a dramatic increase in the price of fuel. Concurrently, the price of water, an essential input into agricultural and industrial production, social infrastructure, public sanitation and household consumption has increased abruptly as a result of a worldwide push to privatize water resources (Barlow and Clarke, 2004).

We are dealing with a major economic and social upheaval, an unprecedented global crisis, characterized by the triangular relationship between water, food and fuel: three fundamental variables, which together affect the very means of human survival.

In very concrete terms, these price hikes impoverish and destroy people's lives. Moreover, the worldwide collapse in living standards is occurring at a time of war. It is intimately related to the military agenda. The war in the Middle East bears a direct relationship to the control over oil and water reserves.

While water is not at present an internationally tradeable or traded commodity in the same way as oil and food staples, it is also the object of market manipulation through the privatization of water. The economic and financial actors operating behind closed doors include:

- the major Wall Street banks and financial houses, including the institutional speculators which play a direct role in commodity markets including the oil and food markets
- The Anglo-American oil giants, including British Petroleum, Exxon-Mobil, Chevron-Texaco, Royal Dutch Shell
- The biotech-agribusiness conglomerates, which own the intellectual property rights on seeds and farm inputs. The biotech companies are also major actors on the New York and Chicago mercantile exchanges
- The water giants including Suez, Veolia and Bechtel-United Utilities, involved in the extensive privatization of the world's water resources
- The Anglo-American military-industrial complex which includes the big five US defense contractors (Lockheed Martin, Raytheon, Northrop Grunman, Boeing and General Dynamics) in alliance with British Aerospace Systems Corporation (BAES) constitutes a powerful overlapping force, closely aligned with Wall Street, the oil giants and the agribusiness-biotech conglomerates.

The Oil Price Bubble

The movement in global prices on the New York and Chicago mercantile exchanges bears no relationship to the costs of producing oil. The spiraling price of crude oil is not the result of a shortage of oil. It is estimated that the cost of a barrel of oil in the Middle East does not exceed 15 dollars. The cost of a barrel of oil extracted from the tar sands of Alberta, Canada, is of the order of $30 (Antoine Ayoub, Radio Canada, May 2008). The price of crude oil is currently in excess of $120 a barrel. This market price is largely the result of the speculative onslaught.

Oil Prices, 1994-March 2008

NYMEX Light Sweet / WTI

Oil Prices, 2006-2008

NYMEX Light Sweet

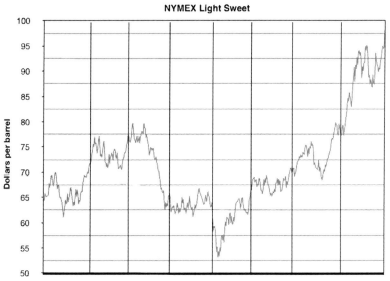

Source: NYMEX

Fuel enters into the production of virtually all areas of manufacturing, agriculture and the services economy. The hikes in fuel prices have contributed, in all major regions of the World, to precipitating tens of thousands of small and medium sized businesses into bankruptcy as well as undermining and potentially paralyzing the channels of domestic and international trade.

The increased cost of gasoline at the retail level is leading to the demise of local level economies, increased industrial concentration and a massive centralization of economic power in the hands of a small number of global corporations. In turn, the hikes in fuel backlash on the urban transit system, schools and hospitals, the trucking industry, intercontinental shipping, airline transportation, tourism, recreation and most public services.

Inflation

The rise in fuel prices unleashes a broader inflationary process that results in a compression of real purchasing power and a consequent worldwide decline in consumer demand. All major sectors of society, including the middle classes in the developed countries are affected.

These price movements are dictated by the commodity markets. They are the result of speculative trade in index funds, futures and options on major commodity markets including the London ICE, the New York and Chicago mercantile exchanges. The dramatic price hikes are not the result of a shortage of fuel, food or water.

The upheaval in the global economy is in fact deliberate. The State's economic and financial policies are controlled by private corporate interests. Speculative trade is not the object of regulatory policies. The economic depression contributes to wealth formation—to enhancing the power of a handful of global corporations. According to William Engdahl, at least 60% of the 128 per barrel price of crude oil comes from unregulated futures speculation by hedge funds, banks and financial groups using the London ICE Futures and New York NYMEX futures exchanges and uncontrolled inter-bank or over-the-counter trading to avoid scrutiny. US margin rules of the government's Commodity Futures Trading Commission allow speculators to buy a crude oil futures contract on the Nymex by having to pay only 6% of the value of the contract. At today's price of $128 per barrel that means a futures trader only has to put up about $8 for every barrel. He borrows the other $120. This extreme 'leverage' of 16 to 1 helps drive prices to wildly unrealistic levels and offset bank losses in sub-prime and other disasters at the expense of the overall population (*Global Research*, May 2008).

Among the main players in the speculative market for crude oil are Goldman Sachs, Morgan Stanley, British Petroleum (BP), the French banking conglomerate Société Générale, Bank of America, the largest Bank in the US, and Switzerland's Mercuria (Miguel Angel Blanco, La Clave, Madrid, June 2008). British Petroleum controls the London based International Petroleum Exchange (IPE), which is one of the world's largest energy futures and options exchanges. IPE's major shareholders include Goldman Sachs and Morgan Stanley. According to Der Spiegel, Morgan Stanley is one of the main institutional actors in the London based speculative oil market (IPE). According to Le Monde, France's Société Générale together with Bank of America and Deutsche Bank have been involved in spreading rumors with a view to pushing up the price of crude oil (See Miguel Angel Blanco, *La Clave*, Madrid, June 2008).

Spiraling Food Prices

The global food crisis, characterized by major hikes in the prices of basic food staples has spearheaded millions of people around the World into starvation and chronic deprivation.

According to the FAO, the price of grain staples has increased by 88% since March 2007. The price of wheat has increased by 181% over a three-year period. The price of rice has increased by 50% over the last three months (Angus, 2008; *GlobalResearch*, April 2008). The price of rice has tripled over a five year period, from approximately 600$ a ton in 2003 to more than 1800$ a ton in May 2008 (see chart below).

The most popular grade of Thailand rice sold for $198 a ton, five years ago and $323 a ton a year ago. In April 2008, the price hit $1,000. Increases are even greater on local markets: in Haiti, the market price of a 50 kilo bag of rice doubled in one week at the end of March 2008. These increases are catastrophic for the 2.6 billion people around the world who live on less than US$2 a day and spend 60 to 80 per cent of their incomes on food. Hundreds of millions cannot afford to eat' (ibid.).

RICE

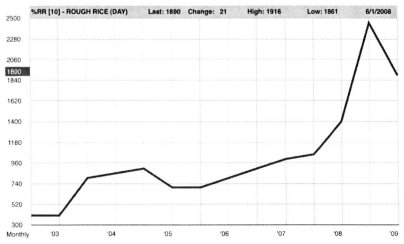

Source: CME Group / Chicago Board of Trade (CBOT)

WHEAT

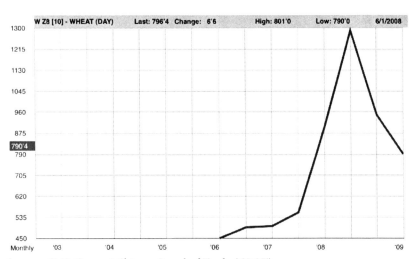

Source: CME Group / Chicago Board of Trade (CBOT)

CORN

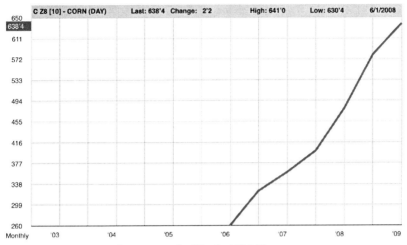

Source: CME Group / Chicago Board of Trade (CBOT)

The main actors in the grain market are Cargill and Archer Daniels Midland (ADM). These two corporate giants control a large share of the global grain market. They are also involved in speculative transactions in futures and options on the NYMEX and the Chicago Board of Trade (CBOT). In the US, 'the world's largest grower of GM crops, Cargill, ADM and competitor Zen Noh between them control 81 percent of all maize exports and 65 percent of all soyabean exports' (Muttitt, 2001).

Background of Agricultural Reform

Since the early 1980s coinciding with the onslaught of the debt crisis, the gamut of neoliberal macroeconomic policy reforms have largely contributed to undermining local agriculture. Over the last 25 years, food farming in developing countries has been destabilized and destroyed by the imposition of IMF-World Bank reforms.

Commodity dumping of grain surpluses from the US, Canada and the European Union has led to the demise of food self-sufficiency and the destruction of the local peasant economy. In turn, this process has resulted in multi-billion dollar profits for Western agribusiness, resulting from import contracts by developing countries, which are no longer able to produce their own food. These preexisting historical conditions of mass poverty have been exacerbated and aggravated by the recent surge in grain prices, which have led in some cases to the doubling of the retail price of food staples. The price hikes has also been exacerbated by the use of corn to produce ethanol. In 2007, global production of corn was of the order of 12.32 billion bushels of which 3.2 billion were used for ethanol production. Almost 40 percent of corn production in the US will be channeled towards ethanol.

Genetically Modified Seeds

Coinciding with the establishment the World Trade Organization (WTO) in 1995, another important historical change has occurred in the structure of global agriculture.

Under the articles of agreement of the WTO, the food giants have been granted unrestricted freedom to enter the seeds' markets of developing countries.

The acquisition of exclusive 'intellectual property rights' over plant varieties by international agroindustrial interests, also favours the destruction of biodiversity. Acting on behalf of a handful of biotech conglomerates GMO seeds have been imposed on farmers, often in the context of 'food aid programmes'. In Ethiopia, for instance, kits of GMO seeds were handed out to impoverished farmers with a view to rehabilitating agricultural production in the wake of a major drought.

The GMO seeds were planted, yielding a harvest. But then the farmer came to realize that the GMO seeds could not be replanted without paying royalties to Monsanto, Arch Daniel Midland et al. Then the farmers discovered that the seeds would harvest only if they used the farm inputs including the fertilizer, insecticide and herbicide, produced and distributed by the biotech agribusiness companies. Entire peasant economies were locked into the grip of the agribusiness conglomerates.

The main biotech giants in GMO include Monsanto, Syngenta, Aventis, DuPont, Dow Chemical, Cargill and Arch Daniel Midland. Breaking The Agricultural Cycle. With the widespread adoption of GMO seeds, a major transition has occurred in the structure and history of settled agriculture since its inception 10,000 years ago. The reproduction of seeds at the village level in local nurseries has been disrupted by the use of genetically modified seeds. The agricultural cycle that enables farmers to store their organic seeds and plant them to reap the next harvest has been broken. This destructive pattern—invariably resulting in famine—is replicated in country after country leading to the worldwide demise of the peasant economy.

The FAO-World Bank Consensus

At the June 2008 FAO Rome Summit on the food crisis, politicians and economic analysts alike embraced the free market consensus: the outbreak of famines was presented as a result of the usual supply, demand and climatic considerations, beyond the control of policymakers. 'The solution': to channel emergency relief to affected areas under the auspices of the World Food Programme (WFP). That is, do not intervene with the interplay of market forces. Ironically, these 'expert opinions' are refuted by the data on global grain production: FAO forecasts for world cereal production point to a record output in 2008.

Contradicting their own textbook explanations, according to the World Bank, world prices are expected to remain high, despite the forecasted increased supply of food staples.

State regulation of the prices of food staples and gasoline is not considered an option in the corridors of the FAO and the World Bank. And of course that is what is taught in the economics departments of America's most prestigious universities. Meanwhile, local level farm-gate prices barely cover production costs, spearheading the peasant economy into bankruptcy.

The Privatization of Water

According to UN sources, which vastly underestimate the seriousness of the water crisis, one billion people worldwide (15% of the World population) have no access to clean water "and 6,000 children die every day because of infections linked to unclean water" (*BBC News*, 24 March 2004).

A handful of global corporations including Suez, Veolia, Bechtel-United Utilities, Thames Water and Germany's RWE-AG are acquiring control and ownership over public water utilities and waste management. Suez and Veolia hold about 70 per cent of the privatized water systems Worldwide.

The privatization of water under World Bank auspices feeds on the collapse of the system of public distribution of safe tap drinking water: "The World Bank serves the interests of water companies both through its regular loan programmes to governments, which often come with conditions that explicitly require the privatization of water provision..." (Barlow and Clarke, 2004). "The modus operandi [in India] is clear—neglect development of water resources [under World Bank budget austerity measures], claim a 'resource crunch' and allow existing systems to deteriorate" (Ninan, 2003).

Meanwhile, the markets for bottled water have been appropriated by a handful of corporations including Coca-Cola, Danone, Nestlé and PepsiCo. These companies not only work hand in glove with the water utility companies, they are linked up to the agribusiness-biotech companies involved in the food industry. Tap water is purchased by Coca-Cola from a municipal water facility and then resold on a retail basis. It is estimated that in the US, 40 per cent of bottled water is tap water (Blumenfeld and Leal, 2007).

In India, Coca-Cola has contributed to the depletion of ground water to the detriment of local communities. Communities across India living around Coca-Cola's bottling plants are experiencing severe water shortages, directly as a result of Coca-Cola's massive extraction of water from the common groundwater resource. The wells have run dry and the hand water pumps do not work any more. Studies, including one by the Central Ground Water Board in India, have confirmed the significant depletion of the water table. When the water is extracted from the common groundwater resource by digging deeper, the water smells and tastes strange. Coca-Cola has been indiscriminately discharging its waste water into the fields around its plant and sometimes into rivers, including the Ganges, in the area. The result has been that the groundwater has been polluted as well as the soil. Public health authorities have posted signs around wells and hand pumps advising the community that the water is unfit for human consumption.

Tests conducted by a variety of agencies, including the government of India, confirmed that Coca-Cola products contained high levels of pesticides, and as a result, the Parliament of India has banned the sale of Coca-Cola in its cafeteria. However, Coca-Cola not only continues to sell drinks laced with poisons in India (that could never be sold in the US and EU), it is also introducing new products in the Indian market. And as if selling drinks with DDT and other pesticides to Indians was not enough, one of Coca-Cola's latest bottling facilities to open in India, in Ballia, is located in an area with a severe contamination of arsenic in its groundwater (India Resource Centre, *Coca-Cola Crisis in India*, undated).

In developing countries, the hikes in fuel prices have increased the costs of boiling tap water by households, which in turn favours the privatization of water resources.

In the more advanced phase of water privatization, the actual ownership of lakes and rivers by private corporations is contemplated. Mesopotamia was not only invaded for its extensive oil resources, the Valley of the two rivers (the Tigris and Euphrates) has extensive water reserves.

Concluding Remarks

We are dealing with a complex and centralized constellation of economic power in which the instruments of market manipulation have a direct bearing on the lives of millions of people.

The prices of food, water, fuel are determined at the global level, beyond the reach of national government policy. The price hikes of these three essential commodities constitute an instrument of 'economic warfare', carried out through the 'free market' on the futures and options exchanges.

These hikes in the price of food, water and fuel are contributing in a very real sense to 'eliminating the poor' through 'starvation deaths'. The sugar-coated bullets of the 'free market' kill our children. The act to kill is instrumented in a detached fashion through computer programme trading on the commodity exchanges, where the global prices of rice, wheat and corn are decided upon ('The Commission on Population Growth and the American Future').

But we are not dealing solely with market concepts. The outbreak of famines in different parts of the World, resulting from spiraling food and fuel prices have broad strategic and geopolitical implications. President Richard Nixon at the outset of his term in office in 1969 asserted "his belief that overpopulation gravely threatens world peace and stability". Henry Kissinger, who at the time was Nixon's National Security adviser, directed various agencies of government to jointly undertake "a study of the impact of world population growth on US security and overseas interests". In March 1970, the US Congress set up a Commission on Population Growth and the American Future (Centre for Research on Population and Security).

The Commission was no ordinary Task Force. It integrated representatives from USAID, the State Department and the Department of Agriculture with CIA and Pentagon officials. Its objective was not to assist developing countries but rather to curb World population with a view to serving US strategic and national security interests. The Commission also viewed population control as a means to ensuring a stable and secure environment for US investors as well as gaining control over developing countries' mineral and petroleum resources.

This Commission completed its work in December 1974 and circulated a classified document entitled *National Security Study Memorandum 200: Implications of Worldwide Population Growth for US Security and Overseas Interests to Designated Secretaries and Agency Heads for their Review and Comments*. In November 1975, the Report and its recommendations were endorsed by President Gerald Ford. It turns out that Kissinger had indeed intimated in the context of the 'National Security Study Memorandum 200' that the recurrence of famines, disease and war could constitute a de facto instrument of population control.

Although the NSSM 200 report did not assign, for obvious reasons, an explicit policy role to famine formation, it nonetheless intimated that the occurrence of famines could, under certain circumstances, provide a de facto solution to overpopulation. Accordingly, those countries where large-scale hunger and malnutrition are already present face the bleak prospect of little, if any, improvement in the food intake in the years ahead barring a major foreign financial food aid programme, more rapid expansion of domestic food production, reduced population growth or some combination of all three. Worse yet, a series of crop disasters could transform some of them into classic Malthusian cases with famines involving millions of people.

While foreign assistance probably will continue to be forthcoming to meet short-term emergency situations like the threat of mass starvation, it is more questionable whether aid donor countries will be prepared to provide the sort of massive food aid called for by the import projections on a long-term continuing basis.

Reduced population growth rates clearly could bring significant relief over the longer term. In the extreme cases where population pressures lead to endemic famine, food riots, and breakdown of social order, those conditions are scarcely conducive to systematic exploration for mineral deposits or the long-term investments required for their exploitation. Short of famine, unless some minimum of popular aspirations for material improvement can be satisfied, and unless the terms of access and exploitation persuade governments and peoples that this aspect of the international economic order has "something in it for them", concessions to foreign companies are likely to be expropriated or subjected to arbitrary intervention. Whether through government action, labour conflicts, sabotage, or civil disturbance, the smooth flow of needed materials will be jeopardized. Although population pressure is obviously not the only factor involved, these types of frustrations are much less likely under conditions of slow or zero population growth (NSC, 2004).

The report concludes with a couple of key questions pertaining to the role of food as 'an instrument of national power', which could be used in the pursuit of US strategic interests. "On what basis should such food resources then be provided? Would food be considered an instrument of national power? Will we be forced to make choices as to whom we can reasonably assist, and if so, should population efforts be a criterion for such assistance? Is the US prepared to accept food rationing to help people who can't/won't control their population growth?" (ibid.). In the words of Henry Kissinger: "Control oil and you control nations; control food and you control the people".

POLITICAL DYNAMICS OF US IMPERIALISM

CHAPTER TEN

'NOT ABOUT TO LOSE CHILE':[1]
DEMOCRATIC SOCIALISM CONFRONTS
THE IMPERIAL STATE

Morris Morley

The US response to democratic socialist rule in Chile between 1970 and 1973 must be placed within the context of its global and regional policy imperatives. Since the late 1940, the US had been locked in a worldwide political, economic and ideological conflict with the Soviet Union. When Richard Nixon entered the White House in January 1969, he confronted a number of interrelated global problems that threatened America's position as the world's dominant power: how to end the war in Vietnam—whose costs had weakened America's ability to compete economically on the world stage with powerful capitalist allies in Europe and Asia; how to maintain the postwar policy of 'containment' of the Soviet Union and China, especially given that the former was now a military superpower; and how to confront a resurgent nationalism in the Third World.

The President and his National Security Council (NSC) Adviser Henry Kissinger quickly concluded that if America was to maintain a stable global order and its status as *the* global hegemon, and solve these various challenges, it had to devise an alternative, more cost effective means of 'containing communism' and pursuing US Cold War foreign policy objectives into the 1970s. The outcome of their thinking was the idea of détente, based on developing a new relationship with the two most powerful communist states. The strategic objective was to gain the participation of the Soviet Union and China in a new international system the White House was intent on constructing, based on the notion of 'linkage' politics, that would commit all participants to ensuring global stability: in return for applying their perceived influence with

---

[1] All footnoted documents are declassified under US Freedom of Information Act. 'Truman had lost China, Kennedy had lost Cuba. Nixon was not about to lose Chile.' CIA Director Richard Helms quoted in Munoz (2008: 67).

Third World nationalist and revolutionary states or movements to end conflicts (especially in Vietnam), and/or dampen down unrest in these regions, Moscow and Beijing would receive significant economic and political rewards. Thus began a process of bridge building, highlighted by Nixon's 1972 path-breaking trips to Beijing, which ultimately led to the restoration of full diplomatic relations, and to Moscow where he signed the Strategic Arms Limitations Treaty (SALT 1) and sought to enmesh the Soviets in a web of trade, technology, investment and mutual cooperation agreements with Washington (Garthoff, 1994: 279–403; Isaacson, 1992: 399–438; Bowker and Williams, 1988: 30–61).

This new emphasis on geopolitics did not imply a downgrading of anticommunist ideology in the shaping of Nixon-Kissinger foreign policy, especially as it related to Western Europe. By the early 1970s, Communist Parties were beginning to emerge as the potential contenders for political power in coalition governments, especially in Italy and Portugal, but also France and even in a post-Franco Spain if the Communist Party was legalized. 'It is hard to imagine', Kissinger told a group of US Ambassadors stationed in European capitals, 'that if one or the other of these [Communist Parties] takes control of a Western government, it will permit the democratic process to operate and thereby face the possibility that it may itself be removed from office....' (Kissinger 1999: 628). Railing against what came to be described as 'Eurocommunism,' he dismissed out of hand the idea of national Communist Parties pursuing foreign policies independently of the Soviet Union and willing to pursue their socialist objectives via the parliamentary system (Kissinger, 1979: 659). This was simply another means of promoting Soviet objectives on the continent 'and a grave threat to the Western Alliance' (Schneidman 2004: 146).

Embedded in Nixon and Kissinger's carefully thought-out conceptual framework were two flawed assumptions that contributed mightily to the ultimate unraveling of the détente strategy. First was a belief that the Soviet Union needed détente more than the US and would be willing to make greater concessions. It would be more receptive to 'self containment' and accept that further efforts to project its power globally, especially in the Third World, were inconsistent with détente. But as far as Moscow was concerned, the whole idea of détente was to reconstruct the international system in such a way that superpower competition could occur, especially in regions of the Third World outside of each other's sphere of influence, without destabilizing effects. Second was the belief that Moscow was responsible for most of the instability in the Third World from which the US deduced, just as unrealistically, that the Soviet Union was therefore in a position to wield maximum pressure on its allies (governments and movements) to weaken or eliminate their opposition to US political and economic interests. Here the White House conflated Moscow's close, fraternal ties to the likes of Vietnam's Ho Chi Minh, Cuba's Fidel Castro, and Angola's Aghostino Neto with Soviet influence to dictate to these and other forces of nationalism and revolution in the Third World whose origins or accession to political power were overwhelmingly a function of internal or indigenous factors.

If an anticommunist outlook co-habited with geopolitics in pursuit of détente with the Soviet Union and China, when it came to Washington's traditional sphere of influence in the Third World—Latin America—waging the Cold War and imperial ambitions continued to drive US policy initiatives. Determined to maintain a strong hold over its informal empire, the White House fashioned an interrelated tripartite strategy: a free market *economic policy* based on eliminating of decades of state regulations, selling off public enterprises, expanding the opportunities for foreign investors and traders at the expense of domestic producers and markets, and imposing greater 'discipline' on workers to lower costs and intensify rates of labour exploitation; a *military strategy* geared to promoting and sustaining in power regimes supportive of this capitalist economic model and capable of resisting nationalist movements or toppling governments advocating alternative non or anti-capitalist development strategies; and a *political strategy* that actively promoted class movements and governments consonant with broader US regional objectives and interests.

At the beginning of the Nixon presidency, however, the region was viewed as marginal to the proposed new global architecture the new administration was intent on constructing. With typical arrogance, Kissinger lectured Chile's Foreign Minister Gabriel Valdez in mid-1969 on the global significance he attached to the Western Hemisphere: 'The axis of history starts in Moscow, goes to Bonn, crosses over to Washington, and then goes to Tokyo. What happens in the South is of no importance' (Dallek, 2007: 229). In a memo to senior White House officials, Nixon defined the region as one of the 'lower priority [foreign policy] items'.[2]

---

[2] Memo to Haldeman, Erlichman and Kissinger, March 2, 1970. Reprinted in Oudes (1989: 99–100).

In October 1969, the President had declared that 'on the diplomatic level we must deal realistically with governments in the inter-American system as they are' irrespective of their origins or methods of rule—except for Cuba (quoted in James D. Cochrane, 1972: 282). Operationally this shift to a policy of maximum flexibility reflected specific priorities: stability and security took precedence over democracy and human rights; autocratic, anticommunist governments committed to political-economic agendas compatible with US interests and willing to work with the imperial state were rewarded with large-scale economic and military aid; popular nationalist and social revolutionary movements, and change-oriented regimes were the targets of economic embargoes and collaborative efforts by Washington and internal opposition forces to crush the former and destabilize the latter. To achieve these outcomes, Nixon stressed the key role played by the region's armed forces and the imperative of maintaining linkages with that most formidable of state institutions in every country in the hemisphere. 'I will never agree with the policy of downgrading the military in Latin America', he told a National Security Council (NSC) meeting in November 1970. "They are power centres subject to our influence".[3]

While such Faustian deals caused periodic concern among sectors of the foreign policy establishment, efforts to contest this Nixon-Kissinger policy approach were limited, typically confined to a small number of individuals, and achieved few victories. When it came to elected or non-elected nationalist governments in the region attempting to assert greater control over their economies and societies, the majority of Congress was reluctant to challenge a White House that invoked the danger of 'falling dominoes', the need to prevent these situations being taken over by radicals and getting 'out of hand', and exaggerated the Soviet 'threat' to, on occasion, justify regime change based on the destructive application of covert subversion, financial pressures, and economic and political sanctions.

During the early 1970s, with the Vietnam War drawing to a close, Washington refocused its gaze on the Western Hemisphere and began a sustained effort to reconsolidate its power and influence which had been weakened by the nationalist political transitions of the previous

---

[3] Memo of Conversation, National Security Council Meeting—Chile (NSSM 97), November 6, 1970.

period that brought to power a number of regimes intent on pursuing domestic and foreign policies that ran counter to the interests of the hegemonic power. The Nixon administration moved aggressively to confront perceived 'hostile' governments in Latin America, typically those intent on imposing limits on US investors within the national economy and pursuing a more independent foreign policy, or those engaged in large-scale socio-economic change designed to move the country out of the US regional political-economic orbit. 'Outsider' economic sanctions complemented 'insider' political-covert strategies based on deepening of ties with key state institutions and societal institutions, separating them from the national project, and gaining their willing collaboration in achieving the imperial state objective-regime change consummated via military coup. These efforts were soon rewarded as anti-communist military ousted these nationalist regimes and assumed political control. The Southern Cone was the epicentre of these pro-US 'regime changes' characterized by high levels of state-authored repression and the implementation of a common [free market] economic model based on increased flows of foreign capital, wage controls and a 'disciplined' labour force, in the process undermining previous efforts to limit the activities of foreign multinationals in the pursuit of greater autonomy.

Chile: Keeping the Left out of Power

By the end of the 1960s, the failure of the multibillion aid programme for Latin America ('Alliance for Progress'), initiated by the Kennedy administration to satisfy popular expectations of social and economic change, triggered a new cycle of nationalist unrest accompanied by a distinct anti-foreign capital, anti-US tinge. Political and military forces advocating greater national control over economic resources and transforming or redefining relations with the regional hegemon assumed political power in Bolivia, Peru and Chile; formidable nationalist movements began to emerge in Argentina and Uruguay; while sympathetic regimes governed in Venezuela, Ecuador and Colombia. These developments, warned an NSC study, indicated, 'a readiness to experiment with radical and extremist solutions' hostile to American interests (quoted in Schmitz, 2006: 93).

The organizational focal point of this nationalist resurgence was the Andean Pact signed by the governments of Chile, Bolivia, Peru,

Ecuador, and Colombia in May 1969 which represented the latest
hemispheric effort at regional economic integration. The agreement
delineated three areas of central concern: the elimination of barriers to
reciprocal intraregional trade; the establishment of a common external
tariff; and the hammering out of joint economic planning strategies.
The centrepiece of the project was a foreign investment code (Decision
24) intended to limit the influence and impact of foreign investors
within the member economies. Despite the formidable array of problems in the hemisphere, the Pact took hold and came to embody the
new ethos of economic nationalism. The reason for its initial success was simple: the policies of each member state were compatible
with the larger project of a common market to promote national
industrialization.

The view from the White House was that modifications in trade
ties and the growth of national industry that did not pose a challenge
to US hegemony could be accommodated. But the internal changes
in some of the regimes that underwrote this regionalist strategy also
implied a shift toward greater autonomy vis-à-vis the US. The combination of support for a regional economic bloc, structural changes
in the domestic political-economies, the nationalization of properties
owned by American investors, and the shift to a more independent
foreign policy were not changes that Nixon was prepared to tolerate,
making such regimes vulnerable to destabilizing counter-measures by
the imperial state. The linchpin of this resurgent hemispheric nationalism, and the prime target of Washington's antagonism, was the
democratic socialist government of Salvador Allende in Chile. In the
words of an NSC staff memo, if allowed to consolidate its rule, such
a government "would create considerable political and psychological
losses to the US: hemispheric cohesion would be threatened; sources
of anti-US policy would be consolidated in the hemisphere"; and it
would be a Cold War victory for the Soviet Union (Kissinger, 1979:
668). To Nixon and Kissinger, the Chilean election had produced a
'cancer' or 'poison' that had to be eliminated lest it spread uncontrol-
lably through the whole regional 'body politic.'[4] Given that détente

---

[4] Transcript of Conversation between President Nixon, Mexican President Luis
Echeverria Alvarez and Alexander Haig Jr, June 15, 1972, Conversation No. 735–1,
Cassette Nos. 2246–2248, Oval Office, White House, *The Nixon Tapes*, National
Security Archive, Washington, D.C. Senior administration officials were attracted to
medical metaphors in discussing the interrelated issues of communism and the "prob-
lem of Chile" in Latin America.

was in part premised on both superpowers acknowledging each others authority within their respective 'spheres of influence', what followed was a White House decision to mobilize all of the resources at its command to destabilize and topple this elected regime from power, in the process severely weakening a regionalist pact that sought to place new limits on foreign capital accumulation and the US presence in Latin America.

As Chile's major political parties began mobilizing for the 1970 presidential elections during the last year of the Frei presidency, Washington policymakers once again expressed their concerns about the possibility of the left gaining national political power. Having funded a major covert action programme to, successfully, forestall this outcome in 1964, the idea of a government led by Salvador Allende had no more appeal six years later—even though there was a greater reluctance this time around, especially in the State Department, to replicate the massive electoral intervention in support of the Christian Democratic Party (PDC) presidential candidate, Eduardo Frei. At the same time, senior State officials in the Bureau of American Republic Affairs (ARA) were willing to support low-level anti-Allende covert political initiatives. In March 1970, a memo from ARA's John Crimmins requested that the interagency '40 Committee' endorse such a proposal as long as it targeted the leftist Popular Unity (UP) coalition and could not be interpreted as providing support to the right-wing National Party candidate, Jorge Alessandri. ARA was above all fearful of the regional consequences of a UP government, that it would bolster 'extremist groups in other countries—most immediately, Bolivia and Peru'.[5] The CIA, on the other hand, also advocated the need for covert intervention but in more traditional Cold War terms: an Allende win was *ipso facto* a win for the Soviet Union and therefore a 'major strategic setback' for the US. To prevent this outcome would send a clear message to Moscow as to "our determination [to] rebuff any Soviet attempt [to] establish another beachhead in the Western Hemisphere".[6]

By mid-year, the White House had designated Chile as a 'high priority' issue. In late July, President Nixon requested an urgent interagency (National Security Study Memorandum 97 or NSSM 97) review of how the US should respond to an Allende presidency.[7] Within a week, the

[5] Memo, Crimmins to Johnson, March 17, 1970.
[6] Memo, CIA, from Santiago for the DCI, May 5, 1970.
[7] National Security Study Memorandum 97, July 24, 1970.

CIA had produced a National Intelligence Estimate (NIE) on Chile detailing the problems Washington was likely to confront depending on the outcome of the September elections. Although bilateral relations would not be trouble-free if either Jorge Alessandri (National Party) or Radimiro Tomic (PDC) became president, both 'appear persuaded of the value of good relations with the US'. By contrast, an Allende government dominated by he Socialist and Communist Parties would produce 'much greater' problems. Apart from the threat to US economic interests in Chile it will likely pose a direct challenge to the US in Latin America and globally which will be 'extremely difficult to manage'. These range from normalizing relations with Cuba and increasing ties with the socialist bloc countries to adopting an 'openly hostile' or neutral stance on key issues involving 'East-West confrontation' at the UN and in 'world affairs generally'.[8]

Soon after, the interdepartmental group (IG) approved NSSM 97, which, for all practical purposes, supplanted the NIE. Its major conclusions treated a Socialist Chile as a threat to US interests in somewhat more measured terms, stating that it would not pose a direct threat to 'vital [US] national interests within Chile'; nor would it 'significantly alter' the global military balance of power. This, however, did not exclude the likelihood of 'tangible economic losses' and significant 'political and psychological costs' if the election resulted in the worst case outcome.[9] Nonetheless, the Principal Deputy Assistant Secretary of State John Hugh Crimmins, who chaired the IG meetings, recalled a consensus that 'the world was not going to come to an end' if Allende won and the White House 'should sort of live with that situation'. Chile's democratic political culture would ensure that 'there was another election down the line'.[10]

Washington's least favoured outcome was confirmed on September 7 when Allende and the UP coalition won a narrow victory over the National Party's Alessandri. The CIA's Directorate of Intelligence produced a same day assessment which basically repeated the conclusions of NSSM 97 and followed it up with a paper for discussion at a '40 Committee' meeting to assess the possibilities for reversing the election result. The military coup option was ruled out on the grounds

    [8] CIA, National Intelligence Estimate, July 30, 1970.
    [9] Memo, National Security Council, August 20, 1970.
    [10] Interview with John Hugh Crimmins, Foreign Affairs Oral History Program, Association for Diplomatic Studies, Arlington, VA.

that the armed forces are 'incapable and unwilling to seize power'. The Agency was almost as pessimistic about a political strategy, which would require the 'unqualified support' of outgoing president Eduardo Frei to 'corral' sufficient PDC and Radical party votes in Congress to elect Alessandri. And while US may have a 'crucial' role to play it must be confined to 'backstopping a Chilean effort'. Whether the US should become involved or not is 'the crux of the issue', NSC staffer Viron Vaky wrote in a memo to Henry Kissinger. He suggested that the 'risks' of an Allende government 'outweighed' the possible unanticipated consequences that might flow from direct US intervention to countermand the election vote. While conceding that Allende "is a serious problem that would cost us a great deal", Vaky was not convinced that the UP leader posed any kind of 'mortal threat to the US' or that this was the start of 'dominos falling' in the region. "The impact of [a] Marxist state in the rest of Latin America", he believed, "is containable".[11]

This was not an assessment that the President wanted to hear. Returning from leave just days after the election, State's John Crimmins encountered a White House that "had gone ape about this—ape. They were frantic, just besides themselves".[12] On September 15, Richard Nixon denounced Allende's victory at a meeting with Central Intelligence Agency (CIA) Director Richard Helms and Kissinger. Terming the result 'unacceptable to the US', the President instructed the head of the covert agency "to prevent Allende from coming to power or to unseat him by whatever means possible". The White House, according to Helms' handwritten notes of the conversation, was determined to 'save Chile!' irrespective of the 'risks involved', and in order to achieve this objective it was necessary to "make the economy scream".[13] The CIA Director recalled that attempting to tell Nixon that no Agency official though it was possible to prevent Allende from being inaugurated as President in early November 'was like talking into a gale' (Frost, 1981: 116).

If Nixon, in Kissinger's words, 'was beside himself' over the election outcome, and took out his frustration on Helms, a similarly apoplectic

---

[11] Memo, Vaky to Kissinger, September 14, 1970.
[12] Interview with John Hugh Crimmins.
[13] Quoted in US Congress, Senate, Select Committee to Study Governmental Operations, Alleged Assassination Plots Involving Foreign Leaders, 94 Cong., 2nd Sess., Report No. 94–465, November 20, 1975, pp. 227, 228.

NSC Adviser directed his wrath at the relevant foreign policy agencies whom he accused of engaging in "a complicated three cornered minuet that kept the problem from high level attention", singling out the State Department's Latin American Bureau for not "put[ting] the chips on anybody" and dismissing the possibility of an Allende victory (quoted in Dallek, 2007: 323). He conjured up the specter of dire global and regional consequences for the US if the vote was allowed to stand. Internationally, it had major implications for the future success of Communist Parties in Western Europe. An NSC aide recalled that Kissinger was especially preoccupied with the growing political support for the Italian Communist Party and the negative message communist participation in Chile's democratic electoral process, and its acceptance of the result, would send to the Italian voter (Hersh, 1983: 270; Kissinger, 1990: 622). Beyond warnings about the threat of 'falling dominoes' across southern Europe, Kissinger also situated Allende's election and the US response 'against the backdrop of the [pro-Moscow] Syrian [government's] invasion of Jordon and our efforts to force the Soviet Union to dismantle its installation for servicing nuclear submarines in the Caribbean' (Kissinger, 1979: 654). Closer to home, its location in the heartland of South America and the democratic origins of the socialist-communist coalition election victory posed a even greater threat to US regional interests than had the Cuban Revolution during the 1960s. What happened in Chile had the potential to "undermine our position in the entire Western Hemisphere...." (Kissinger, 1979: 657).

The day after Richard Helms was given his marching orders, Henry Kissinger held a White House briefing in which he spelled out the broader strategic implications of the election result. Prefacing his remarks with the assertion that an 'irresponsible' populace had almost certainly doomed Chilean democracy because Allende was 'probably a Communist' who headed a 'non-democratic party which tends to make his election pretty irreversible', a gloomy NSC Adviser then launched into a discussion of the 'threat' that a communist Chile posed to the hemisphere, singling out for particular attention Argentina ('which is already deeply divided'), Peru ('which has already been heading in directions that have been difficult to deal with') and Bolivia ("which has already gone in a more leftist, anti-US direction'). Implicitly treating Allende's democratic electoral victory as akin to the Soviet Union forcibly establishing a client regime in one of its Eastern European satellites, he issued an ominous warning: "...I don't think we should delude ourselves that an Allende takover in Chile would not present massive problems for us, and for democratic forces and for pro-US forces in Latin America, and indeed to the whole Western Hemisphere". Washington's dilemma, however, was that current circumstances were not favourable to implementing its policy goal. Realistically, Kissinger acknowledged, "the situation... it not one in which our capacity for influence is very great *at this particular moment* now that matters have reached this particular point".[14]

That said, having failed to prevent the left's political victory, the White House was determined to overturn the result if at all possible. Mobilizing resources to prevent Allende's inauguration as President, Nixon authorized a two-track strategy. Track 1 consisted of a political, economic and propaganda programme to induce the opposition forces to block a formal transfer of power. Track 2 concentrated on efforts to foment a military coup.[15] In a telegram to Santiago on September 28, the head of a special CIA task force on Chile, "instructed his team that every plot, however bizarre must be explored to prod the military into action" (quoted in Streeter, 2004: 7). Kissinger was skeptical about a successful covert operation, terming it a 'long shot' made worse by 'bureaucratic resistance' especially from a 'timid and unsympathetic' State Department.[16] Not surprisingly, given their relative lack of enthusiasm, the senior ARA officials were kept pretty much in the dark about Track 2 programmes.[17] Although the odds were against it, Kissinger directed Ambassador Edward Korry in Santiago to inform the Chilean military leadership that 'we do not want them to be deterred by what they may feel is any ambiguity with respect to our attitude toward the election of Allende' and that if they did block such an outcome the reward would be increased military aid.[18] Meanwhile, the NSC Adviser began chairing interagency meetings to devise a programme of economic sanctions in the event Allende's election was confirmed by the Chilean Congress. "The whole purpose of the meetings", an administration source recalled, "was to ensure that the various aid agencies and

---

[14] US Congress, Senate, Committee on Foreign Relations, Subcommittee on Multinational Corporations, Multinational Corporations and United States Foreign Policy, Part 2, 93rd Cong, March 20, 21, 22, 27, 28, 29, and April 2, 1973, pp. 542–543 (my emphasis).
[15] See US Congress, Alleged Assassination Plots Involving Foreign Leaders, pp. 229–254.
[16] Memo, Kissinger to Nixon, September 17, 1970.
[17] Interview with John Hugh Crimmins.
[18] Memo, Kissinger and Alex Johnson to Ambassador Korry, October 7, 1970.

lending agencies were rejiggered to make sure that [Allende] wasn't to get a penny" (quoted in Hersh, 1974: 19).

Having failed to prevent Allende's accession to the presidency, the Nixon White House redoubled its efforts to make certain that a government they viewed as a profound threat to US interests in Chile, in Latin America, and globally, did not complete its six-year term of office. US policy was not determined by any particular policy decision taken by the Allende government but derived from a commitment to oppose structural ideological developments: the transformation of Chile into a democratic socialist society. Although the changes envisioned were likely to restrict the capacity of US capital to expand in Chile, the nationalization of American property interests, wrote Kissinger, "was not the [primary] issue". While all of the foreign policy departments were committed to seeking redress for affected US investors, the interests and responsibilities of the imperial state were not identical to that of its overseas capitalist class in Chile. "We have the national interest to think about of", he told a group of US corporate executives who supported Treasury Secretary John Connally's proposal for negotiating a quiet government bailout of the corporations and an 'expropriation peace' with Allende (Kissinger, 1979: 656; Morris, 1977: 241–242). What the White House refused to countenance was nationalization of US economic interests in a country where nationalization was linked to a socialist, anti-capitalist development strategy.

With Allende seemingly assured of victory in the congressional vote on October 24, as a result of post-election guarantees negotiated with the PDC, and in the absence of propitious conditions for a military coup, formulating a strategy for dealing with the UP in government now became all the more imperative. A number of key assumptions informed the subsequent policy debate. First, given his 'profound anti-American bias', Allende and the UP '[are] likely to lead opposition to US influence in the hemisphere, to promote policies counter to ours and to seek the adoption of a neutralist Third Word stance by Latin America'. Second, the new government will almost certainly deepen relations with Cuba, the Soviet Union, and the socialist bloc, thereby creating an 'entry point' for these countries to expand their influence in the hemisphere. Third, US investments in Chile will 'almost certainly' be expropriated in due course, possibility without compensation. Fourth, the simple reality of a Marxist government in Chile "is likely to encourage elements opposed to us in other Latin American

countries...."[19] While the State Department expressed particular concern over a possible Chilean 'turn' to the Soviet Union for military
and economic aid, the CIA assessment was that closer relations with
Moscow, however, would not lead Allende "to make Chile a Soviet
vassal...or submit to Soviet domination".[20]

At the end of October, Kissinger received an 'Options Paper on Chile'
prepared by the State Department in consultation with the Department
of Defense (DOD) and the CIA for future consideration by the NSC
which spelled out in much greater detail than earlier memos, policymakers' assumptions regarding an Allende government's regional
and global policies. In addition to its "profound anti-American bias"
that will translate into efforts to 'extirpate' the US presence in Chile
and challenge its influence in the rest of the hemisphere, it is likely
to exploit the OAS "as a forum for advancing its interests principally
at the expense of the US", to encourage other countries in the region
to replicate the Chilean experience, to "become a haven for Latin
American subversives", and will certainly re-establish diplomatic and
economic ties with Cuba. Internationally, it will expand its relations
with the socialist bloc countries in Asia and Eastern Europe while at
the same time seeking 'to avoid dependence' on the Soviet Union. This
presents a potential security threat to the Western Hemisphere if it
leads to a developing military relationship between Santiago and the
Communist world that can only worsen if Chile adopts an 'actively
hostile' stance toward inter-American organizations.[21]

When officials in State's ARA and Policy Planning Bureaus received
copies of the 'Option Paper,' they responded coolly to its more pro-
vocative policy implications. In a briefing memo to Secretary William
Rogers, on the day of Allende's inauguration (November 3), in prepa-
ration for an NSC meeting on Chile that afternoon, they agreed that
the election result was 'clearly a setback for the US' but counseled that
Washington should think carefully about how it treats a democratically-elected government in a region where nationalism is on the rise,
fuelled in large part by a perception of 'US domination'. An approach
based on 'overt' hostility in preference to a more 'restrained' posture,

---

[19] Memo, Vaky to Kissinger, October 18, 1970.
[20] Telegram, Under Secretary of State Irwin to All ARA Diplomatic Posts, October
22, 1970; Memo, CIA, 'Special Report,' October 21, 1970.
[21] Options Paper on Chile, October 28, 1970.

the memo argued, risked the possibility of 'even more serious losses
for us in the hemisphere and elsewhere in the world'. Moreover,
Washington's ability to influence developments in Chile by any means
short of direct military intervention over the next several months was
"marginal at best and could be seriously counterproductive".[22]

As for Moscow's response to Allende's confirmation as President,
State's Bureau of Intelligence and Research (BI&R) reported that the
Soviet Union seemed determined not to 'unduly provoke' Washington
by avoiding any commitment that might be interpreted as helping the
UP to consolidate its hold on political power. Rather, it had adopted
a conservative approach to developing ties with the regime characterized by 'friendly but not effusive public' support. BI&R attributed this
posture not only to the commitments under global détente but also to
Moscow's own domestic economic problems, its existing major international financial commitments to Third World allies, and its concern
over the survival prospects of the Allende government, especially given
Washington's vehement hostility.[23]

In his Council office, Henry Kissinger was projecting a much darker
scenario. A November 5 memo to the President prior to a second NSC
meeting on Chile the next day spelled out the dimensions of 'one of
the most serious challenges ever faced in this hemisphere'. Describing
Allende as "a tough dedicated Marxist...with a profound anti-US
bias", Kissinger hyperventilated that his 'consolidation in power'
would lead to the establishment of "a socialist, Marxist state in Chile",
the total loss of US influence not only in Chile but throughout the
region, and a deepening of ties between Santiago and the socialist bloc.
The consequences of regime consolidation would be bilateral, regional
and global: the billion dollar US investment stake will be immediately
threatened together with the prospect of a default on the approximately $1.5 billion in debt owed to the US government and US private
banks; "Chile would probably become a leader of opposition to us in
the inter-American system...and a focal point for subversion in the
rest of Latin America" and the global impact of a successful democratically elected Marxist government, "especially in Italy", could have a
multiplier effect "significant[ly] affect[ing] the world balance and our

---

[22] Early [undated] November 1970, Briefing Memorandum, ARA, Robert Hur-
witch, Acting and S/PC Arthur Hartman to S/S Rogers, for NSC meeting on Chile,
Nov 3, 1970.
[23] Intelligence Note, BIR, INR/USSR and EE, Dir IM Tobin, October 30, 1970.

own position in it". Thus, Kissinger cautioned against taking a "benign or optimistic view of an Allende regime over the long term" and seeking some kind of accommodation on the grounds that domestically such an approach 'plays into his game plan' and, worse still, a socialist Chile linked to Moscow and Havana "can be even more dangerous for our long-term interests than a very radical regime". His recommendation is predictable: "oppose Allende as strongly as we can and do all we can to keep him from consolidating power".[24]

On November 6, Nixon and his senior foreign policy officials gathered in the Cabinet Room of the White House to discuss the 'problem of Chile.' It quickly became clear that the President himself was preoccupied with the potential regional and global consequences of a consolidated left-wing government in Santiago and, as such, gave short shrift to those in State and the CIA who contemplated an accommodation, under certain circumstances, with this democratically-elected regime. Under Secretary of State John Irwin set the tone of the meeting in his opening sentence. "The problem is", he told the room, "how to bring about his [Allende's] downfall". This, he continued, can only be achieved in collaboration with internal forces opposed to the regime given the limits on "our capability to do it [alone]'. Hostile initiatives should only taken "if we can be sure [they] will have a significant effect on the internal forces there in a way that will hurt Allende and prevent his consolidation". To the President it was "all a matter of degree". If the UP government "is able to get away with" its socialist strategy, it will embolden other Latin governments who are "sitting on the fence". What the region's democracies thought was irrelevant; the main 'game', said Nixon, is in Argentina and Brazil, both governed by military dictatorships.

For Nixon, an even worse scenario than Allende's election would be his ability to consolidate his hold on power and project a positive global image of Chilean socialism. Determined to prevent this happening, he settled on a two-pronged strategy: maintaining a cool and correct public relationship but privately sending 'the message' that Washington opposes his government and also let other Latin American leaders or potential leaders know they are asking for 'trouble' if they think "they can move like Chile and have it both ways". At this point, he told the assembled officials, Chile is 'gone' because

[24] Memo, Kissinger to President, November 5, 1970.

Allende "isn't going to mellow". So, we should try to "hurt him" in any way possible. "I want them to know our policy is negative", Nixon impressed on those present. 'There should be no guarantees'. Likewise, it should be made absolutely clear to other governments in the region that any attempt to replicate what happened in Chile would not be tolerated. "No impression should be permitted in Latin America that they can get away with this, that it's safe to go this way".[25] Following the meeting, Nixon informed his senior policy officials that the public-private tracks would be accompanied by ongoing consultations with the military rulers in Argentina and Brazil, greater efforts to ensure good relations with other pro-US military dictatorships, and attempts to coordinate anti-Chile regional actions.

Indeed, the constraints and options that Nixon policymakers faced in devising a policy for Chile were partly dictated by the course of events in the region where the political landscape at the time of Allende's election provided opportunities for containing any revolutionary 'multiplier' so long as they were tempered by a realistic appreciation of the need to accommodate different non-socialist nationalist development models. The two countries that played a key role in White House efforts to contain Chile were Brazil, a major ally and Peru, a possible adversary.

With the advent of a Marxist Chile, US policymakers increasingly viewed the Brazilian generals and their repressive economic development 'model' as a counterweight to the Chilean experiment, and as Washington's most important regional partner in contesting the forces of political and economic nationalism on the continent. Testifying before Congress in mid-1971, Assistant Secretary of State for Inter-American Affairs Charles Meyer characterized Brazil's development record as 'transcendental'.[26] Some months later, during a White House meeting, an approving Nixon told British Prime Minister Edward Heath that the generals "helped rig the [November 1971] Uruguayan election" to prevent the left-wing *Frente Amplio* winning political office

---

[25] Memo of Conversation, NSC Meeting-Chile (NSSM 97), November 6, 1970; Memo, Kissinger to Secretary of State, et al., Policy Toward Chile—NSDM 93, November 9, 1970.

[26] US Congress, House, Committee on Foreign Affairs, Subcommittee on Inter-American Affairs, New Directions for the 1970s—Part 2: Development Assistance Options for Latin America, 92nd Cong., 1st Sess., February 18, July 12, 19, 26, 27 and August 4, 1971, p. 265.

and creating "another Chile" in Latin America. Brazil, he emphasized was "the key to the [region's] future".[27]

In the case of Peru, the Nixon administration was initially more concerned with neutralizing, not toppling, a possible adversary. In 1968, a military coup in Peru brought to power a nationalist and anticommunist military junta intent on expanding relations with the socialist bloc as part of a more independent foreign policy and committed to a programme of dynamic capitalist-industrial development 'from above'. The latter translated into a policy of selective reforms and sectoral nationalization but one that was not incompatible with private foreign and domestic capital investment. The intent was to redefine, not eliminate, the country's dependence on foreign capital. Overseas investors were welcome, and offered new concessions, provided they adhered to the new "rule of the economic game" (reinvested profits, specific economic sectors off limits to foreign investors, etc.). The sticking point for Washington, however, was the military's decision to expropriate, without compensation, the US-owned International Petroleum Company (IPC).

Ultimately, an accommodation was reached because, unlike Chile, the Peruvian military were not engaged in a socialist transformation; the nationalists generals' process of change was based on modifying the terms of its dependency relationship with the outside world while promoting national industrialization that included a role for foreign capital, compensation to some nationalized US property holders, a continued willingness to negotiate on the IPC issue; and new concessions to foreign capital including major US and foreign companies in the petroleum, mining and industrial sectors. In other words, the nationalist generals were intent on redefining, not eliminating, the country's dependence on foreign investment. Or, as NSC adviser Kissinger told his colleagues at a Senior Review Group (SRG) meeting on Chile in late October 1970, "we judged that Velasco was a nationalist but not unreasonable and that we could keep some lines open to him".[28]

By late 1971, Nixon policymakers began to distinguish between changes *within* capitalist property relations in Peru and changes *away* from capitalism in Chile. Kissinger described the Allende challenge as

---

[27] Memo, "The President's File," From *Kissinger*, December 21, 1971, NSA. Kissinger himself wrote that developing a "special relationship" with Brazil would "serve as a pattern for the dealings of the US with other nations of the hemisphere." Kissinger (1979: 738).

[28] Senior Review Group Minutes, 'Summary of Conclusions,' October 29, 1970.

'fundamentally different' from Peru's capitalist modernization-from-above strategy based on restricted mass mobilization from below (Kissinger, 1979: 657). Moreover, a policy of intransigent opposition in the absence of any significant pressure points in the regime might conceivably provoke the Peruvians to take measures replicating the Chilean pattern. This key political distinction became the basis for negotiating US property nationalizations in one instance and making them a reason for confrontation on the other, and helped explain the shift to a more flexible approach in dealing with Peru—as part of a policy designed to isolate Chile from the rest of the hemisphere. In June 1973, Secretary of State William Rogers made an official visit Peru and declared Washington's support for the military junta's 'constructive nationalism' (*Business Latin America*, 1973: 179).

The existence of democratic-socialist Chile dictated the elaboration of a flexible regional policy to meet what Nixon policymakers defined as a fundamental challenge to US hegemony within its traditional sphere of influence. This meant coming to terms with Peruvian nationalism while moving to expand and deepen its ties to Brazil, promoting that nation as *the* regional powerhouse supportive of its Northern neighbor's larger policy objectives in Latin America. "If the idea gets around in Brazil and Argentina that we are playing along with Allende", said Kissinger, "we will be in trouble".[29]

Destabilizing Allende: The 'Outsider' Strategy

The Chilean economy's vulnerability to US pressures provided a natural target for the Nixon administration as it set about implementing a multi-track destabilization policy. Washington's ability to make the economy 'scream' was immensely facilitated by two key factors: a copper industry, accounting for approximately 90 percent of the country's foreign exchange earnings, largely controlled by American corporations; and Chile's extensive dependence on funds from US public and private sources, as well as US-influenced multilateral development banks (World Bank, Inter-American Development Bank) and international financial institutions (International Monetary Fund), both for day to day operations and long-term development projects. The

[29] Senior Review Group Minutes, 'Summary of Conclusions,' October 29, 1970.

potential consequences for the UP government of these and other susceptible pressure points would soon become all too obvious.

Following Allende's inauguration, the US government systematically went for the economic jugular. First, it terminated all bilateral economic (but not military) aid to an economy that, on a per capita basis, had been the largest recipient of Alliance for Progress funds during the 1960s. Second, it imposed a spare parts embargo that was particularly devastating for a country whose agroindustrial infrastructure was overwhelmingly dependent on purchases of these materials from American firms (NACLA, 1973: 20–21, 26–27).

This cutoff had a profoundly negative impact on the pivotal copper industry's production levels and foreign exchange earnings. Third, between 1970 and 1972, Nixon policy resulted in a precipitous decline in short term US commercial credits (from 78.4 to approximately 6.6%) which further affected the Allende government's ability to purchase replacement parts and machinery for the most critical economic sectors—copper, steel, petroleum, electricity and transportation. Fourth, the White House sought to limit Chile's access to capitalist bloc export markets, most notably in its partially successful effort to place an embargo on Chilean copper sales to Western Europe. Fifth, Washington successfully mobilized support within the global and regional banking institutions for a virtual cutoff of all loans from these sources for the whole period of UP rule. "Our job", recalled Kenneth Guenther, US Alternate Executive Director in the Inter-American Development Bank, "was to make sure that not one shekel left the bank for Allende and for Chile".[30]

Washington also lobbied Chile's foreign creditors to participate in its global credit squeeze on the basis of Chile's "lack of creditworthiness", highlighting domestic economic problems that, in large part, could be attributed to US sanctions. Moreover, at the same time as the White House was denying Chile access to traditional sources of external funding, it instituted its own debt squeeze, demanding that interest payments on that part of the debt owed to US government agencies (accumulated prior to 1970) be made exactly on schedule as compared with the extremely flexible arrangements that operated during the 1960s. Around half of Chile estimated $3.83 billion foreign

---

[30] Interview with Kenneth Guenther. Foreign Affairs Oral History Program, Association for Diplomatic Studies, Arlington, VA.

debt as of December 1970 was owed to US government agencies and
US private lenders (Economist Intelligence Unit, 1973: 15). During the
1972 Paris Club meeting of Chile's creditors, the US justified its refusal
to sign a bilateral rescheduling agreement (the only nation to do so)
on the grounds of the UP government's failure to reach an agreement
on compensations terms for expropriated US properties.

Unlike the credit, financial and trade squeeze, which denied new
economic resources to the government, the debt squeeze sought to
extract financial resources from Chile. By demanding payments on
schedule, US policymakers had a 'no loss' strategy in mind: if Chile
paid up it would have to divert scarce funds from popular programmes
and development projects; if Chile did not pay, its international credit
rating would fall, new loans from non-US sources would not be forthcoming, and the loss of funds to finance of imports would cause an
economic decline generating political discontent.[31] With little alternative but to meet these increased debt obligations, the government
was forced to draw on the country's foreign exchange reserves just to
keep many of its development and social programmes operating—at a
time when the world market price for copper was falling (and did not
recover until mid-1973).

In a porous, dependent society like Chile, these mutually reinforc-
ing US economic sanctions were a formidable instrument in shifting
the internal balance of power against the new government. Over time,
Nixon policy was able to identify gradual economic deterioration
with internal government policy, thus creating the basis for polarizing
Chilean society in a manner favourable to the large property owning
groups and the anti-left political forces.

Allende's efforts to cope with the economic problems resulting from
US sanctions, based on finding alternative sources of funds and new
trading partners, were ultimately not adequate to the task. The Soviet
Union's political support did not translate into significant levels of
economic aid primarily because Moscow was concerned about the survival prospects of the regime given Washington's hostility, and did not
want to become embroiled in a major conflict with the US in its historic sphere of influence and thus risk undermining the new relationship that was being developed under détente. As well, the Brezhnev

---

[31] For a discussion of the Nixon administration debt strategy, see Department of
State, Bureau of Public Affairs, Historical Office, United States Policy Toward Chile,
November 1971–September 1973, Research Project No. 1047-A, May 1976, 43pp.

government (1964–1982) had largely jettisoned the Khrushchev era strategy of using economic aid to cultivate political alliances in the Third World, while paying little or no attention to the needs of the domestic economy (Miller, 1989: 127–47; Nogee and Sloan, 1979: 339–368). As a result, Allende could not at one and the same time honor past external obligations, meet current economic pressures, and develop the economy that, in turn, severely affected his government's ability to budget, plan programmes, and pursue a coherent economic policy.

Destabilizing Chile: The 'Insider' Strategy

The efforts to realize economic dislocation in Chile were paralleled by the deepening of ties between the US and critical sectors of the Chilean state and civil society. The objective was to weaken the capacity of the state to realize a nationalist development project, and to enlist these forces in support of US policy goals. The interagency '40 Committee' approved funds for a multi-track covert programme that included 'political action to divide and weaken' the UP coalition, expanding contacts with the armed forces, and 'providing support to non-Marxist opposition political groups and parties' as well as anti-Allende media outlets.[32] To maximize such efforts, the Nixon administration made a conscious decision not to rupture diplomatic ties with the Allende government that enabled it to collect information, lend support to the political opposition, mount a devastatingly effective covert action programme, and facilitate the flow of financial resources to those internal forces sympathetic to its ultimate 'state against regime' strategy.[33]

The circumstances of Allende's accession to the presidency promised to create formidable institutional obstacles to the new government's efforts to implement a wide-ranging programme of social and economic change in Chile. The UP achieved office in a context of divided political power. Control over the executive branch did not extend to most of the other key state and political institutions. *Congress* remained under opposition control, and time and again was responsible for blocking key legislation proposed by the executive (e.g. bills to introduce a progressive income tax). The *Judiciary* remained an opposition

---

[32] Memo, Kissinger to Nixon, November 25, 1970.
[33] For an extended discussion of the 'state-regime' distinction, see Morley (1994: 1–32).

stronghold throughout the Allende presidency. In return for PDC votes to confirm the September 1970 election outcome, Allende guaranteed that those officials who staffed the *Bureaucracy* in previous governments would retain their positions which effectively meant that the opposition had allies inside the government who were in a position to slowdown or sabotage the implementation of UP programmes. The pre-election guarantee also extended to the *Mass Media* (newspapers, television, radio, films), where the political opposition had a decisive advantage in terms of ownership and control that would not be fundamentally challenged during Allende's tenure. Finally, the majority of the *Armed Forces* leadership had longstanding personal and professional ties with their Pentagon counterparts, which had played an important role in shaping their political outlooks (reinforced by their upper or middle class social origins).

The elite character of country's institutions created a very propitious environment for the US to obstruct the new government's efforts to transform Chile into a democratic socialist society, particularly in light of the former's close relations with the most prominent conservative and centrist in Chilean society; its history of electoral intervention on behalf of the anti-leftist parties since the early 1960s; and the dominating presence of American capital in the most critical sectors of the Chilean economy.

Once in office, the government outlined two sets of economic measures as part of its gradualist 'transition to socialism' strategy: short term impact initiatives (wages increases, price controls, improved educational and health facilities, etc.) designed to consolidate and expand its social base of support; and large-scale, longer-term initiatives directed at transforming the basic structures and organization of the Chilean economy. During 1971 and 1972, there was a massive expropriation and redistribution of agricultural property; the financial sector (banks) came under state control; a range of companies in the industrial sector were nationalized; so to were the US-owned copper mines, along with other American enterprises in the mining and transportation sectors, that became part of an expanding state sector.

The UP was able to implement a large part of its structural socioeconomic programme, despite the institutional constraints it confronted, through a judicious and effective use of legal-bureaucratic machinery that was already in place. The initial success of these policies can be gauged from the significant increase in the UP's electoral and trade union support during the first twelve to fifteen months in office. By early 1972, the political opposition's picture of Chile as a country in the process of 'eco breakdown' stood in sharp contrast to the appraisal by the Inter-American Committee on the Alliance for Progress: "the country's economy is in a situation of full utilization of its productive capacity, followed by a year marked by high growth levels. Unemployment has been reduced markedly and a broad process of redistribution of income and accelerated land reform has been carried out" (OAS, 1972: 148).

But storm clouds were on the horizon. By the latter half of 1971, the internal opposition was beginning to recover from the disarray of the post-election period. The PDC and the National Party had began to mend their fractured relationship while the initial 'panic and paralysis' (Stallings, 1987: 137) that characterized the industrialist class was receding and being replaced by a focus on developing a strategy to contest the government and its economic programme. Meanwhile, the external sanctions regime was beginning to feed into an array of inter-related problems confronting the UP: rising inflation and import costs; shortages of goods; declining private domestic and foreign investment, and foreign currency reserves; the growth of a black market; and wage increases considerably in excess of original projections. Particularly concerning was the failure of domestic production to meet the upward demand for basic foodstuffs occasioned by the rise in workers' wage levels which, in turn, forced the government to divert more of its financial resources to pay for more costly imports as a result of the US sanctions. Substantial falls in the price and production of copper—resulting in direct tax collections falling far short of projected totals—merely added to the emerging fiscal crisis. Not only was the government's ability to make scheduled payments on the almost $4 billion foreign debt it inherited that much more difficult; these problems transformed a $100 million balance of payments surplus in 1970 into a $299m deficit in 1971 (Faundez, 1988: 205, 208).

As the government completed its first twelve months in office, proliferating economic problems accelerated political and ideological differences within UP coalition over the tactics and strategy for achieving the transition to socialism. The 'moderates' led by the Allende wing of the Socialist Party and the Communist Party, and the 'radicals' coalesced around the Socialist Party left clashed over a range of issues: relations with the middle class sectors and the PDC; ties to the extra-parliamentary Movement of the Revolutionary Left (MIR); support for mass mobilization politics; attitudes toward Moscow and the socialist

bloc; agrarian reform strategies; unauthorized factory and land occupations (pressure 'from below'); and, more broadly, the pace and scope
of socioeconomic change.[34] These divergent positions were not easily
reconciled, delaying the submission of critical legislation to take over
'the commanding heights of the economy' and creating other obstacles
that hampered government efforts to pursue a coherent policy programme. Not surprisingly, such intra-coalition disagreements did little
to strengthen the government's ability to withstand attacks by a more
united opposition.

The issue of pressure 'from below' for an accelerated transfer of political, economic and class power, for instance, which surfaced as early as
April 1971, created major tensions within the coalition. In the urban
centres industrial workers began taking over factories and plants on
their own initiative, forcing a rather reluctant Allende—fearful of the
ripple effect of such independent actions—to accede to demands that
they become part of the state sector. In the countryside, pressures on
the government to legitimate farm expropriations were equally strong;
by mid-1972, peasant supporters had illegally occupied around 1700
properties presenting Allende with another largely unwanted problem
(Stallings, 1987: 13); Loveman, 2001: 250).

By early 1972, the most prominent anti-government forces in civil
society had regrouped and begun to develop a focused and organized
counter-response, in particular taking advantage of Allende's gradualist approach to economic transformation-especially as applied to
the critical industrial and commercial sectors. Ranged against the UP
coalition and its lower class base (workers, urban poor and sectors of
the rural population) was the bulk of the upper and middle classes;
large landowners and industrialists; the propertied lower middle class
who abhorred the instability and viewed the government's nationalization policy as a threat to private enterprise and their ability to expand;
retail and wholesale merchants who opposed the government's efforts
to assume direct control over the distribution of goods in order to pre-
empt the black market; those peasants who wanted their own private
plots of land rather than work on collective or state farms; and the
major political parties of the centre-right, the PDC and the National
Party who had put their ideological and political differences aside in
order to jointly oppose the Allende coalition.

[34] See, for example, Haslam (2005: 91, 118–119).

Holding a decisive advantage in seats in both houses of Congress, the opposition political parties signaled their intent to use this power to challenge the constitutionality of the government's programme—to vote against individual proposals, to devise means to limit the executive's traditional power of veto, to censure cabinet ministers and, more generally, displayed an intent to play fast and loose with traditional conventions in implementing measures to obstruct the coalition's objectives.

The UP's resort to legislation and laws 'on the books' to implement its structural changes antagonized sectors of the political opposition based on an earlier government commitment to submit new legislation to Congress to achieve these objectives. In October 1971, the PDC announced a fundamental challenge to the gradualist transition to socialism by submitting a constitutional amendment to the Senate to deprive the Chilean President of 'the regulatory powers on which the government's nationalization policy was based' and make illegal any further takeover of private firms using state funds to become a majority shareholder which had been the strategy employed in the financial sector (Faundez, 1988: 217). The socialist government countered with its own legislation to substantially expand the nationalization sector as part of a broader attempt to increase the power of the executive branch, setting the stage for a major constitutional confrontation. Four months later, following the collapse of negotiations, Congress voted to approve the opposition amendment, which the UP government predictably vetoed. Further negotiations failed to break the deadlock due to a combination of policy differences within the coalition and the PDC's refusal to modify its original stance (Faundez, 1988: 225–26). As this constitutional conflict unfolded, it did so against the background of an emerging electoral collaboration between the PDC and the Nationalist Party, and the appearance of a more coordinated challenge by centre-right political parties and there allies in civil society to the government.

The PDC received considerable support from the Chilean legal profession. The Comptroller-General, responsible for 'implementing the law through governmental decrees', deliberately slowed down the processing of decrees and actively participated in the constitutional debate through efforts to obstruct the government's nationalization programme by, for instance, consistently ruling that decrees requisitioning privately-owned enterprises for the state sector were unlawful (Kaufman 1988: 181). Taking their lead from this 'new approach to legal interpretation', the Supreme Court also repeatedly contested the constitutional basis of government actions (Faundez, 1988: 232–233).

Despite selective nationalizations in the industrial and commercial sectors of the economy, both remained largely under capitalist control and it was precisely in these sectors that the government confronted its most serious internal economic problems. Industrialists stopped investing and cut back on production, used state credits for speculative or political purposes, and transferred capital into foreign bank accounts; the commercial sector resorted to hoarding goods and capital, and selling goods on the black market to circumvent price controls. Meanwhile, just as the new government's initial agricultural reforms were beginning to produce results, thousands of small truck owners responsible for moving goods and foodstuffs from production centres to markets and retail outlets embarked on a series of strikes that had the most devastating impact on the government's social base. The cumulative impact of these multiple internal economic pressures was goods shortages, rising prices, worsening fiscal and trade deficits, skyrocketing inflation, and economic stagnation. The scarcities became a major political problem precisely because the government's income redistribution policies had unleashed consumer demands and expectations among those Chileans long at the bottom of a highly inequitable society that could now not be satisfied.

The political opposition sought to give their efforts a disciplined and focused thrust, and protect their interests, through specific organizational structures with close ties to the centre and right wing political parties called *gremios* or *gremio* associations—confederations of the big landowners and industrialists, the small property owners (truck owners, bus owners, taxi owners, small retail merchants and industrialists), and the salaried professionals (doctors, lawyers, etc.). Because all felt threatened by the new government's policies, the large property owners were able to promote a sense of identity by playing on the theme of a common ownership of property against the property-less working class, a strategy which effectively blunted the differences and traditional conflicts between big and small property owners. Efforts to organize the latter to oppose the government were greatly facilitated by the growing working class pressure on Allende to accelerate the process of change. This merely served to heighten their sense of being embattled in a hostile and chaotic world.

In Washington, the Nixon administration was carefully monitoring these developments as it began to devote more and more time, effort and dollars to what it described as 'the problem of Chile'. To complement and reinforce the internal opposition, and to take advantage of the multiple internal and external pressures that were now beginning to create major dislocations in the Chilean economy, the White House authorized a significant expansion of CIA covert activities.

Covert US support for the centrist and right-wing political parties was a feature of virtually 'every major election in Chile in the decade between 1963 and 1973', enabling the major opposition political parties 'to maintain an anti-government campaign throughout the Allende years'.[35] The PDC was particularly dependent on the Agency for its growth and influence in the decade prior to Allende's election, extending its presence into strategic areas of Chile social as well as political life (religion, unions, education and the civil service)—which Washington fully exploited after 1970 in its effort to destabilize and terminate Popular Unity rule.

CIA expertise and financial support also facilitated a sustained propaganda assault against the government in the newspapers (especially *El Mercurio*), radio stations and on television. The mass media played a key role in influencing popular consciousness by formulating public issues in a manner compatible with US policy objectives. The negative effects of increasing US economic pressures and covert intervention were depicted as the result of government policy, the breakdown of law and order, and an undisciplined labour force. What this did was to exacerbate the inevitable problems and errors that accompany any process of rapid, large-scale social and economic change—in the process, creating at least the appearance of large-scale opposition to the government's policies.

Supported by the traditional elites, the CIA moved to mobilize and finance those social forces most adversely affected by the deteriorating economic conditions and direct their political energies against the UP government. A principal target was the property owning lower middle class which was not only numerous but also concentrated in the capital of Santiago, the nerve centre of government. As a class they exhibited a contradictory attitude toward the state: while opposed to wage and

---

[35] US Congress, Senate, Select Committee on Intelligence, *Covert Action in Chile 1963–1973*, 94th Cong., 1st Sess., December 18, 1975, pp. 9, 29.

price controls, they sought tariff protection, lines of credit and state infrastructure investments. Initially, many of these individuals had been attracted to the UP policies from which they directly benefited: increased access to state credits, rising sales due to wage increases for workers, and greater spending by a frightened upper class. But as Washington's economic blockade began to bite, the lines of credit dried up, spare parts became harder to obtain, and Allende's working class supporters became more militant in demanding a quickened pace of socioeconomic transformation, organizing street rallies on an almost daily basis. To a class who abhorred instability and 'disorder,' the world was becoming an increasingly hostile and threatening place, sentiments that led them to abandon their support of, or at least non-opposition to, the government. They, in turn, became exceedingly receptive to traditional rightist appeals on the need to restore order, defend the sanctity of private property, the family and religion, and to reverse a perceived trend toward economic anarchy—making them available for mobilization by the traditional elites and the CIA who proceeded to organize and channel their resentments in a political direction.

The right-wing political parties and the *gremios* began developing a coordinated strategy in March 1972 centred around a series of strikes that they hoped would weaken and eventually oust the UP government from power—either by forcing Allende to resign or the armed forces to intervene into the political arena. That October, any doubts about the class nature of the conflict were swept away when the Truck Owners' Confederation went on strike, ostensibly over specific economic grievances. Within 48 hours, it had ballooned into the first general strike of the capitalist class as a whole, partly funded by the CIA. The entire *gremialista* movement joined the truckers: the big industrialists called on its members to lock the workers out of their factories; retail shopkeepers closed their doors; private transport firms locked up their vehicles; doctors, lawyers and other professionals closed their practices, and a newly formed *Gremialista Front* performed a coordinating role. Endorsed by the National Party and the PDC, what began as a strike by a single *gremio* triggered an effort to paralyze the economy and was then rapidly transformed into a political strike—an effort to oust Allende from office. Even though the political opposition failed to achieve their strategic objective, economic losses resulting from the strike ran into the hundreds of millions of dollars. At the same time, independent action by factory workers in Santiago's 'industrial belts' prevented lockouts in dozens of enterprises, maintained their operations, and effectively forced the government to issue decrees legitimizing the takeover of more than 50 factories.

Over the next year, the CIA subsidized a series of devastating strikes against the government in the agro-industrial and mining sectors prior to September 1973 that served as a basis for tens of millions of dollars in production and foreign exchange losses. Notable among these was the April–May 1973 strike of thousands of El Teniente copper miners—the 'labour aristocracy' of blue collar workers—organized by the industry *gremio* and supported by the PDC, the National Party, and the extreme right-wing *Patria y Libertad* Party over demands for a 41% salary increase; the June strike by the medical gremios (doctors, chemists, nurses, dentists) who combined specific grievances with a more generalized attack on the government's economic model; and a ruinous political strike in late July, coordinated by a *Gremialista Front*, which resulted in tens of millions of dollars in damage to production (Petras and Morley 1975; Kaufman 1988: 78–9). Given that more than 1000 gremios were actively opposing the government, it is little wonder that the CIA increasingly pursued its objective through those it called "the holders of real power" in Chile (O'Brien, 2007: 248).

Economic destabilization and covert subversion was paralleled by deepening ties between the US and the Chilean armed forces, which had the effect of further separating the most powerful state institution from the national government and its development project, increasing the prospect of their support for White House policy goals. As early as January 1972, the Senate Intelligence Committee's report on *'Covert Action in Chile, 1963–1973'* concluded that the CIA Station "had successfully penetrated" the most likely pro-coup sectors of the armed forces. Agency officials, by their own admission, had 'assets' that were 'drawn from all branches of the Chilean military....' As the level of class conflict intensified, and preparations for the military coup quickened, the Santiago Station moved to give potential plotters support and direction by starting to collect 'operational intelligence' vital to any successful coup such as "arrest lists [and] key government installations that needed to be taken over and government contingency plans...."[36]

---

[36] US Congress, *Covert Action in Chile 1963–1973*, pp. 36, 38, 39.

The combination of US direct intervention into the Chilean political process and the rising level of class conflict precipitated a major debate within the UP government, beginning in late 1972, which revealed a sharp difference of opinion over how to respond to the domestic opposition: whether to consolidate the process of change, reach out to sectors of the middle class (especially the PDC) and emphasize the need to increase productivity; or to accelerate the process of change that was underway (targeting the industrial and commercial sectors) by mobilizing the working class to confront and defeat the capitalist opponents of socialist transition.

By year's end, the *New York Times* reported discussions among senior armed forces officials about the possibility of a military coup against Allende and their increased contacts with the gremio leaders and prominent capitalist supporters of the October 1972 anti-government general strike (Kandell, 1973). On the political right, the National Party, the *gremialista* movement and non-party nationalists were all espousing "the need for an authoritarian political order" (Pollak, 1999: 28, 37, 41). US intelligence sources also reported that the American Embassy in Santiago was becoming a meeting place for extreme right-wing individuals "who were essentially dedicating their lives to the overthrow of Allende—it was like a holy war" (Haslam, 2005: 130).

As this pro-coup activity continued apace, the persistence of internal differences within the UP government undermined efforts to resolve the economic crises and contain lawless behavior by members of the National Party, the proto-fascist *Patria y Libertad* Party and like-minded opposition elements. In April 1973, the confrontation between Congress and the President over the anti-nationalization constitutional amendment flared up again when Chamber of Deputies rejected the government's veto, and the opposition argued that the President was required to promulgate the text within 60 days. Subsequently, the Chamber declared Allende's policies 'unconstitutional and illegal' and voted overwhelmingly for the armed forces to 'defend the constitution' (Angell, 1993: 168).

While the government was still debating whether to consolidate or accelerate the socialist transition, the September 1973 military coup abruptly shattered the Chilean democratic tradition—setting the stage for a rightist counterrevolution based on terror and repression.

Conclusion

Nixon: Well we didn't-as you know-our hand doesn't show on this
           one though
Kissinger: We didn't do it. I mean we helped them...created the condi-
           tions as great as possible (??)
Nixon: That is right

(Telephone Conversation, Sept 16, 1973)

The Nixon-Kissinger destabilization policy could likely not have succeeded in the absence of a permeable Chilean state and civil society,
Allende's commitment to maintaining an open, bargaining democratic
political system which the US and its internal allies exploited to promote
regime change, and the incomplete nature of UP government's socioeconomic transformation. In a context where the new government's
authority was limited to its control over the executive branch, where
sectors of the state apparatus remained linked to the old class structure, and where political channels remained open (thus giving external
forces unfettered access to opposition political parties, employer and
professional organizations, mass media outlets, the military and the
bureaucracy) the US was able to maximize its 'insider' strategy, com-
plementing an equally effective political-economic 'outsider' strategy in
order to bring about the desired outcome. Confronted by a nationalist
regime it defined as inimical to its basic interests, the Nixon administration moved to actively promote instability and conflict between
that regime and the state, disaggregating the latter from the former,
to terminate economic aid (bilateral and multilateral) to the Allende
government, to provide financial and political support to key opposition institutions and individuals, and to encourage the armed forces
to 'change the regime.' The support of these key state institutions and
social class forces was critical to the success of US policy.

Complex forces, internal and external, meshed to create the conditions leading to the September 1973 *golpe*. While the UP government failed to develop a coherent socialist transition strategy, its errors
and incompetence that contributed to the drift toward a burgeoning
economic crisis and stagnation cannot be disassociated from either
the internal class conflict ('sabotage and subversion') or US imperial
state policy. The ties between the Washington, the PDC and right-
wing civilian and military forces inside Chile laid the basis for the
continuous destabilization of the Allende government. Extensive US
funding and penetration of these groups had a profound influence on

the degree and extent of economic dislocation, and deepening social polarization. The Nixon administration was willing to provoke a general societal crisis, a coup, and a military government—to support a transition from democracy to dictatorship—if that was the only means of restoring the optimal conditions for private capital accumulation and crushing the possibilities of a regional economic and political challenge to continued imperial state hegemony, in order to maintain what one scholar in another, early Cold War, context aptly described as a 'closed hemisphere in an open world' (Green, 1971).

Epilogue: Washington Supports 'Foundational Change' in Chile

The Nixon administration's haste to embrace the junta indicated that the issue of a genuine and convincing ideological justification for military intervention was not a high priority for Washington. What mattered above all was that Chile had been rescued from "an anti-American government all the way" and "totalitarianism," and the Southern Cone "from collapse into radicalism."[37] Privately, the President and his NSC Advisor were euphoric over Allende's demise and decried the domestic electorate's lack of appreciation for their contribution to this 'Cold War' victory:

> Kissinger: The Chilean thing is getting consolidated and of course newspapers are bleeding because a pro-Communist government has been overthrown."
> Nixon: Isn't that something. Isn't that something.
> Kissinger: I mean instead of celebrating—in the Eisenhower period we would be heroes.[38]

The Chilean 'transition' brought to power a virulently anti-communist regime determined to implement a rightist revolution in Chile that would eliminate any possibility of the future emergence of a radical, anti-capitalist movement capable of challenging for national political power in Chile; to impose 'stability and order' through the aegis of an autocratic state in order to recreate the optimal conditions for capital accumulation and expansion ('freeing the market').

---

[37] Telephone Conversation, Kissinger/President, September 16, 1973; Kissinger, *Years of Renewal*, p. 753.
[38] Telephone Conversation Kissinger/Nixon, September 16, 1973.

The Pinochet military dictatorship consolidated its rule in the early period through a systematic campaign of terror and bloodshed intended to achieve unchallenged control over the nation's political life in order "to facilitate the long-term transformation of Chile's socioeconomic and political systems...."[39] The core targets of this offensive were the leftist political parties and trade unions, and their supporters, who constituted the political-social base of the Allende government. They had to be—and were—ruthlessly demobilized and denuded of any power to represent their (urban and rural) constituencies. "In the days and weeks [after the coup]," writes Mark Ensalaco, "factories in the [industrial] zone and numerous shanty-towns were raided in massive combined search and destroy operations [which] were intended to sweep up the left's most capable and shantytown organizers."[40] Commenting on the scope and intensity of the junta-directed violence during the six months following the coup, Canada's Ambassador to Chile A.D. Ross sketched an brutal picture: "This 'purification' [physical elimination of the left] has been accomplished mainly by fear—fear caused by the harsh "brutality of the Junta's post-coup methods." "...torture, threats, arbitrary arrest, detention without specific charges and under inhumane conditions, suspicious shootings of prisoners 'while trying to escape,' and other clear violations of basic human rights have occurred on a considerable scale."[41] The disappearances, killings, incarcerations, and torture, Chile's 2004 National [Valech] Commission, concluded was intended "to instill fear, to force people to submit, to obtain information, to destroy an individual's capacity for moral, physical, psychological, and political resistance and opposition to the military regime."[42]

---

[39] Mark Ensalco, *Chile Under Pinochet.* Philadelphia: University of Pennsylvania Press, 2000, p. 34.

[40] Ensalco, *Chile Under Pinochet*, 2000, p. 28.

[41] Despatch/Telegram, Amb (A.D. Ross), Canad Emb, Santiago to S/S for External Affairs, April 23, 1974: Ottawa, Canada NA. According to the 1991 Chilean HR Commission report, over 50% of all those killed by the regime were members of these three organizations. See Lois Hecht Oppenheim, *Politics in Chile.* 2nd ed. Boulder, CO: Westview Press, 1999, p. 119.

[42] Conclusion of the 2004 National [Valech] Commission on Political Imprisonment and Torture, quoted in Peter Kornbluh, "Letter from Chile," *The Nation*, January 31, 2005, p. 23.

This state terror was carried out in a "politically rational [and] calculated" manner[43] to gain specific, interrelated political and economic objectives: it was about transforming the social activist and politically conscious segments who supported the UP government into a passive, atomized mass to serve a capitalist development model based on freeing the market and a privileged role for foreign investment—for which a disciplined and docile labor force was a prerequisite. Over time, with the opposition decimated, the level the repression inevitably ebbed and became more selective. Instead, the regime displayed an increased preference for 'disappearing' opponents as the most effective means of minimizing the publicity attached to other forms of violence against civilians and, simultaneously, maintaining a generalized anxiety among the populace.

Despite the problems and tensions that "internal repression" might produce in the bilateral relationship, Secretary Kissinger made clear to his staff that this would have no bearing on the basic contours of the administration's Chile policy: "we should understand our policy—that however unpleasant they act this government is better for us than Allende was."[44] Elsewhere, he put it equally bluntly: "...we considered the change of government in Chile was on balance favorable—even from the point of view of human rights."[45] There would be no deviation from this bottom line.

[43] Cecilia Menjivar and Nestor Rodriguez, "State Terror in the U.S.-Latin American Interstate Regime," in Menjivar and Rodriguez, eds., When States Kill. Austin: University of Texas Press, 2005, p. 3.
[44] Secretary of State's Staff Meeting on October 1, October 4, 1973.
[45] Henry Kissinger, Years of Upheaval. London: Weidenfeld and Nicolson, 1982, p. 411.

CHAPTER ELEVEN

THE RATIONAL DESTRUCTION OF YUGOSLAVIA

Michael Parenti

In 1999, the US national security state—which has been involved throughout the world in subversion, sabotage, terrorism, torture, drug trafficking, and death squads—launched round-the-clock aerial attacks against Yugoslavia for 78 days, dropping 20,000 tons of bombs and killing thousands of women, children, and men. All this was done out of humanitarian concern for Albanians in Kosovo. Or so we were asked to believe. In the span of a few months, President Clinton bombed four countries: Sudan, Afghanistan, Iraq repeatedly, and Yugoslavia massively. At the same time, the US was involved in proxy wars in Angola, Mexico (Chiapas), Colombia, East Timor, and various other places. And US forces are deployed on every continent and ocean, with some 300 major overseas support bases—all in the name of peace, democracy, national security, and humanitarianism.

While showing themselves ready and willing to bomb Yugoslavia on behalf of an ostensibly oppressed minority in Kosovo, US leaders have made no moves against the Czech Republic for its mistreatment of the Romany people (gypsies), or Britain for oppressing the Catholic minority in Northern Ireland, or the Hutu for the mass murder of a half million Tutsi in Rwanda—not to mention the French who were complicit in that massacre. Nor have US leaders considered launching 'humanitarian bombings' against the Turkish people for what their leaders have done to the Kurds, or the Indonesian people because their generals killed over 200,000 East Timorese and were continuing such slaughter through the summer of 1999, or the Guatemalans for the Guatemalan military's systematic extermination of tens of thousands of Mayan villagers. In such cases, US leaders not only tolerated such atrocities but were actively complicit with the perpetrators—who usually happened to be faithful client-state allies dedicated to helping Washington make the world safe for the *Fortune 500*.

Why then did US leaders wage an unrestrainedly murderous assault upon Yugoslavia?

The Third Worldization of Yugoslavia

Yugoslavia was built on an idea, namely that the Southern Slavs would not remain weak and divided peoples, squabbling among themselves and easy prey to outside imperial interests. Together they could form a substantial territory capable of its own economic development. Indeed, after World War II, socialist Yugoslavia became a viable nation and an economic success. Between 1960 and 1980 it had one of the most vigorous growth rates: a decent standard of living, free medical care and education, a guaranteed right to a job, one-month vacation with pay, a literacy rate of over 90 percent, and a life expectancy of 72 years. Yugoslavia also offered its multi-ethnic citizenry affordable public transportation, housing, and utilities, with a not-for-profit economy that was mostly publicly owned. This was not the kind of country global capitalism would normally tolerate. Still, socialistic Yugoslavia was allowed to exist for 45 years because it was seen as a nonaligned buffer to the Warsaw Pact nations.

The dismemberment and mutilation of Yugoslavia was part of a concerted policy initiated by the US and the other Western powers in 1989. Yugoslavia was the one country in Eastern Europe that would not voluntarily overthrow what remained of its socialist system and install a free-market economic order. In fact, Yugoslavs were proud of their postwar economic development and of their independence from both the Warsaw Pact and NATO. The US goal has been to transform the Yugoslav nation into a Third-World region, a cluster of weak right-wing principalities with the following characteristics:

- incapability of charting an independent course of self-development;
- a shattered economy and natural resources completely accessible to multinational;
- corporate exploitation, including the enormous mineral wealth in Kosovo;
- an impoverished, but literate and skilled population forced to work at subsistence wages, constituting a cheap labour pool that will help depress wages in western Europe and elsewhere;
- dismantled petroleum, engineering, mining, fertilizer, and automobile industries, and various light industries, that offer no further competition with existing Western producers.

US policymakers also want to abolish Yugoslavia's public sector services and social programmes—for the same reason they want to abolish our public sector services and social programmes. The ultimate goal is the privatization and Third Worldization of Yugoslavia, as it is the Third Worldization of the US and every other nation. In some respects, the fury of the West's destruction of Yugoslavia is a backhanded tribute to that nation's success as an alternative form of development, and to the pull it exerted on neighboring populations both East and West.

In the late 1960s and 1970s, Belgrade's leaders, not unlike the Communist leadership in Poland, sought simultaneously to expand the country's industrial base and increase consumer goods, a feat they intended to accomplish by borrowing heavily from the West. But with an enormous IMF debt came the inevitable demand for 'restructuring', a harsh austerity programme that brought wage freezes, cutbacks in public spending, increased unemployment, and the abolition of worker-managed enterprises. Still, much of the economy remained in the not-for-profit public sector, including the Trepca mining complex in Kosovo, described in the New York Times as "war's glittering prize…the most valuable piece of real estate in the Balkans…worth at least $5 billion' in rich deposits of coal, lead, zinc, cadmium, gold, and silver" (*New York Times*, July 8, 1998).[1]

That US leaders have consciously sought to dismember Yugoslavia is not a matter of speculation but of public record. In November 1990, the Bush administration pressured Congress into passing the 1991 Foreign Operations Appropriations Act, which provided that any part of Yugoslavia failing to declare independence within six months would lose US financial support. The law demanded separate elections in each of the six Yugoslav republics, and mandated US State Department approval of both election procedures and results as a condition for any future aid. Aid would go only to the separate republics, not to the Yugoslav government, and only to those forces whom Washington defined as 'democratic', meaning right-wing, free-market, separatist parties.

---

[1] My thanks to James Petras for the interest and support extended to me on repeated occasions regarding the whole conflict waged against Yugoslavia. This essay is written to honour his significant and signal contributions over the years in exposing the workings of US imperialism and capitalist development. He is one of the few American scholar activists who has persisted with intellectual courage and acumen in the service of Marxist social science and politics.

Another goal of US policy has been media monopoly and ideological control. In 1997, in what remained of Serbian Bosnia, the last radio station critical of NATO policy was forcibly shut down by NATO 'peacekeepers'. The story in the *New York Times* took elaborate pains to explain why silencing the only existing dissident Serbian station was necessary for advancing democratic pluralism. The Times used the term 'hardline' eleven times to describe Bosnian Serb leaders who opposed the shutdown and who failed to see it as 'a step toward bringing about responsible news coverage in Bosnia' (*New York Times*, October 10, 1997).

Likewise, a portion of Yugoslav television remained in the hands of people who refused to view the world as do the US State Department, the White House, and the corporate-owned US news media, and this was not to be tolerated. The NATO bombings destroyed the two government TV channels and dozens of local radio and television stations, so that by the summer of 1999 the only TV one could see in Belgrade, when I visited that city, were the private channels along with CNN, German television, and various US programmes. Yugoslavia's sin was not that it had a media monopoly but that the publicly owned portion of its media deviated from the western media monopoly that blankets most of the world, including Yugoslavia itself.

In 1992, another blow was delivered against Belgrade: international sanctions. Led by the US, a freeze was imposed on all trade to and from Yugoslavia, with disastrous results for the economy: hyperinflation, mass unemployment of up to 70 percent, malnourishment, and the collapse of the health care system.[2]

Divide and Conquer

One of the great deceptions, notes Joan Phillips, is that "those who are mainly responsible for the bloodshed in Yugoslavia—not the Serbs, Croats or Muslims, but the Western powers—are depicted as saviours" (Phillips, 1993: 10). While pretending to work for harmony, US lead-

---

[2] For more detailed background information on the stratagems preceding the NATO bombing, see the collection of reports by Ramsey Clark, Sean Gervasi, Sara Flounders, Nadja Tesich, Michel Chossudovsky, and others in *NATO in the Balkans: Voices of Opposition* (New York: International Action Center, 1998).

ers supported the most divisive, reactionary forces from Croatia to Kosovo.

In Croatia, the West's man-of-the-hour was Franjo Tudjman, who claimed in a book he authored in 1989, that "the establishment of Hitler's new European order can be justified by the need to be rid of the Jews", and that only 900,000 Jews, not six million, were killed in the Holocaust. Tudjman's government adopted the fascist Ustasha checkered flag and anthem (*Financial Times*, April 15, 1993). Tudjman presided over the forced evacuation of over half a million Serbs from Croatia between 1991 and 1995, replete with rapes and summary executions.[3] This included the 200,000 from Krajina in 1995, whose expulsion was facilitated by attacks from NATO war planes and missiles. Needless to say, US leaders did nothing to stop and much to assist these atrocities, while the US media looked the other way. Tudjman and his cronies now reside in obscene wealth while the people of Croatia are suffering the afflictions of the free market paradise. Tight controls have been imposed on Croatian media, and anyone who criticizes President Tudjman's government risks incarceration. Yet the White House hails Croatia as a new democracy.

In Bosnia, US leaders supported the Muslim fundamentalist, Alija Izetbegovic, an active Nazi in his youth, who has called for strict religious control over the media and now wants to establish an Islamic Bosnian republic. Izetbegovic himself does not have the support of most Bosnian Muslims. He was decisively outpolled in his bid for the presidency yet managed to take over that office by cutting a mysterious deal with frontrunner Fikret Abdic (Silber and Little, 1995: 11; Johnstone, 1999: 58). Bosnia is now under IMF and NATO regency. It is not permitted to develop its own internal resources, nor allowed to extend credit or self-finance through an independent monetary system. Its state-owned assets, including energy, water, telecommunications, media and transportation, have been sold off to private firms at garage sale prices.

In the former Yugoslavia, NATO powers have put aside neoimperialism and have opted for out-and-out colonial occupation. In early 1999, the democratically elected president of Republika Srpska, the

---

[3] See for instance, Yigal Chazan's report in *The Guardian* (London/Manchester), August 17, 1992.

Serb ministate in Bosnia, who had defeated NATO's chosen candidate, was removed by NATO troops because he proved less than fully cooperative with NATO's "high representative" in Bosnia. The latter retains authority to impose his own solutions and remove elected officials who prove in any way obstructive (Kelly, 1999). This too was represented in the western press as a necessary measure to advance democracy.

In Kosovo, we see the same dreary pattern. The US gave aid and encouragement to violently right-wing separatist forces such as the self-styled Kosovo Liberation Army, previously considered a terrorist organization by Washington. The KLA has been a longtime player in the enormous heroin trade that reaches to Switzerland, Austria, Belgium, Germany, Hungary, the Czech Republic, Norway, and Sweden (*San Francisco Chronicle*, May 5, 1999; *Washington Times*, May 3, 1999). KLA leaders had no social programme other than the stated goal of cleansing Kosovo of all non-Albanians, a campaign that had been going on for decades. Between 1945 and 1998, the non-Albanian Kosovar population of Serbs, Roma, Turks, Gorani (Muslim Slavs), Montenegrins, and several other ethnic groups shrank from some 60 to about 20 percent. Meanwhile, the Albanian population grew from 40 to 80 percent (not the 90 percent repeatedly reported in the press), benefiting from a higher birth rate, a heavy influx of immigrants from Albania, and the systematic intimidation and expulsion of Serbs.

In 1987, in an early untutored moment of truth, the *New York Times* reported: "Ethnic Albanians in the Government have manipulated public funds and regulations to take over land belonging to Serbs.... Slavic Orthodox churches have been attacked, and flags have been torn down. Wells have been poisoned and crops burned. Slavic boys have been knifed, and some young ethnic Albanians have been told by their elders to rape Serbian girls.... As the Slavs flee the protracted violence, Kosovo is becoming what ethnic Albanian nationalists have been demanding for years...an *ethnically pure* Albanian region." (*New York Times*, November 1, 1987). Ironically, while the Serbs were repeatedly charged with ethnic cleansing, Serbia itself is now the only multi-ethnic society left in the former Yugoslavia, with some twenty-six nationality groups including thousands of Albanians who live in and around Belgrade.

Demonizing the Serbs

The propaganda campaign to demonize the Serbs fits the larger policy of the Western powers. The Serbs were targeted for demonization because they were the largest nationality and the one most opposed to the breakup of Yugoslavia. None other than Charles Boyd, former deputy commander of the US European command, commented on it in 1994: "The popular image of this war in Bosnia is one of unrelenting Serb expansionism. Much of what the Croatians call *the occupied territories* is land that has been held by Serbs for more that three centuries. The same is true of most Serb land in Bosnia.... In short the Serbs were not trying to conquer new territory, but merely to hold onto what was already theirs." While US leaders claim they want peace, Boyd concludes, they have encouraged a deepening of the war (*Foreign Affairs*, September–October 1994).

But what of the atrocities they committed? All sides committed atrocities, but the reporting was consistently one-sided. Grisly incidents of Croat and Muslim atrocities against the Serbs rarely made it into the US press, and when they did they were accorded only passing mention.[4] Meanwhile Serb atrocities were played up and sometimes even fabricated, as we shall see. Recently, three Croatian generals were indicted by the Hague War Crimes Tribunal for the bombardment and deaths of Serbs in Krajina and elsewhere. Where were US leaders and US television crews when these war crimes were being committed? John Ranz, chair of Survivors of the Buchenwald Concentration Camp, US, asks: Where were the TV cameras when hundreds of Serbs were slaughtered by Muslims near Srebrenica?[5] The official line, faithfully parroted in the US media, is that the Serbs committed all the atrocities at Srebrenica.

Before uncritically ingesting the atrocity stories dished out by US leaders and the corporate-owned news media, we might recall the five hundred premature babies whom Iraqi soldiers laughingly ripped from incubators in Kuwait, a story repeated and believed until exposed as a total fabrication years later. During the Bosnian war in 1993, the Serbs were accused of having an official policy of rape. "Go forth and rape",

---

[4] For instance, Bonner (1999), a revealing report that has been ignored in the relentless propaganda campaign against the Serbs.

[5] John Ranz in his paid advertisement in the *New York Times*, April 29, 1993.

a Bosnian Serb commander supposedly publicly instructed his troops. The source of that story never could be traced. The commander's name was never produced. As far as we know, no such utterance was ever made. Even the New York Times belatedly ran a tiny retraction, coyly allowing that "the existence of *a systematic rape policy* by the Serbs remains to be proved" (*New York Times*, October 23, 1993).

Bosnian Serb forces supposedly raped anywhere from 25,000 to 100,000 Muslim women. The Bosnian Serb army numbered not more than 30,000 or so, many of whom were engaged in desperate military engagements. A representative from Helsinki Watch noted that stories of massive Serbian rapes originated with the Bosnian Muslim and Croatian governments and had no credible supporting evidence. Common sense would dictate that these stories be treated with the utmost skepticism—and not be used as an excuse for an aggressive and punitive policy against Yugoslavia.

The mass rape propaganda theme was resuscitated in 1999 to justify NATO's renewed attacks on Yugoslavia. A headline in the *San Francisco Examiner* tells us: 'SERB TACTIC IS ORGANIZED RAPE, KOSOVO REFUGEES SAY'. Only at the bottom of the story, in the nineteenth paragraph, do we read that reports gathered by the Kosovo mission of the Organization for Security and Cooperation in Europe found no such organized rape policy. The actual number of rapes were in the dozens "and not many dozens", according to the OSCE spokesperson. This same story did note that the UN War Crimes Tribunal sentenced a Bosnian Croat military commander to ten years in prison for failing to stop his troops from raping Muslim women in 1993—an atrocity we heard little about when it was happening (*San Francisco Examiner*, April 26, 1999).

The Serbs were blamed for the infamous Sarajevo market massacre of 1992. But according to the report leaked out on French TV, Western intelligence knew that it was Muslim operatives who had bombed Bosnian civilians in the marketplace in order to induce NATO involvement. Even international negotiator David Owen, who worked with Cyrus Vance, admitted in his memoir that the NATO powers knew all along that it was a Muslim bomb. However, the well-timed fabrication served its purpose of inducing the United Nations to go along with the US-sponsored sanctions.

On one occasion, the *New York Times* ran a photo purporting to be of Croats grieving over Serbian atrocities when in fact the murders had been committed by Bosnian Muslims. The *Times* printed an obscure retraction the following week (*New York Times*, August 7, 1993).

We repeatedly have seen how 'rogue nations' are designated and demonized. The process is predictably transparent. First, the leaders are targeted. Qaddafi of Libya was a 'Hitlerite megalomaniac' and a 'madman'. Noriega of Panama was a 'a swamp rat', one of the world's worst 'drug thieves and scums', and 'a Hitler admirer'. Saddam Hussein of Iraq was 'the Butcher of Baghdad', a 'madman' and 'worse than Hitler'. Each of these leaders then had their countries attacked by US forces and US-led sanctions. What they really had in common was that each was charting a somewhat independent course of self-development or somehow was not complying with the dictates of the global free market and the US national security state (Parenti, 1995).

Yugoslav president Slobodan Milosevic has been described by Bill Clinton as 'a new Hitler'. Yet he was not always considered so. At first, the Western press, viewing the ex-banker as a bourgeois Serbian nationalist who might hasten the break-up of the federation, hailed him as a 'charismatic personality'. Only later, when they saw him as an obstacle rather than a tool, did they begin to depict him as the demon who 'started all four wars'. This was too much even for the managing editor of the US establishment journal Foreign Affairs, Fareed Zakaria. He noted in the *New York Times* that Milosevic who rules "an impoverished country that has not attacked its neighbours—is no Adolf Hitler. He is not even Saddam Hussein" (*New York Times*, March 28, 1999).

Some opposition radio stations and newspapers were reportedly shut down during the NATO bombing. But, during my trip to Belgrade in August 1999, I observed nongovernmental media and opposition party newspapers going strong. There are more opposition parties in the Yugoslav parliament than in any other European parliament. Yet the government is repeatedly labeled a dictatorship. Milosevic was elected as president of Yugoslavia in a contest that foreign observers said had relatively few violations. As of the end of 1999, he presided over a coalition government that included four parties. Opposition groups openly criticized and demonstrated against his government. Yet he was called a dictator.

The propaganda campaign against Belgrade has been so relentless that prominent personages on the Left—who oppose the NATO policy against Yugoslavia—have felt compelled to genuflect before this demonization orthodoxy.[6] Thus do they reveal themselves as having been influenced by the very media propaganda machine they criticize on so many other issues. To reject the demonized image of Milosevic and of the Serbian people is not to idealize them or claim they are faultless or free of crimes. It is merely to challenge the one-sided propaganda that laid the grounds for NATO's destruction of Yugoslavia.

More Atrocity Stories

Atrocities (murders and rapes) occur in every war, which is not to condone them. Indeed, murders and rapes occur in many peacetime communities. What the media propaganda campaign against Yugoslavia charged was that atrocities were conducted on a mass genocidal scale. Such charges were used to justify the murderous aerial assault by NATO forces.

Up until the bombings began in March 1999, the conflict in Kosovo had taken 2000 lives altogether from both sides, according to Kosovo Albanian sources. Yugoslavian sources had put the figure at 800. In either case, such casualties reveal a limited insurgency, not genocide. The forced expulsion policy began after the NATO bombings, with thousands being uprooted by Serb forces mostly in areas where the KLA was operating or was suspected of operating. In addition, if the unconfirmed reports by the ethnic Albanian refugees can be believed, there was much plundering and instances of summary execution by Serbian paramilitary forces—who were unleashed after the NATO bombing started.

We should keep in mind that tens of thousands fled Kosovo because of the bombings, or because the province was the scene of sustained ground fighting between Yugoslav forces and the KLA, or because they were just afraid and hungry. An Albanian woman crossing into Macedonia was eagerly asked by a news crew if she had been forced out by Serb police. She responded: "There were no Serbs. We were frightened of the [NATO] bombs" (Biggs, 1999: 25). During the bombings, an estimated 70,000 to 100,000 Serbian residents of Kosovo took flight (mostly north but some to the south), as did thousands of Roma and

---

[6] Both Noam Chomsky in his comments on Pacifica Radio, April 7, 1999, and Alexander Cockburn in *The Nation*, May 10, 1999, referred to Serbian 'brutality' and described Milosevic as 'monstrous' without offering any specifics.

other non-Albanian ethnic groups (*Washington Post*, June 6, 1999). Were these people ethnically cleansing themselves? Or were they not fleeing the bombing and the ground war?

The *New York Times* reported that 'a major purpose of the NATO effort is to end the Serb atrocities that drove more than one million Albanians from their homes' (*New York Times*, June 15, 1999). So, we are told to believe, the refugee tide was caused not by the ground war against the KLA and not by the massive NATO bombing but by unspecified atrocities. The bombing, which was the major cause of the refugee problem was now seen as the solution. The refugee problem created in part by the massive aerial attacks was now treated as justification for such attacks, a way of putting pressure on Milosevic to allow "the safe return of ethnic Albanian refugees".[7]

While Kosovo Albanians were leaving in great numbers—usually well-clothed and in good health, some riding their tractors, trucks, or cars, many of them young men of recruitment age—they were described as being 'slaughtered'. Serbian attacks on KLA strongholds and the forced expulsion of Albanian villagers were described as 'genocide'. But experts in surveillance photography and wartime propaganda charged NATO with running a 'propaganda campaign' on Kosovo that lacked any supporting evidence. State Department reports of mass graves and of 100,000 to 500,000 missing Albanian men 'are just ludicrous', according to these independent critics (Radin and Palmer, 1999).

As with the Croatian and Bosnian conflicts, the image of mass killings was hyped once again. The Washington Post reported that 350 ethnic Albanians 'might be buried in mass graves' around a mountain village in western Kosovo. Such speculations were based on sources that NATO officials refused to identify. Getting down to specifics, the article mentions 'four decomposing bodies' discovered near a large ash heap, with no details as to who they might be or how they died (*Washington Post*, July 10, 1999).

An ABC 'Nightline' programme made dramatic and repeated references to the 'Serbian atrocities in Kosovo' while offering no specifics. Ted Kopple asked angry Albanian refugees what they had witnessed? They pointed to an old man in their group who wore a wool hat. The Serbs had thrown the man's hat to the ground and stepped on it,

---

[7] See for instance, Robert Burns, Associated Press report, April 22, 1999.

'because the Serbs knew that his hat was the most important thing to him', they told Kopple, who was appropriately appalled by this one example of a 'war crime' offered in the hour-long programme.

A widely circulated story in the *New York Times*, headlined 'US REPORT OUTLINES SERB ATTACKS IN KOSOVO', tells us that the State Department issued 'the most comprehensive documentary record to date on atrocities'. The report concludes that there had been organized rapes and systematic executions. But reading further into the article, one finds that stories of such crimes "depend almost entirely on information from refugee accounts. There was no suggestion that American intelligence agencies had been able to verify, most, or even many, of the accounts…and the word 'reportedly' and 'allegedly' appear throughout the document" (*New York Times*, May 11, 1999).

British journalist Audrey Gillan (1999) interviewed Kosovo refugees about atrocities and found an impressive lack of evidence. One woman caught him glancing at the watch on her wrist, while her husband told him how all the women had been robbed of their jewelry and other possessions. A spokesperson for the UN High Commissioner for Refugees talked of mass rapes and what sounded like hundreds of killings in three villages. When Gillan pressed him for more precise information, he reduced it drastically to five or six teenage rape victims. But he admitted that he had not spoken to any witnesses and that "we have no way of verifying these reports" (Gillan, 1999).

Gillan noted that some refugees had seen killings and other atrocities, but there was little to suggest that they had seen it on the scale that was being reported. Officials told him of refugees who talked of sixty or more being killed in one village and fifty in another, but Gillan "could not find one eye-witness who actually saw these things happening". It was always in some other village that the mass atrocities seem to have occurred. Yet every day western journalists reported 'hundreds' of rapes and murders. Sometimes they noted in passing that the reports had yet to be substantiated, but then why were such stories being so eagerly publicized?

In contrast to its public assertions, the German Foreign Office privately denied there was any evidence that genocide or ethnic cleansing was a component of Yugoslav policy: "Even in Kosovo, an explicit political persecution linked to Albanian ethnicity is not verifiable.…The actions of the [Yugoslav] security forces [were] not directed against the Kosovo-Albanians as an ethnically defined group, but against the military opponent and its actual or alleged supporters".[8]

Still, Milosevic was indicted as a war criminal, charged with the forced expulsion of Albanian Kosovars, and with summary executions of a hundred or so individuals. Again, alleged crimes that occurred after the NATO bombing had started were used as justification for the bombing. The biggest war criminals of all were the NATO political leaders who orchestrated the aerial campaign of death and destruction.

As the White House saw it, since the stated aim of the aerial attacks was not to kill civilians; there was no liability, only regrettable mistakes. In other words, only the professed intent of an action counted and not its ineluctable effects. But a perpetrator can be judged guilty of willful murder without explicitly intending the death of a particular victim—as with an unlawful act that the perpetrator knew would likely cause death. As George Kenney, a former State Department official under the Bush Administration, put it: "Dropping cluster bombs on highly populated urban areas doesn't result in accidental fatalities. It is purposeful terror bombing".[9]

In the first weeks of the NATO occupation of Kosovo, tens of thousands of Serbs were driven from the province and hundreds were killed by KLA gunmen in what was described in the western press as acts of 'revenge' and 'retaliation', as if the victims were deserving of such a fate. Also numbering among the victims of 'retribution' were the Roma, Gorani, Turks, Montenegrins, and Albanians who had 'collaborated' with the Serbs by speaking Serbian, opposing separatism, and otherwise identifying themselves as Yugoslavs. Others continued to be killed or maimed by the mines planted by the KLA and the Serb military, and by the large number of NATO cluster bombs sprinkled over the land (*Los Angeles Times*, August 22, 1999).

It was repeatedly announced in the first days of the NATO occupation that 10,000 Albanians had been killed by the Serbs (down from the 100,000 and even 500,000 Albanian men supposedly executed during the war). No evidence was ever offered to support the 10,000 figure,

---

[8] Intelligence reports from the German Foreign Office, January 12, 1999 and October 29, 1998 to the German Administrative Courts, translated by Eric Canepa, Brecht Forum, New York, April 20, 1999.

[9] Teach-in, Leo Baeck Temple, Los Angeles, May 23, 1999.

nor even to explain how it was so swiftly determined—even before NATO forces had moved into most of Kosovo.

Repeatedly unsubstantiated references to 'mass graves', each purportedly filled with hundreds or even thousands of Albanian victims also failed to materialize. Through the summer of 1999, the media hype about mass graves devolved into an occasional unspecified reference. The few sites actually unearthed offered up as many as a dozen bodies or sometimes twice that number, but with no certain evidence regarding causes of death or even the nationality of victims. In some cases there was reason to believe the victims were Serbs (Gall, 1999).

Lacking evidence of mass graves, by late August 1999 the *Los Angeles Times* focused on wells "as mass graves in their own right.... Serbian forces apparently stuffed... many bodies of ethnic Albanians into wells during their campaign of terror" (*Los Angeles Times*, August 28, 1999). Apparently? The story itself dwelled on only one village in which the body of a 39-year-old male was found in a well, along with three dead cows and a dog. No cause was given for his death and "no other human remains were discovered". The well's owner was not identified. Again when getting down to specifics, the atrocities seem not endemic but sporadic.

Ethnic Enmity and US 'Diplomacy'

Some people argue that nationalism, not class, is the real motor force behind the Yugoslav conflict. This presumes that class and ethnicity are mutually exclusive forces. In fact, ethnic enmity can be enlisted to serve class interests, as the CIA tried to do with indigenous peoples in Indochina and Nicaragua—and more recently in Bosnia.[10]

When different national groups are living together with some measure of social and material security, they tend to get along. There is intermingling and even intermarriage. But when the economy goes into a tailspin, thanks to sanctions and IMF destabilization, then it becomes easier to induce internecine conflicts and social discombob-

---

[10] It is a matter of public record that the CIA has been active in Bosnia. Consider these headlines: *The Guardian* (Manchester/London), November 17, 1994: "CIA AGENTS TRAINING BOSNIAN ARMY"; *The London Observer*, November 20, 1994: "AMERICA'S SECRET BOSNIA AGENDA"; *The European*, November 25, 1994: "HOW THE CIA HELPS BOSNIA FIGHT BACK".

ulation. In order to hasten that process in Yugoslavia, the Western powers provided the most retrograde separatist elements with every advantage in money, organization, propaganda, arms, hired thugs, and the full might of the US national security state at their backs. Once more the Balkans are to be balkanized.

NATO's attacks on Yugoslavia have been in violation of its own charter, which says it can take military action only in response to aggression committed against one of its members. Yugoslavia attacked no NATO member. US leaders discarded international law and diplomacy. Traditional diplomacy is a process of negotiating disputes through give and take, proposal and counterproposal, a way of pressing one's interests only so far, arriving eventually at a solution that may leave one side more dissatisfied than the other but not to the point of forcing either party to war.

US diplomacy is something else, as evidenced in its dealings with Vietnam, Nicaragua, Panama, Iraq, and now Yugoslavia. It consists of laying down a set of demands that are treated as nonnegotiable, though called 'accords' or 'agreements', as in the Dayton Accords or Rambouillet Agreements. The other side's reluctance to surrender completely to every condition is labeled 'stonewalling', and is publicly misrepresented as an unwillingness to negotiate in good faith. US leaders, we hear, run out of patience as their 'offers' are 'snubbed'. Ultimatums are issued, then aerial destruction is delivered upon the recalcitrant nation so that it might learn to see things the way Washington does.

Milosevic balked because the Rambouillet plan, drawn up by the US State Department, demanded that he hand over a large, rich region of Serbia, that is, Kosovo, to foreign occupation. The plan further stipulated that these foreign troops will have complete occupational power over all of Yugoslavia, with immunity from arrest and with supremacy over Yugoslav police and authorities. Even more revealing of the US agenda, the Rambouillet plan stated: "The economy of Kosovo shall function in accordance with free market principles".

Rational Destruction

While professing to having been discomforted by the aerial destruction of Yugoslavia, many liberals and progressives were convinced that 'this time' the US national security state was really fighting the good fight. "Yes, the bombings don't work. The bombings are stupid!" they said at the time, "but we have to do something". In fact, the bombings were other than stupid: they were profoundly immoral. And in fact they did work; they destroyed much of what was left of Yugoslavia, turning it into a privatized, deindustrialized, recolonized, beggar-poor country of cheap labour, defenseless against capital penetration, so battered that it will never rise again, so shattered that it will never reunite, not even as a viable bourgeois country.

When the productive social capital of any part of the world is obliterated, the potential value of private capital elsewhere is enhanced—especially when the crisis faced today by western capitalism is one of overcapacity. Every agricultural base destroyed by western aerial attacks (as in Iraq) or by NAFTA and GATT (as in Mexico and elsewhere), diminishes the potential competition and increases the market opportunities for multinational corporate agribusiness. To destroy publicly-run Yugoslav factories that produced auto parts, appliances, or fertilizer—or a publicly financed Sudanese plant that produced pharmaceuticals at prices substantially below their western competitors—is to enhance the investment value of western producers. And every television or radio station closed down by NATO troops or blown up by NATO bombs extends the monopolizing dominance of the western media cartels. The aerial destruction of Yugoslavia's social capital served that purpose.

We have yet to understand the full effect of NATO's aggression. Serbia is one of the greatest sources of underground waters in Europe, and the contamination from US depleted uranium and other explosives is being felt in the whole surrounding area all the way to the Black Sea. In Pancevo alone, huge amounts of ammonia were released into the air when NATO bombed the fertilizer factory. In that same city, a petrochemical plant was bombed seven times. After 20,000 tons of crude oil were burnt up in only one bombardment of an oil refinery, a massive cloud of smoke hung in the air for ten days. Some 1,400 tons of ethylene dichloride spilled into the Danube, the source of drinking water for ten million people. Meanwhile, concentrations of vinyl chloride were released into the atmosphere at more than 10,000 times the permitted level. In some areas, people have broken out in red blotches and blisters, and health officials predict sharp increases in cancer rates in the years ahead.[11]

---

[11] Report by Steve Crawshaw in *The London Independent*, reprinted in the *San Francisco Examiner*, July 26, 1999.

National parks and reservations that make Yugoslavia among thirteen of the world's richest bio-diversity countries were bombed. The depleted uranium missiles that NATO used through many parts of the country have a half-life of 4.5 billion years.[12] It is the same depleted uranium that now delivers cancer, birth defects, and premature death upon the people of Iraq. In Novi Sad, I was told that crops were dying because of the contamination. And power transformers could not be repaired because UN sanctions prohibited the importation of replacement parts. The people I spoke to were facing famine and cold in the winter ahead.

With words that might make us question his humanity, the NATO commander, US General Wesley Clark boasted that the aim of the air war was to "demolish, destroy, devastate, degrade, and ultimately eliminate the essential infrastructure" of Yugoslavia. Even if Serbian atrocities had been committed, and I have no doubt that some were, where is the sense of proportionality? Paramilitary killings in Kosovo (which occurred mostly after the aerial war began) are no justification for bombing fifteen cities in hundreds of around-the-clock raids for over two months, spewing hundreds of thousands of tons of highly toxic and carcinogenic chemicals into the water, air, and soil, killing thousands of Serbs, Albanians, Roma, Turks, and others, and destroying bridges, residential areas, and over two hundred hospitals, clinics, schools, and churches, along with the productive capital of an entire nation.

A report released in London in August 1999 by the Economist Intelligence Unit concluded that the enormous damage NATO's aerial war inflicted on Yugoslavia's infrastructure will cause the economy to shrink dramatically in the next few years (*San Francisco Examiner*, August 23, 1999). Gross domestic product will drop by 40 percent this year and remain at levels far below those of a decade ago. Yugoslavia, the report predicted, will become the poorest country in Europe. Mission accomplished.

Postscript

In mid-September 1999, the investigative journalist Diana Johnstone emailed associates in the US that former US ambassador to Croatia,

---

[12] See the communication from Serbian environmentalist Branka Jovanovic: http://beograd.rockbridge.net/greens_from_belgrade.htm; March 31, 1999.

Peter Galbraith, who had backed Tudjman's 'operation storm' that drove 200,000 Serbians (mostly farming families) out of the Krajina region of Croatia four years ago, was recently in Montenegro, chiding Serbian opposition politicians for their reluctance to plunge Yugoslavia into civil war. Such a war would be brief, he assured them, and would "solve all your problems". Another strategy under consideration by US leaders, heard recently in Yugoslavia, is to turn over the northern Serbian province of Vojvodina to Hungary. Vojvodina has some twenty-six nationalities including several hundred thousand persons of Hungarian descent who, on the whole show no signs of wanting to secede, and who certainly are better treated than the larger Hungarian minorities in Rumania and Slovakia. Still, a recent $100 million appropriation from the US Congress fuels separatist activity in what remains of Yugoslavia—at least until Serbia gets a government sufficiently pleasing to the free-market globalists in the West. Johnstone concludes: "With their electric power stations ruined and factories destroyed by NATO bombing, isolated, sanctioned and treated as pariahs by the West, Serbs have the choice between freezing honorably in a homeland plunged into destitution, or following the 'friendly advice' of the same people who have methodically destroyed their country. As the choice is unlikely to be unanimous one way or the other, civil war and further destruction of the country are probable."

CHAPTER TWELVE

JAMES PETRAS ON THE ISRAELI LOBBY, OCCUPIED PALESTINE AND US-ISRAELI MILITARISM

Stephen Lendman

Over his long distinguished career, James Petras authored hundreds of articles and dozens of books on many topics, including social change in Latin America, unmasking globalization as 21st Century imperialism, and the subject of this contribution to his *festschrift*: the power of the Israeli Lobby, Occupied Palestine and US-Israeli militarism. This power gives US imperialism a particular twist in several (the US and Middle Eastern) arenas of international relations, as well as establishing bulwark of US imperialism in a critically important albeit volatile area of the world state system.

This article reviews in depth some of his current writing and analysis from three of his recent books: *The Power of the Israeli Lobby in the US, Rulers and Ruled in the US Empire*, and *Zionism, Militarism and the Decline of US Power.*

The *Power of Israel in the US* (2006) is a work of epic writing documenting the influence of the most powerful lobby in Washington. It extends to the highest levels of government, the business community, academia, the clergy, the mass media, and, as Edward Said once said about the Senate virtually the entire (body) can be marshaled in a matter of hours into coming together for Israel.

The root of its power is in the high proportion of Jewish families among the wealthiest and most dominant in the country. They include billionaires and many others who have created a 'tyranny of Israel over the US' with consequences grave enough to threaten world peace, security, the global economy, and democracy's very future in America and elsewhere. Because of its influence, Washington unconditionally supported all Israeli aggression since 1967. Israel also played a leading role in both US Iraq wars and intervening sanctions, but that's not all. It may press us into war on Iran and its hugely destabilizing effects if it comes. More still, it suppresses open Middle East debate and dissenting opposition to its imperial agenda—regardless of the harm to America or how grievously it violates international law.

Attacking Iraq in 1991, 12 years of punishing sanctions, and then invading and occupying the country in 2003 removed one of Israel's key adversaries, with Iran, Hamas, Hezbollah and Syria remaining. At the same time, it ended Iraq's support of Palestine, allowing Israel to advance further toward its goal of total regional dominance in partnership with Washington.

Committed Israeli support makes this possible from (i) officials at all levels of government; (ii) influential Jewish organizations and lobbying groups like the Conference of Presidents of Major Jewish American Organizations (CPMAJO), the Zionist Organization of America (ZAO), the Anti-Defamation League (ADL), and according to some observers, the single most powerful Washington lobby—AIPAC; as well as (iii) the vast 'Jewish Diaspora', including many thousands of dedicated activists: doctors, lawyers, dentists, philanthropists, key Wall Street figures, major bank executives, Federal Reserve governors, its chairman, other key businessmen, major media bosses, the clergy, academia and journalists given special prominence because of their support of a pro-Israeli agenda, the regime's aggressive war policy, and its most grievous of disturbing crimes of war and against humanity— like the savagery shown Gaza under siege and the Nazi-like blitzkrieg against civilian men, women and children, massacred as if for fun in an electronic war game.

As a result, Israel gets away with mass murder and receives more US aid than all other nations combined and special privileges with it: billions of dollars annually in aid; the latest weapons and technology; low or no interest rate loans; some simply waived and not repaid; additional monetary aid as requested; unrestricted US market access for its products and services; free entry of its immigrants; guaranteed Security Council vetoes for unfavourable to its interests resolutions; freedom to operate covertly inside America, including on US military bases; and Washington's partnership in its aggressive wars, its military agenda, occupation of Palestine, wars against Lebanon, unwarranted attacks on Syria, retention of the Golan Heights, and freedom to commit the most grievous crimes of war and against humanity, including mass-Palestinian incarcerations, free use of torture and as much mass murder as expedient.

Regardless of its harm to America, Israel gets what it wants because the 'Zionist power configuration (ZPC)' extends well beyond the Lobby. It includes a 'complex network of interrelated formal and informal groups, operating at the international, national, regional, and local levels' unconditionally supporting Israel and its agenda of war, colonization and oppression. It influences the selection of political candidates and can defeat incumbents or aspirants daring to criticize Israel. It also shapes major media reporting, suppresses everything unsupportive or critical, and can get academics fired with Norman Finkelstein Exhibit A.

ZPC's fruition came under George Bush to the degree that Ariel Sharon once boasted that: 'We have the US president under our control'. It is likely Israel's next prime minister will say the same about Barack Obama, who Petras terms 'America's First Jewish President' in his November 2008 article by that title. He quoted him asking Israeli president Shimon Peres: 'What can I do for Israel?'

Petras further relates how Obama was spotted, chosen, groomed, vetted, judged safe on all matters for Israel, and may outdo George Bush and the neocons. He discusses the 'conversion and promotion of Obama as an Israel-Firster'—a clear example of how ZPC influence builds 'a near invincible power base in the US political system' under either major party. 'Obama's conversion began through an ideologically diverse, individual, family, and community-based effort'—from local to national prominence with massive political tutoring and funding. It began when Harvard Law School Zionist professor (Martha Minow) spotted him on campus as a 'smart, promising, and politically ambitious' recruit. He then advanced step by step with powerful backers to his current role—a sort of ZPC Manchurian candidate-president and not likely one to disappoint.

As Petras puts it: 'Obama had crossed the River Jordan (and capitulated) to the Zionfascists' and their agenda. Call him George Bush's third term and not 'change to believe in' as wishful thinkers will soon learn. Obama has surrounded himself with a coterie of pro-Israeli zealots from State to Defense to Treasury and all other high-level posts. In this connection Petras justifiably worries about the 'ascent of a minority of ambitious power-driven political operatives acting first and foremost for a militarist colonial power in a strategic region of the world…the biggest threat to world peace and to US democratic values in recent history…. Where does that leave the American people, their rights, their interests and their country's independent foreign policy?' Given the gravest ever global economic crisis, an agenda of continued militarism, a stronger-than-ever alliance with Israel, and the continuation of reckless policies the new administration espouses, be warned that the future under Obama looks grim and frightening.

In his latest January 2009 article titled 'The Politics of An Israeli Extermination Campaign: Backers, Apologists and Arms Suppliers', Petras dissects Israel's war on Gaza, its 'totalitarian vision...ethno-rascist ideology', genocidal agenda, criminal targeting of civilians, and assured continuity under a new Israeli prime minister and Obama as America's 'first Jewish' president.

Gaza, as Petras constructs it, remains totally isolated and for Israel a 'free fire zone (against) the entire population of 1.5 million semi-starved prisoners' living in what Michel Chossudovsky calls a 'concentration camp'—mercilessly under attack round the clock, including with illegal terror weapons. Israel even 'boasts of having systematically planned the extermination campaign—months in advance—up to and including the precise hour and day of the bombing to coincide with inflicting the maximum murder of civilians: the rockets and bombs fell as children were leaving school (and others arriving for afternoon classes), as graduating police cadets were receiving diplomas, and as frantic mothers ran out from their homes to find their sons and daughters'.

Israel and Washington planned the operation collaboratively 'because of (ZPC) influence' over administration and congressional policies under Republicans and Democrats. Strong backing as well comes from media bosses, trade unions, academia, and the entire support network for turkey-shoot mass murder. As Petras describes it there is little hope for an independent US Congressional policy as long as Israel's war of extermination in Gaza (or elsewhere) can be defended by the President, cabinet, House Speaker, leaders of both parties, and virtually the entire Washington establishment with enough power to matter.

Rulers and Ruled in the US Empire

In 2007 Petras' *Rulers and Ruled in the US Empire* was published. Among other topics it discusses 'systemic dimensions' of the US state, evolving changes in the American ruling class, its corporatist system, the use of force and genocidal carnage, Latin American relations and regional events, as well as the power of the Israeli Lobby. In Part II of the book Petras covers the power of Israel and its Lobby in the following terms: (i) how they combined to torpedo the proposal of Jim Baker's Iraq Study Group (ISG) for an alternative Middle East agenda, a proposal that favoured stability and less conflict, a phased withdrawal from Iraq, engaging Iran rather than waging war against Iran, and the policies demanded by 'Big Oil' for a more stable business climate.

Israel, AIPAC and the ZPC make war with Iran their top priority and back candidates supportive of 'Israel's military solution to Iran's (perfectly legal) nuclear enrichment programme'. For Israel and its Lobby, Arabs and Muslims threaten peace, and Washington should unconditionally support its agenda against them. The Lobby wanted war on Iraq and got it. The 2006 Lebanon one as well, targeting Syria, the current Gaza conflict, and more ahead with Iran to neutralize Israel's main regional rival—even at the risk of economic collapse and a possible calamitous world war. Petras calls Washington's permanent war strategy in collaboration with Israel 'an irrational gamble comparable to Hitler's attack on Russia' that doomed him and Germany. Attacking Iran and perhaps Syria and Hezbollah may result in 'greater defeats, greater domestic rebellion' and dark future prospects ahead.

Zionism, Militarism, and the Decline of US Power

In 2008, 'Zionism, Militarism and the Decline of US Power' continued the story. Petras discussed Zionism's destructive influence on America: its stranglehold on US politics, the media and all other important segments of society. He debunked the notion that ZPC influence is like all others, providing convincing evidence of its veto power over war and peace, trade and investment, multi-billion dollar arms sales, and Middle East policies under both major parties.

One example of this power is in the various pretexts advanced for invading and occupying Iraq: the 'weapons of mass destruction' (WMDs), which were known not to exist at the outset; the removal of a dangerous dictator, a valued ally of the US pre-Gulf war; bringing 'democracy' to the region when in fact every effort is made to suppress it; preventing a civil war in occupied Iraq when the presence of the US state was more likely to bring one about; the need for a military victory to retain for the US superpower status; reassuring regional regimes that the US can be relied on for protection and reminding outliers that war against them may be next; and to demonstrate the power of Pax America—that it is willing and able to both fight and defeat whatever the US designates as 'terrorism'.

However, the longer the Iraq and Afghan wars continue, the less convincing these arguments have become. And the more likely that occupation will lead to resistance the greater the economic and political cost, and the increased chance that the US public no longer will put up with permanent wars at a time grave domestic needs should take precedence.

Wars nonetheless persist with possible larger-scale conflict ahead and with perilous consequences. But the Israeli Lobby clearly wants it, and those opposed are intimidated, blackmailed, smeared, pressured, removed from positions of authority, and at times even murdered in ways disguised as unfortunate accidents—a long-time CIA practice against 'uncooperative' leaders and high officials anywhere, including at home. It is in fact difficult to explain why the Israeli lobby is so intent on the projection of state power and military force, but as Petras constructs it, as always with solid empirical data, Israel and its US Lobby want sequential wars for more power as a means of eliminating all regional challengers to the power of the Israeli state. As it turns out, both Congress and the administration are supportive. By all accounts (not just Petras'), with Washington-Israeli regional domination as the goal, the exceedingly high cost and duration of the Palestine conflict are no deterrents.

The ZPC-Israeli Lobby: What is it?

What precisely is the ZPC-Israeli Lobby—a power unlike any other politically! Representing less than 1% of the population, it consists of 'a multiplicity of highly organized, well-financed and centrally-directed structure throughout the US'. It includes scores of political action committees, a dozen or more think tanks, and the '52 major American Jewish organizations grouped under the umbrella listing Conference of Presidents of Major American Jewish Organizations (CPMAJO)'.

Equally or even more important are grassroots Jewish federations and organizations throughout the US, including influential professionals and activist students plus the entire political establishment from Washington to state and local levels.

The ZPC 'octopus', in Petras' account, reaches everywhere—'far beyond the traditional centres of big city power and national politics…into remote towns and cultural spheres' across the country. With powerful mass media backing, its influence is enormous, and only the brave (perhaps foolish) dare opposes it. Yet they do, their numbers grow, and may swell because of Israel's outrageous Gaza slaughter.

Today, the Lobby 'is at or near the peak of its political power', yet remains vulnerable. Hostility against it is growing. Unless stopped, it is heading America toward what Chalmers Johnson views as the dynamic that doomed past empires unwilling to change: 'isolation, overstretch, the uniting of local and global forces opposed to imperialism, and in the end bankruptcy' plus authoritarian rule, the loss of personal freedom, and the end of democracy. America's alliance with Israel and submissiveness to its Lobby hastens the arrival of that kind of future.

Petras again reviewed the possibility of war with Iran and further regional adventurism. He also discussed how top-level Pentagon commanders are replaced by more compliant ones when they are not in accord with Israel and its militarism. He then addressed how this agenda foretells a 'decline of US power' as well as a brief history of military vs. market-driven empire building. He distinguishes between wars of conquest vs. 'large-scale, long-term economic penetration via a combination of investments, loans, credits and trade in which market power and superiority (greater productivity) in the means of production led to...a virtual empire'.

After WW II, European militarism declined. America's advanced for foreign wars, proxy ones, encircling the world with bases, and establishing an unprecedented military-industrial complex for supremacy. Today over $1 trillion annually goes for 'defense' with all spending categories included plus multi-billions more off-the-books and secret CIA, NSA and other undisclosed spending.

America expanded its war-making capacity while Western Europe, Japan, and more recently China and Russia emphasize economic development with predictable results. The US prospered through the 1960s before competition became formidable. Since then, 'European and Japanese (and now Chinese, other Asian, Russian and Latin American) market-based (economies) moved with greater dynamism from domestic to export-led growth and began to challenge (our) predominance in a multiplicity of productive sectors'.

These regions are more dominant as US economic supremacy declines, leaving America only tops in militarism, and that's now stretched to the limit. Why so? Because of decades of off-shoring manufacturing and growing a predominantly service economy. As a result (except for Wall Street and high finance and tech in good times), low wage jobs replaced better-paying ones. Social benefits are being lost, and unions are a shadow of their former selves.

In addition, trade and current account deficits are enormous. The national debt is skyrocketing. Money is created like confetti—what one analyst calls 'toilet paper' and wonders why other countries accept it. The currency is being debased. The groundwork is being laid for a future hyperinflation, and according to one noted economist, a Great Depression does not loom ahead, a 'Very Great Depression' does because of past excesses and hugely counterproductive current policies.

In the book, Petras reviews the empire-building project since WW II that brought the US to its current dilemma. US prosperity peaked in 1999 and ever since declined—now precipitously. Even during a global economic crisis, China, India, Russia, European, Asian and Latin American states are developing their economies and expanding business relationships around the world while America's position is eroding.

The more Washington advances militarism in partnership with Israel, the worse off in the end things will get. History shows that 'imperial wars destroy the productive forces and social networks of targeted countries'. They eat the aggressor's seed corn as well and let market-based economies gain advantage through productive alliances. 'Militarist imperialism has weakened the entire economic fabric of the US empire without any compensatory gains on the military side'. Since WW II, George W. Bush waged the US's only two relatively or somewhat successful conflicts, both against weak opponents, and they were quick and cheap. In contrast, Korea and Southeast Asia were quagmires. So are Iraq and Afghanistan today. Here no end to conflict is in sight, and many hundreds of billions of dollars, badly needed at home, are going to waste or consumed unproductively. The financial resources consumed us staggering in its volume and its impact on the US economy.

In the context of this enormous misallocation of resources, together with the broader impact of the stranglehold of the Israeli lobby over US foreign policy—economic decline, national insolvency, the loss of personal freedom and the erosion of democracy—the prospects for improvement or change are dismal: up for grabs all because of a destructive alliance with Israel.

Even so, what harms America helps the Jewish state, at least in the short run. In that light, Iraq was a great success. Saddam was deposed. A key Palestinians backer was removed. The country was smashed, destroyed and dismembered. Israel's regional dominance increased. It is unimpeded in colonizing and devastating Palestine. Next up perhaps Iran as a regional threat. Syria, Hezbollah and Hamas as well. And proxy wars continue against Pakistan and Somalia, and perhaps future ones in Venezuela, Bolivia, Ecuador—even Russia, with Georgia attacking South Ossetia an early warning.

Petras views the 'Judeo-centric view of the world' as deadly. Believing that 'what is good for the Jews (means) providing unconditional support to an aggressive colonial state' (Israel) it is, he argues, a guaranteed 'formula for global disaster'. A tiny minority of Jews and their supporters back it. In contrast, most Jews and others have no ideological ties to Israel, are dubious of imperial wars, see no advantage in them for themselves and are not comforted by America funding them when that spending is vitally needed at home.

No matter: the worst of policies persist. 'Where will it take us? When will it end?' In the depths of tyranny unless enough people halt 'uncontainable humanitarian calamities whose ramifications impact the entire world' and may end up destroying it and our futures.

Looking Ahead

As this is written, George Bush has but a few days left in office. When published, Obama will be president and a new Israeli prime minister likely elected. Petras looked at the prospects of new leadership of the US state. In December 2008, he reflected on this in an article, whose title—'A Historic Moment: The Election of the Greatest Con-Man in Recent History'—speaks for itself. Unfortunetely, this writer has to wholeheartedly agree with the explicit judgment on Obama. Petras: 'even a cursory analysis of his key campaign advisors and public commitments to Wall Street speculators, civilian militarists, zealous Zionists and corporate lawyers... point(s) to a continuation of the economic and military policies of the Bush administration'.

Make no mistake, he continues: 'Within three weeks of his election, he appointed all the political dregs who brought on the unending wars of the past two decades, the economic policy makers responsible for the financial crash... Obama (speaks to) workers and work(s) for their financial overlords... He promise(s) peace in the Middle East (and) swears undying allegiance to the (ZPC) War Party... serving a foreign colonial power (Israel).

On a bigger stage, Petras argues, admittedly with no empirical evidence, 'Obama will be the perfect incarnation of Melville's Confidence Man. He catches your eye while he picks your pocket'. As Petras sees it, an Obama administration will assure continuity with the worst of George Bush: permanent wars, homeland repression, economic corruption and collapse, the continued pillaging of the national treasury, rewarding 'banksters' for their crimes, debasing the currency, effectively neutralizing organized labour, and destroying what remains of democracy in America—all the while hailing 'change to believe in'.

Only to the degree of even more of the same failed policies heading us to the edge of the abyss. 'Let us (celebrate) our "First Afro-American" Imperial President, (black on the outside, deceptive beneath), who wins by con...rules by guns', and assures the grimmest of grim futures for his own people and damn near all the rest of us as well.

In his January 8/09 article, 'Venezuela: Socialism, Democracy and the Re-Election of President Chávez', Petras comments on the country's February 15 constitutional referendum to allow indefinite re-elections of the President in the context of an effective, working democracy where voters choose their leader and can keep him or her as long as they wish. Since February 1999, Petras notes, Chávez transformed Venezuela from an 'oligarchic electoral politics to democracy', a process labeled by many observers in the US, and many political scientists and sociologists in the liberal tradition, as a 'dictatorship' in the making. Chávez, in this context, overcame a 2002 US-backed coup against a democratically elected regime, a subsequent oil management lockout, and through electoral victories 'strengthened the process of democratization of the state and civil society'. In this context it is not difficult to agree with Petras that allowing (by constitutional change) Chávez to be re-elected 'is essential for the continuation of the democratic process and social welfare of Venezuelans'. For one thing, Chávez 'audacious(ly)' defends 'world peace and humanitarian justice', is strongly opposed to genocidal imperial wars, and he had the courage to expel Israel's ambassador in response to his country's deadly attack and prosecution of the Gaza war. For another, in comparing Chávez to Barack Obama Petras observes: [[a]t a time of Israel's genocidal war, backed by the US and at a time when newly-elected Obama doubles military spending and troops for wars in Afghanistan, Iraq and possibly Iran, the world looks to President Chávez as the world's foremost humanitarian leader, the outstanding defender of freedom, peace, and self-determinination' when so little of them are around and none whatever in Washington or Tel Aviv, whichever party in either country governs. 'Con (and) guns' indeed, when carnage in Gaza rages with the full support of Obama and Congress.

For Palestinians, as for Americans and others across the world, the struggle continues—for peace, social justice, self-determination and liberation. Fortunately for us and even more so for the oppressed in the Middle East and elsewhere, James Petras continues his long-term engagement in this struggle as a committed scholar-activist, critical sociologist, a Marxist and revolutionary.

LIST OF CONTRIBUTORS

BERCH BERBEROGLU is Foundation Professor of Sociology and Chair of the Department of Sociology at the University of Nevada, Reno. He has written and edited 26 books and many articles. Recent books include *Labor and Capital in the Age of Globalization* (2002), *Globalization of Capital and the Nation-State* (2003), *Nationalism and Ethnic Conflict: Class, State, and Nation in the Age of Globalization* (2004), *Globalization and Change: The Transformation of Global Capitalism* (2005), *The State and Revolution in the Twentieth Century: Major Social Transformations of Our Time* (2007) and *Class and Class Conflict in the Age of Globalization* (2008). His latest book is *Globalization in the 21st Century: Labor, Capital and the State on a World Scale* (2010), published by Palgrave Macmillan.

TOM BRASS formerly lectured in the Social and Political Sciences Faculty at the University of Cambridge, UK, and also directed studies for a number of colleges there (Sidney Sussex, Queens'). His academic training is in sociology and anthropology, and he carried out fieldwork in rural Latin America during the 1970s and in India during the 1980s. He edited *The Journal of Peasant Studies* for almost two decades (1990–2008), and has written eleven books and seventy journal articles.

RONALD H. CHILCOTE is Professor of economics and political science at the University of California, Riverside and is the founder and managing editor of *Latin American Perspectives*. He is widely published in the area of Latin American affairs. His many edited and authored books include *Power and the Ruling Classes in Northeast Brazil* (1990), *The Political Economy of Imperialism* (1999), *Imperialism. Theoretical Directions* (2000) and *Theories of Comparative Political Economy* (2000). His monograph *The Portuguese Revolution: State and Class in the Transition to Democracy* will appear in 2010. He also has published two books of photography in an effort to raise awareness of pristine wilderness areas.

RAÚL DELGADO WISE is Director of the Doctoral Program in Development Studies at the University of Zacatecas (Mexico), President of the International Migration and Development Network, and co-Chair of the Critical Development Studies Network. He is author/editor of 14 books and more than 100 essays, including book chapters and refereed articles. Dr. Delgado has been a guest lecturer in North, Central and South America and the Caribbean, Europe, Africa and Asia. He received the annual prize for economics research "Maestro Jesús Silva Herzog" in 1993, and is a member of the Mexican Academy of Sciences, of the National System of Researchers and of several scholarly associations in Canada, the United States, Latin America and Europe. He is editor of the *Journal Migración y Desarrollo*, member of the editorial committee of several academic journals in the US, Chile, Argentina and Mexico, and editor of the book series *Latin America and the New World Order* for Miguel Angel Porrúa.

JOHN BELLAMY FOSTER is a professor of sociology at the University of Oregon and editor of *Monthly Review* (New York). He is the author of numerous books, including, most recently, *Naked Imperialism: The US Struggle for Global Dominance (2006), Critique of Intelligent Design: Materialism versus Creationism from Antiquity to the Present* (with Brett Clark and Richard York, 2008), *The Great Financial Crisis: Causes and Consequences* (with Fred Magdoff, 2009) and *The Ecological Revolution: Making Peace with the Planet* (2009)—all published by Monthly Review Press.

HANNAH HOLLEMAN is from Okmulgee Oklahoma, and a frequent contributor to *Monthly Review*. She is currently a doctoral candidate in sociology at the University of Oregon where her focus is in political economy and environmental sociology. In the broader community she helps organize social justice efforts with an emphasis on underrepresented youth and the transformation of higher education.

ASHOK KUMBAMU was born and brought up in a peasant family in a Telangana village in Southern India. He received his Master's degree in Development Studies from the Institute of Social Studies at The Hague. Currently he is writing a PhD thesis at the University of Alberta, Canada, on the socio-ecological implications of the local adoption, maladaptation and abandonment of genetically modified crops. Recent publications include 'Ecological Modernization and the Gene Revolution: The Case Study of Bt Cotton in India', *Capitalism Nature Socialism*, December 2006.

FERNANDO LEIVA is Associate Professor of Latin American, Caribbean and US Latino Studies at Suny-Albany. He is the author of *Latin American Neostructuralism: The Contradictions of Post-Neoliberal Development* (University of Minnesota Press, 2008). His other books are *Democracy in Chile: The Legacy of September 11, 1973* (with Silvia Nagy-Zekmi) and *Democracy and Poverty in Chile* (with James Petras). HResearch interests include Latin American development theories; the political economy of capitalist restructuring; social movements; and, more recently, critical cultural political economy.

STEPHEN LENDMAN is Research Associate of the Centre of Research on Globalization. Co-hosts The Global Research News Hour on Republic Broadcasting.org.

MORRIS MORLEY is Associate Professor of Politics at Macquarie University, Sydney, Australia, and senior research fellow with the Council on Hemispheric Affairs, Washington DC. He is the co-author (with James Petras) of *US Hegemony Under Siege* (1990), *Latin America in the Time of Cholera* (1992), and *American Global Power and Domestic Decay* (1995); author of *Washington, Somoza and the Sandinistas* (1994); co-author (with Chris McGillion) of *Unfinished Business: America and Cuba after the Cold War* (2002); and the co-editor (with Chris McGillion) of *Cuba, the United States and the Post-Cold War World* (2005).

MICHAEL PARENTI received his PhD in political science from Yale and has taught at a number of colleges and universities. His 21 books include: *The Assassination of Julius Caesar* (New Press); *Contrary Notions: The Michael Parenti Reader* (City Lights); and the forthcoming *God and His Demons* (Prometheus). Over 300 articles of his have been published in scholarly journals, magazines, newspapers, books of collected readings and online publications. He lectures frequently across North America and abroad. Tapes of his talks and interviews have played widely on community radio stations and public access television. For further information, visit: www.MichaelParenti.org.

HENRY VELTMEYER is Professor of Sociology and International Development Studies, Saint Mary's University (Halifax, Canada) and the Universidad Autónoma de Zacatecas in Mexico. Recent publications, include *Unmasking Globalization: Imperialism of the 21st Century* and *What's Left in Latin America*, both co-authored with James Petras.

JAMES PETRAS—SELECTED PUBLICATIONS

America Latina: Mas Alla del Neoliberalismo. Sao Paulo: Xaman, 1999.

Argentina: Entre desintegración y la revolución. Buenos Aires: Editorial la Maza, 2002. [co-author]

Brazil e lula. Petrópolis: Blumenau, 2005.

Capitalist and Socialist Crises in the Late Twentieth Century. Totowa NJ: Rowman & Allenheld, 1984. [co-author]

Cardoso's Brazil: A Land for Sale. Boulder CO: Rowman & Littlefield, 2003. [co-author]

Class, State and Power in the Third World. Mathew Held and Osmun, 1981. [co-author]

Competizione Globale: Imperialismi e Movimienti di Resistencia. Rome: Jaca Book, 2005.

Critical Perspectives on Imperialism and Social Class. New York: Monthly Review. 1978.

Cultivating Revolution: Unites States and Agrarian Reform in Latin America. New York: random House, 1971. [co-author]

Democracy and Poverty in Chile. Boulder CO: Westview press, 1993. [co-author]

Empire or Republic, Global Power, Domestic Decay: The US in the 1990s. Routledge, 1995. [co-author]

Empire with Imperialism: Dynamics of Globalizing Capitalism. London: Zed Books, 2005. Translated into Italian, French, Spanish and German. [co-author]

Ensayos contra el orden: Movimientos sociales en América Latina. Cuenca: Universidad de Cuenca and Quito: Coordinadora de Movimientos Sociales, 2003. [co-author]

Globalización Desenmascarada: El Imperialismo del Siglo XXI. Mexico: Grupo Editoria—Miguel Angel Porrua, 2004. [co-author]

Globalización, Imperialismo y Clase Social. Buenos Aires and Mexico City: Editorial Lumen, 2001. [co-author]

Globalization Unmasked: Imperialism in the 21st Century. London: ZED Press/Halifax: Fernwood Books.

Hegemonia dos Estados Unidos no Nova Milênio. Petrópolis: Editorial Vozes, 2000. [co-author]

Imperial State and Revolution: The United States and Cuba, 1952–1987. Cambridge University Press, 1987.

Juicio a las Multinacionales. Buenos Aires: Editorial Lumen, 2006. [co-author]

La Continuación de la Historia. La Paz: CIDES, 1996.

La Historia Terminable. Txalaparta Navarra, 1994.

Las Dos Caras del Imperialismo. Mexico/Buenos Aires: Grupo Editorial Lumen, 2004. [co-author]

Las privatizaciónes y la desnacionalización en América Latina. Buenos Aires: Libros Prometeo, 2004. [co-editor]

Latin America in the Time of Cholera. Routledge, 1992. [co-author]

Latin America: Bankers, Generals and the Struggle for Social Justice. Rowman & Littlefield, 1986. [co-author]

Latin America: Dependence or Revolution. New York: John Wiley, 1973.

Los intelectuales y la globalización. Quito: Editorial Abya Yala, 2004. [co-author]

Lotte e Regimi in America Latina. Rome: Jaca Book, 2005. [co-author]

Multinationals on Trial: Foreign Investment Matters. London: Ashgate, 2007. In Spanish as

Neoliberalism and Class Conflict in Latin America. London: Macmillan and St. Martin's Press, 1997. [co-author]

Peasants in Revolt. University of Texas Press, 1973. [co-author]

Politics and Social Forces in Chilean Development. Berkeley: University of California, 1969. Spanish edition, 1971.

Politics and Structure in Latin America. New York: Monthly Review, 1970.

Reform or Revolution: Politics and Social Structure in Latin America. New York: Fawcett, 1968. Spanish edition, 1971. [co-editor]

Rulers and Ruled in the US Empire: Bankers, Zionists and Militants. Clarity Press, 2007.

Social Movements and the State: Argentina, Bolivia, Brazil, Ecuador. London: Pluto Press. Spanish edition, Buenos Aires: Editorial Lumen, 2005. [co-author]

System in Crisis: The Dynamics of Free Market Capitalism. London: Zed Books/Halifax: Fernwood Books, 2003. Editions in Spanish, French and Greek. [co-author]

The Dynamics of Social Change in Latin America. London: Macmillan Press, 2000. [co-author]

The New Development Politics. Aldershot UK: Ashgate, 2003.

The Power of Israel in the United States. Clarity Press, 2006.

US Hegemony under Siege. London: Verso, 1990. [co-author]

What's Left in Latin America. Ashgate, 2009. In Spanish as *Espejismos de la izquierda en América Latina.* Buenos Aires: Editorial Lumen, 2009. [co-author]

REFERENCES

Ainslie, Rosalynde. 1977. *Masters and Serfs: Farm Labour in South Africa*. London: IDAF.

Alexander, Robert J. 1973. *Trotskyism in Latin America*. Stanford: Hoover Institution Press. Reviewed by Maitan (1978).

Ali, Tariq and Phil Evans (1980). *Trotsky for Beginners*. New York: Pantheon.

Althusser, Louis, 1971. *Lenin and Philosophy and Other Essays*, London: NLB.

Althusser, Louis, and Etienne Balibar, 1970. *Reading Capital*, London: NLB.

Amaladoss, M. (ed.). 1999. *Globalization and its Victims as Seen by its Victims*. Columbia: South Asia Books.

Amin, Samir, 1974. *Accumulation on a World Scale: A Critique of the Theory of Underdevelopment* (Vols. 1 and 2), London and New York: Monthly Review Press.

Amin, Samir, Arrighi, G. and I. Wallerstein. 1982. *Dynamics of Global Crisis*. New York: Monthly Review Press.

Anderson, Jon Lee. 1997. *Che Guevara. A Revolutionary Life*. New York: Grove Press.

Anderson, Perry. 1999. *The Origins of Postmodernity*. London: Verso.

——. 2002. "Force and Consent", *New Left Review*, 11(17): 5–30.

Andrade, Regis de Castro, 1982. 'Brazil: The Economics of Savage Capitalism', in Manfred Bienefeld and Martin Godfrey (eds.), *The Struggle for Development: National Strategies in an International Context*, Chichester and New York: John Wiley & Sons Limited.

Andreano, Ralph L. 1970. *The New Economic History*. New York: John Wiley & Sons.

Angell, Alan. 1993. "Chile Since 1958", in Leslie Bethel (ed.), *Chile Since Independence*. Cambridge: Cambridge University Press.

Angus, Ian. 2008. "Food Crisis: The greatest demonstration of the historical failure of the capitalist model," *Global Research*, April.

Anti-Slavery and Aborigines Protection Society, 1913. *Portuguese Slavery: Debate in the House of Lords, Wednesday, 23rd July, 1913*, London: Anti-Slavery and Aborigines Protection Society.

Araghi, Farshad. 2008. "The Political Economy of the Financial Crisis." *Economic and Political Weekly* 43(45): 30–32.

Araghi, Farshad and Philip McMichael. 2009. "Capitalism and the World-Historical Crises of Modernity." Paper prepared for the James Petras Festhscrift [araghi@fau.edu].

Arrighi, Giovanni. 2002. "Lineage of Empire," *Historical Materialism*, 10(3): 3–16.

——. 2005. "Hegemony Unravelling—I." *New Left Review* 32 (March–April): 23–80.

Assies, Willem. 2003. "From Rubber Estate to Simple Commodity Production: Agrarian Struggles in the Northern Bolivian Amazon", in Tom Brass (ed.), *Latin American Peasants*. London and Portland OR: Frank Cass Publishers.

Avenas, Denise. 1975. *La pensée de Leon Trotsky*. Toulouse: Privat Editeur.

Ayoub, Antoine, Radio Canada, May 2008.

Banaji, Jairus. 2003. "The Fictions of Free Labour, Contract, Coercion, and So-called Unfree Labour." *Historical Materialism* 11(3).

Bandeira, Luiz Alberto Moniz. 1962. *O caminho da revolução brasileira*. Rio de Janeiro.

——. 1978. "Origins e evolução do PTB". *Encontros com a Civilização Brasileira* 4, Octobre; 95–116.

Banxico. 2006. "Remesas familiares", in www.banxico.org.mx. Accessed September 18, 2007.

Baran, Paul. 1960. *The Political Economy of Growth*. New York: Promethius. Originally published in 1957 by Monthly Review Press.

Barlow Maude and Tony Clarke. 2004. *Water Privatization: The World Bank's Latest Market Fantasy*. Ottawa: Polaris Institute.

Barnet, Richard and John Cavenagh. 1994. *Global Dreams: Imperial Corporations and the New World Order*. New York: Simon & Schuster.

Bartra, Armando. 2003. *Cosecha de ira: economía política de la contrarreforma agraria*. Mexico City: Itaca.

Baruch, Knei-Paz. 1979. *The Social and Political Thought of Leon Trotsky*. Oxford: Oxford University Press.

Beams, Nick. 1998. *The Significance and Implications of Globalization: A Marxist Assessment*. Southfield: Mehring Books.

Bedoya Garland, Eduardo, and Alvaro Bedoya Silva-Santisteban, 2005a. *Enganche y Servidumbre por Deudas en Bolivia*, Geneva: International Labour Organization.

——. 2005b. *Trabajo Forsozo en la Extracción de la Madera en la Amazonia Peruana*. Geneva: International Labour Organization.

Beer, M. 1939. *An Inquiry into Physiocracy*. London: George Allen & Unwin.

Bello, Walden. 2006. "The Capitalist Conjuncture: Over-accumulation, Financial Crises and the Threat from Globalisation." *Third Word Quarterly* 27(8).

——. (2009). "The Global Collapse: A Non-orthodox View." *Z Net*, February 22. [http://www.zmag.org/znet/viewArticle/20638.

Belloc, Hilaire, 1924. *Economics for Helen*, New York: G.P. Putnam's Sons.

Berberoglu, Berch. 1987. *The Internationalization of Capital: Imperialism and Capitalist Development on a World Scale*. New York: Praeger.

——. 1992. *The Legacy of Empire: Economic Decline and Class Polarization in the United States*. New York: Praeger.

——. 1994. *Class Structure and Social Transformation*. New York: Praeger.

——. 2001. *Political Sociology: A Comparative/Historical Approach*, 2nd edition. Boulder CO: Rowman and Littlefield.

——. 2002. *Labour and Capital in the Age of Globalization*. Lanham MD: Rowman and Littlefield.

——. 2003. *Globalization of Capital and the Nation-State: Imperialism, Class Struggle, and the State in the Age of Global Capitalism*. Lanham MD: Rowman and Littlefield.

——. 2005. *Globalization and Change: The Transformation of Global Capitalism*. Lanham, MD: Lexington Books.

——. 2007. *The State and Revolution in the Twentieth Century*. Lanham MD: Rowman and Littlefield.

——. 2009. *Class and Class Conflict in the Age of Globalization*. Lanham MD: Lexington Books.

Bernstein, Peter W. and Annalyn Swan. 2007. *All the Money in the World: How the Fortune 400 Make-and Spend-Their Fortunes*. New York: Alfred A. Knopf.

Best, Steven and Douglas Kellner. 1997. *The Postmodern Turn*. New York: Guilford Press.

Beynon, Huw, 1973. *Working for Ford*, London: Allen Lane.

Biggs, Brooke Shelby. 1999. "Failure to Inform." *San Francisco Bay Guardian*, May 5, 1999.

Bina, Cyrus and Chuck Davis. 2002. "Dynamics of Globalization: Transnational Capital and the International Labour Movement", in Berch Berberoglu (ed.), *Labour and Capital in the Age of Globalization*. Boulder: Rowman and Littlefield Publishers.

Blanco, Hugo. 1972. *Land or Death: The Peasant Struggle in Peru*. New York: Pathfinder Press.

Blanco, Miguel Angel. *La Clave*, Madrid, June.

Blum, William. 2000. *Rogue State, A Guide to the World's Only Superpower*. Common Courage Press: Monroe.

Blumenfeld, Jared and Susan Leal. 2007. "The Real Cost of Bottled Water." *San Francisco Chronicle*, February 18.

Bonner, Raymond. 1999. "War Crimes Panel Finds Croat Troops 'Cleansed' the Serbs", *New York Times*, March 21.

Bonnet, Michel. 2000. "Child Labour in the Light of Bonded Labour", in Bernard Schlemmer (ed.), *The Exploited Child*. London and Paris: Zed Books and l'Institut de Recherche pour le Développement.

Borón, Atilio. A. 2005. *Empire and Imperialism. A Critical Reading of Michael Hardt and Antonio Negri*. Zed Books: London.

Bouhdiba, Abdelwahab, 1982. *Exploitation of Child Labour*, New York: United Nations.

Bowker, Gordon, and John Carrier (eds.), 1976. *Race and Ethnic Relations*, London: Hutchinson & Co (Publishers) Ltd.

Bowker, Mike and Phil Williams. 1988. *Superpower Détente: A Reappraisal*. London: Sage Publications.

Brass, Tom. 1994. "Some Observations on Unfree Labour, Capitalist Restructuring, and Deproletarianization", *International Review of Social History* 39(2).

——. 1995. Reply to Utsa Patnaik: If the Cap Fits…", *International Review of Social History* 40(1).

——. 1999. *Towards a Comparative Political Economy of Unfree Labour: Case Studies and Debates*. London and Portland OR: Frank Cass Publishers.

——. 2000. *Peasants, Populism, and Postmodernism: The Return of the Agrarian Myth*. London: Frank Cass.

——. 2002. "Rural Labour in Agrarian Transitions: The Semi-Feudal Thesis Revisited", *Journal of Contemporary Asia* 32(4).

——. 2003. "Why Unfree Labour is Not 'So-Called': The Fictions of Jairus Banaji." *The Journal of Peasant Studies* 31(1).

——. 2004. "Medieval Working Practices. British Agriculture and the Return of the Gangmaster", *The Journal of Peasant Studies* 31(2).

——. 2005. "Late Antiquity as Early Capitalism?" *The Journal of Peasant Studies* 32(1).

Brass, Tom and Marcel van der Linden (eds.). 1997. *Free and Unfree Labour: The Debate Continues*. Bern: Peter Lang, AG.

Braverman, Harry. 1974. *Labour and Monopoly Capital: The Degradation of Work in the Twentieth Century*. New York and London: Monthly Review Press.

Brecher, Jeremy, Tim Costello, and Brendan Smith. 2000. *Globalization from Below: The Power of Solidarity*. Boston: South End Press.

Bright, John. 1865. *Speeches of John Bright, M.P., on the American Question*. Boston: Little, Brown, and Company.

Bromley, Simon. 2003. "Reflections on Empire, Imperialism and United States Hegemony", *Historical Materialism* 11(3): 17–68.

——. 2004. "American Power and the Future of International Order", pp. 145–183 in *Ordering the International: History, Change and Transformation*, ed. William Brown, Simon Bromley and Suma Athreya. Pluto Press and the Open University: London.

Brooks, David and Jonathan Fox. 2004. "Ten Years of Cross-Border Dialogues", Americas Program, Interhemispheric Resource Center, in www.irc-online.org .Accessed August 10, 2007.

Bukharin, Nikolai c. 1930. *Imperialism and World Economy*. London: Martin Lawrence Limited.

——. 1972. *Imperialism and World Economy*. The Merlin Press: London.

Business Latin America. 1973. "Secretary Rogers' Latin America Tour Brings No Concrete Changes in Policy," June 7.

Byres, Terence J. 1996. *Capitalism from Above and Capitalism from Below: An Essay in Comparative Political Economy*. London: Macmillan Press.

——. 1999. "Rural Labour Relations in India: Persistent Themes, Common Processes and Differential Outcomes", *The Journal of Peasant Studies* 26(2–3).

——. 2005. "Neoliberalism and Primitive Accumulation in Less Developed Countries", in Alfredo Saad-Filho and Deborah Johnston (eds.), *Neoliberalism*. London: Pluto Press.

Cadbury, William A., 1909. *Labour in Portuguese West Africa*, London: George Routledge and Sons, Ltd.

Cadena, Guadalupe. 2005. "Manufactura, en la ruta de la "desindustrialización." *El Financiero*, August 16.

Callinicos, Alex. 1990. *Against Postmodernism: a Marxist Critique*. New York: St. Martin's Press.

——. 1990. *Trotskyism: Concepts in Social Thought*. Minneapolis: University of Minnesota Press.

Campos, José Roberto (1981). *O que é trotskyismo*. São Paulo: Coleção Primeiros Passos (40), Editora Brasiliense.

Cândido Filho, José. 1982. *O movimento operário: o sindicato, o partido*. Petropólis: Editora Vozes.

Canterbery, E. Ray. 2000. *Wall Street Capitalism: The Theory of the Bondholding Class*. River Edge, New Jersey: World Scientific Publishing.

Castañeda, Jorge G. 1997. *Compañero: The Life and Death of Che Guevara*. New York: Alfred A. Knopf.

Castillo, H. 1995. "Review: Democracy and Poverty in Chile: The Limits to Electoral Politics by James Petras," *The Hispanic American Historical Review* 75(4): 722–723.

CEPAL. 2002. *Globalización y desarrollo*. Santiago: CEPAL/ILPES/ONU.

Champlin, Dell and Eric Hake. 2006. "Immigration as Industrial Strategy in American Meatpacking," *Review of Political Economy*, 18(1): 49–70.

Chilcote, Ronald H. 1974. *The Brazilian Communist Party: Conflict and Integration, 1922–1972*. New York: Oxford University Press.

——. 1984. *Theories of Development and Underdevelopment*. Boulder: Westview Press.

——. 1992. "From Popular Power to Bourgeois Democracy: The Case of Portugal", in James Kurth and James Petras, pp. 128–159 in *Mediterranean Paradoxes: The Politics and Social Structure of Southern Europe*. Oxford: Berg Publishers.

——. 1993. "Left Political Ideology and Practice", pp. 171–86 in Barry Carr and Steve Ellner (eds.), *The Latin American Left: From the Fall of Allende to Perestroika*. Boulder: Westview Press.

Chilcote, Ronald H. and Joel Edelstein (eds.). 1974. *Latin America: The Struggle with Dependency and Beyond*. New York: Schenkman and Wiley.

Chomsky, Noam. 2001. *9–11*. Seven Stories Press: New York.

Coats, A.W. and Ross M. Robertson (eds.). 1969. *Essays in American Economic History*. London: Edward Arnold Publishers.

Cochrane, James D. 1972. "US Policy Toward Recognition of Governments and Promotion of Democracy in Latin America Since 1963," *Journal of Latin American Studies* 4(2).

Coggiola, Osvaldo Luis Angel. 1983. "Le mouvement trotskyste en Argentine: 1929–1959." Paris: Ph.D Dissertation: Ecole d'Hautes Etudes en Sciences Sociales, University of Paris. Pp. 629. In the Arquivo E Leunroth, Unicamp 0/2874, Campinas, Brazil.

Cohen, Robin. 1987. *The New Helots: Migrants in the New International Division of Labour*. Aldershot: Gower Publishing.

CONAPO. 2008. Migración internacional, in www.conapo.gob.mx accessed January 15, 2009.

Conrad, Alfred H. and John R. Meyer. 1965. *Studies in Economic History*. London: Chapman & Hall.

Cook, Allen. 1982. *Akin to Slavery: Prison Labour in South Africa*. London: IDAF.

Corrigan, Philip. 1977. "Feudal Relics or Capitalist Monuments? Notes on the Sociology of Unfree Labour", *Sociology* 11(3).

Council of Economic Advisers. 2008. *Economic Report of the President 2008*, Table B-91: Corporate Profits by Industry, 1959–2008.

Cypher, James. 1993. "The Ideology of Economic Science in the Selling of NAFTA: The Political Economy of Elite Decision-Making," *Review of Radical Political Economics* 25(4): 146–163.

Cypher, James and Raúl Delgado Wise. 2007. "Restructuring Mexico, Realigning Dependency: Harnessing Mexican Labour Power in the NAFTA Era," *Working Chapter*, Doctorado en Estudios del Desarrollo, Universidad Autónoma de Zacatecas.

Dallek, Robert. 2007. *Nixon and Kissinger: Partners in Power*. New York: Harper Collins.

Dange, S.A. 1949. *India from Primitive Communism to Slavery*. Bombay: People's Publishing House Ltd.

Day, Richard B. 1973. *Leon Trotsky and the Politics of Economic Isolation*. London: Cambridge University Press.

Delgado Wise, Raúl, Humberto Márquez and Héctor Rodríguez. 2004. "Organizaciones transnacionales de migrantes y desarrollo regional en Zacatecas," *Migraciones internacionales* 2(4).

Delgado Wise, Raúl and Humberto Márquez Covarrubias. 2005. "Migración, políticas públicas y desarrollo. Reflexiones en torno al caso de México," presented at the Seminario Problemas y Desafíos de la Migración y el Desarrollo en América, Red Internacional de Migración y Desarrollo, April 7–9, Cuernavaca.

Delgado Wise, Raúl and James Cypher. 2005. "The Strategic Role of Labour in Mexico's Subordinated Integration into the US Production System Under NAFTA", Working Document 12/11/2005, Doctorado en Estudios del Desarrollo, Universidad Autónoma de Zacatecas.

Desai, Meghnad. 2000. "Underconsumption", pp. 552–4 in *A Dictionary of Marxist Thought*, ed. Tom Bottomore. Maya Publishers: New Delhi.

Deutscher, Isaac. 1954. *The Prophet Armed: Trotsky 1879–1921*. London: Oxford University Press.

——. 1959. *The Prophet Unarmed: Trotsky 1921–1929*. London: Oxford University Press.

——. 1963. *The Prophet Outcast: Trotsky 1929–1940*. London: Oxford University Press.

—— (ed.). 1964. *The Age of Permanent Revolution: A Trotskyist Anthology*. New York: Dell Publishing.

Dilke, Sir Charles W., 1968 [1885]. *Industrial Remuneration Conference: The Report of the Proceedings and Papers* (Reprints of Economic Classics), New York: Augustus M. Kelley Publishers.

Dobb, Maurice. 1940. *Political Economy and Capitalism*, London: Routledge & Kegan Paul.

——. 1946. *Studies in the Development of Capitalism*. London: George Routledge & Sons.

Domhoff, William G. 2009. "Wealth, Income and Power," September 2005 (updated April 2009).

Dos Santos, Theotônio. 1970. "The Structure of Dependence," *American Economic Review* 60 (May), 231–236.

——. 1973. *Socialismo e fascismo-el Nuevo carácter de dependencia e el dilemma latinoamericano.* Buenos Aires: Periferia.

Dubois, Pierre, 1976. *Sabotage in Industry*, Harmondsworth: Penguin Books.

Dulles, John W.F. 1983. *Brazilian Communism, 1935–1945: Repression during World Upheaval.* Austin: University of Texas Press.

Economist Intelligence Unit. 1973. *Quarterly Economic Review of Chile*, Annual Supplement.

Edmunds, John C. 1996. "Securities: New World Wealth Machine," *Foreign Policy*, No. 104, Fall: 118–33. http://www.foreignpolicy.com/Ning/archive/archive/104/worldwealthmachine.PDF.

Elster, Jon. 1986. "The Theory of Combined and Uneven Development: A Critique", pp. 54–77 in John Roemer (ed.), *Analytical Marxism.* New York: Cambridge University Press.

Engahl, William. 2008. *Global Research*, May.

Engels, Frederick. 1985 [1868]. "Review of Volume One of Capital for The Fortnightly Review", Karl Marx Frederick Engels. *Collected Works*, Vol. 20. London: Lawrence & Wishart.

Engerman, Stanley L. 1973 [1967]. "The Effects of Slavery Upon the Southern Economy: A Review of the Recent Debate", in Peter Temin (ed.).

Engerman, Stanley L. and Eugene D. Genovese (eds.). 1975. *Race and Slavery in the Western Hemisphere: Quantitative Studies.* Princeton, NJ: Princeton University Press.

Ercelawn, A. and M. Nauman. 2004. "Unfree Labour in South Asia: Debt Bondage at Brick Kilns in Pakistan", *Economic and Political Weekly* XXXIX (22).

Falk, Richard. 1999. *Predatory Globalization: A* Critique. Malden Mass.: Blackwell.

Farnam, Henry W., 1938. *Chapters in the History of Social Legislation in the United States to 1860*, Washington, DC: Carnegie Institute.

Faundez, Julio. 1988. *Marxism and Democracy in Chile.* New Haven: Yale University Press.

Faux, Jeff. 2006. *The Global Class War.* Hoboken. John Wiley & Sons: New Jersey.

Federal Reserve Board. 2009. "Ponds and Streams: Wealth and Income in the US, 1989–2007," http://www.federalreserve.gov/Pubs/feds/2009/200913/200913abs.html.

Fernandes, Florestán. 1981a. *A revolução burguesa no Brasil.* 3d edn. Rio de Janeiro: Zahar Editores.

——. 1981b. "Entrevista: Florestán Fernandes, a pessoa e o político," *Nova Escrita Ensaio* 4 (December), 9–39. Interview with various intellectuals, including J. Chasin, Heleieth Saffioti and others.

Financial Times (London), April 15, 1993.

Fishman, Walda-Katz, Jerome Scott, and Ife Modupe. 2005. "Global Capitalism, Class Struggle, and Social Transformation," in Berch Berberoglu (ed), *Globalization and Change: The Transformation of Global Capitalism.* Lanham, MD: Lexington Books.

Flynn, Elizabeth Gurley. 1916. *Sabotage: The Conscious Withdrawal of the Workers' Industrial Efficiency.* Cleveland, OH: IWW.

Fogel, Robert William. 1975. "Preface", in Stanley L. Engerman and Eugene D. Genovese (eds.).

Fogel, Robert W. and Stanley W. Engerman. 1974. *Time on the Cross*: Vol. I—*The Economics of American Negro Slavery.* London: Wildwood House.

Forbes, October 6. 2008. "The 400 Richest People in America".

——. December 25. 2008. "The Richest People in America".

Foreign Affairs, September/October 1994.

Foster, John B. 2002. "Monopoly Capital and the New Globalization," *Monthly Review* 53(8), January.

Foster, John Bellamy and Fred Magdoff. 2008. "Financial Implosion and Stagnation: Back to the Real Economy," *Monthly Review* 60(6), December: 1–10.

——. 2009. *The Great Financial Crisis: Causes and Consequences*. New York: Monthly Review Press.

Fotopoulos, Takis and Alexandros Gezerlis. 2002. "Hardt and Negri's Empire: A New Communist Manifesto or a Reformist Welcome to Neoliberal Globalization?" *Democracy & Nature*, 8(2): 319–330.

Fox, Jonathan. 2005. "Repensar lo rural ante la globalización. La sociedad civil migrante," *Migración y desarrollo* No. 5: 35–58.

Frank, André Gunder. 1966. "The Development of Underdevelopment," *Monthly Review* 18 (September), 17–31.

——. 1967. *Capitalism and Underdevelopment in Latin America: Historical Studies of Chile and Brazil*. New York: Monthly Review Press.

——. 1977. "On So-Called Primitive Accumulation," *Dialectical Anthropology* 2(2).

——. 1978. *Dependent Accumulation and Underdevelopment*. London: Macmillan Press.

——. 1980. *Crisis in the World Economy*. New York: Holmes & Meier.

——. 1981. *Crisis in the Third World*. New York: Holmes & Meier.

——. 1981. *Reflections on the World Economic Crisis*. New York: Monthly Review Press.

Frank, Pierre. 1979. *The Fourth International*. London: Ink Links.

Fröbel, Folker, Jürgen Heinrichs and Otto Kreye. 1980. *The New International Division of Labour. Structural Unemployment in Industrialised Countries and Industrialisation in Developing Countries*. Cambridge, Cambridge University Press.

Frondizi, Silvo. 1947. *La integración mundial, última etapa del capitalismo (respuesta a una crítica)*, Buenos Aires: Praxis. 2d edition, 1954.

——. 1957. *La realidad argentina: ensayo de interpretación sociológica*. Buenos Aires: Praxis, 2 edn, 2 Vols.

——. 1960. *La revolución cubana: su significación histórica*. Montevideo: Editorial Ciencias Políticas.

Frost, David. 1981. "An Interview with Richard Helms, May 22–23, 1978," *Studies in Intelligence*, Fall.

Gall, Carlotta. 1999. "Belgrade Sees Grave Site as Proof NATO Fails to Protect Serbs," *New York Times*, August 27.

Garthoff, Raymond. 1994. *Détente and Confrontation*. Washington DC: The Brookings Institution.

Geras, Norman. 1975. "Rosa Luxemburg After 1905," *New Left Review* 89, January–February; 3–46.

——. 2000. "Luxemburg", pp. 327–29 in *A Dictionary of Marxist Thought*. ed. Tom Bottomore. Maya Publisher: New Delhi.

Gerstein, Ira. 1977. "Theories of the World Economy and Imperialism", *Insurgent Sociologist* 7(2), Spring.

Giddens, Anthony, and Gavin Mackenzie (eds.), 1982. *Social Class and the Division of Labour*, Cambridge: Cambridge University Press.

Gillan, Audrey. 1999. "What's the Story?" *London Review of Books*, May 27.

Girguli, Sivia, Selene Gaspar and Paula Leite. 2007. *La migración mexicana y el mercado de trabajo estadounidense*. CONAPO: Mexico.

Goldman, Michael. 2005. *Imperial Nature: The World Bank and Struggles for Social Justice in the Age of Globalization*. Yale University Press: New Haven and London.

González Casanova, Pablo. 1969. "Internal Colonialism and National Development," pp. 118–139 in Irving Louis Horowitx, Josué de Castro, and John Gerassi (eds), *Latin American Radicalism*. New York: Vintage.

Gorender, Jacob(o). 1987. *Combate nas trevas. A esquerda brasileira: das ilusões perdidas à luta armada.* 3d ed. São Paulo: Serie Temas (3), Editora Atica.

Government of India, 1931. *Royal Commission on Labour in India: Evidence, Vol. II— Part 2 (Punjab, Delhi and Ajmer-Merwara),* London: HMSO.

Government of India, Ministry of Labour, 1979. *Report of the Committee on Child Labour,* Delhi: Government of India Press.

Gowan, Peter. 2001. "Neoliberal Cosmopolitanism", *New Left Review* 11 (September–October): 79–93.

Green, David. 1971. *The Containment of Latin America.* Chicago: Quadrangle Books.

Green, Peter. 2002. "The Passage from Imperialism to Empire: A Commentary on *Empire* of Michael Hardt and Antonio Negri". *Historical Materialism* 10(1): 29–77.

Guarnizo, Luis Eduardo. 2003. "The Economics of Transnational Living," *International Migration Review* 37(3): 666–699.

Guérin, Daniel. 1956 [1951]. *Negroes on the March: A Frenchman's Report on the American Negro Struggle.* London and New York: New Park Publications.

Gulbenkian Commission. 1996. *Open the Social Sciences: Report of the Gulbenkian Commission on the Restructuring of the Social Sciences.* Stanford CA: Stanford University Press.

Halliday, Fred. 2001. *The World at 2000.* New York: St. Martin's.

Hardt, Michael and Antonio Negri. 2000. *Empire.* Harvard University Press: Cambridge and London.

Hart, Célia. 2004. "Socialism in One Country and the Cuban Revolution," See text at http://www.marxist.com/Latinam/cuba_celia_hart100504.html. Her collected works are at http://www.marxists.org/archive/celia-hart/index.htm.

——. 2007. "How Can You not be a Trotskyist in the Cuban Revolution!" Interview with David Rey. July 6, 2007. Published in Spanish in *El Militante* (Buenos Aires) and available at http://www.marxist.com/Latinam/cuba_celia_hart100504.htmlthrough The Walter Lippmann Web Site: Célia Hart Collection and the Marxists Internet Archive.

Hart, Jeffrey Hart. 1992. *Rival Capitalists: International Competitiveness in the United States, Japan, and Western Europe.* Ithaca, NY: Cornell University Press.

Harvey, David. 1989. *The Condition of Postmodernity: An Enquiry into the Origins of Cultural Change.* Oxford UK and Cambridge Mass: Blackwell.

——. 2003. *The New Imperialism.* Oxford University Press: London.

——. 2007. "Neoliberalism as Creative Destruction", *The Annals of the American Academy of Political and Social Science* 160(1): 21–44.

Haslam, Jonathan. 2005. *The Nixon Administration and the Death of Allende's Chile.* London: Verso.

Hersh, Seymour M. 1974. "Kissinger Called Chile Strategist," *New York Times,* September 15.

——. 1983. *The Price of Power.* New York: Summit Books.

Herskovits, Melville J. and Mitchell Harwitz (eds.). 1964. *Economic Transition in Africa.* London: Routledge and Kegan Paul.

Hobsbawm, E.J. 1964 [1958]. "History and "The Dark Satanic Mills", in *Labouring Men: Studies in the History of Labour.* London: Weidenfeld and Nicolson.

Hodges, Donald C. 1974. *The Latin American Revolution: Politics and Strategy from Apro-Marxism to Guevarism.* New York: William Morrow.

Hodgson, Geoff. 1975. *Trotsky and Fatalistic Marxism.* Nottingham: Spokesman Books.

Hohman, Elmo Paul, 1928. *The American Whaleman: A Study of Life and Labor in the Whaling Industry,* New York, London and Toronto: Longmans, Green and Co.

House of Commons Environment, Food and Rural Affairs Committee, 2003. *Gangmasters* (Fourteenth Report of Session 2002–03). London: The Stationery Office.

Houtart, Francois and Francois Polet (eds.). 2001. *The Other Davos Summit: The Globalization of Resistance to the World Economic System.* London: Zed Books.

Howard, Andrew. 2005. "Global Capital and Labour Internationalism: Workers' Response to Global Capitalism," in Berch Berberoglu (ed.), *Globalization and Change: The Transformation of Global Capitalism.* Lenham, Md: Lexington Books.

Howard, M.C. and J.E. King. 1989/1992. *A History of Marxian Economics.* Vol. 1— (1883–1929) and Vol. 2 (1929–1990). Princeton: Princeton University Press.

Howe, Irving (ed.). 1976. *The Basic Writings of Trotsky.* New York: Random House.

IFAD. 2007. *Sending Money Home. Worldwide Remittance Flows to Developing Countries.* Rome: International Fund for Agricultural Development.

INEGI. 2006. *Conteo de población y vivienda.* Mexico: INEGI.

Ingram, J.K. 1895. *A History of Slavery and Serfdom.* London: Adam and Charles Black.

INM. 2005. *Propuesta de política migratoria integral en la frontera sur de México.* Instituto Nacional de Migración: Mexico DF.

International Trotskyism 1929–1985. Durham, North Carolina: Duke University Press.

Isaacson, Walter. 1992. *Kissinger.* New York: Simon & Schuster.

Jameson, Fredric. 1991. *Postmodernism Or The Cultural Logic of Late Capitalism.* Durham: Duke University Press.

Johnson, Simon. "The Quiet Coup," *The Atlantic*, May 2009, 53. http://www.theatlantic.com/doc/200905/imf-advice.

Johnstone, Diana. 1999. "Alija Izetbegovic: Islamic Hero of the Western World," *Covert Action Quarterly*, Winter.

Kandell, Jonathan. 1973. "Chilean Officers Tell How They Began to Plan the Takeover Last November," *New York Times*, September 27.

Kaufman, Edy. 1988. *Crisis in Allende's Chile.* New York: Praeger.

Kautsky, Karl. 1910 [1891]. *The Class Struggle* (Erfurt Programme). Chicago, IL: Charles H. Kerr.

——. 1936. *The Economic Doctrines of Karl Marx.* Hampstead: NCLC Publishing Society.

——. 1983. "Imperialism", pp. 74–96 in *Karl Kautsky: Selected Political Writings*, ed. Patrick Goode. The Macmillan Press: London.

——. 1984 [1894/95]. "The Competitive Capacity of Small-scale Enterprise in Agriculture", in A. Hussain and K. Tribe (eds.), *Paths of Development in Capitalist Agriculture.* London: Macmillan.

——. 1988 [1899]. *The Agrarian Question*, 2 Vols. London: Zwan Publications.

Kelly, Michael. 1999. "The Clinton Doctrine is a Fraud, and Kosovo Proves It," *Boston Globe*, July 1.

Kennickell, Arthur B. (Federal Reserve Board). 2004. "Currents and Undercurrents: Changes in the Distribution of Wealth, 1989–2004," http://www.federalreserve.gov/Pubs/oss/oss2/papers/concentration.2004.5.pdf.

Kissinger, Henry. 1979. *The White House Years.* Sydney: Hodder and Stoughton.

——. 1990. *Years of Renewal.* New York: Simon & Schuster.

Kloby, Jerry. 2003. *Inequality, Power, and Development: Issues in Political Sociology*, 2nd Edn. New York: Humanity Books.

Knapp, Peter and Alan J. Spector. 1991. *Crisis and Change: Basic Questions of Marxist Sociology.* Chicago: Nelson-Hall, Publishers.

Knei-Paz, Baruch. 1977. "Trotsky, Marxism and the Revolution of Backwardness", in S. Avineri (ed.) (1977).

Kornbluh, Joyce L. (ed.), 1968. *Rebel Voices: An I.W.W. Anthology*, Ann Arbor, MI: The University of Michigan Press.

Kornbluh, Peter. 2003. *The Pinochet File*. New York: The New Press.

Krissman, Fred. 1997. "California's Agricultural Labor Market: Historical Variations in the Use of Unfree Labour, c. 1797-1994", in Tom Brass and Marcel van der Linden (eds.) (1997).

Krugman, Paul. 2009. "Making Banking Boring," *New York Times*, April 10.

Kuczynski, Jürgen. 1939. *The Condition of the Workers in Great Britain, Germany and the Soviet Union, 1932-1938*. London: Left Book Club/Victor Gollancz.

Kumbamu, Ashok. 2006. "Ecological Modernization and the Gene Revolution: The Case Study of Bt Cotton in India", *Capitalism Nature Socialism* 17(4): 7-31.

Lawrence, Felicity. 2004. *Not on the Label: What Really Goes into the Food on Your Plate*. London: Penguin Books.

Laxer, Gordon. 2003. "Radical Transformative Nationalisms Confront the US Empire", *Current Sociology* 51(2): 133-152.

——. 2005. "Popular National Sovereignty and the US Empire", *Journal of World-Systems Research* IX (2): 317-353.

Leiva, F.I. and J. Petras. 1986. "Chile's Poor in the Struggle for Democracy," *Latin American Perspectives* 13(4): 5-25.

——. 1987. "Chile: New Urban Movements and the Transition to Democracy," *Monthly Review* 39.

Lenin, V.I. 1963 [1913]. "Child Labour in Peasant Farming", *Collected Works*, Vol. 19. Moscow: Foreign Languages Publishing House.

——. 1964a [1899]. "The Development of Capitalism in Russia", *Collected Works*, Vol. 3. Moscow: Foreign Languages Publishing House.

——. 1964b [1918]. "Karl Marx: A Brief Biographical Sketch with an Exposition of Marxism", *Collected Works*, Vol. 21. London: Lawrence and Wishart.

——. 1965. *Imperialism, the Highest Stage of Capitalism*. Foreign Language Press: Peking.

——. 1972. Introduction to *Imperialism and World Economy*, Nikolai Bukharin 9-14.

——. 1975. *Selected Works in Three Volumes*. Vol. 2. Moscow: Progress Publishers.

Levy, Adrian, and Cathy Scott-Clark, 2004, 'He won, Russia lost', *The Guardian Weekend*, 8 May.

Lichtenstein, Alex, 1996. *Twice The Work of Free Labor: The Political Economy of Convict Labor in the New South*, London: Verso.

Lieten, G.K. 2003. *Power, Politics and Rural Development: Essays on India*. Delhi: Manohar.

Lipietz, Alain. 1987. *Mirages and Miracles: The Crisis in Global Fordism*. London: Verso.

Lituchy, Barry. 1993. "Media Deception and the Yugoslav Civil War", in *NATO in the Balkans*.

Lora, Guillermo (1977). *A History of the Bolivian Labour Movement 1848-1971*. Cambridge: Cambridge University Press.

Los Angeles Times, August 22, 1999.

——, August 28, 1999.

Loveman, Brian. 2001. *Chile: The Legacy of Hispanic Capitalism*. New York: Oxford University Press.

Löwy, Michael. 1975. "Is there a Law of Arrested and Un-combined Development?" *Latin American Perspectives* 2 (4): 118-120.

——. 1973. *The Marxism of Che Guevara*. New York: Monthly Review Press.

——. 1981. *The Politics of Combined and Uneven Development: The Theory of Permanent Revolution*. London: New Left Books.

Luxemburg, Rosa. 1951 [1913]. *The Accumulation of Capital*. London: Faber and Faber.

——. 1972. "The Accumulation of Capital: An Anti-critique", pp. 47–150 in *Imperialism and the Accumulation of Capital*, ed. Kenneth J. Tarbuck. Penguin Press: London.
Magdoff, Harry. 2003. *Imperialism without Colonies*. Monthly Review Press: New York.
Magdoff, Harry and Paul M. Sweezy. 1990. "The Editors Comment," *Monthly Review* 42, No. 7 (December: 37–38.
Maitan, Livio. 1978. "Apontes para una historia del trotskismo en América Latina," *Combate* 32 (1978).
Mandel, Ernest. 1968. *Marxist Economic Theory*, Vols. 1 and 2. London: The Merlin Press.
——. 1975. *Late Capitalism*. London: New Left Books.
——. 1979. *Trotsky: A Study of the Dynamic of his Thought*. London: New Left Books.
——. 1983. "In Defense of Permanent Revolution," *Intercontinental Press* 21, August 8, pp. 444–463. Reply to Doug Jenness.
Mantega, Guido. 1982. "Raizes e formação da economia política brasileira: a fase estagnacionista." São Paulo: Tese de Doutoramento, Faculdade de Filosofia, Letras e Ciências Humanas da Universidade de São Paulo.
Manzo, Kate. 2005. "Modern Slavery, Global Capitalism and Deproletarianisation in West Africa," *Review of African Political Economy*, No. 106.
Marglin, Stephen and Juliet Schor. 1990. *The Golden Age of Capitalism: Reinterpreting the Post-War Experience*. Oxford: Clarendon Press.
Marini, Ruy Mauro. 1969. *Subdessarrollo y revolución*. Mexico City: Siglo Veintiuno Editores.
——. 1973. *Dialéctica de la dependencia*. Mexico City: Ediciones Era.
——. 1978. "World Capitalist Accumulation and Sub-Imperialism," *Two Thirds* 1 (Fall): 29–39.
Márquez Covarrubias, Humberto. 2006. "El desarrollo participativo transnacional basado en las organizaciones de migrantes," *Problemas del desarrollo* 37 (144): 121–144.
Martins, Ernesto. 1967. "A donde vamos?" Rio de Janeiro (?), mimeo. Gorender (1987: 39) cites an essay "Na história da POLOP. Um pouco da história da esquerda brasileira," and essays in Em Tempo (October 4, 1979 and April 17, 1980).
Martins, José de Souza. 1997. "The Reappearance of Slavery and the Reproduction of Capital on the Brazilian Frontier", in Tom Brass and Marcel van der Linden (eds.) [1997].
Marx, Karl. 1913. *A Contribution to the Critique of Political Economy*. Chicago IL: Charles H. Kerr & Company.
——. 1972 [1861–63]. *Theories of Surplus Value—Part III*. London: Lawrence & Wishart.
——. 1976a [1867]. *Capital*, Vol. 1. Harmondsworth: Penguin Books.
——. 1976b [1847]. "The Poverty of Philosophy", Karl Marx Frederick Engels, *Collected Works*, Vol. 6. London: Lawrence & Wishart.
——. 1984 [1861]. "The Civil War in the United States", Karl Marx Frederick Engels, *Collected Works*, Vol. 19. London: Lawrence & Wishart.
——. 1985 [1866]. "Instructions for the Delegates of the Provisional General Council: The Different Questions", Karl Marx Frederick Engels, *Collected Works*, Vol. 20. London: Lawrence & Wishart.
——. 1986 [1857–58]. "Economic Manuscripts of 1857–58", Karl Marx Frederick Engels, *Collected Works*, Vol. 28. London: Lawrence & Wishart.
——. 1992. *Capital*, Vol. II. Penguin Books: London and New York.
Marx, Karl, and Fredrick Engels. 1957. *On Religion*. Moscow: Foreign Languages Publishing House.
——. 1976 [1848]. "Manifesto of the Communist Party", in Karl Marx and Fredrick Engels, *Collected Works*, Vol. 6. London: Lawrence and Wishart.

Mavrakis, Kostas. 1976. *On Trotskyism: Problems of Theory and History*. London: Routledge and Kegan Paul.

McMichael, Philip. 2004. *Development and Social Change*. Pine Forge Press: Thousand Oaks and New Delhi.

Miles, Robert. 1987. *Capitalism and Unfree Labour: Anomaly or Necessity?* London: Tavistock Publications.

Mill, John Stuart. 1849a. *Principles of Political Economy*, Vol. 1. London: John W. Parker.

———, 1849b, *Principles of Political Economy*, Vol. 2. London: John W. Parker.

Miller, Nicola. 1989. *Soviet Relations with Latin America, 1959–1987*. Cambridge: Cambridge University Press.

Mintz, Sidney W. 1977. "The So-Called World System: Local Initiative and Local Response," *Dialectical Anthropology* 2(4).

———. 1985. *Sweetness and Power: The Place of Sugar in Modern History*. New York: Viking.

Mittelman, James H. and Norani Othman (eds.). 2002. *Capturing Globalization*. New York: Routledge.

Moniz, Edmundo. 1980. "A crise mundial do imperialism e Rosa Luxemburgo," *Encontros com a Civilização Brasileira* 25 (July), 195–202.

Moore, David (ed.). 2007. *The World Bank: Development, Poverty, Hegemony*. University of Kwazulu Natal Press: Scottsville.

Moreno, Nahuel. 1974. *El golpe gorila de 1955: las posiciones del Trotskismo*. Buenos Aires: Editora Pluma.

Morley, Morris. 1994. *Washington, Somoza and the Sandinistas: State and Regime in US Policy Toward Nicaragua, 1969–1981*. New York: Cambridge University Press.

Morris, Roger. 1977. *Uncertain Greatness*. New York: Harper & Row.

Morton, Adam David. 2009. "Reflections on Uneven Development: Mexican Revolution, Primitive Accumulation, Passive Revolution," Nottingham. Paper presented as the inaugural address of the Latin American Perspectives Fellowship at the University of California, Riverside, January 2008, and revised for publication in *Latin American Perspectives* 37 (1) January 2010: 7–34.

Moyers, Bill and Michael Winship. 2009, "Mortgaging the Whitehouse," *Truthout*, May 2. http://www.truthout.org/050209Z.

Munck, Ronaldo. 1984. "Revolutionary Trends in Latin America," Montreal. *Occasional Monograph Series, No. 17*, Centre for Developing Area Studies, McGill University. Chapter 3, pp. 79–118, entitled "Trotskyism in Latin America."

Munoz, Heraldo. 2008. *The Dictator's Shadow*. New York: Basic Books.

Muttitt, Greg. 2001. "Control Freaks, Cargill and ADM," *The Ecologist*, March.

NACLA. 1973. "Chile; Facing the Blockade," *NACLA's Latin America and Empire Report*, January.

New York Times, November 1, 1987.

———, October 23, 1993.

———, October 10, 1997.

———, July 8, 1998.

———, March 28, 1999.

———, May 11, 1999.

———, June 15, 1999.

Nieboer, H.J. 1910. *Slavery as an Industrial System*. The Hague: Martinus Nijhoff.

Ninan, Ann. 2003. "Private Water, Public Misery," India Resource Center, April 16.

Nogee, Joseph L. and John W. Sloan. 1979. "Allende's Chile and the Soviet Union," *Journal of Inter-American Studies* 21(3), August.

Novack, George. 1970. "Critique of Frank's Thesis of Capitalist Underdevelopment," *Intercontinental Press* 15 (November).

———. 1972. *Understanding History: Marxist Essays*. New York: Pathfinder.

——. 1976. "The Law of Uneven and Combined Development and Latin America," *Latin American Perspectives* 3(2): 100–06.

NSC-National Security Council. 2004. *National Security Study Memorandum 200: Implications of Worldwide Population Growth for US Security and Overseas Interests.* Washington DC.

O'Brien, Thomas F. 2007. *Making the Americas.* Albuquerque: University of New Mexico Press.

O'Connor, James. 1970. *The Origins of Socialism in Cuba.* Ithaca: Cornell University Press.

——. 1989. "Uneven and Combined Development and Ecological Crisis: A Theoretical Introduction," *Race and Class* 30(3): 1–11.

OAS-Organization of American States, Inter-American Committee on the Alliance for Progress. 1972. *Domestic Efforts and Needs for External Financing for the Development of Chile.* Subcommittee on Chile, April 24–28.

OCDE. 2005. "La emigración de mexicanos a Estados Unidos," *Comercio Exterior* 55(2): 148–165.

ONU. 2006. "Seguimiento de la población mundial, con especial referencia a la migración internacional y el desarrollo," *Informe del Secretario General*, E/CN.9/2006/3, January 25.

Oshinsky, David M. 1997. *Worse Than Slavery: Parchman Farm and the Ordeal of Jim Crow Justice.* New York: Free Press.

Oudes, Bruce (ed.). 1989. *Richard Nixon's Secret Files.* New York: Harper & Row.

Page, Thomas Nelson. 1919 [1892]. *The Old South: Essays Social and Political.* New York: The Chautauqua Press.

Panitch, Leo and Colin Leys (eds.). 2003. *The New Imperial Challenge.* New York: Monthly Review Press.

Panitch, Leo and Sam Gindin. 2003. "Global Capitalism and American Empire", pp. 1–42 in *The Socialist Register 2004*, eds. Leo Panitch and Colin Leys. Merlin Press: London.

Parenti, Michael. 1995. *Against Empire.* San Francisco: City Lights Books.

Parker, William N. (ed.). 1970. T*he Structure of the Cotton Economy of the Antebellum South.* Washington DC: The Agricultural History Society.

Payer, Cheryl. 1974. *The Debt Trap: The IMF and the Third World.* New York: Monthly Review Press.

——. 1982. *The World Bank: A Critical Analysis.* New York: Monthly Review Press.

Peñaloza, Juan Ramón. 1953. *Trotsky ante la revolución nacional latinoamerica.* Buenos Aires: Editorial Indo América.

Petras, James. 1969b. *Politics and Social Forces in Chilean Development.* Berkeley and Los Angeles: The University of California Press.

——. 1969c. "Chile," *New Left Review* 1 (54).

——. 1970. *Politics and Structure in Latin America.* New York: Monthly Review.

——. 1973. *Latin America: Dependence or Revolution.* New York: John Wiley.

——. 1975. "The Chilean Junta Besieged: Generals Without Bankers," *The Nation* 220(25): 784–786.

——. 1978. *Critical Perspectives on Imperialism and Social Class.* New York: Monthly Review Press.

——. 1981. *Class, State, and Power in the Third World.* Montclair, NJ: Allanheld, Osmun.

——. 1983. "The Chicago Boys Flunk Out in Chile," *The Nation* 236(7): 193–211.

——. 1986. "Death in Chile: On the murder of a journalist and long-time friend," *Monthly Review* 38(November): 56–59.

——. 1987. "The Anatomy of State Terror: Chile, El Salvador and Brazil," *Science & Society* 51(Fall): 314–38.

——. 1988. "The New Class Basis of Chilean Politics," *New Left Review* 1(172).

——. 1990. "The Metamorphosis of Latin American Intellectuals," *Latin American Perspectives* 17(2): 102–112.

——. 1998. "Allende: Relevant Today?" *Canadian Dimension* 32(5): 39–41.

——. 1998. *The Left Strikes Back: Class Conflict in Latin America in the Age of Neoliberalism*. Boulder, CO: Westview Press.

——. 2002. "A Rose by Any Other Name? The Fragrance of Imperialism", *The Journal of Peasant Studies* 29(2): 135–160.

——. 2003. *The New Development Politics: The Age of Empire Building and New Social Movements*. Ashgate Publishing: Aldershot.

——. 2006. "Chile's New President: Washington's Best Ally?" *Counterpunch*, January 25, 2006.

——. 2006. "Mesoamerica Comes to North America: The Dialectics of the Migrant Workers' Movement". Retrieved January 6, 2009 from http://petras.lahaine.org/articulo.php?p=6&more=1&c=1.

——. 2007. "The Great Financial Crisis or Who's Got a Turd in his Briefcase?," James Petras website, August 24, 2007, http://petras.lahaine.org/articulo.php?p=1707&more=1&c=1.

——. 2007. *Rules and Ruled in the US Empire. Bankers, Zionists, Militants*. Atlanta: Clarity Press.

Petras, James and Christian Davenport. 1990. "The Changing Wealth of the US Ruling Class," *Monthly Review* 42, No. 7, December: 33–37.

Petras, J. and F.I. Leiva. 1988. "Chile. The Authoritarian Transition to Electoral Politics: A critique," *Latin American Perspectives* 15(3): 97–114.

Petras, J., F.I. Leiva, with H. Veltmeyer. 1994. *Democracy and Poverty in Chile: The Limits of Electoral Politics*. Boulder CO: Westview Press.

Petras, J. and H. Zemelman. 1972. *Peasants in Revolt: A Chilean Case Study, 1965–1971*. Austin and London: Institute of Latin American Studies/University of Texas Press.

Petras, James and Henry Veltmeyer. 2000. "Globalization or Imperialism?" *Cambridge Review of International Affairs* XIV(1), Autumn–Winter: 41–82.

——. 2001. *Globalization Unmasked: Imperialism in the 21st Century*. London: ZED Press/Halifax: Fernwood Books/Zed Books.

——. 2003. *System in Crisis: The Dynamics of Free Market Capitalism*. London: Zed Books/Halifax: Fernwood Books.

——. 2005. *Empire with Imperialism*. Halifax: Fernwood Books and London: ZED Press.

——. 2005a. "Globalization or Imperialism?" in *Power: A Critical Reader*, eds. Daniel Egan and Levon Chorbajian. Prentice Hall: New York.

——. 2007. *Multinationals on Trial: Foreign Investment Matters*. London: Ashgate.

——. 2007. "Social Movements and the State: Political Power Dynamics in Latin America", pp. 239–260 in R.A. Della Buono and José Bell Lara (eds.), *Imperialism, Neoliberalism and Social Struggles in Latin America*. Leiden and Boston: Brill.

——. 2007a. "Neoliberalism and Imperialism in Latin America: Dynamics and Responses", *International Review of Modern Sociology* 33, Special Issue.

——. 2008. "Camponeses numa era de globalização neoliberal: América Latina em movimento", pp. 79–120 in Eliane Tomiasi and Joe Edmilson Fabrini (eds.), *Campesinato e territórios em disputa*. Sao Paulo: Editora Expressão Popular.

——. 2008. "World Development: Globalization or Imperialism?" in H. Veltmeyer (ed.).

——. 2009. "A Class Perspective on Ecology and Indigenous Movements: Diversity with Inequality is not Social Justice," in L. Vasapollo and R. Martufi (eds.).

Petras, James and Maurice Zeitlin. 1968. *Reform or Revolution: Politics and Social Structure in Latin America*. New York: Fawcett.

———. 1968. "Agrarian Radicalism in Chile," *The British Journal of Sociology* 19(3): 254–270.

———. 1969. *El radicalismo político de la clase trabajadora chilena*. Buenos Aires: Centro Editor de América Latina.

Petras, James and Morris Morley. 1975. *The United States and Chile: Imperialism and the Overthrow of the Allende Government*. New York: Monthly Review Press.

Petras, J. and S. Vieux. 1990. "The Chilean Economic Miracle: An Empirical Critique," *Critical Sociology* 17(2): 57–72.

Philippon, Thomas and Ariel Reshef. 2008, "Wages and Human Capital in the US Finance Industry: 1909–2006," December, 3–4, figure1. http://pages.stern.nyu.edu/~tphilipp/papers/pr_rev15.pdf

Phillips, Brian. 1998. *Global Production and Domestic Decay: Plant Closings in the US*. New York: Garland.

Phillips, Joan. 1993. "Breaking the Selective Silence," *Living Marxism*, April.

Phillips, Kevin. 2006. *American Theocracy*. New York: Viking.

Phillips, Ulrich Bonnell. 1918. *American Negro Slavery: A Survey of the Supply, Employment and Control of Negro Labor as Determined by the Plantation Regime*. New York: Appleton and Company.

Plekhanov, Georgi, 1976 [1893]. 'Essays on the History of Materialism', *Selected Philosophical Works*, Vol. II, London: Lawrence and Wishart.

Polet, Francois (ed.). 2007. *The State of Resistance: Popular Struggles in the Global South*.

Pollak, Marcelo. 1999. *The New Right in Chile 1973–1989*. Basingstoke: MacMillan.

Prado Jr., Caio. 1966. *A revolução brasileira*. São Paulo: Editora Brasiliense.

Puga, Cristina. 2004. *Los empresarios organizados y el Tratado de Libre Comercio de América del Norte*. Miguel Ángel Porrúa: Mexico D.

Radin, Charles and Louise Palmer. 1999. "Experts Voice Doubts on Claims of Genocide: Little Evidence for NATO Assertions," *San Francisco Chronicle*, April 22.

Ramos, Jorge Abelardo. 1952. *La revolución nacional en Latinoamérica*. Buenos Aires: Ediciones del Mar Dulce.

Raptis, Michel. 1974. *Revolution and Counter-Revolution in Chile*. London: Alison and Busby.

Reuters.com, March 12. 2009. "US Household Wealth Falls $11.2 Trillion in 2008".

Rew, R.H. 1913 [1892]. "The Migration of Agricultural Labourers,' in *An Agricultural Faggot: A Collection of Papers on Agricultural Subjects*. Westminster: P.S. King & Son.

Robinson, William 2004. *A Theory of global Capitalism*. Baltimore: John Hopkins University Press.

Romagnolo, David. 1975. "The So-called Law of Uneven and Combined Development," *Latin American Perspectives* 2 (Spring), 7–31.

Rosenberg, J. 2005. "Globalisation Theory: A Post-Mortem," *International Politics* 42 (1).

Ross, Andrew (ed.). 1997. *No Sweat: Fashion, Free Trade, and the Rights of Garment Workers*. London: Verso.

Ross, Robert J.S. and Kent C. Trachte. 1990. *Global Capitalism: The New Leviathan*. Albany: State University of New York Press.

San Francisco Chronicle, May 5, 1999.

San Francisco Examiner, April 26, 1999.

———, August 23, 1999.

Santos, Mário dos and Ricardo Guerra Vidal. 1982. "A esquerda brasileira e o PT," *Internacionalismo* 2 (January–April): 19–36.

Sassen, Saskia. 2007. *A Sociology of Globalization*. New York: W.W. Norton.

Schäffle, A. 1893. *The Theory and Policy of Labour Protection*. London: Swan Sonnenschein & Co.

Schmitz, David F. 2006. *The United States and Right Wing Dictatorships.* New York: Cambridge University Press.

Schnee, Heinrich, 1926. *German Colonization: Past and Future*, London: George Allen & Unwin Ltd.

Schneidman, Witney W. 2004. *Engaging Africa.* Dallas: University Press of America.

Segal, Ronald. 1979. *Leon Trotsky.* New York: Pantheon.

Silber, Laura and Allan Little. 1999. *Yugoslavia: Death of a Nation.* London: Penguin.

Singleton-Gates, Peter, and Maurice Girodias, 1959. *The Black Diaries: An Account of Roger Casement's Life and Times with a Collection of his Diaries and Public Writings*, London: Sidgwick and Jackson Ltd.

Sklair, Leslie. 1995. *Sociology of the Global System.* Baltimore: Johns Hopkins University Press.

——. 2001. *The Transnational Capitalist Class.* Malden, Mass.: Blackwell Publishers.

Smith, Adam. 1812 [1776]. *An Inquiry into the Nature and Causes of the Wealth of Nations*, Vols. I–III. London: Cadell and Davies.

Smith, Murray E.G. 1996–1997. "Revisiting Trotsky: Reflections on the Stalinist Debacle and Trotskyism as Alternative," *Rethinking Marxism* 9, No. 3 (Fall), 40–67.

Sombart, Werner. 1967. *Luxury and Capitalism.* Ann Arbor, MI: The University of Michigan Press.

Stallings, Barbara. 1987. *Class Conflict and Economic Development in Chile.* Stanford: Stanford University Press.

Stavenhagen, Rodolfo. 1968. "Seven Fallacies about Latin America," pp. 13–31 in James Petras and Maurice Zeitlin (eds.), *Latin America: Reform or Revolution?* Greenwich, Connecticut: Fawcett Putlications.

Stevis, Dimitris and Terry Boswell. 2008. *Globalization and Labour: Democratizing Global Governance.* Lanham, Md.: Rowman and Littlefield.

Streeter, Stephen M. 2004. "Destabilizing Chile: the United States and the Overthrow of Allende," Latin American Studies Association International Congress. Las Vegas, October 7.

Sutch, Richard. 1975. "The Treatment Received by American Slaves: A Critical Review of the Evidence Presented in Time on the Cross," *Explorations in Economic History* 12(4).

Sutcliffe, Bob. 2006. "Imperialism Old and New: A Comment on David Harvey's *The New Imperialism* and Ellen Meiksins Wood's *Empire of Capital*", *Historical Materialism*, 14(4): 59–78.

Sweezy, Paul M. 1946. *The Theory of Capitalist Development: Principles of Marxian Political Economy.* London: Dennis Dobson Limited.

——. 1994. "Triumph of Financial Capital," *Monthly Review* 46, No. 2, June: 1–11.

Sweezy, Paul and Harry Magdoff. 1988. *The Irreversible Crisis.* Monthly Review Press.

Szymanski, Albert. 1978. *The Capitalist State and the Politics of Class.* Cambridge Mass.: Winthrop.

——. 1981. *The Logic of Imperialism.* New York: Praeger.

Tarbuck, J. Kennet. 197. *Imperialism and the Accumulation of Capital.* Penguin

Temin, Peter (ed.). 1973. *New Economic History.* Harmondsworth: Penguin Books.

The Guardian (London/Manchester), "Yigal Chazan's Report, August 17, 1992.

Trotsky, Leon. 1957. *History of the Russian Revolution.* Ann Arbor: University of Michigan Press.

——. 1959. *The Russian Revolution: The Overthrow of Tzarism and The Triumph of the Soviets.* Selected and Edited by F.W. Dupee. Garden City New York: Doubleday Anchor. Drawn from Leon Trotsky, *The History of the Russian Revolution.*

——. 1961. *Por los estados unidos socialistas de América Latina.* Buenos Aires: Editorial Coyoacán.

———. 1964a. "The Theory of Permanent Revolution", pp. 62ff in Isaac Deutscher (ed), *The Age of Permanent Revolution*.
———. 1964b. *The Age of Permanent Revolution: A Trotsky Anthology*. New York: Dell Publishing. Edited by Isaac Deutscher.
———. 1970 [1930]. *The Permanent Revolution*. New York: Pathfinder Press. Pioneer Press, 1962.
———. 1973. *The Spanish Revolution* (1931–39). New York: Pathfinder Press.
———. 1976. *Towards Socialism or Capitalism?* London: New Park Publications.
Tuden, Arthur and Leonard Plotnicov (eds.). 1970. *Social Stratification in Africa*. New York: The Free Press.
Turchetto, Maria. 2003. "The Empire Strikes Back: On Hardt and Negri", *Historical Materialism* 11(1): 23–36.
Uchitelle, Louis. 2007. "The Richest of the Rich, Proud of a New Gilded Age," *New York Times*, July 15.
United Nations and International Labour Office. 1953. *Report of the Ad Hoc Committee on Forced Labour*, Geneva: UN/ILO.
Valle, Martín. 1981. "História do Trotskyismo argentino' (de sua origem até 1945)," *Internacionalismo* Part 1 in 1 (October), 95–lll; Part 2 in 2 (January–April 1982): 89–106.
Vasapollo, Luciano and Rita Martufi (eds.). *Armonia con la madre terra la nuestra america del vivir bien a cura di* Rome: Jaca Books.
Veltmeyer, Henry. 2002. "The Politics of Language: Deconstructing Post-Development Discourse," *Canadian Journal of Development Studies* XX 11(3): 597–624.
——— (ed.). 2008. *New Perspectives on Globalization and Antiglobalization: Prospects for a New World Order?* Aldershot, UK: Ashgate.
——— (ed.). 2009. *Critical Development Studies: Tools for Change*. Halifax: Fernwood Books and London: Pluto Books.
Veltmeyer, Henry and James Petras. 1997. *The Dynamics of Social Change in Latin America*. London: Macmillan Press.
———. 2000. *Economic Liberalism and Class Conflict in Latin America*. London: Macmillan Press/New York: St. Martin's Press.
Vitale, Luis. 1967. *Interpretación marxista de la historia de Chile*. Santiago: Edicions de Prensa Latinoamericana.
———. 1968. "Latin America: Feudal or Capitalist?' pp. 32–43 in James Petras and Maurice Zeitlin (eds.), *Latin America: Reform or Revolution?* Greenwich Connecticut: Fawcett Publications.
Volkogonov, Dimitri. 1996. *The Eternal Revolutionary*. New York: Free Press.
Wagner, Helmut, ed. 2000. *Globalization and Unemployment*. New York: Springer.
Wakefield, Edward Gibbon. 1849. *A View of the Art of Colonization, with Present Reference to the British Empire*. London: John W. Parker, West Strand.
Wald, Alan. 1994–1995. "The End of American Trotskyism?" *Against the Current*. Part 1, 19 (November–December 1994), 29–32; Part 2, 19 (January–February 1994), 34–38; Part 3, 19 (March–April 1995), 33–37.
Walker, Francis A. 1888. *Political Economy*. London: Macmillan and Co.
Wall Street Journal, May 21, 2009. "US Rescue Aid Entrenches Itself."
Wallerstein, Immanuel. 1974. *The Modern World-System: Capitalist Agriculture and the Origins of the European World-Economy in the Sixteenth Century*. New York: Academic Press, Inc.
———. 1979. *The Capitalist World Economy*. Cambridge: Cambridge University Press.
Warren, Bill. 1980. *Imperialism, Pioneer of Capitalism*. London: Verso.
Washington Post, June 6, 1999.
———, July 10, 1999.
Washington Times, May 3, 1999.

Waterman, Peter. 1998. *Globalization, Social Movements, and the New Internationalisms.*
Waters, Malcolm. 1995. *Globalization: The Reader.* New York: Routledge.
Weber, Max. 1927. *General Economic History.* London: George Allen & Unwin.
———. 1947. *Theory of Social and Economic Organization.* London: William Hodge & Co.
Wilson, Edmund. 1972. *To the Finland Station.* New York: Farrar, Straus & Giroux and London: Macmillan.
Wolf, Eric R. 1982. *Europe and the People Without History.* Berkeley and Los Angeles CA: University of California Press.
Wood, Ellen Meiksins. 2003. *Empire of Capital.* Verso: London and New York.
World Bank. 1975. *Land Reform: Sector Policy Paper.* Washington DC: World Bank.
Zimbalist, A. and J. Petras. 1975. *Workers' Control in Allende's Chile.* Nottingham: Institute for Workers' Control.
Žižek, Slavoj. 2001. "Have Michael Hardt and Antonio Negri Rewritten the *Communist Manifesto* for the Twenty-First Century?" *Rethinking Marxism* 13(3/4): 190–198.
Zúñiga, Victor and Rubén Hernández-León, eds. 2005. *New Destinations: Mexican Immigration in the United States.* New York: Russel Sage Foundation.

INDEX

accumulation
  capital: 69, 74, 76, 92, 156, 227, 252
  primitive: 67, 68, 83, 115–125, 144
  regime: 32, 36
activists: 3, 20, 32–3, 36, 257, 274
Africa: 3, 67, 88, 163, 286
  South Africa: 67, 90, 93–4
agrarian
  capitalist: 84, 95–7, 107, 110, 126
  question: 95, 98, 106, 113
  reform: 57, 65, 92, 211, 244
  relations: 98
  revolution: 51, 99
  sector: 94, 118
  society: 9
  transformation: 95, 131
agribusiness: 67, 80, 93, 102, 106, 127, 206, 211–4, 270
agriculture
  capitalist: 106, 108
  colonial: 84
  labour: 96, 109, 124
  precapitalist: 46
  Third World: 95, 119
agroexports: 31, 92, 126, 185, 211–2, 239
Albania: 255, 260, 264–8, 271
Allende, Salvador: 13, 19–20, 26–8, 30–1, 34–6, 61, 226–254
Alliance for Progress: 22, 225, 239, 243
Amin, Samir: 11, 121
analysis
  bourgeois: 9
  class: 4, 6–10, 12–13, 18
  critical: 15
  empirical: 5, 11, 14, 135 137
  Marxist: 4, 68, 104, 172
  radical: 4
  social: 6, 18
  sociological: 8, 13
  structural: 7, 26–7
Argentina: 42, 53–8, 63, 225, 230, 235–6, 238
armed forces: 32, 224, 229, 241–2, 249–251
Asia: 3–4, 141, 163, 198, 221, 233, 279–280
authoritarian: 34–5, 41, 250, 279

Bachelet, Michelle: 35
backwardness: 42–6, 52–53, 57, 64, 84, 86, 99
banks
  bailout: 30, 192, 199
  debts: 30, 234
  development: 46, 238
  globalization: 156
  loans: 146
  local: 173
  nationalisaton: 201
  political power: 199
Baran, Paul: 44, 46, 52, 61, 197
Bello, Walden: 6, 11–12, 85, 178, 205
Blanco (Hugo): 54
Bolivia: 28, 35, 42, 45, 51, 53, 55, 57, 225, 227, 230, 281
Bosnia: 258–265, 268
Braverman, Harry: 79–80
Brazil: 35, 44–5, 51–3, 55, 57, 59–64, 120, 123, 235–8, 285
Bressano, Hugo: 55
Bretton Woods: 143, 147, 204
bureaucracy: 21–22, 32, 34, 58–9, 80, 231, 242, 251
Bush, George W.: 5, 257, 275, 280–2

capital
  accumulation: 69, 74, 76, 92, 156, 227, 252
  capitalist class: 6, 11, 16, 32, 35, 89, 92, 114, 137, 156–9, 164–6, 176, 185, 191–201, 232, 248
  capitalist development: 4, 7, 9–19, 37, 43, 45, 47, 49, 52, 62, 65, 68, 75, 79, 96, 105–107, 110, 117, 123, 133, 139, 149, 159, 223, 232, 254, 257
  capitalist manifesto: 5
  capitalist production: 4, 6–7, 11, 75, 83, 103–4, 113, 117–8, 137, 157, 166
  capitalist reproduction: 101, 105, 116, 165
  capitalist system: 3, 5, 12–13, 62, 68, 101, 110, 116, 118, 121, 127–128, 137, 142, 154, 157–9, 163–4, 166
  foreign: 34, 51, 65, 225, 227, 237
  monopoly: 11, 44, 46, 56, 138, 140, 155, 157, 167

Castañeda, Carlos: 57
Castro, Fidel: 42, 54, 57, 223
Central Intelligence Agency: 216, 227–8,
    231, 233, 235, 247–9, 268, 278
CEPAL, see ECLAC
change:
    agent of: 153, 188–190
    political: 4
    process of: 9, 189, 237, 246–7, 250
    radical: 3–4, 41
    social: 3, 9–10, 23, 155, 273
    socioeconomic: 35, 244, 248
Chicago Boys: 29–31
Chile:
    agriculture: 31
    Christian Democratic Party: 21, 227
    CIA: 227–8, 231, 233, 235, 247–9,
        268, 278
    communist league: 54
    communist party: 53
    counter-revolution: 20, 32, 225, 252
    democracy: 33, 35, 221, 226–7, 230,
        232, 238, 242, 247
    development: 21, 27, 34, 240–1
    economy: 29, 31, 238, 242–243, 247
    industrialization: 20, 30
    and Kissinger, Henry: 215–7, 221–6,
        229–238, 241, 251–2, 254
    military: 231, 237, 249, 251
    nationalization: 245
    and Nixon, Richard: 215, 221–7, 229,
        231–2, 235–241, 251–2
    peasants: 25–6
    purification: 253
    revolutionary left: 25, 27
    ruling class: 27, 29, 34
    socialism: 235
    socialist party: 53, 54
    transition: 34
    US intervention: 13, 28, 227–9, 232–4,
        239, 241, 250, 252
    working class: 21, 24, 35
China: 67, 124, 163–4, 182, 221, 223,
    268, 279, 280
CIA: see Central Intelligence Agency
class
    analysis: 4, 6–13, 18
    -based movements: 3
    consciousness: 20–1, 25, 35
    dominant: 20, 96
    dynamics: 6, 36
    formation: 125–6
    middle: 21–2, 27, 208, 242–4, 250
    movements: 3, 223

power: 16, 22, 34, 191, 244
    ruling: 27, 49, 148, 167, 186, 191–3,
        196, 199–201, 276
    struggle: 3, 6, 14, 16, 18–19, 27, 63,
        77, 82, 87, 95–97, 100–1, 105, 107,
        111, 114, 117, 121–2, 125–130,
        153–7, 165–9, 189
    upper: 248
    war: 4, 6–9
    working: 7–8, 19, 21, 24–6, 35, 48, 51,
        79, 81, 95, 98, 103, 114–5, 121, 126,
        137, 148, 153, 155, 157, 159–160,
        162, 166–8, 246, 250
cold war: 139–140, 164, 221, 223, 226–7,
    252
Colombia: 225–6, 255
colonial(ism): 53, 299
colonies: 51, 62, 63, 65, 84, 105, 141, 173
commodity
    -ies: 72, 88, 90–94, 98, 137–8, 144,
        203, 215
    dumping: 211
    exchange: 215
    market: 206, 208
    production: 79, 138
communism: 46, 50, 221–2, 226, 297, 298
Communist Manifesto: 46, 102, 133
Communist Party: 33, 53–4, 60, 222,
    230, 243
competition: 56, 73, 81, 83, 98, 102,
    112–4, 123, 129, 138, 158–9, 164, 222,
    256, 270, 279
Conference of Presidents of Major
    Jewish Organizations (CPMAJO): 274,
    278
conservative
    approach: 234
    counterrevolution: 7
    neo-: 5
consumption: 46, 125, 135, 205, 214
    bourgeois: 71
    domestic: 104
    family: 186
    household: 205
    means of: 136
    under-: 135, 137
contradictions
    capitalist: 154, 158, 165–6, 169
    class: 16, 167, 169
    imperialist: 55, 139, 148
    labour: 18, 67
    marxism: 59, 99
cooperation: 5, 8, 63, 138–140, 149, 163,
    222, 262

corporations: 28, 30, 94, 141, 144–6, 154, 156–9, 166, 176, 180, 197, 203–4, 208, 213–5, 231–2
crisis
 debt: 203, 211
 ecological: 12, 46
 economic: 30–1, 97, 191, 203, 251, 275, 280
 financial: 6, 12, 144, 196, 200–1, 243, 286
 food: 12, 89, 205, 209 213
 global: 6, 12, 159, 162, 204, 205
 production: 4, 7, 11
 propensity toward: 11–12, 17
 systemic: 6–7, 12, 18
 water: 213
Critical Sociology: 12, 13–14, 18
Croatia: 259, 261–2, 265, 271–2
Cuba: 5, 8, 29, 41–2, 46, 53, 57, 120, 145, 221, 223–4, 228, 232–3, 287
Cuban Revolution: see revolution, Cuban
culture: 44, 80, 140, 174
 backward: 45
 political: 23, 228
 primitive: 44
Czech Republic: 42, 255, 260

debt
 bank: 30
 bondage: 67, 69, 77, 92, 102, 110–1, 121, 123, 129, 131, 174
 crisis: 203, 211
 foreign: 177, 186, 197, 239–240, 243
 IMF: 257
 mechanism: 108
 national: 160, 234, 280
democracy
 bourgeois: 51, 96, 99
 Chilean: 230
 Christian: 23
 and development: 178
 full: 65
 genuine: 32
 parliamentary: 22, 24, 222
 transition from: 63, 252
 transition to: 32–33, 282
Department of Defence (DOD): 233
dependency: 41–3, 49, 51–2, 55–6, 61, 63, 65, 146, 184, 237
deproletarianization: 79, 94–5, 97–8, 100, 104, 115, 126, 130–1
deskilling: 78–82, 84, 129

development
 capitalist: 4–5, 7, 9–19, 24, 37, 43–52, 62, 65, 68, 75, 79, 96, 105–107, 110, 117, 123–4, 133, 139, 149, 154, 159, 216, 223, 236, 254, 257
 combined: 45–8, 50, 62
 economic: 7, 9, 80, 87, 92, 119, 236, 256
 dialectic: 14–15, 27, 35, 105, 118, 126–7, 143, 160, 168, 173, 178–179, 185, 189–190
dictatorship: 13, 20, 28, 29, 32, 35, 99, 235–6, 252–3, 263, 282
discourse
 globalization: 11, 15
 market: 32
 nationalist: 17
 postmodern: 9, 11
Dos Santos, Theotônio: 52–3, 55, 60–1, 63–4

ECLAC: see Economic Commission for Latin America and the Caribbean
ecological
 crisis: 12, 46
 limits: 13
Economic Commission for Latin America and the Caribbean: 184
economic development: see development, economic
economy
 capitalist: 101, 114, 181, 201
 globalized: 144
 market: 75
 peasant: 108–109, 124, 211–3
 political: 7, 10, 12–13, 15, 17–18, 44, 52, 67–69, 71, 81, 83, 87, 116, 128, 145, 147, 153, 155–6, 164, 173, 197
 service: 279
 subsistence: 75, 115, 127, 171–2, 176, 185–6, 256
 United States: 158, 184, 194, 197, 199, 201
 world: 5, 64, 129, 138–9, 158–9, 162, 164, 198
Ecuador: 25, 225, 226 281
elites: 20–25, 34, 173, 177–9, 181, 184, 187, 190, 247–8
emigrants: 171, 182
employment: 24, 70–3, 76, 79–80, 82, 88, 90–3, 97–8, 101–2, 107, 109, 111–2, 114, 122, 124, 127, 130–1, 146, 160, 164, 173, 185, 187, 243, 257–8
Engels: 46, 49, 98, 100, 102–5

England: 49, 51, 70, 77, 83–5, 101, 104
enterprise
    agricultural: 75, 93, 102, 108, 127
    American: 242
    capitalist: 67–9, 77, 82, 88, 102, 112, 123
    commercial: 77, 88, 123
    large-scale: 106, 108–9
    private: 30, 244–5
    rural: 106
    small-scale: 108
    worker-managed: 257
environment: 35, 124, 162, 187, 271
Eritrea: 204
European Union: 145–6, 163, 211
exploitation
    capitalist: 160
    colonial: 62
    corporate: 256
    labour: 3, 14, 31, 52, 155–160, 162, 164–6, 174, 189, 223
    market: 32, 143
    migrant: 174
    national: 28, 49, 189
    periphery: 52, 63, 217
    super-: 31, 52, 63, 160, 164
    women and children: 83, 107
    worker: 52, 155, 157, 166
export
    agriculture: 31, 92, 126, 185, 211
    capital: 138, 156, 158–9, 165
    commodities: 138
    export-led: 180–2, 185, 279
    labour: 91, 180–2, 184, 186
    manufactures: 180–1, 186
    people: 172–3, 177, 179
    processing zones: 67

fascism: 63, 99, 115, 126
Fernandes, Florestán: 61
feudal
    -ism: 42, 57, 64, 92, 94, 142
    aristocracy: 57
    lords: 57, 92, 97–8, 142
    thesis: 94–97, 100, 104, 119, 122, 128–130
Filho, Cándido: 59
financialization: 191, 193, 195, 197–9, 201
food crisis: see crisis, food
Forbes: 192–7
forced migration: see migration, forced
forces of production: see production, forces of

Foreign Direct Investment: see Investment, Foreign Direct
foreign exchange: 176, 238–240, 249
Fourth International: 43, 50, 54, 56, 59–60
Frank, Andre Gunder: 44, 52, 118, 121
freedom
    capital: 212
    forces: 5, 203
    labour: 14, 69, 106–7, 113
    personal: 279–280
    political: 8
    slavery: 76, 103
    unfreedom: 67–9, 72, 74–5, 77–8, 81, 84, 87, 91, 93–94, 96–97, 100, 111, 114–5, 117, 120, 126, 130–1
Friedman, Milton: 30–1
Frondizi, Silvio: 42, 55–6, 61
fuel, prices: 203–217

G8: 145–6
Gaza: 274, 276–7, 279, 282–3
genetically modified seeds: 212, 286
Germany: 63, 76, 105, 110, 114–5, 126, 145–156, 213, 260, 277
Gilly, Adolfo: 47, 58
globalization
    capitalist: 154, 157, 162, 165, 167
    neoliberal: 4–5, 8–9, 13, 16, 144, 147–9, 153–169, 172, 189
GMO: see Genetically Modified Seeds
Gonzalez, Casanova Pablo: 53
governance, global: 6
grassroots
    activists: 20, 33
    cadre: 36
    leaders: 32–3, 37
    movement: 26, 35
Great Depression: 191, 199–200, 204, 280
Green Revolution: 82, 131
growth
    agriculture: 119
    demographic: 74, 81, 215–7
    economic: 4, 9, 91, 186, 194, 197–200, 243
    engine: 7
    enterprise: 108
    exponential: 182, 256
    export-led: 182, 279
    monopolies: 138, 155
    multinationals: 28
    negative: 183
    poverty: 165

pro-: 11
proletariat: 108
remittances: 186
wages: 197
with equity: 21
Guatemala: 54, 58, 204, 255
Guevara, Ernesto 'Che': 42, 57–59

Harvey, David: 10, 121, 143-7, 156,
   178
health: 115, 127, 160, 175-6, 181, 184,
   214, 242, 258, 265, 270
hegemony
   bourgeoisie: 48
   capital: 21, 35, 120
   dollar: 201
   ideological: 16, 169
   imperialist: 143, 144, 179, 252
   neoliberal: 145
   United States: 5, 140, 149, 226, 238
historical materialism: 46
Hodges, Donald C.: 43, 55
humanitarian: 73, 74, 88, 134, 147, 255,
   281-2

IADB: see Inter-American Development
   Bank
IDB: see Inter-American Development
   Bank
IMF: see International Monetary Fund
immigration: 148, 175-6
impasse, theoretical: 6-7
imperial state: see State, imperial
import
   contracts: 211
   costs: 243
   projections: 216
   regime: 181
   substitution: 20
India: 67, 95-96, 101-2, 149, 204, 214-5,
   285-6
indigenous
   communities: 8, 11
   migration: 182
   peoples: 268
   population: 89
industrialization: 9, 20, 51, 65, 70, 122,
   226, 237
industry
   bourgeois: 105
   British: 111
   capitalist: 112, 116
   construction: 111
   copper: 238-239

domestic: 75, 110-111
food: 214
heavy: 114
large-scale: 75, 105-111
local: 160
manufacturing: 158, 160
maquiladora: 180
mining: 112
modern: 81, 83, 102, 105
national: 226
private: 198
subsidies: 101
trucking: 208
whaling: 77
workers: 67, 70, 77, 79, 102, 107, 109,
   111, 173
inequality: 160, 177
inflation: 29-30, 208, 243, 246, 280
insurgents: 3-4, 8, 11, 26
Inter-American Development Bank
   (IDB): 171, 233-4, 238-9, 243
interimperialist: 163-4
international cooperation: 5, 8
International Monetary Fund: 145, 171,
   177, 179-180, 211, 257, 259, 268
international trade: see trade,
   international
internationalism: 58, 99, 167-8
interventionist
   foreign policy: 162
   state: 162
investment
   capital: 70, 75, 237
   corporate: 144
   Foreign Direct: 5, 171, 181, 186
   long-term: 197, 216
   speculative: 30, 178, 192-4
   transnational: 163
   United States: 163, 232-234
Iran: 145, 273-282
Iraq: 28, 141, 163, 204, 255, 261, 263,
   269-282
Israel: 17, 173-283

Japan: 145-6, 163-4, 279
jobs: 6, 82, 131, 160, 175, 181, 280
junta: 27-30, 237-8, 252-3

Kaplan, Marcos: 56, 61
Kautsky, Karl: 15, 100, 106-9, 116, 135,
   137-142
Kenya: 204
Kissinger, Henry: 215-7, 221-6,
   229-238, 241, 251-2, 254

Kosovo: 255–271
Kuwait: 261

labour
  agricultural: 77, 83, 87, 92, 96, 101,
    109, 112, 124
  exploitation: 3, 14, 31, 52, 63, 83, 107,
    142, 155–166, 168, 174, 189, 223
  exportation: 181
  industrial: 67, 80, 93
  market: 101, 114, 130, 175, 179, 182,
    185
  migrant: 91, 105, 174–6
  movement: 3, 21, 55, 162, 166
  power: 14, 97–98, 118, 124, 126–7,
    142
  productivity: 70, 136
  reserve army: 81, 94, 101, 107, 112,
    126–131
  rural: 8, 11, 20, 80, 92, 95, 111
  unfree: 14, 67–142
  wage: 96, 98, 106, 112–3, 119–120,
    136, 142, 157, 166
laissez faire: 82, 92, 125, 130
Latin America, Left (the): 22, 24, 27, 33,
  35, 42, 54, 61, 225–231, 236, 253
Lenin, Vladimir Ilyich: 15, 43–9, 53,
  60–65, 100–1, 106, 110–3, 116, 124,
  133–142, 148, 166, 167
liberalism: 6, 10, 30, 51, 85, 106, 151,
  180
Liga Comunista de Chile: 54
Löwy, Michael: 41, 45, 47–8, 57, 60
Luxemburg, Rosa: 44, 60–1, 117–9, 121,
  135–8

Mandel, Ernest: 43, 48–49, 100 114–5,
  126–7
Mantega, Guido: 44, 45, 52, 63–5
manufacturing: 87, 107, 111, 158, 160,
  181, 186, 193, 195–6, 208
maquiladora: 91, 180–1
Mariategui, Carlos: 51
Marini, Ruy Mauro: 52, 60–4
market
  capitalist: 120, 155–7, 160, 166–7, 189
  common: 226
  expansion: 76, 91, 95, 137, 252
  free: 30, 31, 91, 113, 138, 141, 203,
    213, 215, 223, 259, 269
  -friendly: 9
  grain: 211–2, 280
  home: 93, 181
  ideology: 30

labour: 101, 114, 130, 175, 179, 182,
  185
  manipulation: 205–6, 215
  mass: 93
  world: 47, 57, 133, 141, 240
Marx
  Karl: 136
  marxism: 6–7, 14, 18, 33, 43, 49, 62,
    79, 94–100, 172
  marxist theory: 39, 64, 68, 95, 97–100,
    122, 128, 130
  marxist tradition: 3, 5, 14
materialism: 6, 46
means of production: see production,
  means of
metropoles: 51–3, 63, 65
Mexico: 42–43, 45, 47, 51, 54, 58, 61, 91,
  147, 172, 176, 179–188, 255,
  270
middle class: see Class, middle
Middle East: 16, 163, 206, 273, 276–7,
  281, 283
migrant: see migration
migration
  and development: 14
  -development nexus: 171–190
  forced: 14–15, 172–4, 177, 190
  labour: 67, 76–7, 82, 85, 89–93, 105,
    109, 124, 127, 131, 171, 172, 174–9,
    188–189
  United States: 36, 85, 89–91, 176,
    182–3, 188–9, 274
militants: 20, 32–3, 54, 58, 62, 248
military
  aid: 224, 231
  coup: 27, 29, 225, 228, 231, 237, 249,
    250
  dictatorship: 20, 28, 235–6, 253
  dominance: 140
  expenditure: 162–3
  force: 5, 8, 15, 140, 149, 157, 166, 179,
    251, 264, 278
  government: 252
  intervention: 134, 147, 157, 234
  junta: 28, 29, 237, 238
  occupation: 204
  power: 5, 142, 148, 157
  regime: 31, 34
  United States: 5, 15, 140, 147–8,
    162–3, 206, 223, 236, 274, 277,
    280–2
Mill, John Stuart: 68–9, 72–3, 76, 86, 94,
  100, 128
miners: 23, 25–6, 101

modernization: 9–10, 46, 52, 238
monetary policies: 12
monopoly
-ies: 16, 56, 138, 148, 157, 162, 165,
  167
capitalism: 11, 44, 46, 56, 138, 140,
  155, 157, 167
transnational: 16, 157, 162, 167
Monsanto: 212
Morales, Evo: 55
movement
  anti-imperialist: 3
  class-based: 3, 223
  labour: 55
  liberation: 3, 162, 283
  nationalist: 53, 223, 225
  popular: 8, 27, 36
  protest: 204
  revolutionary: 224
  social: 11, 34–5, 52, 224. 287
  socialist: 32
  Trotskyist: 53
Mozambique: 204
multinational corporations: 28, 144, 225,
  231, 256, 270
muslims: 258–263, 277

NAFTA: see North American Free Trade
  Agreement
national development: see development,
  national
National Security Council (NSC): 221,
  224, 228
National Security Study Memorandum
  200 (NSSM 200): 216, 227
nationalism: 60–1, 221, 223, 226, 233,
  236, 238, 268, 285
  developmental: 61
NATO: see North Atlantic Treaty
  Organization
neoclassical: 7, 87, 128–130
neoimperialism: 5
neoliberal globalization: see
  globalization, neoliberal
neoliberal policies: see policy,
  neoliberal
neoliberalism: 10, 30, 106, 151, 180
neostructuralism: 287
New World Order: 5–8, 16, 140, 149,
  204
non-capitalist: 79, 99, 104, 117–9, 133,
  136–7, 142
North American Free Trade Agreement
  (NAFTA): 179–180, 182, 184, 186–8,
  270

North Atlantic Treaty Organization:
  256, 258–272
North Korea: 145

Organización Latinoamericana de
  Solidaridad (OLAS): 54
outsourcing: 123, 181
overproduction: see production, over-

Page, Thomas Nelson: 86
Partido Obrero Revolucionario (POR):
  43–55
Partido Revolucionario de Trabajadores
  (PRT): 54
Partido Socialista Revolucionário (PSR):
  59
Partido Socialista de Trabajadores
  (PST): 54
Partido Trabalhista Brasileiro (PTB),
peasant
  de-peasantization: 124
  economy: 108–9, 124, 211, 213
  feudal: 99
  industry: 112
  insurgent: 26
  landless: 8
  peasantry: 8, 21, 23, 25–6, 46, 48–9,
    99, 109–110, 149
  poor: 48–9, 69, 92, 96, 130
  producers: 11
  rich: 97
  smallholders: 92, 117–8
permanent revolution: see revolution,
  permanent
Peru: 51, 54, 78, 225, 227, 230,
  236–238
Phillips, Ulrich Bonnell: 86–9
Pinochet, Gen. Augustus: 20, 29, 31–2,
  253
Polet, François: 167
policy
  destabilization: 238, 249, 252, 268
  economic: 116, 148, 194, 211, 223,
    281
  immigration: 176
  monetary: 12
  neoliberal: 7, 171
  postwar: 221
  United States foreign: 16–17, 149,
    163, 198, 223–6, 230–2, 235, 237,
    275, 280
political forces: 21, 27, 240
political stability: 21
political system: 22, 24–5, 34, 251, 253,
  275

politico-ideological: 97
popular insurrection: 49–50
popular resistance: 31
Popular Unity (UP): 20, 26, 32, 227, 247
Portugal: 49, 222, 296
Posada, Juan: 53, 60
postmodern
   -ism: 7, 10, 97
   discourse: 9
   perspective: 7, 10
   Pivot: 6, 12
Prebisch, Raúl: 52
pre-capitalism: 9, 44, 46–7, 94, 95, 121,
   142, 158
primitive accumulation: see
   accumulation, primitive
private enterprise: see enterprise, private
private property: see Property, private
privatization: 90, 125, 155, 206, 213–5,
   257
production
   agricultural: 126
   biological: 73, 93, 173
   capitalist: 4, 6, 7, 11, 75, 81, 83, 104,
      113, 116, 157, 166
   commodity: 79, 293
   crisis: 4, 6, 7, 11, 12
   decline: 203
   food: 79, 216
   forces of: 49, 52–3, 136–7
   global: 4, 147, 212–3
   of knowledge: 36–7, 146
   means of: 42, 49, 90, 98, 118, 121,
      129, 191
   mechanization: 82
   mode of: 7, 46, 83, 105, 108, 116–7,
      119–120, 124, 135
   over-: 4, 12
   processes of: 80, 85, 117, 158, 166
   relations: 68–9, 80, 93, 95–7, 100, 102,
      105, 117–8, 121, 124
   system: 6, 110, 154
   of wealth: 73
proletariat
   (de)proletarianization: 79, 94–98, 100,
      104, 115, 126, 130–1
   growth of: 108
   revolution: 48
   rule of: 51
property: 26, 34, 50, 71–2, 85, 90, 98,
   107, 129, 146, 232, 237, 238, 240, 242,
   246–7
   intellectual: 206, 212
   private: 114, 144, 248

radical change: see change, radical
radicalism: 25–6, 252
recession: 162–164, 193
regime
   authoritarian: 34, 41
   capitalist: 130
   change: 224–225, 251
   client: 147, 230
   conservative: 5
   elected: 21, 32, 227, 282
   labour: 67, 84, 121, 126
   nationalist: 225
   Pinochet: 29, 32
   puppet: 143
   repressive: 164
   social: 49
   socialist: 13
remittances: 171–2, 176–8, 182, 185–6
Reserve Army of Labour: see labour,
   reserve army
resistance
   bureaucratic: 231
   forces of: 11, 13
   to global capital: 143
   popular: 31
   social: 187
reterritorialization: 135
revolution
   change: 5, 7–8, 13
   Cuban: 22, 28–9, 41, 45, 48, 54,
      59–60, 230
   intellectual: 19, 37, 154
   leadership: 168
   permanent: 44, 47–9, 52, 57–8, 62,
      64–5, 99
   process: 45, 48–9, 62
   technological: 4, 104
   world: 48, 60, 64, 99
Revolutionary Workers Party:
   see Partido Revolucionario de
   Trabajadores
ruling class: see class, ruling
rural
   bourgeoisie: 98
   capitalism: 124
   landless workers: 8
   peasantry: 8
   wages: 92
Russia: 43–51, 64–5, 76, 99, 101, 110–2,
   124–5, 129, 145–6, 164, 277, 279–281
ruthless criticism: 20, 33, 37

Sachs, Eric: 60
Sachs, Goldman: 200, 209

securitization: 198–9
semi-feudal
-ism: 42, 94
framework: 95–6
thesis: 94–7, 100, 104, 119, 122,
128–130, 295
Serbia: 258, 260, 262–5, 267–272
slavery: 70–6, 78, 80, 85–9, 93, 98, 101,
103–5, 107–8, 111, 115, 120, 122–3,
126–7
smallholding: 120
Smith, Adam: 68–72, 75, 91
social change: *see* change, social
social movements: *see* movement,
social
social transformation: *see*
transformation, societal
socialism
actually existing: 129
building: 57
democratic: 53, 221, 226, 232, 242
path to: 56
revolutionary: 48–50, 53, 57, 62–4
transition to: 42, 50, 56, 64, 242–5
Socialist Revolutionary Party: *see* Partido
Socialista Revolucionário (PSR)
Socialist Workers' Party: *see* Partido
Socialista de Trabajadores (PST)
sociology
academic: 17
of crisis: 17
critical: 12–14, 18
of globalization: 18
of imperialism: 17
mainstream: 22
political: 4
South Africa: 67, 90, 93–4
South America: 49, 131, 230, 286
Soviet Union: 58–60, 125, 221–3,
226–7, 230, 232–4
Spain: 49, 57, 98–99, 222
speculative trade: *see* trade, speculative
stability
political: 21, 144, 215
socioeconomic: 171–7, 186
(in)stability: 193, 222, 244, 248, 251
Stalin,
Joseph: 42–3, 48
Stalinism: 43, 52, 55–6, 58, 99
state
bourgeois: 48–9
colonial: 281
development: 5, 8, 204

imperial: 16, 18, 27–8, 141, 143–9,
154–7, 160, 162–6, 169, 172–6, 221,
224–6, 232, 252, 290
interventionist: 162
nation-: 8, 17, 154, 285
power: 11, 15–16, 149, 168, 278
regulation: 175, 213, 223
Stavenhagen, Rodolfo: 53
Strategic Arms Limitations Treaty
(SALT 1): 222
structural adjustment: 5, 16, 171–2,
179–180
structural analysis: 7, 26–7
structural dynamics: 179, 187–8
structuralism: 6–7, 12
structuralist: 52, 184
post-structuralist: 9, 10
superexploitation: 31, 52, 63, 160, 164,
167
super-imperialism: 140
surplus
extraction: 52, 115
labour: 102, 116, 142, 173
population: 81, 83, 112, 172–3
value: 5, 51, 81, 114, 117, 136–7, 165
sweatshops: 67, 111, 160
Sweezy, Paul: 11, 61, 81, 138, 191, 194,
197
Szymanski, Albert: 156–7, 166, 168

tenant
labour: 71
peasants: 142
share: 71, 76
Third International: 41, 43
Third World: 28, 60, 82, 94, 107, 118–9,
126, 145, 147, 153, 157–8, 160, 163,
164, 171, 173, 221–3, 234, 241, 256,
257, 289
trade
international: 208
regional: 141, 226
speculative: 208
union: 33, 83, 114, 174, 188–9, 242,
253, 276
transformation
agrarian: 95, 113, 131
bourgeois: 64
capitalist: 4, 20, 64, 97–8, 124, 153–5,
159, 169
economic: 244, 248, 251, 253
labour: 79, 81, 117, 125
manufacturing: 101

political: 253
socialist: 63, 237
societal: 9, 16, 28, 35, 37, 165,
176–177, 187–9, 248, 253
structural: 20, 31, 35, 119
systemic: 96, 130
transnational
capital: 35, 141, 155, 160, 167
capitalism: 155
corporations: 141, 145–6, 154, 156–7,
166, 180
monopolies: 16, 157, 162, 167
Trotsky, Leon: 41–65, 98–100, 113
Trotskyism: 43, 53, 55–6, 61–4, 99

ultra-imperialism: 137–140
underdevelopment: 42–9, 52, 55–6,
62–4, 75, 92–3, 171, 173–4, 177–9
unemployment: 81, 83, 101, 107, 160,
164, 173, 185, 187, 243, 257, 258
United Nations Conference on Trade
and Development (UNCTAD): 146
United Nations Development
Programme (UNDP): 171
United States (US):
capital: 141, 158, 163, 177, 180, 197
and Chile: 13, 19, 21, 28, 223–254
economy: 158, 160, 184, 197, 199,
201
empire: 15, 140–1, 149
foreign policy: 16, 149
hegemony: 149, 226, 238
imperialism: 5, 13, 15–16, 55, 140,
158, 163, 172, 178–9, 187, 219
intervention: 13, 28, 147, 229
and Mexico: 180–184
and the Middle East: 16
policy: 28, 41, 141, 179, 200, 223,
240–1
sphere: 28, 148, 215, 223–5, 230
Uruguay: 225, 236

Vargas, Getúlio: 51, 62
Velvet Glove: 5, 8, 149
Venezuela: 14, 28, 58, 145, 225, 281–2
Vitale, Luis: 42, 53–56

wage
capitalist: 98, 112
decline: 78, 160
incentives: 75
labour: 96, 98, 106, 112–3, 119–120,
136, 142, 157, 166
minimum: 91, 115, 127, 204
rural: 92
Washington Consensus: 11, 148, 179
wealth holders: 196–7
Weber, Max: 69, 74–8, 85–8, 94, 128
Werneck, Sodré Nelson: 61
Western Alliance: 222
workers: see labour
Workforce
cheap: 173
free: 72, 90, 98, 120
immigrant: 85, 91, 93, 174–6
qualified: 174, 183–5
restructuring: 104, 110, 128
rural: 8, 11, 20, 92, 95, 111–2
working class: see Class, working
World Bank: 92, 145, 159–160, 171, 178,
180, 211, 213–4, 238
World Food Programme (WFP): 213
World System: 10, 18, 37, 133, 137
World Trade Organization (WTO): 212

Yugoslavia: 16, 255–272

Zeitlin, Maurice: 4, 25
Zionism, 17, 273–7, 281
Zionist Organization of America (ZAO):
274
Zionist power configuration (ZPC): 274
Zuñiga, 182